Contents

Figures

A History of Everyday Life in Scotland, 1800 to 1900

A History of Everyday Life in Scotland

SERIES EDITORS: CHRISTOPHER A. WHATLEY AND ELIZABETH FOYSTER

A History of Everyday Life in Scotland, 1800 to 1900

Edited by Trevor Griffiths and Graeme Morton

Edinburgh University Press

Edinburgh University Press Ltd
22 George Square, Edinburgh
www.euppublishing.com

Reprinted 2011

Typeset in 10/12pt Goudy Old Style by
Servis Filmsetting Ltd, Stockport, Cheshire, and
printed and bound in Great Britain by
CPI Antony Rowe, Chippenham and Eastbourne

A CIP record for this book is available from the British Library

ISBN 978 0 7486 2169 9 (hardback)
ISBN 978 0 7486 2170 5 (paperback)

Published with the support of the Edinburgh University
Scholarly Publishing Initiatives Fund.

Acknowledgements

With such a long gestation, as is all too often the case with any edited collection, we are particularly grateful for the persistent enthusiasm and continued robust health of all those involved. Such forbearance has enabled us to get to this point. VoIP telephones and budget airlines helped us to deal with the vagaries of transatlantic editing in an age of incessant software updates. Our series editors and Edinburgh University Press have been unfailing in their patience, encouragement and their insight into the most appropriate point at which to suggest that, just perhaps, progress should be doing what it should, progressing. Pushing us along with great energy as we entered the final stages of pulling the volume together was Anna Millward. She hunted down citations tenaciously and guided us through the dark arts of the style guidelines; we are deeply grateful for her help. Welcome research assistance came from Elizabeth Ritchie (UHI Millennium Institute) and financial support from the University of Guelph allowing us to include more of the striking images than we could have hoped.

Personal thanks go to our families and friends for bearing with us throughout this venture. On the Griffiths side to Mrs Mary Griffiths, Janet and Kelvin Lawton, Malcolm Cook and David Jarman; on the Morton side to Angela, Sam and Evie. Great cheer, and the occasional flash of inspiration, came from Scott, Amber, Stewart, Angel and Timothy – for which we give blessings. Our respective institutions, the universities of Edinburgh and Guelph, have been unfailingly supportive and we are grateful for their continued dedication to Scottish historical research. Finally, we wish to thank our students who, knowingly or otherwise, have pushed us to think more widely and deeply about the topics we examine here – and it is to them, and to future scholars, that we offer this volume.

Midlothian & Ontario
2010

Series Editors' Foreword

Elizabeth Foyster and Christopher A. Whatley

The four books in this series examine the ordinary, routine, daily behaviour, experiences and beliefs of Scottish people from medieval times until the present day. Their focus is on the 'common people', that is, most of the population, the ordinary folk below the ranks of the aristocracy, substantial landowners, opulent merchants, major industrialists, bankers and financiers, even if it is true that people from relatively humble beginnings have managed periodically to haul themselves into the ranks of the nation's social elite. Contributors in each volume describe the landscapes and living spaces that formed the familiar contexts for daily life. The events and activities that determined how individuals spent their time are explored, including the experiences of work and leisure, and ranging in duration from those that affected the passage of a single day, through those that impinged on peoples' lives according to the calendar or the seasons and weather, to those that were commonly experienced over the course of the life-cycle. Scottish people made sense of their everyday lives, it is argued, through ritual and belief, by their interactions with others and by self-reflection.

As a whole, the series aims to provide a richer and more closely observed history of the social, economic and cultural lives of ordinary Scots than has been published previously. This is not to suggest that accounts and analyses of the everyday in Scotland have not been written. They have.[1] And this present series of four volumes overlaps with the publication of the fourteen volumes of the *Scottish Life and Society* series, sponsored by the European Ethnological Research Centre in Edinburgh, led by Alexander Fenton. The first volume in this series was published in 2000, with others following at intervals through to 2008. Unlike the series of which this volume is part, which is structured by chronological periods in which selected broad themes are studied, each of the books in the *Scottish Life and Society* series has been organised around a particular topic, including: farming and rural life; domestic life; boats, fishing and the sea; and religion.[2] They are substantial, multi-authored volumes, and eclectic in the range of subjects and sub-topics covered, entirely befitting the series sub-title, *A Compendium of Scottish Ethnology*. It represents a monumental resource for future researchers.[3] Where appropriate, contributors to this series *A History of Everyday Life in Scotland* have drawn upon the *Scottish Life and Society* team's findings. Rather than clashing, however, or overlapping to the point of repetition, the two series complement each other, with ours concentrating more on continuities and change, and historical explanations for this, and written, mainly but not entirely, by professional historians. Together, both series offer readers a heady mix of historical information, and an array of approaches, analytical styles and depths and insights.

The everyday had a context, or contexts. At the individual level what was everyday altered across time and often differed according to class, gender, age, religion and ethnic group. It was also shaped by national and regional surroundings, and could vary between urban and rural environments, highland and lowland, inland and coastal settings, the northern and western islands.[4] Contributors pay attention to regional and local variations and peculiarities, especially with regard to language, dialect, practices and customs. The series reveals aspects of the everyday that were distinctively Scottish, but it also shows how the everyday lives of Scots were influenced by other cultures and nations. This resulted from travel, trading relations, or migration by Scots who lived and worked abroad, both temporarily and permanently. Indirectly, Scots read and learned of the shared or conflicting ideas and practices of everyday life in near and distant lands. Contributors to the series can point to inter-national differences and similarities because of the pioneering work on the everyday that has been conducted by historians on other countries across a range of periods. While relatively little has been published specifically on the everyday in Scotland or even Britain, we are fortunate to be able to draw upon an extensive body of historical research for Europe and the Americas.[5]

The roots of this historical endeavour, and the approaches that this series takes, lie in a range of developments within the discipline. In Britain, the interest of social historians – often with a Marxist perspective – in writing 'history from below', has brought the lives of working-class people to centre stage.[6] In Scotland the study of 'new' social history was pioneered by T. C. Smout, with his seminal *History of the Scottish People, 1560–1830* (1969), although Smout's approach was liberal rather than leftist.[7] This was followed in subsequent decades by a surge of research on a range of topics, and a plethora of publications written by a small army of historians examining different historical periods, including the same author's *Century of the Scottish People, 1830–1950* (1986).[8] Furth of Scotland, *Annaliste* historians, such as Fernand Braudel, focused attention on the material culture of daily life, and a later generation of French and then Italian historians narrowed the scale of study to produce 'microhistories'. These examined in detail the history of one individual, village or incident in order to understand the wider *mentalité* of the societies of which they were a part.[9] Historians in Germany have addressed the issue of the everyday most directly, where the concept of *Alltagsgeschichte* ('the history of everyday life') was conceived, and continues to be the source of lively debate.[10] Preceding, running alongside and occasionally influencing historical work has been the study of everyday life by academics in other disciplines, including ethnology, sociology, social anthropology, geography, psychology and cultural theory.[11] Academics from these disciplines contribute to some of the volumes of this series.

What can the reader expect from this series, and how does the content of the books that comprise it differ from other social histories of Scotland?

First, by uncovering the everyday, we provide fresh insights into a diverse range of historical topics. Whereas much social history can focus on the structures, ideals or prescriptions that were intended to govern daily living, this series examines the practices and realities of life experience. Although not the primary purpose of the series, people's experiences of major change, like wars, famine and environmental disaster, are incorporated. The result is to demonstrate how the extraordinary affected the ordinary. But as Alexander Fenton correctly observed of Scottish rural society some years ago, broad trends, big ideas and eye-catching technologies only explain so much; how they impacted on the everyday depended on local conditions and responses. As important for understanding the everyday lives of ordinary people, and the pace and nature of change, were, for example, how small-scale pieces of equipment were adopted and used, and how things were done in the home or barn or yard far from power centres that passed legislation or, from which sprang – as in the case of Edinburgh and east-central Scotland in the early eighteenth century – models for and aids to agrarian improvement. But on Orkney even in the later eighteenth century weighing machines – the pundlar and the pindlar – weights and measures, and the commonly used, one-stilt plough, had been in use since Viking times.[12] Change on the ground was invariably slow, piecemeal and indigenous rather than spectacular.[13]

Examples and case studies of aspects of everyday life in these volumes also enhance our understanding of some long-standing subjects of debate within Scottish history. Hence, readers will gain new insights about the role of the kirk in social and moral discipline, the impact of enclosure and the Clearances in the Lowlands as well as the Highlands, the struggles between popular and elite forms of culture, standards of living, and the significance of 'public' and 'private' spaces in daily life. In addition, the exploration of the everyday has allowed our contributors to cover less familiar historical territory – some of which has posed considerable challenges. We discover how Scottish people's fears, anxieties and perceptions of danger changed over time, we learn about the importance of gestures as well as forms of verbal and written communication and we begin to recover how ordinary Scots experienced their sensory worlds of taste, sound, sight and touch. The everyday enables historians to engage with important emerging topics within the discipline of history, for example, the history of the Scottish landscape and the environment. Chapters in the books in the series explore the changing relationship with and impact of Scots upon their natural environment.[14] The series also demonstrates how women, whose lives were once considered too everyday and mundane to merit serious academic study, played a central part in the negotiation and management of particularly home and family daily life.[15] In addition, women could play an active role in everyday life beyond the domestic scene, as recent research has begun to reveal.[16] Scottish men's gendered identities were also constructed and experienced in the context of the everyday.

The contributors to this series have been able to write these histories not, on the whole, because they have discovered vast quantities of new evidence in the archives, although much original material has been uncovered. Rather, a new history has emerged because they have asked novel questions of material with which they were familiar, and have pieced together a wide range of what was often unused information from both primary and secondary sources. Undoubtedly, writing the history of the everyday presents unique problems of evidence for the historian. These problems can vary with historical period; those researching the everyday in medieval times can face a dearth of written sources, while it is easy to be overwhelmed by the mass of information available for the twentieth century. However, there are also more fundamental issues of evidence at stake that have to be faced by all historians of the everyday. As Braudel recognised, 'everyday life consists of the little things one hardly notices in time and space'.[17] Everyday life could be so banal, repetitive, tedious, boring, easily forgotten or taken for granted that our predecessors rarely bothered to record it. Sometimes this means we have to read 'against the grain' of the sources that do survive. In other words, examining the exceptional incident or object to deduce its opposite. For the most part, however, writing about the everyday necessitates the laborious sorting through and amalgamation of fragments of the past: written, visual and material. Contributors to this series have found evidence of the everyday in artefacts, archaeological sites, buildings, diaries, letters, autobiographies, polite and popular literature, trial records of church, burgh and state courts, estate papers, directories, prints, maps, photographs and oral testimony. It is the incidental comment, remark or observation, chance survival, brief glimpse or snapshot that often contains a clue to and even the core of the everyday. The historian's task is to put these details together, 'as in a jigsaw puzzle', so that we can present to readers a picture of the everyday.[18]

What the reader will not get from the series is a complete or comprehensive compendium of everyday life. This, as indicated earlier, is to be found elsewhere. It has not been our intention to list or describe all everyday objects and occurrences, even if this were practicably possible. Rather, our purpose is to explain and analyse the everyday as well as record it. The methodological tools used by contributors are diverse, and reflect their differing disciplinary backgrounds. This is especially the case in the twentieth century volume, where interdisciplinary approaches are most widely employed.

The second distinctive contribution of this series to our understanding of the Scottish past is concerned with what it reveals about historical change.

Across the series the reader can expect to find enduring continuities within everyday life, but also transformations, some rapid, but most long and drawn out. These can be observed by the historian; how far and in what ways they were experienced by ordinary people is harder to know. Yet it is clear that, over time, changes did occur in everyday life, as new ways of working, forms of social organisation, products, sights and sounds expanded the experiences of ordinary Scots. Even the fundamentals that comprise everyday life – what people ate and drank, where they slept, what they wore, where they worked and how they travelled from A to B – were indisputably transformed. Even so, these volumes also present evidence of elements of everyday life stubbornly resistant to change. The consecutive volumes in this series do not signify a set of breaks with the last, or a turning point in all aspects of the everyday. Hence, to take some examples: Scots continued to trust self-administered and home-made cures for illness even as medicine became professionalised and institutionalised; oral culture continued to thrive long after literacy had become the norm; and families and their communities continued to mark birth, marriage and death as significant rites of passage. Ale is still widely drunk at the start of the twenty-first century; and walking and other earlier forms of transport, the use of the bicycle, for example, are growing in popularity. The enduring qualities of everyday life have attracted comment. For the Marxist cultural theorist Henri Lefebvre, the everyday in more recent times offered a glimmer of hope in capitalist societies, because it revealed 'a corrective to the spectacularizing discourse of modernity'. Despite industrial and technological change, the humdrum and main concerns of everyday life for many people remained little altered.[19] Historians have noted people's determination to maintain the routines of daily life in the face of dramatic change, such as during periods of crisis and conflict.[20] Our predecessors shared our need for food, drink and shelter, and our yearning for love and affection, but when other parts of their lives faced serious disruption, the relative importance of fulfilling these needs had to be adjusted. Scots could be proud of 'making do' in times of hardship, and of the fact that daily life 'went on' despite the havoc and destruction around them. This series looks more closely at why particular aspects of the everyday were so hard to disrupt.

By so doing, revealing perspective is provided upon the meaning for ordinary Scots of 'great events', such as wars, which traditionally have been seen as the key moments of change in Scottish – and other nations' – history. Arguably, it was in the context of the 'non-event-ness' of the everyday that the vast majority of Scots spent their lives.[21] Indeed, as Dorothee Wierling has observed, 'most persons have *nothing but* . . . ordinary everyday life'.[22] Studying the history of everyday life is about retrieving the history of what most people did most of the time.

The series demonstrates that the speed of change in everyday life could vary between that experienced within the space of a generation, to barely perceptible shifts across centuries. However, the series also offers some explanations for what brought about change when it occurred. More important is how change was accommodated within the everyday; this was a social process. The seeds for change in Scottish society were frequently contained within the everyday. The everyday was often 'political'. Studying the everyday allows us to see how ordinary people could exercise power over their lives to resist, counter, accommodate or adapt to the changes they encountered. As Ben Highmore has observed, everyday life often serves in helping people to cope with 'the shock of the new'. The everyday becomes the setting:

> for making the unfamiliar familiar; for getting accustomed to the disruption of custom; for struggling to incorporate the new; for adjusting to different ways of living. The everyday marks the success and failure of this process. It witnesses the absorption of the most revolutionary of inventions into the landscape of the mundane. Radical transformations in all walks of life become 'second nature'.[23]

In short, it is by examining the minutiae of people's daily lives that we can uncover the significance of historical change as this affected ordinary people.

Above all – and this is our third aim – the series aims to provide an accessible history that will interest, excite and engage with the reader. This should not be difficult to achieve given the degree of public interest in the everyday. From the popularity of 'reality' TV shows where individuals are exposed to reconstructed life as their Iron Age ancestors might have lived it, for instance, to the fact that it is often the kitchens and servants' living quarters of stately homes which attract the most visitors and curiosity, it is clear that there is an appetite to find out more about the everyday. This is because the history of the everyday is one to which most people can relate, or at least with which we can empathise. It is the bread and butter of life in the past. This is not to suggest that the reader will find any straightforward or single narrative of everyday life in these volumes. The history of the everyday is complex in the extreme: the range of experience is immense, what evidence we do have is often contradictory and there are enormous black holes in our knowledge and understanding. The books in the series reflect all of this, but they have also identified patterns and processes that make some sense of the everyday life of the Scots over the centuries in all of its diversity.

Notes

1 A classic in its time was H. G. Graham, *The Social Life of Scotland in the Eighteenth Century* (London, 1899), while Marjory Plant's *Domestic Life of Scotland in the Eighteenth Century* (Edinburgh, 1948), and Marion Lochhead's *The Scots Household*

in the Eighteenth Century (Edinburgh, 1948), broke new ground in revealing much about everyday life in and around the home. It was Alexander (Sandy) Fenton, however, who led the way in Scotland in modern exploration of the everyday, particularly that of rural society: see, for example, A. Fenton, *Scottish Country Life* (Edinburgh, 1976, 1977; East Linton, 1999), and *The Northern Isles: Orkney and Shetland* (Edinburgh, 1978; East Linton,1997).

2   *Scottish Life and Society: A Compendium of Scottish Ethnology*, 14 vols (John Donald, in association with The European Ethnological Research Centre and The National Museums of Scotland).

3   Perhaps the most enduring research tool deriving from the project will be H. Holmes and F. Macdonald (eds), *Scottish Life and Society: Bibliography for Scottish Ethnology*, vol. 14 (Edinburgh, 2003).

4   For a fine study of the impact of environmental factors and changing international conditions upon a locality, and aspects of everyday life in the northern isles, see H. D. Smith, *Shetland Life and Trade, 1550–1914* (Edinburgh, 1984).

5   See, for example, C. Dyer, *Everyday Life in Medieval England* (London, 1994); S. Wilson, *The Magical Universe: Everyday Ritual and Magic in Pre-Modern Europe* (London, 2000); R. Sarti, *Europe at Home: Family and Material Culture 1500–1800* (New Haven, 2002); R. Braun, *Industrialisation and Everyday Life*, trans. S. H. Tenison (Cambridge, 1990); S. Fitzpatrick, *Everyday Stalinism. Ordinary Life in Extraordinary Times: Soviet Russia in the 1930s* (Oxford, 1999); 'The Everyday Life in America series' edited by Richard Balkin; and M. Wasserman, *Everyday Life and Politics in Nineteenth-Century Mexico: Men, Women and War* (Albuquerque, 2000).

6   The work of E. P. Thompson was especially important in this regard, notably his seminal *The Making of the English Working Class* (London, 1965). See also the collection of his essays in *Customs in Common* (London, 1991). Thompson pays little attention to Scotland; more inclusive – and comparative – is Keith Wrightson's *Earthly Necessities: Economic Lives in Early Modern Britain* (New Haven, 2000), which contains much on everyday lives and how these were affected by the emergence of the market economy.

7   Marxist analyses of Scottish society appeared later, for example, T. Dickson (ed.), *Scottish Capitalism: Class, State and Nation from before the Union to the Present* (London, 1980); Dickson also edited *Capital and Class in Scotland* (Edinburgh, 1982).

8   Some sense of what has been achieved over the past half century or so can be seen in the bibliographies that accompany each of the chapters in R. A. Houston and W. W. Knox's *New Penguin History of Scotland from the Earliest Times to the Present Day* (London, 2001).

9   See, for example, F. Braudel, *Civilization and Capitalism 15th–18th Century Vol. I: The Structures of Everyday Life: The Limits of the Possible*, trans. S. Reynolds (London, 1981); E. Le Roy Ladurie, *Montaillou: Cathars and Catholics in a French Village 1294–1324*, trans. Barbara Bray (Harmondsworth, 1980); and C. Ginzburg, *The Cheese and the Worms: The Cosmos of a Sixteenth-Century Miller*, trans. J. and A. Tedeschi (Baltimore, 1980).

10 See, for example, A. Lüdtke (ed.), *The History of Everyday Life: Reconstructing Historical Experiences and Ways of Life*, trans. W. Templer (Princeton, 1995).

11 See, for example, A. J. Weigert, *Sociology of Everyday Life* (London, 1981); J. M. White, *Everyday Life of the North American Indian* (New York, 2003); T. Friberg, *Everyday Life: Women's Adaptive Strategies in Time and Space*, trans. M. Gray (Stockholm, 1993); G. M. Davies and R. H. Logie (eds), *Memory in Everyday Life* (Amsterdam, 1993); H. Lefebvre, *Critique of Everyday Life*, 2 vols (London, 1991 and 2002); Michel de Certeau, *The Practice of Everyday Life*, trans. S. Rendall (Berkeley, 1984); and M. Certeau, L. Giard and P. Mayol, *The Practice of Everyday Life Volume 2: Living and Cooking*, trans. T. J. Tomasik (Minneapolis, 1998).

12 W. S. Hewison (ed.), *The Diary of Patrick Fea of Stove, Orkney, 1766–96* (East Linton, 1997), pp. 21, 24.

13 Fenton, *Scottish Country Life*, p. v.

14 See T. C. Smout, *Nature Contested: Environmental History in Scotland and Northern England Since 1600* (Edinburgh, 2000); and for a study which looks more closely at the relationship between one element of the environment, trees, and aspects of everyday life, T. C. Smout (ed.), *People and Woods in Scotland: A History* (Edinburgh, 2003).

15 For discussion of the links between women and the everyday see, D. Wierling, 'The history of everyday life and gender relations: on historical and historio-graphical relationships', in Lüdtke, *History of Everyday Life*, pp. 149–68.

16 See, for example, E. Ewan and M. M. Meikle (eds), *Women in Scotland, c.1100–c.1750* (East Linton, 1999); L. Abrams, E. Gordon, D. Simonton and E. J. Yeo (eds), *Gender in Scottish History since 1700* (Edinburgh, 2006); W. W. Knox, *Lives of Scottish Women: Women and Scottish Society, 1800–1980* (Edinburgh, 2006). A pioneering if eccentric account of women's role in popular protest was J. D. Young's *Women and Popular Struggles: A History of Scottish and Women Working-Class Women, 1500–1984* (Edinburgh, 1985).

17 Braudel, *Civilization and Capitalism*, p. 29.

18 Sarti, *Europe at Home*, p. 1.

19 J. Moran, 'History, memory and the everyday', *Rethinking History*, 8:1 (2004), pp. 54–7.

20 See, for example, N. Longmate, *How We Lived Then: A History of Everyday Life During the Second World War* (London, 1971).

21 The concept of 'non-event-ness' is taken from B. Highmore, *Everyday Life and Cultural Theory* (London, 2002), p. 34.

22 Wierling, 'The history of everyday life', p. 151; the emphasis is in the original.

23 Highmore, *Everyday Life*, p. 2.

Introduction

Structures of Everyday Life in Scotland, 1800 to 1900

Trevor Griffiths and Graeme Morton

Narratives of nineteenth-century Scotland have, more often than not, been preoccupied with the impact of change, unprecedented both in its pace and its extent.[1] Through the impact of industrialisation and its close cousin urbanisation, society is seen to have been transformed from the small-scale and personal, to larger-scale, concentrated patterns of urban living, carrying with them recurrent concerns over anomie and alienation. In the process, all aspects of the everyday were affected. In terms of social relations, a sense of locality, capable of transcending differences of income and status, gave way to a more sharply stratified social structure, which for the first time it was possible to describe in terms of class. A more self-consciously urban middle class emerged, no longer content to serve the needs of, and bow the knee to, rural wealth, while new forms of productive activity also gave rise to something approximating a united working class.[2] These new social formations were but one manifestation of a wider reordering of society around new conceptions of time, space and function. Time, one of the key building blocks of the everyday experience, was subject to fundamental change, becoming more standardised across areas, as communications and more rapid transit effaced physical difference. It was also subject to more precise measurement, a boon to a transport system reliant on an accurate timetable and a necessity for the effective functioning of more modern and centralised forms of industry, which depended primarily on punctuality in attendance and regularity of effort.[3] The result was a bifurcation in the structuring of time, between that spent at work and that devoted to what came to be defined as 'leisure', in which obligations were less pressing and greater discretion could be exercised over the uses to which time was put. Over the decades, the balance between work and non-work time would shift irregularly but invariably in favour of the latter, as statutory and negotiated limits were imposed on hours of toil.[4] For most, the key periods of change came towards the end of the century, the point at which living standards for the majority showed a marked and sustained improvement, so that for the first time the everyday was no longer dominated by the need to subsist, but could involve decisions over the deployment of resources informed by choice and expressive of underlying values and preferences.[5]

Time was not the only facet of the everyday experience to be subject to

reordering along what some perceived to be more 'rational' lines. In the new
urban civilisation of the nineteenth century, the use of space became more
specialised and closely defined. For a growing portion of the population,
work and home were increasingly physically separable, giving enhanced
significance to the temporal limits now placed on work. In addition, the
all-purpose meeting place, the focus for transacting key aspects of the
everyday business of the locality, was replaced by spaces with distinct and
defined functions, a process furthered in certain instances by the impact of
legislation. Over time, then, the public house was transformed from a place
for transacting all manner of business and a setting for sports fixtures, to a
space devoted to the consumption of alcohol.[6] By the end of the century, it
formed part of an increasingly regulated urban society, in which the structures of governance were applied to stemming the threat of physical and
moral degradation brought about by living in polluted and over-crowded
conditions. These agencies had themselves been subject to rationalisation,
with specialist organisations emerging to deal with problems of public health
and policing.[7] The emergence of institutions to address specific social problems also entailed a progressive narrowing in the previously all-embracing
authority of the Church in Scottish society. At the end of the century, for
all that high levels of membership and formal adherence offered evidence of
underlying religiosity, the churches' ability to mould the moral universe of
Scots appeared compromised by developments which weakened adherence
to religion's wider social mission: the physical separation of the classes, and
the lure of alternative uses of free time that divested leisure of any broader
spiritual function.[8]

What continuities that remained in parish life were strained further by
the enlargement of Scotland's population, doubling in size from 2.37 million
in 1831 to 4.76 million in 1911. The dynamics of this growth were far from
uniform, and these book-end snapshots from the census exclude the hundreds of thousands who had taken themselves off to England and the near
2 million Scots who had left for overseas in the intervening decades, but do
enumerate returning Scots and immigrants from south of the border and
from Ireland. Those that remained should not be seen as any less mobile, with
regular internal migrations, short-term, seasonal as well as permanent moves
made in search of work, cash income, charity, or simply a less arduous life.
All but the north-east of Scotland witnessed depopulation in the rural areas,
but most of these parishes experienced some periods of growth as well as
decline. The towns were frequently the destination, and by the count of the
1911 census nearly half of Scotland's people are to be found in the industrial
concentrations of the western Lowlands. Looking at the period as a whole,
rates of fertility were higher in Scotland than in England, but rates of nuptiality were lower. When Scots did marry they did so earlier than their contemporaries in England and tended to have their children soon after their vows
were blessed. Consistently over the period Scotland was a predominantly

young and female society, but disease and illness were frequent fractures in the lives of all. Some threats were epidemic, with cholera the great scourge of 1831–2, 1848–9, 1852–4 and 1866–7 and typhus most virulent in 1836–7 and 1846–7 but also endemic alongside various respiratory diseases that attacked the weakened bodies of urban dwellers, their health hampered by impoverishment, the hardship of industrial work and a degree of unsanitary housing and overcrowding not found in the rural areas. Death within the family was a lived reality, as the chapters from Andrew Blaikie and Stewart J. Brown confirm. Infant mortality was the great skew upon the death rate, not reducing significantly in this century and with the 1890s seeing a marked rise in its occurrence. Medical intervention would struggle to overcome social ills, and while inoculation against smallpox began at the start of the century, was commonplace in the 1840s and compulsory in 1863, the overall death rate was slow to come down until after the 1870s. Debate raged over miasma or contagion as the cause behind the spread of disease, just as disagreements tumbled forth as to the most effective means of alleviating its ravages. How much longer, bemoaned the Edinburgh University physician, William Pulteney Alison, in 1840, could it be said that the state should not intervene? There was inevitably much regional variation in all the great signifiers of the population's characteristics, with the Kirk continuing to embroil itself in the moral dilemma of illegitimate and pre-nuptial pregnancy, but by 1901 most of the nation was heading towards the 'demographic transition', from high rates of fertility and death to what in modern Western society is regarded as low rates in each. Yet such a transformation, uneven as it was between parishes, should not detract from understanding the century as one where the vulnerability of life was the constant experience.[9]

Given such compelling indications of underlying change, it is tempting to see the nineteenth century as, in effect, the midwife of modern society. Yet if change was profound, it was not unqualified. In all areas touching the everyday, important aspects of continuity can be identified. In particular, the impact of industrialisation has been re-evaluated to emphasise the degree to which innovation in the techniques and organisation of production was more limited in extent and less productive of wider social effects.[10] For many workers, it is argued, the employment experience remained little altered over the bulk of the period, while even where change was marked, the absence of modernisation in management techniques ensured that sources of difference within the workforce, reflecting hierarchies of income and skill had renewed salience.[11] As a result, any propensity to recast the everyday in terms of class distinction must be resisted. Recent research has also done much to modify our perception of other aspects of the social experience. The reordering of time that so characterised the new industrial order was, it is emphasised, more selective in its impact than had been thought. Here, the modern preoccupation with issues of gender difference has offered important new insights. So, while it is acknowledged that male industrial workers experienced work and non-work as progressively discrete phases of time, for most women, increasingly tied to the home by strengthening adherence to ideas of separate spheres, no such demarcation was evident. Instead, a structuring of time familiar from the pre-industrial age, where the boundaries between work and non-work were less clearly drawn, remained the norm.[12] If the burden of domestic management was, to a degree, lifted by improvements in living standards over the final quarter of the nineteenth century, problems of subsistence were never entirely alleviated. The uncertainties induced by irregular income flows, liable to fluctuation and interruption in cases of illness and unemployment, made families frequently dependent on external assistance if equilibrium was to be maintained. The most immediate and accessible sources of help, particularly in the short term, were those living in close physical proximity who shared many of the same problems. Social surveys consistently noted the importance of assistance, both material and financial, proffered within urban neighbourhoods.[13] The effect was to emphasise enduring ties of locality within seemingly undifferentiated urban settlements. So, while increasing flows of people and information over greater distances gave evidence of the progressive irruption of national into local patterns of living and thought, the needs and structures of everyday living suggest that their impact was qualified at best. The locality remained an important source of assistance and information, allowing families to navigate the hazards of living in late nineteenth-century Scotland. The institutional underpinnings of life reflected this wider reality, from savings organisations to sports clubs and more conventional agencies of spiritual succour. Central to this still vital civil society was the Church, its position buttressed by a range of denominational organisations designed to appeal to and hold in particular groups within the congregation, from mothers to youths, the latter through such agencies as William Smith's Boys' Brigade.[14] While the Church fulfilled a similar parochial role to that encountered elsewhere in urban Britain, the peculiarities of Calvinist ideology gave it a broader national significance.

This orthodoxy was capable of throwing up some strange debates. One that caught the eye of Henry Cockburn was the Revd Andrew Thomson's refusal to open his church for a service marking the unexpected death of Princess Charlotte on 6 November 1817. The day of her demise, Thomson insisted, was not the Sabbath. Cockburn's take was that although 'we sons of Calvin' always despise a royal proclamation requiring such services, it was still 'natural decency and piety' that such should take place. In the end Thomson's was the only church where the gates were closed while 'crowds rolled into every other', and no pamphlet war, or disarming sermon finally given on the Sunday, could persuade anyone to agree with Thomson's view that 'everybody was wrong except himself'.[15] A few years later Cockburn tells of another agitation throughout the land caused by George IV, when the monarch compelled the British people not to pray for his estranged wife Caroline. While it was perhaps proper for such requests to come from the head of the Church of England, the Scottish Presbyterians, 'who own no earthly head, kicked'. As Cockburn rhetorically pointed out, 'What right had the Crown to put words in the mouths of praying Presbyterians?' and, with glee, noted that the again discomfited Thomson immediately tried to persuade the General Assembly to deny the royal claim to the throne, a proposal which the Assembly managed to evade.[16]

The ubiquity of the Church and of its ideas reflects the often dynamic interplay between change and continuity to which historians of the everyday in the nineteenth century must be sensitive. Their work is assisted to a degree by the diversity and extent of the material available, both written and pictorial, which taken together facilitate the exploration of the various themes encapsulated by the idea of the everyday.

The development and growth of all manner of written and printed output in this century has left a variety of such sources. There are very few ordinary (or other) voices recorded for us to listen to, but the choice of language, speech pattern and vocabulary is there to be read. A definition of orality forms when we clarify what it is not: 'literacy, the literary, writing, print and elite culture', yet its evidence persists within a variety of written forms.[17] Recalibration of the relative prevalence of English, Scots and Gaelic in this century, and in that which preceded it, have been analysed within stadialist models of historical development. This linguistic balance permeates notions of cultural centrality, peripherality and inferiority as variable rates of social and economic improvement are contrasted. Yet it is an intellectual construct that works against understandings of the everyday because its explanation of social progress downplays the continued relevance of languages, dialects and speech patterns that are in decline. By directing our academic gaze towards the ordinary people and what they spoke, wrote and read about we find unevenness in the direction of these structural changes. As Donald Meek contends regarding one notable case, 'there is not a century in which Gaelic literature has been more greatly mistaken than this one'. His argument flows from observing that it was a time when economic and social dislocations meant the Gaelic-speaking areas were 'compelled by circumstances to find new voices and to develop less vulnerable modes of existence and self-preservation'.[18]

In a number of respects the same argument applies to the Scots language. Ubiquitous in this period was the penmanship of William Latto (1823–99), writing in Scots as Tammas Bodkin, known throughout Scotland in the second half of the century for his regular column in the *People's Journal*. Active until 1898, Latto's writings offered reflection on world events in a language understood by ordinary Scots. His impact differed and widened when his writings were transferred from newspaper to book form, Anglicised and projected as rural and 'couthy'. While the repackaged version is the one that survives, it is the earlier ephemeral newspaper publications that made his writings a vital feature of life, published weekly, re-read and re-circulated daily.[19]

These and writings like them were not divorced from the political economy of their day. William Alexander (1826–94) in his most celebrated work, *Johnny Gibb of Gushetneuk* (1871), has the eponymous hero following J. S. Mill's thinking on land ownership, placing value on the common man.[20] Alexander is an author who dealt with urban issues and contemporary social and political concerns yet is someone, William Donaldson laments, who has been identified erroneously with the worst nostalgia and rural parochialism of the Kailyard school. Donaldson's research shows that these publications worked best when there was a local paper with a deep local attachment, or a particular national paper with high number of working-class readers, with the *People's Journal* the most notable example.[21] Alexander added the role of reporter to that of critic, commenting on the changes that have followed faster transportation, as Alastair Durie argues in his chapter, and when visiting the Glasgow Saltmarket in 1865, exclaiming:

> Pity me! what a coontless multitude o' folk! What a warld o' wretchedness, want, an' misery! What a congregation o' rogues an' vagabonds o' baith sexes! Whaur did they a' come frae? Whaur are they a' guan till? On what business are they bent? Hoo do they manage to pick up a livelihood? . . . Hundreds o' them, I doot, live like the fowls o' the air – unable to tell i' the mornin when they get up whaur their breakfast is to come frae'.[22]

Bodkin was also read commenting on life around him, on the Afghan war, on royal marriage, on elections as well as on more prosaic activities (for some at least) of buying a lobster, bathing in the sea off St Andrews and engaging in proverbial philosophy.[23] The persistence of the Scots language in the modern newspaper continued a tradition of popular publishing, with the chapbook and broadside literature achieving some of the widest of audiences among the lower classes. Its transience and its ubiquity, sustained by its low cost, made it a literature of the people.[24] It offered life stories on love and marriage, on politics and religion, and on the history of the people, placing them in the constitutional structure of Britain. For some, such literature was celebrated in reviews for its humour and pathos.[25] It became a means for the Scottish countrymen to be described and appreciated for who they were.

The value of *Johnny Gibb* to the historian of the everyday is that the chosen dialect is central to the narrative and not employed solely as a cultural signifier. While his work was reviewed in the newspapers where his readership among speakers of Scots was to be found, it was not considered by the influential *Edinburgh Review* until 1883, after the third edition, which is perhaps suggestive of how easily overlooked this kind of literature can be.[26] It is also tempting to see its use of Scots as the death throes of a fast-disappearing language, or the cultural outcome of nostalgia, although a more meditated response suggests it is evidence of a language still in use outside of high public discourse. It was just as relevant in everyday speech for those who used it, as English was to others. It makes us consider the wider point informing the chapters in this volume that the everyday is not a 'trend', or a 'majority', but a lived reality to those involved. We should not be surprised to find when we continue this theme of written oral language a conflict between dialects: 'Da skülmaisters hae nae bishiness ta interfere wi' wir guid midder tongue. We pay dem fur learnin' bairns English, no fur unlearnin' wir Shetlan' speech . . .'.[27] This was an Aberdeenshire-speaking school-master trying to stamp out the Shetland dialect, a battle unexpected in the narrative trend of Anglicisation. Whatever the cultural critique, one spoke the language norms of one's family and community. Earlier in the century, Walter Scott had been congratulated for his use of Scots and English to differentiate the nationality of his characters. James Beattie's *Scotticisms* (1771) was re-published as *The Grammarian* in 1838, and while the use of unfashionable Scots words came to be employed as an ethnic marker, and presented with negative connotations, it was reading that was absorbed from within the Scottish nation just as it was a literary trope used to differentiate within a narrative.[28] But again this trend is not straightforward. John Galt's *The Entail* (1823) was described in the *Literary Gazette* as being 'eminently Scottish' and written in a 'provincial dialect than can hardly be intelligible beyond the western parts of that ancient kingdom'.[29] Yet along with *The Provost* (1822) it is regarded as among Galt's most perceptive work, bringing satire home to the small towns in which the two novels are rooted. J. M. Barrie's *A Window in Thrums* (1889) also presented rather broad Scotch to its readership, but as one commentator suggests, to the Scot of the north-east 'the realism is strangely striking and impressive'.[30] Nor should we assume Hugh McDairmid's creation of Lallans as part of an early twentieth-century counter-reaction to Kailyardism to be simply evidence of a re-routing from a cultural diversion. His attempt to reclaim Scotland's lowland language indicates that it was the power of the language in text, rather that in speech, which most connected the people with themselves and with their land.

Technological change within the period also makes available to us new forms of visual record in the photograph in both still and, towards the end of the century, moving form. There is an obvious attraction in the apparent immediacy with which everyday detail is caught by the camera, and contemporaries readily celebrated the capacity of the photograph to encapsulate reality with a fidelity that justified claims to scientific exactitude. The accuracy of the image was widely praised and for early exhibitors of the moving picture became a major selling point, as the large numbers filmed leaving work or attending local events were encouraged to attend screenings in order to 'see yourselves as others see you'.[31] Yet this also makes explicit the degree to which the images selected for reproduction were chosen more on grounds of commercial viability than documentary fidelity. The cameras of firms such as Washington Wilson of Aberdeen and Valentine and Sons of Dundee were thus drawn to views of Scotland and the Scots that resonated beyond the nation. In the process, a certain documentary record was bequeathed of particular geographical and occupational communities. As R. J. Morris has noted, fisherfolk figure disproportionately in the photographs of the period, satisfying as they did prevailing notions of the picturesque in ways that perhaps more representative urban trades could not.[32] We can interrogate such images for their content, both intended and incidental. So, the film of workers leaving the Camperdown Jute Works in Dundee, taken in 1912, presents in moving form a specific labour force, its age and gender balance, in which the dress of the young operatives is seen to replicate that of their elders. Yet it is also the quietness of the surrounding streets, populated by the occasional slow-moving tram and horse-drawn cart that helps to convey something of the auditory and environmental nature of the everyday even in this industrialised area.[33] The utility of such sources extends beyond their subject matter, as we are also told something of their intended audience and the manner in which they were consumed. The still photograph thus has much to convey on the tourist gaze in nineteenth-century Scotland and the particular images, replicated over time, that were deemed to capture the essence of the nation. It is in the ideas it conveys as much as in the information it imparts that the value of the visual resides.

EVERYDAY LIFE IN SCOTLAND, 1800 TO 1900

The chapters in this volume examine the lives of the Scottish people under the changes and continuities that enveloped the nineteenth century. Some of the most visible transformations are reflected in the Scottish landscape and in the work and society found in rural areas. Rental or ownership of land remained essential to many livelihoods, being a constant in the lives of Scots as either producers or consumers. The nation was home to a predominantly rural population in the first half of the century, and living in the country-side continued to be an actual or recent experience for many even in later decades. As more people relocated in search of opportunities and relief from the hard toil of rural work, concomitant pressure was placed on rural communities to increase productivity in order to feed the towns and cities with their burgeoning populations. That the emotional pull of the land remained in the blood came from practical experience; its availability best secured a safety net when hunger threatened. Without doubt the key attraction of emigration, to North America especially, was the promise of sufficient land upon which a basic standard of living could be secured. Land had long been assigned a fundamental place in society through biblical reference: 'And God blessed them, and God said unto them, be fruitful and multiply, and replenish the earth, and subdue it . . .'.[34] It was a call to stewardship by the people and a confidence in society's ability to control nature over the ages, and especially in this century of 'progress'.

Mairi Stewart and Fiona Watson explain in their chapter that land remained a fundamental continuity in the everyday lives of the Scots even when faced with the shards of modernity. The development of the steam engine and other new technologies impacted not only in the towns, but also on the countryside, on the built landscape of rural settlements as on woodlands, hedging and field structures. Using government reports, estate records, maps and the voluminous comparative evidence found in the Old and New Statistical Accounts, they explain the changing relationship between living and working on the land and its effects on the environment. Contemporary comment from those (non-tourist) visitors to the Highlands and Islands, and also the poetry from those who lived there, they argue show contemporaries conscious that long-worked jobs were under change, especially with the creation of the great deer estates in the second half of the century. We know from a number of vantage points that commercialisation of agriculture was not new in this period, and Stewart and Watson show how the introduction of lowland breeds of sheep, and moves to mixed farming were accompanied by emerging knowledge of fertilisers and of productivity gains from enclosure and changing patterns of crop rotation. This was new knowledge underpinned by scientific ideas of agriculture first developed in the Improvement phase of the Enlightenment. The reclamation of unproductive land and investment in infrastructural improvements, in docks, roads, bridges and fencing contributed to the visual impact on the topography of Scotland. Both clearing and re-forestation, separating grassland and woodland were to alter what was grown. This was not a world in stasis, it was life of remarkable drudgery, but one where small and much more dramatic changes were also happening. It was normal to find people moving around the rural world just as they continued to take on temporary seasonal migrations to the towns and cities. These were changes that required hard work and a variety of skills, and made toil a constant part of the day with little demarcation between productive employment and leisure. Some developments caused their own problems. The greater nutritional value of the potato compared with alternatives helped families to stay on the land, yet the blight that came in 1846 led to an estimated 150,000 Highland Scots having the fragility of their situation challenged further.

One feature of this period identified by Stewart and Watson that did much to change the daily and seasonal work patterns of agricultural workers was the creation of the sporting estate. It was a different kind of commercialisation from that seen elsewhere and one not directly linked to rational management of the land. Deer forests and grouse moors were introduced and developed, in part because the Improvers had moved away from the shieling. Sporting estates impacted on the jobs and income offered, with gamekeepers, gillies and beaters much in demand along with all the support and services required for these (urban) visitors.

Occupations associated with land, and its ideological importance to the Scots, are important, but so was access to some means of growing food or keeping small animals. The very necessities of Scotland, the food grown or purchased, the goods made, bartered or bought, are essential signifiers, as W. Hamish Fraser argues, to who the Scots were as a people. Food, drink, warmth, cleanliness and clothing were the basics of Scottish life in this century, as in others, their consumption split by social class and cultural variation, including what for some was luxury and for others necessity. Fraser reminds us that we know much about the lives of the very poor from the numerous government reports and other inquiries into their lives and that we know a fair bit about the middle classes from their aspirations of respectability and industriousness, including their guidance on how ordinary lives should be led. Again the Old and New Statistical Accounts provide insight. Fraser outlines the common foods found in the Scottish diet: the importance of oatmeal was central despite much regional variation in the consumption of other foods. Potato, of course, became popular, but dairy produce was something for the market rather than the dinner table. Fish was consumed differently in the regions and salt was important as a preserver, allowing the fish from the north-east to be exported as far as way as Jamaica. Meat was not eaten frequently in the decades before the 1840s and the consumption of fruit and vegetables was much more common in the rural areas than in the towns. Consumption of tea was one of the most interesting barometers of social class suggests Fraser; its classification as an everyday or luxury item reflected societal mores, and its consumption often debated as to its health qualities, including its ability, when sweetened, to fill an empty stomach. Fraser explains that dairy products would be more often found in the Scottish diet in the second half of the century, although milk, often rightly he suggests, was eyed with suspicion.

Keeping warm would also see important changes in this period, notably a move away from dependence on peat to the burning of coal in a fireplace with a metal grate. Only by the 1840s would gas lighting start to be used, with whale or fish oil being lit prior to that. Fraser suggests that cooking in the overcrowded Scottish home was never a straightforward proposition, hence, the attraction of preparing simple meals of bread, cheese and butter. Clothing was kept in use by repair and alteration. Underwear would be changed to help with personal cleanliness, although it was difficult to preserve substantial supplies mould and damp free. Just keeping hunger at bay and clothing on one's back, shoes for one's feet, and not just on Sunday, was an everyday concern for the majority. Thrift and self-help were mores that developed around industriousness as the means of keeping a life or family economy functioning when income was scarce or irregular. We learn that the middle class of the second half of the century were caught up with trying to match their lifestyles with incomes that were often overly stretched, but at least they could generally obtain the privacy and cleanliness denied those living in the tenements. The middle class moved in fashion and soft furnishings towards the overly ornate, with the separate parlour being a preserve of respectability even when unjustified by the space left for daily use in the remainder of the property. The structures of class in nineteenth-century Scotland were to play out in a number of small and otherwise insignificant cultural variations, in diet, clothing and at the table around which one sat.

All living Scots were born, but how birth was treated in different social situations and at different times of adult life had much variation. The chapter from Andrew Blaikie explores the customs that form around the birth of a child, the act that all experience coming into the world. Until the mid-twentieth century, he argues, both birth and death were most likely to have taken place within the home, thus making these most individual acts a family experience. These were cultural episodes that took place as part of the inter-play of popular customs and institutional change, particularly of the Church of Scotland. Attitudes to pre-marital sex and illegitimate births were forged in this axis, but were also considered in terms of local economic resources, notably the availability of work, land and a home. Rates of nuptiality, Blaikie suggests, were heavily dependent on confidence that a viable nuclear family could be established. One must be aware of how middle-class moralists mis-read immorality as a function of modernisation, a mis-reading that a number of contributions to this volume suggest was widely held. The health of illegitimate babies and infants contributed to a higher death rate than those born legitimately. Infant mortality fuelled a persistently high death rate throughout this century, and it also justified the increasingly wide range of funeral customs that proliferated, led in part by the very public and long-lasting mourning of Albert, the Prince Consort, by Victoria. Family size was slowly reducing, but the preference for large families persisted. Still, shows Blaikie, changes in family size alongside other cultural norms indicate a re-evaluation of children as wanted for themselves rather than simply valued as economic resources. Greater control over when births were likely to happen, and improvements in sanitation that began to mitigate the endemic and episodic challenges to health, contributed to making the fragility of life less precarious, although this was no Whiggish progress and the death rate was reluctant to diminish in this century.

One of the key features of Blaikie's chapter is its focus on the challenging cultural situation within which the Kirk Session imposed discipline and parochial morality among the Scottish people. Challenged by individualism but especially customs borne out of economic circumstances which deterred against marriage, this discipline was invariably regionally marked. As shown in the case study of Banffshire and Aberdeenshire, 'unmarried motherhood was', Blaikie concludes, 'remarkable only for its normality'. The thesis that a 'Victorian crisis of faith' followed such a breakdown in church discipline, and that secularisation grew on the back of modernisation, is challenged by Stewart J. Brown. One important way that the Church of Scotland reformed itself here was its move away from an unbending definition of the Westminster Confession of Faith where one would not know whether one was elect and destined for heaven or damned without salvation: it was a concern that could prick a conscience, or a rebuke, at almost any level. The change would be towards the social intervention of evangelism and the belief that all could be saved. The sermon, Brown shows, remained central to maintaining the tenets of Presbyterianism throughout Scotland, its absorption in mind and spirit part of the debate over the respective merits of the extemporised or scripted oration. Hierarchies of social class were maintained through pew rents and the variability of cost, or of no cost, was a feature in the competing attraction of eloquent preachers. Brown shows that customs began to change in the second half of the century when church interiors became more ornate, although it was not until 1866 that the Church of Scotland permitted the use of organs to provide musical accompaniment. The sacrament of Holy Communion was an occasion for much introspection upon personal worthiness and, at the start of the century, these were great events built up over days and weeks. The baptism was the second sacrament in the Church of Scotland, most commonly taking place in the home rather than in the church (as Blaikie has also explored). Personal moralities, Brown shows, were presented around the birth and although popular understandings hasted the child to baptism lest it die 'in limbo', there was no doctrinal basis for this belief. Kirk discipline was widely linked to ideas of self-help and industriousness, confirmed by notions of respectability. Yet chastisement would increasingly be ignored or would result in departure from the congregation, a particular danger for the Church of Scotland after the Disruption in 1843. Its apparent loss of adherents revealed by the Religious Census of 1851, and the rise of religious pluralism in the second half of the century, was an important change in how Scotland worshipped but one that did not appear to diminish religiosity. The alliance of the United Presbyterian Church and the Free Church to disestablish the Church of Scotland was a sign of how, while Scotland remained predominantly Presbyterian and strongly religious, no one Church could dominate as the Kirk had previously done.

The ripping apart of the Established Church of Scotland in 1843 was the apogee of decade-long spiritual and temporal clashes, founded on much longer-lasting concerns, and its social impact was to subvert the link between parish and relief, ushering in the state to increase slowly its role in welfare provision. This period also saw invigoration of the charitable associational activity of the Scots, often strengthening the relevance of points of doctrine and Evangelicalism within Presbyterianism. It contributed to a strand of Protestantism that fuelled a variety of religious conflict and violence. An example showing the associational side to this incitement was the Edinburgh Association for Promoting Evangelical Religion on the Continent, which met in 1841 'to carry the gospel into nations where Popery and Infidelity reign' and to raise money to support theological schools.[35] Another was the Scottish Association for Opposing Prevalent Errors, formed in 1845, which castigated 'Popery, Puseyism and INFIDELITY' as superstitions at variance with Christianity.[36] Upping further the rhetorical stakes, the Edinburgh Irish Mission and Protestant Institute formed the following year to 'save the British Constitution' from 'Ireland's terrorism' as 'Jesuits and priests glide into our drawing rooms'.[37] In 1850 that city's Protestant Publication Society issued a third plea for the creation of a National Protestant Confederation and Protestant Electoral Unions throughout Britain to divide electors between 'sincere Protestants, who hold the principles of the Reformation and the Revolution . . .' and 'Papists, pseudo-Protestants and infidels who unite together . . .'[38] It was the passing of the Catholic Emancipation Act in 1829 and state funding for Maynooth Seminary College, a key preoccupation of mid-century politics, which brought the Scottish Protestant Alliance together to issue its manifesto in 1854.[39]

The everyday influence of Christianity was pervasive. In song, in art and reading, to take the most obvious examples, religious themes abounded. They were not incompatible with less formal religious beliefs and regionally specific moral imperatives. In chapbook accounts from the late eighteenth and early part of the nineteenth centuries, stories of sexual awakenings and worldly advice would permeate tales of adolescence and family life.[40] Informal religious beliefs in paganism, fairies and other unexplainable phenomena co-existed alongside biblical scripture despite the efforts of many a preacher and the secular sciences. Hugh Miller, the Free Church stonemason, doubted whether fairy inhabitants could survive the 'light of science', yet such beliefs persisted; in one case a mother claimed her baby had become a changeling, a suggestion that could mask infanticide, but here the infant had been taken to a neighbouring township, dropped in the river where miraculously it was transformed back into the mother's own child again.[41] The work done on Celtic beliefs in fairies by the Tiree minister, John Gregorson Campbell (1834–91), shows the seriousness and commonality of such beliefs. As Elizabeth Ritchie explains, Campbell keeps his commentary to a minimum preferring to let the ordinary voice of the sentiment, and strength of belief, come to the fore.[42] It was a constant undercurrent of late Victorian Highland religious life, while throughout Scotland spiritualists and mesmerists were a new connection to the 'other world'. The most successful of them all was the Glasgow-born Daniel Dunglas Home (1833–86), who not only withstood the investigations of other conjurors but the reputations of royalty, celebrities and scientists.[43]

Formal religion was not to be undermined by such beliefs and informal practices were for many no contradiction in their lives. Widely in society God would be thanked and appealed to in equal measure, for the rain and sun of the seasons and called upon to guide life's decision making. Writing from the north-east of Scotland and reflecting on the year 1889 as the most memorable ever because of his marriage, James Wilson prayed: 'May that Providence for the future guide and direct our every step in life, and trusting entirely to His Almighty care, we would look forward to the coming year with faith and hope, trusting that for not only ourselves but all our friends and relations it may prove both a happy and prosperous one.'[44]

How the people of Scotland traversed their landscape was one of the more dramatic transformations of this century. The road system, Alastair Durie explains, was now home to the trap, the cart and the stagecoach rather than the sledge and packhorse. Steamships were to offer regular sailings around Britain's coasts and, most dramatically of all, the railway was to move people and goods around with the greatest of speed, the first wave of track and stations being laid down in the 1830s and 1840s, the next growth coming in the 1860s. Much change, certainly, but some older forms of transportation persisted. The canals were still important for moving goods and people in the early part of this century as were riverboats and horse-drawn stagecoaches. Horses were found pulling tramcars in the streets of the 1870s, although pulley systems and electrical motors would later take on this work. The railway, of course, was the noisy interloper, but even the much quieter bicycle in the 1890s and the motorbus and car in the first decade of the next century, Durie notes, added in their own ways to the whizzing by of human kind. Such developments in the speed and reach of mass transportation enabled new kinds of leisure activities to be followed. The Lowland and English elite fascination with hunting and fishing in the Highlands had its impact on local employment and on an evolving landscape. Durie shows how the development of the railway led to the creation of new occupations; along with concentrations of carters and vendors there were porters and other support workers in and around the railway station. Railway hotels and lodging houses were established for commercial travellers and tourists alike. Steamers allowed cheap fun for a works or community outing and were especially popular during the 'fair holiday' weeks, often gaining a negative reputation for boisterousness and drunkenness. Tourists brought money into local economies, not for souvenirs, although local produce would be bought, but for the fetching and carrying of bags and equipment and all the servicing needed for those making the most of their leisure time. If the labouring classes were not sailing down the Clyde on their time off, which the chapter from Trevor Griffiths shows to be formalised from the 1870s, then they might make use of railway specials to take themselves to the seaside or to other sources of fresh air and (perhaps) restorative waters.

From the starting point that that leisure was the time left over after work, Griffiths begins his chapter with an examination of changing processes in the work place, especially the increasingly prominence of the clock and time discipline. The irregularity of pre-industrial patterns was threatened, as was the undisciplined nature of leisure and sporting activities. This was no simple change, Griffiths shows, with the modernisation of work and leisure developing haphazardly across the country, with much regional and sectoral variation. Work discipline took many forms: pay being docked; corporal punishment; bullying; and invasive supervision. The discipline of the clock was also applied, although workers would look for ways to circumnavigate the pressure. And just as traditional and modern work practices co-existed long into the century, so too, Griffiths argues, can it be said of leisure activities. While there was control imposed on the cruelties of cat and bull baiting, and of cock fighting, still there would continue unregulated underground or under a blind eye bare-knuckle fighting, vulgar freak shows and other amusements. Again local variation abounded, making the everyday experience of work and leisure an experience difficult to summarise. Seasonal changes were apparent, and work would be impacted by international trade cycles. Fire and harvest festivals were strong community events with the hiring fair becoming a means of recruitment to industry, but it was also an occasion for boisterous behaviour and numerous others forms of socialising. Firms would organise the workers' day out or support a brass band. Again these could be lively affairs, with much consumption of alcohol and the feeling of St Monday persisting to mid-century. But it was Saturday that became the important day off, and this was the day on which leisure activities were to be encouraged. Still, for many, working days were not regular, and often continued until the job was done, irrespective of the hour. Nor was there any clear divide between work and home, work and leisure, for women. Women found it hard to find the time for discrete leisure, just as their work patterns were slowest to accede to modern patterns.

Maintaining the morality of the Scottish people during their time away from work was not only the preserve of the churches and home missionaries. The apparatus of local state intervention was based on local as well as national freedoms. As William Knox and Alan McKinlay explain, the origins of policing in Scotland were a symbiosis of 'watching' and control over public infrastructure. It was the creation of a structure to stop vice becoming commonplace, to stop it becoming, or developing further as a feature of the everyday. The scandal of the Burke and Hare trials in 1828–9, for example, would offer much detail on the life of immigrant Irishmen and of those with whom they associated in the tumble down housing of Edinburgh's vennels. The accusations of murder and the beliefs of the resurrectionists were printed to excess as early forms of newspaper supplement, with attention focused on the phrenological characteristics of the defendants and those of their nation.[45] Vice, generally linked to drunkenness and the arrival of identifiable outsiders competing for jobs or relief from poverty, were strong motifs in demands for an efficient system of policing throughout the country. That much of the early police legislation was enacted to maintain social order in the towns and cities, especially attempting to manage public order under pressure from sectarian conflict, is a point picked up by Knox and McKinlay.

Alcohol, inevitably, contributed to much public disturbance. 'In the hour of National Danger, Apathy is Crime' the inhabitants of Edinburgh were addressed in 1832.[46] The despairing commentator questioned how Scots could claim their northern part of the British Isles had a superior culture given the hideousness of the scene in Edinburgh's High Street on a Sabbath morning. The city inhabitants were reminded that 2,438 were counted as drunk and disorderly in the period 15 July to 15 August in that year of franchise reform.[47] Little had apparently improved over the next two decades, with one newspaper investigation concluding there were 400 public houses open on the Sabbath in the capital.[48] The temperance movement, in which John Dunlop was the leading campaigner, identified this as a hideous vice, crippling the Scottish character. At the time of the amalgamation into the Scottish Temperance Society in 1832 there were fourteen societies in Glasgow with around 8,000 members.[49] The Scottish Temperance League chose 5 November 1844 as the day to form in Falkirk, a group that grew into an average membership of 12,000 with an income of £7,000 over the century.[50] As much as Scotland was a society of ubiquitous drinkers, so it was a society brimming with disapprobation against that very act. The work of the temperance groups was preached in the church and in the meeting hall.

Adding to a slowly growing literature that challenges the notion of the straightforward and steady rise of order and sobriety in Victorian Scotland, Knox and McKinlay examine how respectability and rough culture ebbed and flowed, especially after 1850. They first examine the extent to which petty property crime remained a common survival strategy for the very poor, as it had been in the eighteenth century. The defence of property as a mark of social order was, they show, a particularly powerful motor of legislative and attitudinal changes. The moral overseeing of the poor, their education, their health, their neighbourhoods and their street activities of begging, gambling and simply hanging around, came at various times to the attention of reformers worried about the economic impact of the 'disaffected'. It tended to be young men and it tended to be crimes against property that were the most prevalent, and criminal activity appeared to be closely linked to intemperance. Knox and McKinlay conclude their analysis with the wider point that most crime was petty and deemed actionable by courts influenced by prevalent bourgeois moralities and values.

Religious disorder was at times linked to sporting occasions, represented most clearly by sectarian divides in the football teams of Dundee, Edinburgh and Glasgow, and both were contributing elements of gang culture. That women were involved in public disorder as well as political and gender struggles is shown in a number of different examples by Knox and McKinlay. Their evidence throughout shows how the people of Scotland were faced by a developing police force more concerned with maintaining social order than detecting or preventing crime, and how after 1850 its emphasis fell on the implementation of middle-class defined behaviours. For some the police increasingly took on a role once reserved for the military, to others they were nothing more than the frontline of class-based moralising; the policeman was not always deemed friend by the working classes.

Much of this control was developed in response to urbanisation: the developing urban world threw up dramatic changes in how space was conceived, used and lived in. Urban space was shaped within the buildings and the spaces between them, and space was managed, R. J. Morris tells us, by rituals of place which did much to teach the Scots who they were. Prestige space and its reverse, the slums and the broken down areas of the towns, also taught Scots their social demarcations of class, of ethnicity, religion and of gender. Boundaries were important, either the common land being ridden by the burgesses of Selkirk or Hawick, or the Glasgow parish expanding its tax base under police legislation. These urban boundary extensions, Morris contends, were about creating communities where there was much in common, maintaining public order and public health, and were a means of resolving disputes, avoiding boundaries becoming barriers.

The urban landscape can be explored in maps and in photographs to show the impact of the industrial system as it developed in towns small and large. There were areas designated for trade and exchange, there was light added from streetlamps and order imposed through street design as much as the urban policeman. There were divisions in space between areas for walking and areas for transport, especially the 'furious' motorised vehicles and – for some – the 'frightening' pedal-powered bicycles (of the kind that Durie identifies). There were areas for shopping, some more accessible to middle-class women than others. The street was formalised where, Morris notes, social groups identified and made allowances for each other as they used the street for different purposes and at different times of the day. The noise and the rhythm of the street were much altered from the previous century. Walking, we learn, was a skill that needed to be adapted, and still does as urban landscapes evolve; 'going for a walk' then became a trip to the countryside for exercise and recreation. It is the railway that Morris identifies as being the key non-space in the city, a 'place of anxiety, a place of transition'. Other places had greater meaning, particularly those created for the purpose of commemoration, enabling the Scots to forge a social memory and identity no matter how fractured and wide changing the urban landscape had become.

Attachment to locality is also seen to underpin Graeme Morton's examination of identity in the everyday. Personal identities are produced and reproduced in the course of social interaction, yet their conscious articulation is of little relevance without challenge or test to trigger awareness.[51] Still, identity claims are made all the time in ways that are so banal that too often their essence is missed. Their apparent irrelevance, Morton argues, is their significance, because they are a constant part of life. As one group of researchers spells out their pervasiveness, 'We claim identity, we attribute identity to others, and we receive the claims of others.'[52] Some of these claims are accessible, some less so; some are fixed, some are fluid; some are projected back upon ourselves from afar.

From this basis Morton suggests there is insight to be gained by shifting the historical gaze away from ethnicity or heightened moments of commemoration towards the everyday projection and reception of identity claims. Such evidence can be unearthed as the Scots managed their society in a period of sometimes jarring and incessantly uneven change. One way contemporaries attempted to fix the personal identity markers of their day was by establishing connections to key interpretations of their past. It was, suggests Morton, a means of maintaining rootedness in the nation as well as in the locality of place. Museum collections show how contemporaries made accessible a suitable past for fear its bond with the present was being lost. The library thus functioned among a number of naturalist, mechanics' and philosophical societies, as did the small permanent collection of artefacts or sometimes the more extensive ad hoc exhibition. Aberdeen's Mechanics' Institution, for instance, designed an exhibition of Fine Arts, Natural History, Philosophy, Machinery, Manufactures, Antiquities, and Curiosities in 1840 in hope of raising sufficient funds to establish a permanent home for their objects.[53] Their rooms and display cases contained much variety, including working locomotive engines; a diving-bell; a letter press; paper in various stages of manufacture; a cheetah or hunting leopard; a vampire bat; Borland's Patent Water-Meter; a Lunar Circle and Sun Dial; portraits of Alexander Bannerman, Esq. and MP, Cleopatra and Stirling Castle; Mr Laing's painting of *John Knox Preaching before the Lords of the Congregation*, styled after Sir David Wilkie; a French image of Ossian; plus a glass case of famous staffs: from Charles Edward Stuart, Napoleon Bonaparte's gift of a staff to Mr George Thom, master, on his voyage to St Helena, plus the stick presented by Robert Burns to Mr Thomson of Edinburgh in 1793. The intention of the exhibitors was to situate the north-east of their day within a chosen story of the historical nation, to make the narrative receptive to all, and to fix it in time and in place.

Other organised responses to the dislocations of urban and industrial change were apparent in societies and associations established to help those deemed to be casualties of the age. These organisations, Morton contends, were formed in an image of Scotland as a Christian nation, where religion pervaded almost all aspects of personal daily life through patterns of speech, in thoughts and prayers over even the smallest matters, and in motivations of guilt, salvation and the benefits of Providence. In the identity claims of associational culture, there was emphasis on morality, piety and self-help as ideals underpinned by formal and informal religious observance. In part a reaction to the signs of secularisation, in part a means of social discipline, it was adjudged a Christian duty to intervene in the lives of the poorest. Study of the ragged school movement and the Magdalene institutions indicate how middle-class moralists aimed for social regulation imbued by predetermined ideas of how 'saved' lives were to be lived in daily routine. Religion informed so much of the institutional day, not just Sunday, and was a constant point of reference for (generally) young men and women taught the habits of industry and the skills of economy. Many inevitably rejected the moralists, and even those who aspired to their promptings could never hope to obtain all the necessary ideals, but such a life formed an identity of the Scot sustained sometimes in its breech as much as in its observance.

Morton argues further that these ideals were rooted in various interpretations of Scotland as place, a theme he takes up in the examination of local attachment to community and region. From maps to diaries there are signs of how the Scots imagined the everyday world around them. Analysis of the highland journal of Queen Victoria shows a monarch's annotations of her everyday life and of those whom she observed during her time in Scotland. Yet the great impact of the published dairy was to commodify the Highlands as the antonym of modernity and all the changes that entailed. In deer farms and grouse moors, in the homeliness of Victoria, the Highlands presented a place consumed for its ordinariness, its everyday qualities seemingly protected from the disarray of the times. Divorced from the historical reality of lived lives, celebration of the ordinary was mined from this and similar attachments to place. Festivals of harvest, fire, sport and a preferred past, like so many aspects of community formation examined in this volume, offer the historian evidence of the endemic networks of self-identification that were formed in the localities of Scotland.

Notes

1 Among recent overviews of nineteenth-century Scotland, the following are especially useful: T. C. Smout, *A Century of the Scottish People, 1830–1950* (London and New Haven, 1986); S. G. and O. Checkland, *Industry and Ethos: Scotland, 1832–1914* (London, 1984); W. Hamish Fraser and R. J. Morris (eds), *People and Society in Scotland. Volume II, 1830–1914* (Edinburgh, 1990); T. M. Devine, *The Scottish Nation, 1700–2000* (London, 1999); G. Morton and R. J. Morris, 'Civil Society, Governance and Nation, 1832–1914', in R. A. Houston and W. W. J. Knox (eds), *The New Penguin History of Scotland: From the Earliest Times to the Present Day* (London, 2001), pp. 355–416; T. M. Devine, C. H. Lee and G. C. Peden (eds), *The Transformation of Scotland: The Economy since 1700* (Edinburgh, 2005).

2 For a classic statement of this view, albeit in an English context, see H. Perkin, *Origins of Modern English Society, 1780–1800* (London, 1969).

3 E. P. Thompson, 'Time, Work-Discipline and Industrial Capitalism' *Past and Present* (December 1967), 56–97.

4 M. A. Bienefeld, *Working Hours in British Industry: An Economic History* (London, 1972) provides a reliable guide to the principal changes through the period.

5 G. R. Boyer, 'Living Standards, 1860–1914', in R. Floud and P Johnson (eds),

The Cambridge Economic History of Modern Britain. Volume II: Economic Maturity, 1860–1939 (Cambridge, 2004), pp. 280–313.

6   B. Harrison, *Drink and the Victorians: The Temperance Question in England, 1815–1872* (London, 1971); T. Collins and W. Vamplew, *Mud, Sweat and Beers: A Cultural History of Sport and Alcohol* (Oxford and New York, 2002).

7   R. J. Morris, 'Urbanisation and Scotland', in Fraser and Morris (eds), *People and Society in Scotland*, pp. 73–102; T. Hart, 'Urban Growth and Municipal Government: Glasgow in a Comparative Context, 1846–1914', in A. Slaven and D. H. Aldcroft (eds), *Business, Banking and Urban History* (Edinburgh, 1982), pp. 193–219.

8   C. G. Brown, *Religion and Society in Scotland since 1707* (Edinburgh, 1997), esp. ch. 6; C. G Brown, 'Religion, Class and Church Growth', in Fraser and Morris (eds), *People and Society in Scotland*, pp. 310–35.

9   M. Anderson and D. J. Morse, 'The People', pp. 8–13, 15, 22–4, 31–4, and A. Crowther, 'Poverty, Health and Welfare', pp. 265–8, 282, both in Fraser and Morris (eds), *People and Society in Scotland*, II; M. Anderson and D. J. Morse, 'High Fertility, High Emigration, Low Nuptiality: Adjustment Processes in Scotland's Demographic Experience, 1861–1914, Part I', *Population Studies*, 47: 1 (March 1993), 5–25, and 'Part II', *Population Studies*, 47: 2 (July 1993), 319–43.

10 D. Cannadine, 'The Present and the Past in the English Industrial Revolution, 1880–1980', *Past and Present*, 103 (1984), 131–72, provides a useful overview of the changing historiography on this key if contested aspect of the period.

11 W. Lazonick, 'Employment Relations in Manufacturing and International Competition', in R. Floud and D. McCloskey (eds), *The Economic History of Britain since 1700. Volume 2: 1860–1939*, 2nd edn (Cambridge, 1994), pp. 90–116.

12 Although relating to a slightly later period, the oral testimony collected in C. Langhamer, *Women's Leisure in England, 1920–1960* (Manchester, 2000), offers useful perspectives on the female experience of and attitudes to time.

13 E. Ross, 'Women's Neighbourhood Sharing in London before World War I', *History Workshop Journal*, 15 (1983), 4–27; E. Ross, *Love and Toil: Motherhood in Outcast London, 1870–1918* (Oxford, 1993).

14 F. P. Gibbon, *William A. Smith of the Boys' Brigade* (London, 1934); R. S. Peacock, *Pioneer of Boyhood: The Story of Sir William A. Smith, Founder of the Boys' Brigade* (Glasgow, 1954).

15 H. Cockburn, *Memorials of His Time* (Edinburgh, 1856), pp. 337–8.

16 Cockburn, *Memorials*, pp. 371–2.

17 L. Davis and M. N. McLane, 'Orality and Public Poetry', in I. Brown, S. Manning, M. Pittock and T. Clancy (eds), *Edinburgh History of Scottish Literature*, Vol. II (Edinburgh, 2006), p. 125.

18 D. E. Meek, 'Gaelic Literature in the Nineteenth Century', in Brown *et al.* (eds), *Edinburgh History of Scottish Literature*, p. 253.

19 W. Donaldson, *The Language of the People: Scots Prose from the Victorian Revival* (Aberdeen, 1989), p. 7.

20 See Donaldson's edited version of this book and of Alexander's *My Uncle the Baillie*; W. Donaldson, 'Alexander, William (1826–1894)', *Oxford Dictionary of National Biography* (Oxford, 2004); online edn, May 2006, available at: http://www.oxforddnb.com/view/article/39241 (accessed 18 July 2008).

21 Donaldson, *Language of the People*, p. 14.

22 'Bodkin in the Saltmarket', 8 April 1865, in Donaldson, *Language of the People*, p. 58

23 Donaldson, *Language of the People*, pp. 47–90.

24 E. J. Cowan and M. Paterson, *Folk in Print: Scotland's Chapbook Heritage 1750–1850* (Edinburgh, 2007), ch. 1.

25 E. Letley, *From Galt to Douglas Brown: Nineteenth-century Fiction and Scots Language* (Edinburgh, 1988), p. 220.

26 Letley, *From Galt to Douglas Brown*, pp. 133–4.

27 Donaldson, *Language of the People*, p. 117.

28 Letley, *From Galt to Douglas Brown*, p. 51.

29 *The Literary Gazette*, 21 December 1822, p. 800 cited in Letley, *From Galt to Douglas Brown*, p. 50.

30 Letley, *From Galt to Douglas Brown*, p. 222.

31 V. Toulmin, *Electric Edwardians: The Story of the Mitchell and Kenyon Collection* (London, 2007).

32 R. J. Morris, *Scotland 1907: The Many Scotlands of Valentine and Sons, Photographers* (Edinburgh, 2007), p. 8; A. J. Durie, *George Washington Wilson in St Andrews and Fife* (Aberdeen, 1994); A. J. Durie, *Scotland for the Holidays: Tourism in Scotland, c.1780–1939* (East Linton, 2003); T. Normand, *Scottish Photography: A History* (Edinburgh, 2007).

33 Scottish Screen Archive, 0771, 'A Glimpse of the Camperdown Works'.

34 Genesis (1:28; 9:2).

35 *The Edinburgh Association for Promoting Evangelical Religion on the Continent*, 26 January 1841; *Edinburgh Continental Association*, No. V, March 1843.

36 *Scottish Association for Opposing Prevalent Errors* (March 1847), pp. 1, 3; *Report of the Scottish Association for Opposing Prevalent Errors* (Edinburgh, 1848), p. 1.

37 *Missions for the Conversion of Irish Romanists in the Large Towns of England and Scotland explained and recommended, being the Report of the Edinburgh Irish Mission for the Year 1851, with a list of subscriptions* (Edinburgh, 1852), pp. 2–3.

38 *Plea for a National Protestant Confederation. and Protestant Electoral Unions throughout the Kingdom* (Edinburgh, 1850), p. 4.

39 *Manifesto of the Scottish Protestant Alliance; or Reasons for an enlarged basis of Union and Action for the Overthrow of Popery in every form* (Edinburgh, 1854), pp. 3, 5.

40 For one study of this literature, see: K. Saffery, 'Chapbooks and Audiences: an Examination of Representations of Family in Scottish Chapbooks, 1801–1829', MA, University of Guelph, 2007.

41 H. Miller, *Scenes and Legends of the North of Scotland* (Edinburgh, 1835), p. 2; R. Black, (ed.), *The Gaelic Otherworld: John Gregorson Campbell's 'Superstitions of the Highlands and Islands of Scotland' and 'Witchcraft and Second Sight in the Highlands and Islands'* (Edinburgh, 2005), p. lvii.

42 E. Ritchie, 'Review', *International Review of Scottish Studies*, 31 (2006), 139–40.

43 P. Lamont, 'Spiritualism and a Mid-Victorian Crisis of Evidence', *The Historical Journal*, 47:4 (2004), 897–920.

44 *Journal of My Life and Everyday Doings, 1879–81, 1885–92, James Wilson, farmer in Banffshire*, P. Hillis (ed.) (Edinburgh, 2008), p. 315 (30 November 1889).

45 G. MacGregor, *The History of the Burke and Hare Trials and of the Resurrectionist Times* (Glasgow, 1884); D. A. Symonds, *Notorious Murders, Black Lanterns, & Moveable Goods: the Transformation of Edinburgh's Underworld in the Early Nineteenth Century* (Akron, 2006).

46 *Address to the Inhabitants of Edinburgh on the necessity of removing the causes of crime which now disgrace the city, Edinburgh* (Edinburgh, 1832), p. 1.

47 *Address to the Inhabitants of Edinburgh*, p. 9.

48 From the 'Scottish Press', 16 March 1850.

49 A. Aird, *Glimpses of old Glasgow* (Glasgow, 1894), p. 215.

50 Aird, *Glimpses of old Glasgow*, p. 216.

51 Jenkins, 'Rethinking Ethnicity', p. 209.

52 R. Kiely, F. Bechhofer, R. Stewart and D. McCrone, 'The Markers and Rules of Scottish National Identity', *The Sociological Review*, 49:1 (2001), 34–7.

53 *Catalogue of the Exhibition of objects illustrative of the Fine Arts, Natural History, Philosophy, Machinery, Manufactures, Antiquities, Curiosities, etc. in connection with the Aberdeen Mechanics' Institution* (Aberdeen, 1840).

Chapter 1

Land, the Landscape and People in the Nineteenth Century

Mairi Stewart and Fiona Watson

INTRODUCTION

Landscape is ever-changing, whether that change is dramatic like a land-slip, or gradual like the meandering river; whether it is the result of natural processes or driven by human intervention. The way that the land is used by people also changes, even as part of the seasonal cycle. Take the field, for example, which ripples with barley in late summer, after which the stubble is given over to grazing in autumn and winter. Each shift in the form of cultivation changes the face of the countryside even on an annual basis. However, this form of rotational agriculture – the growing of grass leys one year, oats or barley in the next and then perhaps potatoes or turnips in the following year – became prevalent in the Scottish country-side only in the nineteenth century. This seasonality also dictated the way the people who spent most of their working lives on the land carried out their everyday lives. And even though by the beginning of that century the proportion of the Scottish population living in the countryside was falling dramatically, nevertheless two-thirds were still rural dwellers, even if they were not all directly employed in agriculture.[1] An expansion of towns and villages in the countryside, where agriculture still formed a part of daily life, if only with the keeping of a cow and raising of subsistence vegetables such as kale and potatoes, ensured a retention of a land-centred culture. Smaller burghs like Nairn and Elgin, at the bottom of the urban hierarchy for most of their history, continued to have an important agri-cultural function – both arable and pastoral – after 1800. Throughout the century, most people in Scotland retained close ties with the land, even city dwellers, many of whom had family still living in the countryside and had known rural life at first-hand.

At the macro scale, land-use change can fundamentally transform the landscape, often to the point of near or total obliteration of what was there before, with considerable repercussions for local populations. It could be argued that the nineteenth century witnessed a period of unprecedented change in land use, creating a landscape which had more in common with the twenty-first century than with what went immediately before, though the stimulus and origins of this transformation were rooted in the eighteenth century (and, indeed, earlier in some parts of Scotland). That is not to deny the impact of the progress of the Improvement era in the late eighteenth century, which some commentators regard as having been revolutionary in nature.[2] This might be a valid conclusion for the more profitable grain growing and dairy producing counties of the Lothians, Fife and the west of Scotland, but in other parts of Scotland improvement was slow to take off and the most significant landscape changes occurred well into the nineteenth century.

Even those areas which had been so unequivocally transformed, structurally and physically, in the second half of the eighteenth century, continued to be altered and improved as new methods of farming, the advent of steam and other new technologies increased profitability, and investment in infrastructure, machinery, housing (domestic and farm) and land reclamation proceeded apace. Many present-day landscape features have their origins in the nineteenth century – substantial clusters of assorted stone farm buildings, today frequently converted to expensive country retreats, roads and farm tracks lined with splendid old oak and ash trees, large rectilinear fields enclosed by dyke, hedge or ditch, now largely amalgamated, and the field systems themselves, delineated now by only an occasional tree or solitary hawthorn indicating former boundaries.

It is usually assumed that the Highland landscape was less affected by late eighteenth- and nineteenth-century land-use developments, though the social and economic consequences are acknowledged. However, consider the line of croft houses with strips of fields extending down to the shore; mile upon mile of stone dykes, often reaching to the summit of mountains; the strategically located sheep fank, built from stone scavenged from deserted touns; or the line of stone grouse butts stretched out across heather moorland. Even the antecedents of twentieth-century commercial conifer-based forestry in the uplands can be found in the nineteenth century.

This chapter considers some key changes in land use and the landscape of the nineteenth century – agricultural and settlement re-organisation, woodland and trees and sporting developments – all of which are intertwined and which influenced the Scottish landscape, albeit with variable effects. Continuity and change plays its part, as always, both impacting on those who lived and worked in the countryside. It is not possible to present here a detailed review of how the re-shaping of the Scottish countryside during the nineteenth century changed the lives of its population. The complexity and spatial diversity of nineteenth-century land-use systems ensured that generalisations based on the experience of one locality cannot easily be applied more widely. The purpose of this chapter is simply to provide some insight into land-use change and how that affected the people who depended on the land, drawing on examples from various parts of Scotland.

Figure 1.1   *Achiltibuie, Ross-shire. A crofting township dating from the early nineteenth century when Cromarty Estate re-organised the landscape in order to turn large areas into sheep farms. © Royal Commission on the Ancient and Historical Monuments of Scotland; C/40130. Licensor www.scran.ac.uk.*

SOURCES

By the nineteenth century, the sources – particularly archival material – which can be drawn on to construct a picture of the countryside, country life and land management become richer, more detailed and more widespread. Estate records become voluminous, providing extensive records of the minutiae of estate organisation and management. However, there is no doubt that they principally and inevitably depict a one-sided view of society: that of the landowners. There exists in the documentary evidence little detail regarding the tenantry's opinions and preoccupations, and even less on the subordinate cottars and servants.

The profusion of estate plans and surveys that emerged during the latter half of the eighteenth century in response to the drive to re-organise estates by their owners provides a good baseline for comparison with nineteenth-century maps, particularly the first edition of the Ordnance Survey (hereafter OS), truly the first large-scale and comprehensive topographic survey of Great Britain (at a scale of 1:10560). The OS was completed for Scotland between 1843 and 1882 and provides perhaps the most accurate and detailed portrayal of the Scottish landscape before the twentieth century, at a time when it was being transformed almost beyond recognition from that which existed only 100 years earlier.[3] Although Smout *et al.* (2003) question the ability of this map series to capture the nuances of woodland and scrub prevailing in the Scottish (mainly highland) landscape, it remains a hugely informative source for historians and geographers interested in the changing nature of the land. Another important, though often maligned, source is the Statistical Accounts of Scotland (often referred to as the Old and New Statistical Account, hereafter OSA and NSA). These offer the basis for some comparison between parish life in the late eighteenth and mid-nineteenth centuries. Though the accounts have been heavily criticised for deliberate bias, they nonetheless provide a good deal of information about the changing face of Scottish society.[4] As a result, it is possible to chart the progress of improvement in agriculture and the impact this had on the parish and its population.

In addition, there are a plethora of government reports and parliamentary commissions, set up to look into various aspects of rural life from the 1840s until the end of the century and, indeed, into the next. Ian Levitt and Christopher Smout, for example, utilised the report of the Poor Law Commission of 1843 to offer a picture of the state of the poor in mid-century.[5] The quantity of travellers' accounts swelled in the nineteenth century, in no small measure thanks to the success of Sir Walter Scott in depicting Scotland, and the Highlands in particular, in romantic tones and hues, which suited early Victorian aesthetic sensibilities and precipitated a tourist boom. However, the unfamiliarity with the society which they were describing makes many tourist accounts problematic as a source for social history. The very nature of their romantic ramblings are in some ways less useful to modern historians than the more critical accounts of the early eighteenth century, such as those by Daniel Defoe and Edmund Burt.[6] However, though not strictly speaking travelogues, the likes of the circuit journeys of Henry Cockburn and reminiscences of engineer Joseph Mitchell provide valuable insights, as do the novels of William Alexander in relation to the north-east.[7]

Such literary sources provide contrasting impressions of the land and how the environment and the people who populated it have since changed. Few written sources survive from the ordinary country folk, but their views are hinted at in song, poetry and superstition, much of which has been collected since the nineteenth century. Though open to interpretation, these can provide considerable insight into the often descriptively lyrical and occasionally humorous temperament of the native inhabitants.

A GLIMPSE OF THE OLD WAYS

Perhaps one of the most evocative voices of the Highlands, one which provides a glimpse of the old ways and a comment on the new, is that of Duncan Ban Macintyre (or Donnchadh Bàn Mac an t-Saoir in his native Gaelic). He was born in 1724 at Drumliart at the head of Glenorchy and died in Edinburgh in 1812. Towards the end of a long life, the first part of which had been spent as a gamekeeper in the hills of Breadalbane, Macintyre, one of Gaeldom's most admired poets, composed 'Farewell to the Bens', which includes the following lines:

> As I gazed on every side of me
> I could not but be sorrowful,
> for wood and heather have run out,
> nor live the men who flourished there;
> there's not a deer to hunt there,
> there's not a bird or roe there,
> and the few that have not died out
> have departed from it utterly.[8]

From this poem, one gets an impression not only of ecological deterioration, but also of the depopulation of his homeland. Is this simply the lament of the old, a longing for the glory of past times when, as a young man, he had traversed the hills in youthful health and enthusiasm for his daily pursuits? As an historical source, the poetry of Duncan Ban Macintyre (as of any other poet) must be interpreted with caution. And yet he evokes a sense of something truly altered from the landscape of his youth and early middle age.

Duncan was a gamekeeper when gamekeepering was in transition. There is no indication that the poet had ever taken part in one of the great deer hunts of old, though he must surely have been aware of what that entailed – the huge numbers of men and beasts and the grand social context. However, his own job had been reduced to one of policing the bounds of the forest and culling deer for the earl's dining table.[9] Although aristocratic hunting had not completely gone out of favour, it was not until ten years after he died that the hills of his home territory, which had been converted to a sheep walk in the late eighteenth century, were re-developed as deer forest. In 1820 the 2nd Marquis of Breadalbane converted an area 20 miles long by 12 miles broad from roughly the Kingshouse in Glencoe down towards Bridge of Orchy into Blackmount deer forest, which became one of the earliest of the new type of hunting reserves emerging in the early nineteenth century and reaching their heyday towards the close of that century.

With Macintyre's poetry there is a clear sense of his intimacy with the

hills. It would be impossible to substantiate his claims of ecological degen-
eration from documentary sources and verification of ecological change can
be achieved only through collaboration with palaeoecologists. What does
seem certain is that the parish of Glenorchy and its environs underwent substantial change in the early nineteenth century. The parish minister, Duncan
McLean, writing for the NSA, thus states in rather florid language:

> The aboriginal population of the parish of Glenurchy (not of Inishail) has been
> nearly supplanted by adventurers from the neighbouring district of Breadalbane,
> who now occupy the far largest share of the parish. There are a few, and only a few
> shoots, from the stems that supplied the ancient population.[10]

It is certainly documented elsewhere that the Glenorchy population had
decreased by this time, as it did in neighbouring parishes.[11] Lowland breeds
of sheep had been introduced, and mixed farming practices based on summer
and winter touns had largely been replaced by sheep farming and deer forest.
This was not untypical for the upper reaches of many parishes in this part of
the central Highlands. The penetration of sheep into the Highlands (followed
by deer forest creation) would continue well into the century. For example,
Argyllshire had 278,000 sheep in 1800, 827,000 in 1855 and over 1 million by
1880.[12] For the Highlands, at least, it was to be a century of dislocation, eviction and emigration, though as Tom Devine has argued, the transformation
and dislocation of population in the Lowlands was no less severe. However,
the latter tended to have a stronger economic base, and its inhabitants were
arguably better able to withstand the vicissitudes of change.[13]

Factors contributing to changes in land use and landscape

There is a veritable library of books and papers written on the subject of the
transformation of Scottish society and its economy in the eighteenth and
nineteenth centuries. It is a period that has spawned considerable debate
concerning the modernisation of agriculture, especially whether or not it
was revolutionary. In particular, much has been written on the subject of the
Highland Clearances, its causes and consequences.[14]

The key forces at play during the nineteenth century were rapid urbanisation and the concomitant industrial take-off, as a result of which by 1901
almost 60 per cent of Scotland's people were living in urban areas (that
is, of over 5,000 inhabitants), and many were working in industries such
as coal, shipbuilding, engineering, textiles and the metallurgical sector.[15]
Industrialisation in the first half of the century was concentrated on
the textile industries, when hand-loom weaving declined as urban-based
powered weaving spread, thus precipitating a wave of migrants from countryside to city. Until around 1830 most Scots still laboured on the land, at
home or in the workshop rather than in large urban factories, but this would
soon change.

At the same time, the fruits of eighteenth-century endeavours to advance and commercialise agriculture were truly felt in the Scottish countryside in the following century, resulting in a major re-shaping of social and farming structures and the re-design and modernisation of the landscape. Urban and rural life was still deeply intertwined, so, for example, market gardening for potatoes, hay, grain and turnips to feed the teeming populations (and their horses) became common around Scotland's major cities. Agriculture developed regional specialisations, with dairying, orchards and market gardening developing within reach of the expanding urban markets. The Clyde valley, long a producer of fruit, became particularly noted for orchards, as did Strathmore and the Carse of Gowrie, close to Dundee, especially when new methods of draining allowed these low lying, relatively sodden, lands to become highly productive.[16]

Industrial landscapes sprang up in the countryside, particularly in the central belt, Lanarkshire and Ayrshire, where coal mining really took off and hundreds of small pits opened up. This not only precipitated new building, viaducts and aqueducts, spoil heaps and pools, but changed the nature of many small villages and introduced atrocious work conditions for men, women and children, and not much better living conditions. With industrialisation came urbanisation, especially in the latter half of the nineteenth century, and with it Scotland was transformed from a nation largely of rural dwellers to one mainly of urbanites.

Alongside these physical and socio-economic changes, developments in the philosophy of agriculture, as well as in science and technology, continued to affect how the land was viewed and used. The development of scientific or 'High' farming led to new ways of approaching agriculture and numerous experiments in fertilising, crop rotations and draining were tried, the results occupying the pages of such influential journals as the *Transactions of the Highland and Agricultural Society of Scotland*. As the general population's reliance on peat as a fuel became less marked – excepting the poor and many Highland communities – and coal became an affordable household fuel, so the dependence on peatlands, once highly valued especially in small Scottish towns and burghs, became objects of reclamation. The peat was stripped or burned and used as fertiliser and the land manured and cultivated, or, increasingly, planted up with trees, which became extremely fashionable in the nineteenth century.

Politics and developing global networks also played their part in the transformation of the Scottish countryside. Wars, most notably the Napoleonic Wars at the beginning of the century, impacted on all aspects of life, especially with the cessation of hostilities, which resulted in an economic depression in Britain. Most areas of the British economy experienced some difficulty in the years after 1815; cattle prices halved between 1810 and 1830, for example.[17] War had also provided a source of employment for men, most notably from the Highlands, who otherwise may have had few alternatives in their home territory. The expansion of the Empire also fuelled demand for goods and services, such as army personnel in volatile colonies such as India, or in creating the railways of many parts of the world. Scotland became the powerhouse of the British Empire and men and women flocked to the coal mining areas, to the shipyards and engineering towns; cogs in the mighty wheels of British imperialism.

Technological advances worked against, as well as for, the interests of rural life. Advances in steam technology in the maritime sphere allowed the importation of vast quantities of raw materials from around the world. On the one hand, this permitted the use of the hugely important guano from Peru as a fertiliser. On the other hand, cotton from the southern US states (except during the American Civil War), jute from India, sugar from the West Indies, to name but a few – all these imports had major implications for home-based industries and for agriculture. The development of refrigeration also had a monumental impact, allowing lamb and beef to be imported from as far afield as New Zealand and the vast prairies of the American Midwest. This contributed to the agricultural depression of the 1880s, which affected the whole of the sector in Britain. In the Highlands, the sheep industry went into decline, opening the way for the creation of even more deer forests. The revolution in rural transport with the construction of parish and turnpike roads, canals and eventually railways, allied to the advent of steamships, provided great stimulus to the opening up of the Highlands for tourists and sportsmen alike, as well as for the movement of people and livestock. The days of the drover, if not gone, were certainly numbered by the mid-nineteenth century.

The robustness of the agricultural economy, the alteration in how farms operated and the use of new technologies may have ameliorated the effects of the weather, which had played a pivotal role in people's everyday lives in the past. However, climate still played a part, especially in those areas where the economic base was already fragile. As will be discussed later, poor harvests, disease and famine would continue to haunt the Highlands in the nineteenth century. In 1836, for example, it was reported that at Lawers, on Lochtayside, the adverse weather reduced the hay crop by a third and there was no aftermath forage on the stubble.[18] This was nothing compared with what was to come when, in 1846, potato blight hit the Highlands. It was not only the impact that weather had on crops that could precipitate calamity; storms could also cause immense damage, as happened as a result of the 'muckle spate' (big flood). In August 1829, a mighty storm lashed Scotland, particularly the north-east, for two whole days, affecting the Nairn, the Findhorn, the Lossie and the Spey. Flash floods crashed down from the sources of all the great Grampian rivers, taking bridges, houses, trees and crops on their way and depositing massive sheets of sand and gravel downstream on valuable agricultural land. Meander cut-offs occurred and many new channels were excavated. Mar Lodge, near Braemar, was badly damaged, its dining room swept away. Amazingly, only eight lives were lost, although it is thought that the flood rendered at least 289 families destitute and requiring charitable relief. It has been estimated that the flood led to losses for estate owners approaching £2.83 million (2005 prices).[19] Such episodes remind us of the effect of nature in reshaping the Scottish landscape and the lives of those in its path.

LARGE-SCALE ENCLOSURE AND RE-ORGANISATION OF AGRICULTURE AND SETTLEMENT

The re-shaping of rural society and the modification of farm structures to produce more commercially efficient units of production was undoubtedly a key feature of eighteenth-century Scotland. Nevertheless, the effects of the Improvement era continued well into the nineteenth century, and, arguably, improvement remained a key feature of agriculture and land management throughout the century. Enclosure – one of the key features of the Improvement era – had become a defining feature of the new form of Scottish agriculture, spreading through both lowland and highland Scotland in the first half of the nineteenth century, the geographical extent and abundance of dyke and hedge continuing to increase at a phenomenal rate.

Ironically, it was often at the urban–rural interface that change was particularly slow in coming. Even in 1800, it was possible to find landscapes which still had more in common with that of earlier centuries than with the new improved countryside. Certainly this could be said of the landscape around Nairn in the late eighteenth century.

The agricultural commentator, Andrew Wight, touring Scotland for the Commissioners of the Annexed Estates in the last quarter of the eighteenth century, was naturally most impressed with those whom he found applying new farming methods, including rotations, drainage, enclosure and improved manuring. However, he says of the town land west of Nairn that 'though the soil is good, and capable of high improvement, little has been done by the languid inhabitants'.[20] We are told that the 'field around the town', more than 400 acres, were 'formerly runrigg or acre and acre alternately; but owning to an excambion . . . about 4 years ago, the different proprietors will now have it in their power . . . to enclose their lands'. This was, in effect, a medieval landscape still operating at the close of the eighteenth century.[21]

However, the 'winds of improvement' were already beginning to blow through Nairnshire, driving forward both the desire and the ability to make everything and everyone more productive. This resulted in a profound change of attitude towards pieces of land such as peat mosses; previously well regulated and valuable natural resources, they were now regarded as 'waste', with all the connotations of unproductiveness and squandering of a resource associated with the word. For Nairn and other small Scottish towns hovering on the edge of financial insolvency, altering the physical condition of land through a change in its function also presented their town councils with a means of reducing their debts. The income could be used for infrastructural projects such as bridges and harbours which were regarded as essential for economic development.[22]

By the 1840s, when the NSA were published, agriculture in Nairnshire had, indeed, changed markedly. The ministers describe great improvements, including rotations with fallow, enclosure, drainage and the use of lime, marl and bone dust. Several of the ministers take the opportunity to describe the 'old' agriculture, which was by then largely abandoned. No longer was there an 'ancient attachment to the hog-stye and dunghill, which usually block-aded the entrance to their houses'. Instead, lime and bone-dust were increasingly used, the latter a significant element of trade through Nairn's small port.[23] The use of these fertilisers was greatly facilitated by the improvement in transportation, particularly in roads from the late eighteenth century, and in the mid-nineteenth century by the railway.

A feature of 'improvement' agriculture was the reclamation of 'waste' land. The increasing availability and use of lime allowed areas of muir and rough pasture to be brought under cultivation.[24] Estate owners and gentle-men farmers were becoming more adventurous, trying different methods of reclamation and experimenting with a variety of manures. From the 1830s to the end of the century, the pages of the *Transactions of the Highland & Agricultural Society of Scotland* are replete with discourse on waste land reclamation experimentation.[25]

This sort of transformation is vividly captured on the first edition OS maps. Placed alongside a range of eighteenth-century town and estate plans it offers a glimpse of the physical and bio-geographical transformation of a landscape in the process of being re-shaped almost beyond recognition.

On Lochtayside, for example, it is possible to compare land-use change instigated between 1769, when the Earl of Breadalbane commissioned a survey of the area, and 1861 from the OS. The 1769 survey was initiated at a time when estate re-organisation was being considered and included suggestions for improvements such as where a wood might be grubbed up and turned over to cultivation. It is an exceptional piece of work, which has been shown to be highly accurate.[26] The alteration of landscape is quite vividly expressed in comparing the plan for the farms of Ardvoile and Ballemore on north Lochtayside with the same area in 1861. In 1769, the impression is of an organic landscape on a pre-improvement model – essentially an infield–outfield system, based upon a contrast between land that was intensively cultivated and that from which the yield was more intermittent and marginal – whereas 100 years later the changes have been realised to the extent that there are rationalised systems of separate woodland and grassland management forming a rectilinear enclosed field system. That the system prior to this was multi-use is demonstrated by the surveyor, Farquharson's comment in 1769: 'There are some outfields common to the whole farm . . . and what

Figure 1.2 *Landscape change on Lochtayside, Perthshire, 1769–1861. A rationalised system of separate woodland and grassland management with enclosed fields, parkland and shooting lodge replacing the old pre-improvement landscape. Left: John Farquharson's 1769 Survey of the North Side of Loch Tay (original held by National Archives of Scotland) RHP 973/1 map 3. Reproduced courtesy of the Royal Commission on the Ancient and Historical Monuments of Scotland (National Archives of Scotland). Right: Ordnance Survey Maps – six-inch edition, Scotland, 1843–1882, Perthshire and Clackmannanshire, Sheet LXVIII, 1861 (1867). Reproduced by permission of the National Library of Scotland.*

is still more against improvement one person eats the grass of the field among the firs by the lochside and another reaps the corn.' By 1861, not only are the named farms of the previous period lost, but Ardvoile has been superseded by the gardens and parkland of Morenish shooting lodge, which had been built in 1844 to cater for shooting parties.[27]

The population on Lochtayside rose steadily during the latter half of the eighteenth century, and, unlike the north and west Highlands, peaked around the turn of the century before beginning to decline, so the social and economic problems precipitated by these changes were probably not as acute here as in some other parts of the Highlands, where the population continued to increase during the first half of the century. The communal agriculture of Lochtayside, based largely on cattle, was being replaced, as elsewhere in the Highlands, by a rural economy with a much greater emphasis on sheep production, and supporting a much reduced population. Those who had become excess to the requirements of the agricultural economy had either left the district, or were absorbed by the developing rural service and small-scale industrial centres such as Killin, Kenmore and Aberfeldy.[28] Although there had been specialised craftsmen such as the boatwright and shoemaker in rural areas, it is likely that specialisation increased in the nineteenth century, and more and more of the needs of the local farming population were met by the tradesmen who populated developing villages. In this respect, the population history of this period is not entirely a straightforward story of migration from the rural environment to the urban one (or abroad); there was also a degree of population redistribution within the rural environment.

This period also witnessed the abandonment of farms, which in 1769 were present above the road on Loch Tayside. At the end of the 1790s there was a wholesale re-allocation and redefinition of 'lots' and a concomitant expansion into land previously used as outfield, mainly above the road, which had been cultivated only intermittently. This came at a time, during the Napoleonic wars, when as William Marshall put it 'the barons of north Perthshire had . . . large tenantries kept as fighting forces'.[29] Estate policy was then for retention and sub-division. The Breadalbane Fencibles were disbanded in 1802 and, with less need for fighting men and an acceptance by landowners that emigration was necessary, the population on the estate began to fall.

By 1821 some fifty-seven of 136 lots distributed across the lochside are described as 'above the road' or 'high lots', though not all of these were either new or on the outfields.[30] However, by the time of the OS mapping 40 years later, most of these lots had become uninhabited. Abandonment did not take place overnight – many tenants hung on for decades, probably by taking on non-agricultural work. For example, a family of Mallochs attempted to convert outfield to a permanent arable holding, perhaps in a way not dissimilar to settlers on the mid-western plains of North America, though without the added problem of hostile indigenous assaults. Though we know little of the trials and tribulations of their attempts at colonisation other than periods of arrears, it must have been a struggle and the men of this particular family sought to supplement their agricultural income by becoming dykers. Eventually, they abandoned the land and it became grazing for an adjacent low ground farm, though Mallochs continued on Lochtayside at least until the end of the century. This family's history was in no way unusual and today only a handful of families that lived on Lochtayside at the time of the 1769 survey remain in the district, and, of those, most are to be found in the rural service centres such as Aberfeldy and Killin.

This re-shaping of the landscape and changes in land use could come about only through human endeavour and graft. People's lives and their day-to-day activities changed in response to land-use and landscape change. With fewer, but generally larger, farms and therefore fewer tenants, there was increasing specialisation in the countryside in what we might call country crafts such as dyking and masonry work, tailoring, ploughing and so on. An explosion in the construction of boundaries – fences, dykes, hedges – required men to become more focused on one or two crafts rather than being involved directly in agricultural production. The re-building of farms and settlements, which proceeded at an unparalleled rate particularly in the latter half of the nineteenth century, and the expansion of rural villages and towns, not to mention the increase in new sporting lodges and associated paraphernalia, all required masons and this became an important rural trade. Such tradesmen mainly lived in the expanding towns and villages, where they might have a garden and often kept a cow, which was taken out to the common grazing by a young herd each day. They were, however, tradesmen or labourers first and agriculturists second.

James Kennedy, a long-time resident of Strathtay in Perthshire, wrote in 1927 of the valley as it was in the 1850s. He recalled that there were eight shoemakers in the 6 miles of the strath between Aberfeldy and Grandtully, of which about a half had workshops outside their houses (where much of the gossip about daily life in the locality took place). Most of the shoemakers were, however, itinerant and plied their trade in the homes of their clients. Similarly tailors would come to the house and make, with up to three apprentices, a man's suit in a day, costing 3s. 6d. with victuals – breakfast, dinner and tea – being part of the deal.[31] In this respect, they were carrying on a long-standing tradition. What is different is the sheer numbers. There were also seven blacksmiths, five millers, six joiners, two slaters and six grocers. Tradesmen could now offer their services to a population which, though largely still agriculturally-focused, no longer relied on their own labours to feed and clothe themselves or provide the roof over their head and furniture for their homes, as they had traditionally done.

Joseph Mitchell, who together with his father, John, was responsible for supervision of much of the Highland road, bridge and harbour building that flourished during the middle decades of the nineteenth century, recollected that 'in Elgin, Forres and Nairn and neighbouring villages, colonies of masons existed outnumbering the requirements of each locality, but they found employment in the Highlands', on the Caledonian Canal and numerous other public works that were being constructed across the Highland landscape in the process of opening up the region to commerce and trade. He described how these skilled workmen spent from March until November away from home working on the canal, housed nearby 'in houses or huts', as many as thirty per dwelling, sleeping on rudimentary bunks and cooking for themselves. The day started at 6 am with breakfast at 9 am and a similar fare of porridge and oaten bannocks at 2 pm, followed by a supper of potatoes and herring at 8 pm. Sunday was a day of rest.[32]

Within the urban environment, change also affected the landscape, not least because of the increases in population. This was not just a feature of expanding cities like Glasgow; even humble backwaters experienced a considerable transition. In Nairn, for example, in 1792 the number of souls in town and parish was at least 2,400, divided into 1,100 for the town itself and less than 1,300 in the country part of the parish. However, the urban population had already nearly doubled, since it was said that about 40 years previously there were only 600 inhabitants in the town. Fifty years later, in 1842, the urban population suffered a slight decline to 1,074, while the rural element had increased to 2,318, bringing the total to 3,392.[33]

In order to cope with this expansion, Nairn's council decided, in 1830, to look into whether or not they should adopt the regulations contained within a bill for establishing 'a General System of Police in the Burghs of Scotland'. These burgh police would, among other things, be responsible for ensuring that the streets were clear of obstacles, including dung hills, but it was noted that this would have serious implications for hundreds of poor people whose subsistence was derived mainly from the value of their manure and who would be more materially injured by declaring it the property of the commissioners. Currently, these people collected it carefully for the use of neighbouring farmers who, in exchange, allowed them to raise potatoes on their ground, effectively providing for a large part of their subsistence for the following year.[34] Along with the burgh's expansion, its poor had also increased.

THE VICTORIAN ERA: DEPOPULATION AND DEVELOPMENT

Despite the many innovations and advances in farming techniques, growth was not linear, and during the course of the nineteenth century depression and slump in farm incomes was not uncommon, though it varied between sectors. Most areas of the British economy experienced some difficulty in the years after 1815 with the end of the Napoleonic Wars. As has been noted, cattle prices halved between 1810 and 1830.[35] Though sheep prices stagnated they did not experience the collapse of other commodities, and so, for the Highlands, this further inculcated sheep – in the minds of the landowners at least – as the only viable form of commercial pastoralism that would generate sufficient profit, with all its implications for further clearance and dispossession.

By the 1840s, however, improved agriculture had triumphed throughout the Lowlands, and Scottish farming, criticised for its backwardness in earlier years, had now become internationally renowned as a model of efficiency for others to follow. The Highlands, on the other hand, had become hefted to the sheep and those who still lived on the land were greatly reliant on the potato. Although grown in Scotland from the early eighteenth century, the potato was still relatively uncommon by 1750 – on Lochtayside, for example, it was not cultivated at all in 1769, though by 1783 it was being grown on the lochside, but still at relatively modest levels.[36] Thereafter, there was an extraordinary expansion in its cultivation, particularly in the north and west Highlands where it became the staple for an increasingly impoverished population.[37] It was a crop that yielded far more nutrition per well-manured acre than the old cereals and, though still requiring back-breaking effort to dig the lazy beds and manure them with seaweed and the like, it became indispensable in the Highlands by the 1840s. This is clearly demonstrated in a letter written by a Breadalbane estate tenant to its factor, James Wyllie, in 1845. In it, the tenant, Donald Duff, complains of poverty and asks for an additional allowance of meal, 'as the potatoes never grow in this place with any attention I have in my power to give them'. In fact, he said he would prefer to be moved to any place where the potato could be reared. Unfortunately, it is not stated in which part of the vast Breadalbane estate Duff's farm is located; however, that he should feel so reliant on one crop underlines the level of dependence that had developed in a relatively short time.[38]

The following year, 1846, the blight came. Much has been written about this grim episode in modern Scottish history, which lasted almost a decade and had a devastating impact on many parts of the Highlands, creating a major stimulus to mass emigration.[39] On Lochtayside in 1846, it was said that no fields were free of the disease and that there would certainly not be enough either for seed or for use. One report thought the potatoes so bad that it would be dangerous to feed them to pigs much less to humans; if they appeared sound when lifted they were gone by the next day – 'the very smell of them when boiled is enough to bring a disease among the people without eating any of them'.[40]

Osgood Mackenzie, a child at the time, described the impact of the famine that occurred as a result of the blight for the people of Gairloch in Wester Ross, where his mother and uncle, Dr John Mackenzie, ran the family estate. He recalls that his mother never left the district for three years while she created paid work (in food or money) for all able-bodied men on the estate, which kept them and their families from starving, and into the bargain created a network of roads – the so-called destitution roads – in a district which hitherto had contained almost none other than a few cattle tracks.[41] According to Mackenzie, his mother raised £10,000 from government and charitable relief funds, which enabled them to guarantee the prevention of starvation on the property. She was described as 'deserving of the highest praise for her benevolent care of the poor'.[42] In 1845 Lady Mackenzie and her brother-in-law also tried to re-organise the local economy by introducing a new settlement pattern as a means of maintaining the estate population against the current trend.[43]

Despite the philanthropy of some Scottish landlords and effective action by the government of the day, which averted the kind of catastrophe that befell the Irish during this same period, the potato blight turned an already impoverished population into one riven with despair, desperation and disease. It became for many an indescribable horror, which it is thought affected around 150,000 people, with the number of deaths resulting from famine diseases such as typhus and diarrhoea increasing considerably. For some lairds, it was the last straw; they emerged broke from this crisis and were forced to sell all or part of their estates. For others, it prompted efforts to accelerate 'assisted' emigration, often of the poorest and most destitute of their estates' inhabitants, resulting in some of the most notorious Clearances of this period.[44] For much of the north and west Highlands the potato blight led to the total decimation of its economic base. From 1841 until 1861 around one-third of the population left and many thousands either died on the voyage to the New World, or on its shores in the vast quarantine areas that had been created to try to stop the spread of disease into the general population. In one such place, Grosse Ile on the St Lawrence river downstream of Quebec City, 5,300 perished; many were Highlanders from the likes of Barra, the Uists and Skye, who had attempted to escape the misery of famine, but who were simply already too weakened by starvation to survive in the ships that were often stinking hell-holes, rotten with disease.[45]

For those who stayed on, disease continued to strike the potato crop periodically and life did not become any easier as it began to run its course. Even though the worst had passed by 1857, the estate manager for Mackintosh of Mackintosh, based at Moy Hall in Inverness-shire, was writing to his laird, then on tour in Europe with his family, that poor weather had befallen them, resulting in a bad harvest, and disease was in the potatoes.[46] It was a biological check that, alongside periodic bad weather conditions, would continue to hinder attempts at economic advancement for the region. Indeed, it has been argued that poor weather, bad harvests and the re-emergence of blight, alongside other factors such as a dramatic failure of earnings from the fishing industry, helped precipitate the crofter agitations of the early 1880s.[47]

One way that the Highland population managed to supplement a meagre living was to head for the Lowlands in search of seasonal work. Seasonal migration of this sort was already well established by the end of the eighteenth century, but, by the time of the potato famine, had become so important to many Highlanders that it has been suggested that it could account for half or more of their means of subsistence.[48] In Skye, for example, it was reckoned that, of a total male population of 3,243 in the parish of Strath, 500 left annually for the Lowlands.[49] Demand for this temporary workforce was possible because Lowland agriculture itself had radically changed. The needs of improved agriculture were different to that which had existed under the old system. The more intensive cultivation of the land through ploughing, the adoption of new crops, particularly the more extensive use of turnips, and innovation in rotations ensured that the working year started to alter and lengthen. This development favoured the hiring of full-time workers, married servants hired by the year, especially those at the top of their social hierarchy – the ploughmen. Also, single male and female servants were employed for six months, undertaking the more menial tasks such as hoeing, weeding, singling and lifting as well as the all-important grain harvest. A married ploughman could expect to be given a house, garden, the keep of a cow and other privileges as part of his wage reward; his wife was often required to provide her labour at harvest time in lieu of rent.

It was to these large, highly productive lowland farms that many Highlanders (and Irish) swarmed each year to earn sufficient wages to sustain their families at home and pay for the rent of their crofts. Though some eventually moved permanently to the Lowlands for more stable employment in agriculture or countless other expanding sectors such as construction, domestic service or textiles, many remained rooted to the land. As one observer noted, the 'attachment to their native soil' was not removed by 'years of intercourse with the more advanced districts'.[50] The contrast that many seasonal migrants must have experienced between the highly commercial and intensive farming of the Lothians and the economically fragile crofting system that had developed during the course of the century must have been extreme. The English radical social commentator, William Cobbett, riding through East Lothian in the 1830s, found much to criticise, but also saw, 'such cornfields, such fields of turnips, such turnips in those fields, such stack-yards, and such a total absence of dwelling-houses, as never, surely, were before seen in any country upon earth'.[51] As the century progressed, larger and larger farms with clusters of specialised farm buildings, housing farmer, livestock, machinery and farm labour, were constructed, encircled by their large rectangular-shaped fields, devoid of weed or marshy corner. The physical face of agriculture was changing as larger, more elaborate and better designed farm steadings spread across the countryside. To this day, many of these imposing buildings survive as a lasting memorial to the prosperous days of 'High Farming' in Victorian Scotland.

The Highlands also experienced a rationalisation in the agricultural landscape with the creation of large home farms in most straths and glens, a somewhat less grand mirroring of the richer parts of the Scottish countryside to the south of the Highland boundary line, but nevertheless a clear parallel. Even in the overcrowded and impoverished crofting heartland of the north and west, large farms with their associated steadings became a feature of the landscape. Elsewhere, thanks to mass emigration, the population started to decrease and those who remained were invariably relocated from the more fertile glens to the poorer coastal lands. They left behind a desolate lack of habitation in once populated inland glens, save for a scatter of isolated shepherd or gamekeeper houses.

This period of relative stability came to an end in the later 1870s. Bad weather, at its worst in the winter of 1878/9, combined with structural changes in the global supply of food resulting in the importation of refrigerated beef and lamb from North America and Australasia, brought forth another agricultural depression. During 1879 the situation deteriorated to the point where the government appointed a Royal Commission to enquire into the cause of agricultural distress. As a result, the situation for tenants improved significantly with the introduction of benefits such as compensation for improvement.[52] At the same time, others experienced yet another transformation of the landscape, with implications for their way of life, through the rise of the sporting estate.

SPORTING DEVELOPMENTS

The sporting estate emerged as a distinctive entity in the early nineteenth century and reached its heyday around the close of that century. It was a quintessentially Victorian phenomenon; yet it was rooted firmly in antiquity and has proved an enduring entity that has withstood economic, social and political challenges to its hegemony in Highland society almost since its inception. The roots of the sporting estate lie firmly in the history and culture of the Highlands, which was by then wrestling with significant economic and social changes. Its creation coincided with a time of significant change in Highland society and its economy, not least a cataclysmic depopulation linked to fundamental economic and structural transformation.[53]

The sporting estate emerged as a new form of commercialisation, this time of the historic leisure pursuits of the landed aristocracy, expanding on the craze for shooting which had already begun in the late eighteenth century (see Alastair Durie, Chapter 5, below). Stemming as it did out of the direct interests of the traditional landholding class, this enabled the sporting estate to remain ostensibly rooted in land-focused rural society even when owners and clients began to emerge from among the emerging urban industrial elites and growing middle classes. However, the sporting estate may arguably have provided a degree of stability and social cohesion for Highland rural society at a time of rapid depopulation, substituting for the patriarchal relations which had begun to unravel in the eighteenth century with the disintegration of the traditional clan economy. Gamekeepers, gillies and others required to service the sportsman were invariably local men (and women), who knew the hills and could adapt to the new requirements of the landed classes, as they always had done. Of course, not all were natives of the glen and, indeed, there was considerable movement of men in such occupations from one estate to another, as is still the case today. In fact, as the trend for renting deer forests grew in the second half of the century, more and more staff would come up from the south with the deer forest or grouse moor lessee and his guests. This could cause problems for the estate proprietor and his manager, as revealed in the letters written by Mackintosh of Mackintosh's estate manager, John Bisset, to his employer, while the latter was abroad on a European tour: 'Mr Lister and party have left Moy Hall except the Gamekeeper who is left to shoot all he can until the season ends, I must say they have been the most mean set that I ever met with.'[54]

The history of deer forest and grouse moor is also intricately linked to that of the nineteenth-century expansion of sheep farming in the Highlands. As already described, the later eighteenth century heralded the expansion of large-scale commercial sheep farming to the southern and central Highlands. Giving over established grazing ground of black cattle or native Highland sheep to large flocks of Lowland breeds of sheep had several effects. For one, tenants could no longer regularly send their livestock to the summer pastures, or shielings. The 'Improver' movement clearly despised the use of shielings, which involved a 'train of evils' such as the practice of driving live-stock over other tenants' and even the proprietor's ground, and were keen to do away with the practice. Allied to this was its perceived incompatibility with, and eventual subordination to, the use of upland grazings for sheep farming. Its discontinuance was also said to be affected by the introduction of new arable farming practices, especially the introduction of flax and pota-toes, which required looking after over the summer months when the tenants were traditionally at the shielings.[55] The penetration of the lowland flocks into the Highlands was, however, not as swift as is sometimes implied. It was also patchy; some areas were turned into sheep walks as early as the 1770s and others, like Gairloch, remained firmly cattle country well into the nine-teenth century. The memoir of Dr John Mackenzie of Gairloch describes the importance of black cattle in that locality during the early years of the nineteenth century, and the intentional exclusion of sheep on the part of the estate until around the 1830s. He provides a detailed account of the gathering and milking of the cows at their Gairloch property before they were sent off to the shieling ground.[56] This very distinctive feature of summer farm life in the Highlands, which had been the cornerstone of agricultural activity and social interaction, was by this time on the cusp of extinction.

On a bright August day sometime in the early 1840s, Charles St John, the renowned Victorian sportsman–naturalist, was on a deer-stalking expedition in the upper reaches of the River Findhorn in Inverness-shire.[57] Having left behind the relative civilisation of lower Strathdearn, 'with here and there a

black hut perched on a green knoll, dotted with groves of the rugged and
ancient-looking birch-trees. . . . About these solitary abodes, too, small
patches of oats and potatoes', he headed for the source of Findhorn, deep in
the heart of the Monadhliaths, led by a shepherd guide. In *Wild Sports and
Natural History of the Highlands*, St John relates his encounter with a group of
shepherds, 'in the highest building on the river, if building it can be termed
. . . a small shealing, or summer residence of the shepherds, called I believe,
Dahlvaik'. He details the interior of the hut and their mid-morning repast
of oatmeal and hot water, 'each man then produced from some recess of his
plaid a long wooden spoon'. The men spoke only Gaelic, his guide only a
little English. It was a meeting of two cultures, observed by an Englishman
in pursuit of deer, while these men went about their daily lives as shepherds,
little knowing that their days tending sheep in that remote glen were numbered. St John, who endured considerable physical hardship during this trek
in search of deer (which he knew would be elusive because of the presence of
sheep), was enthralled with the place:

> Beautiful in its grand and wild solitude is the glen where the Findhorn takes its
> rise; seldom does the foot of man pass by it. It is too remote even for the sports-
> man; and the grouse cock crows in peace, and struts without fear of pointer or
> gun . . . The red deer . . . seldom is he annoyed by the presence of mankind,
> unless a chance shepherd or poacher from Badenoch happens to wander in that
> direction.[58]

He adds: 'I do not know a district in Scotland that would make a better deer-
forest than that immediately around and to the west of Coignafern . . . It is
almost a pity that the Mac Intosh does not turn the district into a forest.'
The Mackintosh did. Within a decade it was deer forest and sheep and their
shepherds were replaced by deer, the sportsman and his retinue, few of them
permanently living in the glen.[59] In 1755, the population of the parish of
Moy and Dalarossie, within which Coignafearn lies, amounted to 1,693. By
the 1790s, the number was 1,813. In 1831, a decade prior to St John's visit,
the population had decreased to 1,098. By 1881 there were only 822 inhabitants of the parish, of whom 634 were Gaelic speakers. The greatest loss of
population was during the first three decades of the nineteenth century and,
according to the minister, can be attributed to mass emigration, following
the creation of sheep farms.[60] It seems likely that the population of the upper
part of the parish was the first to decline with the introduction of sheep. By
the 1850s, the estate manager was complaining to his laird that it was becoming difficult to get labourers, a result of 'such wages going in Morayshire
and further down the country together with the great inducement given to
Emigrants'.[61] It is unlikely that the four shepherds that St John encountered
would still have been found within the bounds of Coignafearn or Strathdearn
a decade later, though given that one of them was already acting as a guide to
this early Victorian sportsman, it is entirely possible that he had become a

gamekeeper or the like. It was not unusual for find men changing occupation, or moving from one locality (or country) to another at this time.

The sporting estate was in reality a continually evolving phenomenon, adapting – or not – to wider social and economic conditions, despite the veneer of tradition which helped the concept to take off and endure. Deer forests and the exploitation of large tracts of land for the purpose of commercialised sport had become one of the most visible aspects of landholding in the Highlands by the late nineteenth century. Indeed, it could be argued that this was one of the dominant perceptions of the region, either by critics of such a system or by sportsmen. As more and more southern industrialists and other prosperous businessmen, stalwarts of the British Empire, coveted their own deer forest or grouse moor, the traditional estates began to hive off parts of their often extensive landholdings to such men, who viewed their participation in such sports as a status symbol. This was especially true after 1852, when Queen Victoria purchased Balmoral on Deeside, having first rented the hunting lodge in 1848. The great exception was the Sutherland estates, whose owners expanded their landholding to over 1 million acres by the end of the century.

When Charles St John was writing about his sporting pursuits in the 1840s, deer stalking was still mainly confined to the landed class and a few adventurous sportsmen. There were probably around forty deer forests in the Highlands and, although not numerically insignificant, among this number were tracts of land, like the forests of Mar, Atholl and other

Figure 1.3   *Red deer stalking in Glenfeshie, Inverness-shire, c. 1900. © Highland Folk Museum. Licensor www.scran.ac.uk.*

Cairngorm estates, which had probably never ceased to be hunting grounds for their aristocratic owners. By 1895, this number had increased to 117, covering some 2.5 million acres. The phenomenon reached its peak in 1912, when it totalled 3.5 million acres. In Ross and Cromarty this amounted to a staggering 46 per cent of the county's total land area.[62]

It is not easy to summarise the social impact of sporting developments in the nineteenth century without the risk of oversimplifying the complex social, economic and political forces at work during this period.[63] However, in the sources that remain to us it is certainly true that the voice of those who lived and worked on sporting estates is largely absent. Unquestionably, there was considerable resentment in the crofting world about the use of land previously occupied by crofters, which had subsequently been turned into a playground for the rich. This culminated in the so-called Crofters' War and precipitated a string of government commissions looking into the land question, most notably the Napier Commission in 1884, and especially the Deer Forest Commission of 1892. The celebrated raid in November 1897 on Lady Matheson's Park deer forest in Lewis is one of the few examples of physical resistance to the system. While not wishing to belittle the significance of the social impact of the creation of sporting estates in large parts of the Highlands, in reality the lives of many Highland people became dependent – directly and indirectly – upon these activities. Willie Orr calculated that in Scotland in 1851 there were some 1,944 gamekeepers employed, while by 1901 this had risen to 5,367.[64] This does not account for the seasonal work for gillies, beaters, pony and kennel boys, and other employees during the combined grouse and shooting season from mid-August until December, to which must be added the shooting lodge staff, road- and dyke-making employment, in addition to the benefits accruing to subsidiary commercial activities such as laundries and tweed manufacturers. Durie estimates that as many as 10,000 beaters were required in the Highlands during the grouse season from August until September, significantly more, he suggests, than was required for deer stalking. He relates that the day labourer in Glenesk in the 1820s, whose normal wage was 1s. 6d., could make from 3s. to 5s. per day acting as a gillie or attendant on walking up days for wealthy visitors during the grouse season.[65]

Developing grouse moors appears to have created fewer problems and offered more opportunities for locals than was true with deer forests, which took land that could be used for grazing. Grouse and sheep could and did co-exist, although there were some debates over stocking levels. Sheep and deer stalking did not mix and the winter raiding by deer on crops was much resented and the cause of considerable hardship for an already pressed agricultural population, particularly in the western Highlands and Islands. In districts where hunting had long been pursued by the elite, the tenantry seemed to have fared better. Developing the Forest of Mar in Deeside as a sporting estate in Victorian times was not therefore a complete change of direction.

However, it marked a period when hunting for deer and game birds became the principal activity on the estate, almost to the exclusion of all others, including farming and forestry. Hunting was no longer merely an aristocratic pastime but a serious commercial enterprise.

The Mar estate had long been associated with exploitation of its extensive pine woods, but after the Napoleonic Wars timber slumped in price, along with wool. Letting out land to paying customers provided a lucrative alternative to sheep and trees. The owner, the 4th Earl of Fife, moved with the times and, when the opportunity arose, he cleared or took farms 'in-hand', removing both sheep and people. By 1843 the last tenant farmer left the north side of the Dee, enabling the earl to run the area entirely as a deer forest. Shooting parties flocked to Deeside in autumn. The gentlemen stalked hundreds of deer and bagged thousands of grouse, ptarmigan, blackcock and wood pigeon, while their keepers killed scores of eagles, peregrine, goshawk, crows and foxes, which might prey on them. Meanwhile the ladies took carriage drives around the pleasure grounds, had picnics on the lawn and arranged dinners and balls in grand rooms festooned with the trophies of the chase, quite oblivious to the impact that this lifestyle was having on rural life. Local people had little choice but to adapt to this new shift in estate policy, or leave.

It was not only the landscape that was transformed in the nineteenth century; the entire way of life in these glens changed. Down through the ages Mar folk had lived and worked in a wooded land. They may have been farmers, but they also traded in wood and illicit whisky. They depended on the trees to shelter their sheep and cattle, to keep a roof over their heads and provide some cash to keep them going when their crops failed and cattle starved. One of the last attempts at timber speculation by a local man came to grief and probably heralded the end of this form of exploitation. Alexander Davidson, known locally as 'Rough Sanie' and more usually a poacher and smuggler, turned to a legitimate enterprise. Having bought the rights to fell Derry wood, he is said to have remodelled the dam to ease the passage of the logs. The cost of this, however, far exceeded his calculations. To make matters worse, he then agreed to sell £200 worth of standing timber back to the earl, who had decided that such a felling operation would harm the estate's amenities. Unfortunately, the earl was made bankrupt soon after and couldn't pay 'Rough Sanie' what he was owed. The final blow came with the 'muckle spate' of 1829, which broke the Derry Dam and proceeded down the Dee, washing away all in its path. This proved the ruin of 'Rough Sanie' as a timber merchant at least, though he soon moved with the times and became widely know for his exploits and prowess as a poacher.[66] The earl's fortunes eventually improved, but traditional timber dealing had had its day.

By 1851, Mar estate employed fifteen gamekeepers, while there was only one sawmiller and three carpenters left to carry on the timber working tradition. Centuries of woodsmanship passed down through the generations was seeping away as the old families left or turned their hand to other occupations. For some families like the McHardys, a name synonymous with the district who had been sheep farmers at the beginning of the century, their great knowledge of the hills was diverted into tending deer instead.

The Mar estate was one of a relatively small number of estates, like Glenfeshie, Glenmore and Glenfiddich, where hunting had been, if not always the principal function, then at least up until the early nineteenth century a constant activity besides forestry and agriculture. Though Mar sustained an agricultural population until the nineteenth century, when sheep farming was largely usurped by deer forest, many Highland estates retained a mixed economy, with only the high tops and hill pasture given over to sheep or deer. Mackintosh of Mackintosh, for example, at the beginning of the nineteenth century held extensive lands from Lochaber in the west through Badenoch and Strathspey and as far east as Daviot, near Inverness. It is evident from the series of letters written to him by his manager, John Bisset, at Moy Hall, his ancestral home near Tomatin, that even by the 1850s there were several activities and concerns that Bisset was required to oversee. These included the letting of the shooting and meeting the needs of those renting the shootings and ensuring that they were well maintained, in addition to managing the farming operation and employing farm labour. Bisset, for example, in a letter in October 1856 from his employer, was asked to give the labourers a harvest ball or 'harvest home'.[67] His letters to his employer include reference to problems with staff and at one point he defended a suggestion that on an occasion he had been seen to be drunk in Inverness.

Around 1870 Mackintosh sold Glen Mazeran, a tributary of Strathdearn downstream of Coignafearn, to John Fowler, whose engineering firm built the Forth Bridge. Fowler had previously been a tenant. Other traditional estates retained their ownership in their deer forests, letting them out to a string of industrialists, brewing magnates and American millionaires, although towards the end of the century several of these trophy hunters themselves became proprietors of their own deer forest. The Mackenzies of Gairloch converted some 2,000 acres, creating Flowerdale deer forest in 1847, while remaining in essence a mixed economy including sheep and crofting. The population often fell back to fishing and large numbers of the Gairloch men migrated to Caithness and the east coast to work in the herring fishing. The destitution roads became the means for easier access for sportsmen, alongside the railways, which opened up the Highlands to tourists and sportsmen.

The landscape and its ecology were undoubtedly affected by these shifts in land management, though in ways that it is difficult to quantify. The predator–prey balance must surely have changed as deer and game numbers rose and management favoured quarry species. Osgood Mackenzie, a voracious hunter in his day, recalled that in his father's time at the beginning of the century, 'The vermin consisted of all kinds of beasts and birds, a good many of which are now extinct.' The last red kite, which is said to have 'swarmed' the district in his father's time, had already become extinct by his own. So too were pine martens, polecats and badgers, although he recalls them being abundant in his youth.[68] Heather burning, or muirburn as it was commonly known, had become an essential element of the new sheep farming. It also became a central part of the sporting estate's annual cycle, as part of the effort to increase the carrying capacity of the land for grouse and other game, as well as for sheep. By the beginning of the twentieth century, the combined effects of sheep farming and sport on the landscape of the Highlands was to create upland landscapes divided by substantial stone dykes and iron and wire fences, invariably crossing miles of high ground and sometimes meeting at hill summits as can still be seen in Glenshee, where the marches of three counties meet at the summit of Glas Maol. The effort involved in building these impressive marches must have been colossal. Such boundaries were built, not just because they could be, but because of the conflicts that arose between sheep and deer. So, in 1884, Mackintosh of Mackintosh's keeper at Coignafearn was in correspondence with Lord Lovat's sheep manager about the latter's sheep trespassing on his deer forest. By 1889, the estate accepted a quotation of iron and wire fencing for 18,930 yards for a march fence between its lands, and those of Belleville in Strathspey, Cluny in Badenoch and Dochfour (the latter presumably holding a property on the north side of the Monadhliaths), a distance of 10 miles or more. On the nearby Ardverikie estate, its owner, Sir John Ramsden, spent £180,000 on 76 miles of internal fencing, 43 miles of march fencing (shared with his neighbours), 473 miles of drains, 20 miles of carriage road and 18 miles of pony paths; eighteen houses were built and thirteen were restored.[69] By the end of the century roads, fences, grouse butts and occasional bothies had replaced the shieling, and in some places communities of men, women and children working the land and tending their livestock, characteristic of the previous century.

There is a sense, rightly or wrongly, that what befell the Highlands during the nineteenth century was somehow unjust, despite the fact that something had to give with the overwhelming population pressure pushing the carrying capacity of the land to breaking point. As Smout so eloquently puts it, 'The grouse moor and deer forest between them changed a landscape of use, full of farmers working the hills at field and shieling, to a landscape of delight, kept empty of people.'[70]

WOODLAND AND FOREST

Samuel Johnson, the great eighteenth-century English writer, in describing his tour of Scotland in 1773, famously wrote that 'a tree might be a show in Scotland as a horse in Venice'.[71] Admittedly, Scotland at that time may have had somewhat less woodland than the more sylvan landscapes of many districts of England, but that is too simple an explanation for his initial response to the Scottish countryside. The nature of the landscapes of these two neighbouring countries – particularly between north and south – was profoundly different. Johnson, when he ventured out of London into the English countryside, would have been accustomed to seeing a well-populated landscape with many manors and stately homes surrounded by great parklands and plantations, a countryside of ancient hedgerows and scattered copses – the kind of landscape that he grew up with in Staffordshire. At the time of his visit, Scotland, particularly the Lowlands, was still largely unenclosed and he would have undoubtedly observed small villages of little more than a dozen or more households dispersed across the countryside, still virtually bereft of hedges, ditches, dykes, roads and any of the other man-made constructions. In Scotland the hedgerow was predominantly a creation of the Improvement era, one means of dividing up the large fields. Of course, his comments related specifically to his travels through Fife, which was evidently then 'in uniform nakedness, except that in the road between Kirkcaldy and Cowper, I pass for a few yards between two hedges'.[72] Once he ventured into the Highlands, where most woodland was to be found, it would have been far from a treeless scene over which he cast his critical gaze.

Smout recently estimated that woodland cover in Scotland was likely, by the beginning of the nineteenth century, to be up to 9 per cent (as opposed to 4 per cent previously estimated) of the land area. More than half of this, he conjectured, was probably composed of uncommercial, scrubby pasture or montane scrub. He suggested that at that time planted woodland of non-native or native species accounted for only about one-fifth of this total. By 1900, Smout's estimate for total woodland cover amounts to around 6 per cent. From these figures he deduced that perhaps half the ancient semi-natural woods surviving around 1800 had been lost 100 years later. In short, native woodland declined as plantations increased and replaced them during this period.[73] What, therefore, is the explanation that underlies these rather startling statistics? And how did this relate to the transformation of the lives of rural dwellers during the course of the nineteenth century?

Scotland's people have probably always had a complex relationship with their woods, which they both exploited and venerated. Certainly, as soon as we have enough information to form an opinion, it is clear that they served a wide range of purposes, some firmly utilitarian, others more recreational. They were also valued for their beauty and spiritual value. Trees were an integral part of rural society and its economy until the Victorian period. At the same time, local requirements for the produce of woods for everyday life in Scotland, which was still largely rural based, remained substantial. Outside Scottish cities and burghs houses required a range of types of wood for their construction; most importantly for roofing, which was predominantly locally sourced. Farm implements, household utensils, furniture and even harnesses were usually made of wood. This varied over the country, but where the countryside was still well wooded, such as the west Highlands, wood produce continued to be essential for daily life well into the nineteenth century and the people knew which properties of a tree would best suit each implement or use. In the early nineteenth century on Lochtayside these included: alder for cabers; birch for hand barrows; fir (Scots pine) for fencing corn and for 'dealls' (sawn timber planks); hazel for firewood; young oak for byre construction; ash for corn stacks, hoops and carts; oak for slade (sledge) rungs; and even ash for shinty sticks.[74] The increased specialisation already mentioned is evident for Lochtayside from the roup rolls of wood sold in the period between 1790 and 1850, when larger amounts of timber were being sold to fewer people, who tended to be sawmillers, wheelwrights and cabinetmakers.

As the value of the native woods increased in the late eighteenth century, so too did their supervision, which became more proactive and interventionist. If they were oak woods, for example, they were generally managed as coppice. However, brush or 'barren' species were less desirable and removed, and 'vacancies' were filled in with oak, in a form of enrichment planting. This was probably the first sustained attempt at changing the composition of these woods in their history. The rising value of oak woods in particular led to increasing conflict between the needs of the people – for pasture and wood products – and the needs of the commercialising landowners. Pilfering had always been part and parcel of the way woods were used and was sometimes unofficially sanctioned, as long as fines might be extracted for the misdeeds.

Up until the mid-nineteenth century, woodkeepers were employed on Lochtayside and in many other estates where woodland was perceived as an asset for the landowner. Around 1815 a new woodkeeper, Malcolm Macgregor, was brought to Breadalbane from Glenorchy. He very enthusiastically produced several long reports on the state of the woods on the western half of Lochtayside, Glendochart, Glenlochay and Edinample (Lochearnside), from which much can be learned about both his experiences and views, not to mention the views of the estate owner, on woodland management. Macgregor's remit included apprehending transgressors, who would then be fined, or worse.[75] He found many injures to trees caused not just by trespassing livestock, but often by bark stripping (dyeing was a commonly cited use for alder bark), as well as the taking of living and dead trees, and parts of them. Being an outsider probably helped him in this task, though on one occasion, Macgregor informed his superiors that a bottle of whisky had been left in his house, to induce him not to take a transgressor to court! The offence in this case was removing ferns (probably bracken for roofing) from an enclosed wood without permission, a practice which was increasingly viewed as detrimental to the woods, both because of the damage inflicted on the dykes and due to the disturbance of game. In fact the 4th Earl of Breadalbane eventually prohibited anyone from entering the wood enclosures, although this must have been a particularly difficult directive to police.[76] However, as farmers and country dwellers relied less and less on their own skills to build and repair their housing and produce their own farm and household implements, the pressure to resort to stealing was progressively reduced as the century progressed.

With agricultural change, particularly the emphasis on sheep and loss of summer pastures from many tenancies, the traditional reservation of low pasture during summer was often no longer possible; valley land and lower parts of hill pasture, which often supported some kind of woodland, were pressed into service in summer to accommodate the new breeds of sheep. The decline of semi-natural woodland during this period therefore became inevitable, although it must have been a slow process given the enduring nature of trees and woodlands.

Furthermore, in the course of the nineteenth century the emphasis began to shift from the 'natural' woods to plantation forestry based on conifers. In the Highlands, two developments substantially affected the extent and character of the native woods: the coming of modern sheep farming and the arrival of forestry. Coppice woodland became less important, although it was still utilised, at least until the end of the century, where markets could be found for the produce. Bark had gradually become less profitable following the end of the Napoleonic Wars and most of the coppice woods had lost their value by the 1850s, becoming once more pasture for the increasing number of new breeds of sheep, particularly in the Highlands. Many woods also became game sanctuaries and the number of gamekeepers steadily increased, employed to protect the woods for the game and keep out trespassing locals, who might damage fences and disturb the laird's quarry. Certainly, this was an era when the majority of the Scottish population appear to have become alienated from the woods, often excluded in favour of deer and game. Perhaps more than at any time in the past, the woods became the 'preserve of the few'.

The great trend of the late eighteenth and early nineteenth centuries, linked to the drive for agricultural 'improvement', was tree planting, epitomised by the efforts of 'Planter' John, 4th Duke of Atholl (1755–1830). He transplanted over fourteen million larch seedlings alone onto his Perthshire estate between 1774 and 1826. Most of these were planted in a monoculture, in an attempt to furnish a profitable timber resource to supply the British Navy. It was a tremendous effort, which changed the face of the Atholl hills, but while a number of ships were built during the lifetime of the 4th duke, by the time many of these trees reached maturity the markets had once again become unfavourable for home-grown timber. Cheap and apparently limitless supplies of timber were coming from the Baltic, Scandinavia, North America and indeed other parts of the British Empire. However, this later trend did not deter further extensive plantings in the Highlands. On Ardverikie estate, Sir John Ramsden, whose foremost interest was hunting, from the 1870s onwards planted some 10,400 acres of his 42,000-acre estate with some thirty-four million trees, mostly of the newly imported firs from North America.[77]

Planting was not just for profit; landscape enhancement and game cover were also important. 'Planter' John notably commented that 'Planting ought to be carried on for Beauty, Effect and Profit.' One-upmanship probably also played a part in the spread of new and interesting trees and shrubs, which started to appear in Scotland when David Douglas and other plant explorers returned with seed from North America. Western hemlock, Sitka spruce, western red cedar and Lawson's cypress were among the North American introductions, which were often planted with other exotics like Norway spruce, Grand fir and beech to create ornamental policies and parklands. Beech, larch and Norway spruce were also increasingly planted in 'vacancies' in existing semi-natural woods.

In the Lowlands, plantations also became a common feature of the landscape, not just around elite houses. With less reliance on rough grazings, expansion of plantations on moorland and on less valuable agricultural land proceeded apace. While some estate owners and gentlemen farmers tried to reclaim these 'wastes' for agricultural purposes, this often proved to be unsuccessful or at least unprofitable. They then resorted to tree cover, which proved much more successful. As well as offering potential returns – admittedly in the long term – these plantations of larch and pine provided excellent game cover, especially if ground cover such as rhododendron was included in the planting lists.

There was a time in Scotland when every aspect of life required woodland produce and the woods around settlements were an integral part of daily life, whether for livestock, fun or utility. In the well-wooded parts of Scotland, they also provided revenue for the landholder and tenant alike, as we have seen with Mar. On the other side of the Cairngorms, it is known that the Grants of Rothiemurchus were able to realise an incredible annual revenue of between £10,000 and £20,000 during the Napoleonic Wars. For all that, Elizabeth Grant, one of the daughters of the laird during this period, later commented, 'The Wood manufacture was our staple, on it depended our prosperity . . . while it flourished so did we . . . when it fell the Laird had only to go back to black cattle again . . . It was a false stimulus, said the political economists. If so, we paid for it.' Despite this rather gloomy assessment of the estate's finances at the beginning of the nineteenth century, the Grants maintained an interest in utilising their extensive Caledonian pine forest.[78]

The Rothiemurchus woods evidently also provided employment to local people, and there is a sense that the local people lived as much by the trees as by their livestock and farming. Elizabeth Grant provided a wonderful description of one of the key occupations relating to this trade – the floaters, that is, the men, who punted and jostled the felled pine logs down the river Spey to Garmouth on the Moray Firth. They mostly came from around Ballindalloch, on the middle reaches of the Spey, but there were many locals employed too. Most of the work was done in autumn and winter and dams were created in the woods to assist the thrusting logs when they were set upon their journey to the sea. She recounted: 'The night before a run, the man in charge of that particular sluice set off up to the hill, a walk of miles partly over an untracked moor, and reaching the spot long before daylight opened the heavy gates; out rushed the torrent, travelling so quickly as to reach the deposit of timber in time for the meeting of the woodmen.' It must have been a spectacular sight – certainly the young Grant children were enthralled as they watched this operation near Loch an Eilean – but it was a dangerous occupation. One young lad froze to death, having been sent to open the sluice gates on a stormy night well up the glen. But it also brought laughter and mirth to those involved. The floaters' ball was held around Christmas: 'As the harvest home was given to the farm, this entertainment belonged to the forest.'[79] Rothiemurchus, however, like many neighbouring estates in the nineteenth century, sought revenue from sporting interests and the woods became less important to the proprietors. The vast stands of Scots pine, birch, alder and willows endured and were worked in some form through the nineteenth century and into the twentieth century. Rather than grandiose schemes of exploitation, local use on a smaller scale seems to have developed. For areas such as Strathspey, where woods remained a significant feature of the landscape, the relationship between people and woods continued.

CONCLUSION: A CENTURY OF CHANGE

Nothing remains the same. A boulder perched on a hillside for millennia, deposited there by a receding glacier some 10,000 years ago, is finally dislodged after centuries of weathering and crashes down the hillside. The landscape will never look the same again for those who remember how that hillside looked before the boulder plunged down the slope. To those who view the scene for the first time thereafter, the landscape will be accepted in its new form, without realising that a mighty boulder once dominated that landscape.

Landscape – and how it is perceived and valued by people – is ever-changing, evolving according to its own physical requirements and responding to the needs of society. The interaction between people and the land, the way that it is used and viewed created the landscape and the context for the daily lives of most Scots in the past. During the nineteenth century there developed an overwhelming imperative to dominate nature, where before it had seemed static, almost unalterable. Increasingly, nature became a focus for 'improvement', and in time, across the land it is likely that change was realised to a far greater extent than had ever been known before in terms of human impact. This can be traced to a number of key forces, most prominently the transformation of the economy and society in the nineteenth century. This could be achieved only by technological innovation, which allowed the economy, both manufacturing and agricultural, to develop in ways simply not possible in the eighteenth century.

Caught within these various forces for change those who occupied the land had to adapt or leave. And yet there was something about the land that seems to have proved enduring and hard to let go of. Many persisted with a basic allegiance to their place of birth, whether as an Uist crofter, north-east ploughman or Clydesdale dairyman. That is not to say that those that lived and worked on the land in this period did not have a hard life, not just by twenty-first century standards, but also by the standards of the day. The daily drudgery of clearing the land, draining, sowing, ploughing, reaping, weeding, gathering, milking, lifting and a host of other arduous jobs. As one newspaper reported:

> Six days shalt thou labour and do all
> That you are able;
> On the Sabbath-day wash the horses' legs
> And tiddy up the stable.[80]

John McPhail was born in 1848 in Mull, during the potato famine. At the time his father, Donald, was ploughman to the minister at Bunessan in the Ross of Mull. His elder brother, Dugald, was born the year the blight broke

Figure 1.4   *A landscape in transition. Rigs near Coupar Angus, Perthshire. Mid-nineteenth-century print showing a field containing rigs being sown. © Scottish Life Archive. Licensor www.scran.ac.uk.*

out in 1846. John had at least ten younger siblings, born in several parts of Argyll in the following 15 years. His parents clearly moved around a bit before settling on a croft near Connel Ferry just outside Oban in the 1860s. During a reasonably long lifetime – some 74 years – John McPhail was at various times an innkeeper, gamekeeper, policeman and possibly a soldier in the Ashanti Wars of the 1870s. He finally settled on the croft that his father had passed on to him when, at around 70 years old, Donald and his wife, along with several of their other children, emigrated to Canada in the 1880s.

John McPhail had two sons, both of whom emigrated to Canada. His six daughters – some of whom would also end up in Canada – almost all went into domestic service in various parts of Scotland. This family history can be replicated a thousand times over for many Highland families. It demonstrates the extent of internal migration and prevalence of emigration, as well as the need to adapt to the prevailing economic conditions and to follow opportunities where they arose. A man could quite easily be both a gamekeeper and a crofter in his lifetime and reach an advanced age, having been born into extreme poverty and famine conditions. John McPhail never let this or the loss of two brothers – one in a mining accident in Montana and another in Australia – overcome the essential determination of the human spirit to survive and endure.

The process of change that began in the eighteenth century (and earlier in some parts of Scotland) reached its zenith in the nineteenth century. As one Highlander recalled:

> I saw with childish sorrow, impotent wrath and awful wonder at man's inhumanity to man, the harsh and sweeping Roro and Morenish clearances, and heard much talk about others which were said to be as bad if not worse. A comparison of the census returns for 1831 with those of 1861 will show how the second Marquis reduced the rural population on his large estates, while the inhabitants of certain villages were allowed, or, as at Aberfeldy, encouraged to increase.[81]

Such changes created the landscape with which we are still familiar today, though the fields which teemed with hard-wrought activity are now populated by the occasional mammoth tractor and its various agricultural accessories. Today for most of the Scottish population (and for those beyond its bounds) land is for delight. Few of us depend upon the land for our living. However, that which we find attractive – the high tops, the verdant forests, the hedge-lined fields – are all a product of the nineteenth century, when they were still alive with people, albeit fewer than in previous centuries. Few today would wish to go back to life for the majority in the nineteenth century, even if poverty and unremitting hard work was lightened by the kind of communal bonds that have probably disappeared forever. It is easy to romanticise that, just as it is easy to romanticise the experience of living much closer to nature, which could overwhelm at least as often as it sustained. Of course, nature itself had no idea that it was supposed to be doing something different in the nineteenth century than that which it had done before, any more than it pays any attention to 'Scotland' or 'the Highlands' or 'the Lowlands'. Equally, changes on the ground are always a product of both the activities of man, sometimes decades and even centuries before, as well as the painstaking actions and reactions of landscapes and ecosystems over an even longer period. And yet, it is striking, as this story has unfolded, how much changed and how near it was to our own time. For those whose everyday lives were transformed only two centuries ago at most, alongside landscapes fundamentally altered thanks to the ideas and desires of a new technologically-driven economy, we can only wonder at the harsh realities of that transition, and the resilience of both nature and the human spirit to endure it.

Notes

1 In 1844 35 per cent of the population lived in towns with populations greater than 5,000 (in 1971 this was 74 per cent); T. C. Smout, *A Century of the Scottish People, 1830–1950* (London, 1986). The proportion of the population employed in agriculture fell from 25 per cent in the mid-nineteenth century to 11 per cent in the early twentieth century, see: R. H. Campbell and T. M. Devine, 'The Rural Experience', in W. H. Fraser and R. J. Morris (eds), *People and Society in Scotland, vol. 2, 1830–1914*, (Edinburgh, 1990), p. 46.

2 T. M. Devine argues thus, using the cases of Angus, Fife, Ayrshire and Lanark, *The Transformation of Rural Scotland: Social Change and the Agrarian Economy, 1660–1815* (Edinburgh, 1994), pp. 164, 166.

3 J. H. Andrews, *History in the Ordnance Map: An Introduction for Irish Readers* (Dublin, 1974).

4 I. Whyte, *Agriculture and Society in Seventeenth-Century Scotland* (Edinburgh, 1979), pp. 3–4; C. Dingwall, 'Sources of Woodland History: the Statistical Accounts', Paper presented at Scottish Woodland History Discussion Group conference, Stirling, 1996.

5 I. Levitt and T. C. Smout, *The State of the Scottish Working Class in 1843* (Edinburgh, 1979).

6 E. Burt, *Letters from a Gentleman in the North of Scotland to his Friend in London*, 2 vols (London, 1754); D. Defoe, *A Tour Through the Whole Island of Great Britain*, G. D. H. Cole and D. C. Browning (eds) (London, 1974).

7 Lord H. Cockburn, *Circuit Journeys* (Edinburgh, 1975); J. Mitchell, *Reminiscences of my Life in the Highlands* (Newton Abbot, 1971); W. Alexander, *Johnny Gibb of Gushetneuk in the Parish of Pyketillim* (East Linton, 1995).

8 A. McLeod (trans.), *The Songs of Duncan Ban Macintyre* (Edinburgh, 1978), 'Farewell to the Bens'. Thanks to Meg Bateman for information and advice about Gaelic poetry and Duncan Ban MacIntyre.

9 See B. Dugan, 'The Social and Economic History of the Blackmount Deer Forest 1820–1900', Unpublished Ph.D. thesis, Glasgow University, 2004. Dugan cites several references to the forester's responsibilities, including 'the forest of Corichbay to serve the family when at the caste or when the earl please to dispose

of the deer' (GD112/41/3). Other similar references for the early eighteenth century suggest that the forester has an annual cull to achieve (e.g. eight deer between May and November).

10 New Statistical Account [NSA], 1843, *Parish of Glenorchy*, 98.

11 Population of Glenorchy parish (1801) 1,851, (1831) 1,806, (1861) 1,307, (1871) 1,054, (1881) 1,105 and of neighbouring Killin: (1801) 2,048, (1831) 2,002, (1861) 1,520, (1871) 1,856, the latter as the gazetteer says, 'many of them navvies', on the building of the railway, available at: http://www.geo.ed.ac.uk/scotgaz/parishes/parhistory466.html. The Old Statistical Account [OSA] recorded that there were approximately 20,000 sheep in the parish by 1792. According to OSA there were 1,669 inhabitants in 1792, considerably less than the population 10 years later.

12 E. Richards, *A History of the Highland Clearances*, vol. 1 (London, 1982), p. 176.

13 See Richards, *Highland Clearances*, and T. M. Devine, *Clearance and Improvement: Land, Power and People in Scotland, 1700–1900* (Edinburgh, 2006). Also W. Orr, *Deer Forests, Landlords and Crofters: the Western Highlands in Victorian and Edwardian Time* (Edinburgh, 1982) and J. Hunter, *The Making of the Crofting Community* (Edinburgh, 1976).

14 See G. Whittington, 'Agriculture and Society in Lowland Scotland, 1750–1870', in G. Whittington and I. Whyte (eds), *An Historical Geography of Scotland*, (London, 1983). Also I. Whyte, 'Rural Transformation and Lowland Society', in A. Cooke *et al.* (eds), *Modern Scottish History: 1707 to the present, vol. 1, The Transformation of Scotland, 1707–1850*, (East Linton, 1998) and Devine, *Transformation of Rural Scotland*, p. 165. For the Highlands, Richards, *Highland Clearances* and Hunter, *Crofting Community*.

15 T. M. Devine, *Exploring the Scottish Past: Themes in the History of Scottish Society* (East Linton, 1995), p. 117.

16 P. Sansum, M. J. Stewart and F. J. Watson, *A Preliminary History of the Clyde Valley Woodlands* (commissioned technical report for SNH, published by Highland Birchwoods, July 2005).

17 T. M. Devine, 'The Transformation of Agriculture: Cultivation and Clearance', in T. M. Devine, C. H. Lee and G. C. Peden (eds), *The Transformation of Scotland: the economy since 1700* (Edinburgh, 2005), p. 92.

18 J. G. Harrison and B. Lawers, *A Report for The Royal Commission on the Ancient And Historical Monuments of Scotland* [RCAHMS], July 2003 From Harrison Report. National Archives of Scotland [NAS]: GD112/16/14/4, Item 16–20, reports by ground officers on crops in Lawers etc. 1836.

19 Sir T. D. Lauder, *An account of the great floods of August 1829, in the province of Moray, and adjoining districts* (Edinburgh, 1830). For estimates of damage incurred, L. McEwen and A. Werritty, '"The Muckle Spate of 1829": the Physical and Societal Impact of a Catastrophic Flood on the River Findhorn, Scottish Highlands', *Transactions of the Institute of British Geographers*, 32:1 (January 2007), 66–89 (24).

20 A. Wight, *Present State of Husbandry in Scotland*, 4 vols (Edinburgh, 1778–84), vol. 4, pp. 1, 374.

21 OSA, XXIX, vol. 12, *Parish of Nairn. By The Rev. Mr. John Morrison*, p. 393.

22 In 1789, the council had to borrow £100 to pay off their debts (Highland Regional Archive [HRA] D231/A/4, 85). A few years earlier they had resolved to lease their moor ground in order to 'increase their funds of the Community' (HRA D231/A/4, 5 June 1786). By 1800, they had almost raised the funds for a new bridge and in 1806 the council opened a subscription for a new pier (HRA D231/A/4, 5 June 1806).

23 NSA, vol. 13, p. 15; NSA, vol. 14, *Ardersier*, p. 473; NSA, vol. 13, p. 4.

24 C. Rampini, *A History of Moray and Nairn* (Edinburgh, 1897), p. 299.

25 For example, *Transactions of the Highland Agricultural Society of Scotland* [THASS], 2nd series, 1837, pp. 97–121, THASS, 3rd series, 1843, pp. 452–5.

26 Work carried out by RCAHMS as part of the Ben Lawers Historic Landscape Project has ground-truthed the plans and found them to be very accurate and very useful as a means to identify and date ruins on the lochside.

27 NAS: RHP973, 3.

28 M. J. Stewart, 'The Growth of Aberfeldy in the Second Half of the 19th Century, Unpublished MA diss., Glasgow University, 1984.

29 W. Marshall, *General View of the Agriculture of the Central Highlands* (London, 1794), pp. 24, 27.

30 From Harrison Report: GD112/16/13/4/16, *State of cropping and sown grass on Lochtayside*, 1821.

31 J. Kennedy, *Folklore and Reminiscences of Strathtay and Grandtully* (Perth, 1927), p. 55.

32 J. Mitchell, *Reminiscences*, 35.

33 NSA XIII, *Nairn*, pp. 1–6.

34 HRA 1/1/5, p. 23.

35 Devine, 'The Transformation of Agriculture: Cultivation and Clearance', in Devine, Lee and Peden (eds), *The Transformation of Scotland*, p. 92.

36 From Harrison Report, ch. 5: GD112/16/13/1, item 2, *Sowing and Souming*, c. 1769; GD112/16/13/1, item 10, *Sowing and Souming*, 1783.

37 For a full analysis of the famine see, T. M. Devine, *The Great Highland Famine: Hunger, Emigration and the Scottish Highlands in the Nineteenth Century* (Edinburgh, 1996).

38 NAS: GD112/74/80/1. *Letters from J. F. Wyllie to Breadalbane and Barcaldine*, 21 November 1845.

39 Devine, *Great Highland Famine*; Hunter, *Crofting Community*; Richards, *Highland Clearances*.

40 Harrison Report, ch. 5: GD112/16/7/2, item 51, *Report on the Potato Crop*, 1846.

41 O. Mackenzie, *A Hundred Years in the Highlands* (London, 1949; reprinted 1965), p. 37.

42 Devine, *Great Highland Famine*, p. 89, quote from Relief Correspondence, Mr Trevelyan to Sir E. Coffin, p. 28, December 1846.

43 Richards, *Highland Clearances*, 411.

44 T. M. Devine, *Clanship to Crofters' War: the Social Transformation of the Scottish Highlands* (Manchester, 1994), p. 151; Richards, *Highland Clearances* (reprinted 2008), ch. 13.

45 Devine 'The Transformation of Agriculture: Cultivation and Clearance', p. 86;
    J. Hunter, *A Dance Called America: the Scottish Highlands, the United States and
    Canada* (Edinburgh, 1994), p. 115. Death rates on ships were around 10 per cent
    and could be as much as 40 per cent (Hunter, *Crofting Community*, p. 113).

46 NAS: GD176/2253/23, *Letters to the Mackintosh, travelling in Europe, from John
    Bisset, manager at Moy Hall, reporting on farming and household matters*, 10
    September 1857.

47 E. A. Cameron, 'Poverty, Protest and Politics: Perceptions of the Scottish
    Highlands in the 1880s', in D. Broun and M. Macgregor (eds), *Miorun Mor nan
    Gall, 'The Great Ill-Will of the Lowlander?' Lowland Perceptions of the Scottish
    Highlands, Medieval and Modern*, (Glasgow, 2007).

48 Devine, *Exploring the Scottish Past*, p. 145, quoting from Sir John McNeill enquiry
    into conditions in Western Isles in 1851.

49 Devine, *Great Highland Famine*, p. 148, quoting Sir John MacNeill.

50 Sir John MacNeill quoted in Smout, *History of the Scottish People*, p. 66.

51 Quoted from D. K. Cameron, *Ballad and the Plough* (Edinburgh, 2008), p. 7.

52 British Parliamentary Papers, vol. 18: *The Final Report from the Royal
    Commissioners on Agriculture, with Minutes of Evidence*, Part III, Digest of
    Evidence, Parts II and III, and appendix, 1882.

53 See Devine, *From Clanship to Crofters' War*, and Orr, *Deer Forests, Landlords and
    Crofters*. Also, P. Gaskell, *Morven Transformed: a Highland Parish in the 19th
    Century* (Cambridge, 1996) and J. Hunter 'Sheep And Deer: Highland Sheep
    Farming, 1850–1900', *Northern Scotland*, 1:2 (1973), pp. 199–222.

54 NAS: GD176/2253/27. Letters to the Mackintosh, travelling in Europe, from
    John Bisset, manager at Moy Hall, reporting on farming and household matters,
    16 October 1857.

55 Marshall, *A General View of the Agriculture of the Central Highlands of Scotland*,
    pp. 31, 45. See A. Bil, *The Shieling, 1600–1840: the Case of the Central Scottish
    Highlands* (Edinburgh, 1990) for a full discussion of shielings and the causes of
    decline.

56 Mackenzie, *Hundred Years in the Highlands*, p. 25.

57 C. St. John, *Short Sketches of the Wild Sports and Natural History of the Highlands/
    by Charles St. John* (London, 1872), p. 291.

58 St. John, *Short Sketches*, p. 293.

59 At the head of Strathdearn some of the crofters' grazing was taken to form
    Coignafearn forest, although this initiative was accomplished in an 'amicable
    manner' with appropriate rent reductions, Deer Forest Commission, Q48,583.

60 NSA, *Parish of Moy and Dalarossie*, available at: http://stat-acc-scot.edina.ac.uk/
    link/1834-45/Inverness/Moy%20and%20Dalarossie/14/106.

61 NAS: GD176/2253/18, 2 May 1857.

62 Orr, *Deer Forests, Landlords and Crofters*, p. 48.

63 See Orr, *Deer Forests, Landlords and Crofters*; D. Hart-Davis, *Monarchs of the
    Glen: a History of Deer-stalking in the Scottish Highlands* (London, 1978); Hunter,
    Crofting Community; E. Cameron, *The Life and Times of Charles Fraser Mackintosh,
    Crofter MP* (Aberdeen, 2000). See Devine, *From Clanship to Crofters' War*.

64 Orr, *Deer Forests, Landlords and Crofters*, p. 216. At the same time the number of shepherds reached a peak of 10,281 in 1881, falling to 9,647 in 1901.

65 A. Durie, '"Unconscious Benefactors": Grouse-Shooting in Scotland, 1780–1914', *International Journal of the History of Sport*, 15:3 (1998), 68, the wages data comes from Fenton, 'Two Nineteenth-century Day Labourers' Account Books in Glenesk in Angus', *Scottish Local Historian*, 33 (1995), 17.

66 M. J. Stewart and F. J. Watson, *Mar Lodge Estate, Its Woods and People* (Edinburgh, National Trust for Scotland, 2004). See also Hart-Davis, *Monarchs of the Glen*, pp. 51–3.

67 NAS: GD176/2253/1–36. *Letters to the Mackintosh, travelling in Europe, from John Bisset, manager at Moy Hall, reporting on farming and household matters.*

68 Mackenzie, *Hundred Years in the Highlands*, p. 64.

69 NAS: GD176/1378/2 *Letter from Walter Archibald, Sheep Manager to Lord Lovat to Mr Hugh Kennedy, Keeper, Coignafearn, 26 February 1884*; NAS: GD176/1378/3, *Lochrin Ironworks, Coatbridge, 1 April 1889*; Orr, *Deer Forests, Landlords and Crofters*, p. 96.

70 T. C. Smout, *Nature Contested: Environmental History in Scotland and Northern England since 1600* (Edinburgh, 2000), p. 133.

71 S. Johnson, in I. McGowan (ed.), *Journey to the Hebrides*, (Edinburgh, 1996), p. 8.

72 Johnson, *Journey to the Hebrides*, p. 8.

73 T. C. Smout, A. R. Macdonald and F. Watson, *A History of the Native Woodlands of Scotland, 1500–1920* (Edinburgh, 2005), pp. 67–8.

74 M. J. Stewart, 'The Utilisation and Management of Lochtayside's Semi-Natural Woodlands between 1650 and 1850', Unpublished M.Phil. thesis, St Andrews University, 1997; NAS: GD 16/10/5.

75 NAS: GD 112/16/13/10.

76 NAS: GD 112/16/10/2.

77 M. J. Stewart and F. Watson, 'Preserve of the Few – Used by All. Scotland's Woodland History 1500–1850', *Scottish Forestry*, 58:4 (Winter 2004); S. House and C. Dingwall, '"A Nation of Planters": Introducing the New Trees, 1650–1900', in T. C. Smout (ed.), *People and Woods in Scotland. A History* (Edinburgh, 2003), p. 156.

78 E. Grant, *Memoirs of a Highland Lady*, vol. 1, A. Tod (ed.) (Edinburgh, 1988), p. 225.

79 Grant, *Memoirs of a Highland Lady*, pp. 267–75.

80 A rhyme about ploughmen from the *Fife Herald and Journal* in 1903, taken from Smout, *Scottish People*, p. 83.

81 D. Campbell, *Reminiscences and Reflections of an Octogenarian Highlander* (Inverness, 1910).

Chapter 2

Necessities in the Nineteenth Century

W. Hamish Fraser

> Even our bodies, the foods we eat and the physical nature of our surroundings are 'objects' of the material world. All these serve to define who and what we are, both to ourselves and others. As objects they are our alter egos, our parallel selves, because our use and understanding of them communicate 'us' and our identity as effectively as the spoken word.[1]

As interest in people as consumers has grown in recent decades, there has been a recognition that what people buy and what they display tells us much about them. Goods are the means by which people identify themselves as members of a particular culture. According to the sociologist Pierre Bourdieu it is taste that 'classifies the classifier', while the cultural theorist, Jean Baudrillard, has argued that people become what they buy. Although levels of income clearly can shape the choices that people have, even necessities – what people regard as essentials – are shaped by how they perceive their own social world. People, as much as possible, choose to buy what they see as appropriate to their social position or their aspirations. As so many of those commenting on working-class mores in the nineteenth century and providing 'improving' advice failed to recognise, wants could go beyond simple needs to the desire to maintain a particular standard and standing in the social world. Security in the all too likely eventuality of a crisis, a desire for a 'decent burial', the concern to keep up with neighbours, the desire to impress one's peers were all powerful influences in shaping how people spent their money. For those on a weekly wage this required immensely careful financial planning.[2]

Necessities I am taking to mean goods that minister to physical needs – food and drink, warmth, cleanliness and clothing. Just how to structure a chapter on these is problematic because there are huge geographical variations, class variations and changes over time. As in all things connected with the home, there are also individual character variations. The divisions between the 'respectable' and the 'rough', with all kinds of gradations in between were real enough, although complex, and account after account emphasises the contrast there could be between houses in the same street, one with an apparent level of comfort and cleanliness, the other a hovel. Within social classes, there are many different strata with different incomes, different aspirations, different values and different interests. Also, what are rare luxuries at one time or for one social group can become necessities at other times and for other social groups. The class differences constructed through consumption are often about what are regarded as 'necessities' and what as 'luxuries'.[3]

One of the difficulties with class variations is the fact that we know a great deal of the life of the very poor. It was they who were visited, investigated, inquired into and, where possible, 'improved'. We know even more about the really wealthy, multiple-servant households, where there are inventories, paintings and even photographs of the actual content of houses to fall back on. It is much more difficult to get information on the food, fashion and life style of the skilled working class or the lower middle class. One can get their aspirations and what producers and others wanted them to aspire to, in recipe books, domestic economy manuals and advertisements. How far the reality tied in with the advice books or the fashion brochures is more problematic.

As regards chronology, it is possible broadly to divide the century into three periods. The first period from 1800 to the 1840s was a time of huge social change, much movement of population and considerable social mobility, by no means all upwards; Scotland moved rapidly from a rural to an urban society. The mid-century decades from the end of the 1840s until the 1870s were a time when substantial groups were gaining from the huge industrial changes taking place. There were shorter hours and, for some, rising living standards and a big expansion in the middle class. The third period from the late 1870s is one when, thanks to the falling price of foodstuffs in particular, the standard of living of the mass of the population was rising and a recognisably 'modern' pattern of consumption was appearing.

1800–1840s

Many of the ministers compiling the material for the New Statistical Account (NSA) at the end of the 1830s were agreed that there had been a marked alteration in dress, diet, furnishings and manners among all social classes since the Old Statistical Account (OSA) in the 1790s. Food, of course, is the absolute fundamental, with 60 to 70 per cent of expenditure on average going on food, a substantially higher percentage than in England, where more was spent on housing. For the early period, we are fortunate in having Christopher Smout, Alex Gibson and Ian Levitt's splendid work on the state of the working-class diet in 1843 based on the NSA and on the Scottish Poor Law Commission. As they point out, 'from the point of view of what they ate they had infinitely more in common with the standards of the pre-industrial past than with the standards of the present day'.[4] They bring out the extensive regional variations, although the centrality of oatmeal in the diet is pretty universal outside the western Highlands, where oats did not grow particularly well, but were imported from elsewhere in the country. Barley, or the poorer bere, was more common in the north-west, wheat in Fife and the Lothians. Oatmeal was consumed in prodigious quantities as porridge, brose and oatcakes. In the Carse of Gowrie, the consumption was reputedly 36 ozs (1 kg) of oatmeal per man per day, with oatmeal and milk eaten three times a day. An Angus farm servant's diet in 1813 consisted of porridge or brose for breakfast, oatcakes with butter and skimmed milk for dinner and sowens – oats steeped until they begin to ferment (the English equivalent is flummery) – or potatoes for supper.[5] Working as a nurseryman in Edinburgh in 1831, Alexander Somerville and his fellow bothy-dwelling workers had a small measure of porridge for breakfast served with 'sour dook', 'a kind of rank butter-milk peculiar to Edinburgh', potatoes and salt and an occasional herring for dinner and 'sour dook' and oatmeal for supper. They never saw meat and seldom bread.[6]

In 1845, investigators from *The Times* visiting the Highlands found that few of the working classes or, even small farmers, 'ever taste animal food, with the exception of salt herring, or mutton of such sheep as are unfit for market; but live upon porridge of oatmeal, on potatoes, with or without a little milk or butter, as the case may be, and such other seasoning as the kail-yard may supply'.[7] As late as 1869, a report claimed that oatmeal remained 'the leading article of daily subsistence amongst ninety per cent of the families of the labouring classes in Scotland'.[8]

In the Highlands, the potato, which in the mid-eighteenth century had still been something of a luxury, was now pretty general, helping, until famine hit in the 1840s, to sustain a rapidly rising population. A survey of 1808 said that potato patches were more or less universal in Inverness-shire and that half the inhabitants lived mainly on potatoes for eight to nine months of the year.[9] Potatoes with salt was also a staple meal in many parts of the Lowlands and potatoes still formed a part of the wages of many farm servants well into the nineteenth century. The north-east combined both: an Urquhart labourer was consuming 8–10 lbs (about 4 kg) of potatoes a day and ½ lb of oatmeal (227g) together with a quart of milk.[10] Alexander Fenton suggests that married men with wives to cook for them could generally hope for potatoes, while the unmarried, cooking for themselves, stuck to oatmeal. There were also differences between those who ate in the kitchen with the farmer's family and those who had to fend for themselves. Treatment did, of course, vary from farm to farm, and in William Alexander's wonderful evocation of Aberdeenshire farm life in the 1840s at Clinkstyle, while the farmer and his family had bread, oatcakes, cheese and butter for tea, the men had boiled turnip and 'turnip brose' every night for a week.[11]

According to Gibson and Smout, other dairy produce was produced largely for the market. This certainly seems to have been the pattern in the north and in Ayrshire. Quite a lot of cheese making was going on in crofts and farms in the summer months, with production in Ayrshire and

Galloway becoming more commercialised. Fishwives with their creels would barter fish for cheese, butter and meal. Intriguingly, eggs rarely seem to be mentioned so, presumably, there was little keeping of hens.

Fish was popular in some areas. After 1815, herring fishing spread from the west to the Moray Firth and southwards. In Lanark, potatoes with herring were common for dinner, while salt herring was a staple of the Highlands well into the twentieth century. The salt tax was not repealed until 1823, so, where salt could not be produced from the sea, fish would be smoked. Excise men in Ross-shire were seizing huge quantities of illicit salt being smuggled from the west coast to Inverness in the years after Waterloo.[12] According to a Fyvie diary, the demand for salt in the city of Aberdeen in 1823, when the tax was lifted, was such that supplies ran out.[13]

With the new cheapness of salting and the possibilities of packing some in ice, fish were being transported over greater distances. Salt-cured herring went for export to Ireland and the West Indies early in the century and later to Russia, the Baltic States and Germany. Salted turbot and cod from Orkney and the Hebrides were finding their way to Edinburgh, while there was less of the once plentiful salmon around. Salmon was going further afield. Pickled and ice-packed salmon were going from Banff to London. But there were problems with fish among the working class in the cities. It went off quickly, but also was not seen as nutritious. Jockeys wanting to lose weight were fed fish. It did not have the carbohydrates to give the sense of being filled up that most manual workers demanded. On the other hand, because it did deteriorate rapidly, fish could be purchased cheaply from dealers at the end of the week.

Meat consumption was pretty limited, although poaching was endemic and by no means confined to the Highlands. So rabbits and venison perhaps appeared more often than was admitted. Meat consumption was rising in the industrialising south. In industrial Blantyre in the late 1830s, competition between butchers' shops was leading to lower prices and to a 'considerable amount' of meat consumption each week. At the same time, several butchers' shops had opened in Aberdeen 'in the last few years', and so meat could be 'obtained on any day of the week'.[14] In Larbert, the use of butcher meat had 'greatly increased' in the previous decade.[15]

As for fruit and vegetables, the difference between town and country was marked. In rural areas, kale and cabbage were available, being grown in the kailyard, even in the Hebrides, by the early nineteenth century. But a lack of green vegetables in the Hebrides contributed to scurvy and skin problems, while in Orkney, where they ate cabbage with their fish, there was apparently no scurvy.[16] In Hamilton and other parts of Clydeside in the late 1830s, a great proportion of houses had orchards, growing pears and apples and soft fruit.[17] Apples, plums, greengages, gooseberries and cherries were all available. A Lewis man saw strawberries, known as North Carolinas, being grown in Gairloch for the first time in 1820.[18] Kale-wives from Musselburgh ('old gin-drinking women' according to Cockburn) sold vegetables and fruit from creels in the streets of Edinburgh, while those from the Clyde valley went into Glasgow.

There was also an extensive range of other vegetables available for the better off. The remarkable Christian Johnston, editor of *Tait's Edinburgh Magazine*, produced her *Cook and Housewife's Manual* under the pseudonym of Mrs Margaret Dods, of the Cleikum Inn, St Ronan's, in 1826, and it went through sixteen editions over the next fifty years.[19] The first edition declared that vegetable markets had improved wonderfully both in terms of numbers and quality, with prices coming down. What is striking is the sheer range of vegetables that seemed to be available: 'where a turnip, cabbage, or leek, was twenty years ago the only vegetable *luxury* food on a Scottish gentleman's table, we see now a regular succession of not merely broccoli, cauliflower and peas, but the more recondite asparagus, sea kale, endive and artichoke'. Onions, cucumbers and celery all get a mention and must have been being produced locally together with a range of herbs, fennel, basil, tarragon and garlic.[20] How much nutrition there was in the vegetables is questionable since the advice was to boil vegetables well – cabbage up to an hour, swedes for four hours, asparagus half an hour. Most vegetables found their way into the easily-cooked broth and this was widely recommended as a quick meal. One has to ask, however, why this variety of vegetables did not appear to filter very far down the social scale even in the 1920s, never mind the 1820s.

New foreign tastes were coming in among the better off. The influence of French cuisine is evident in 'Meg Dods'. Not surprisingly the Indian influence was also apparent in the recipes, with Mullagatawny soup, Indian pickle and curry with Patna rice. The tenth edition of 1854 comments on the range of spices and fresh and dried fruit now available and accessible 'even among the working classes'. There was also evidence of Italian influence, which grew over time. Macaroni served with Parmesan cheese (often as a pudding course),[21] and Bologna sausage are both in the recipe book for 1829. By 1854 other pastas are appearing. While this was aimed at a growing middle class, servants saw the kind of food that was available among the well-to-do, so one would expect knowledge of it to filter down.

Much to the concern of many of the ministers of the NSA, tea was gaining in popularity among women. 'Other more real and substantial comforts are often sacrificed to obtain this enervating luxury' bemoaned the minister of St Fergus. The minister of Fortingall, near Perth, found it 'almost incredible' how much was expended on tea by the peasantry.[22] Interestingly, they were making exactly the same point in the OSA in the 1790s and Christian Johnston had condemned 'the universal and excessive use of tea' in her 1829 manual, arguing that 'the teapot drains the soup-pot'. One of the attractions of tea for the less well-off must have been the warmth that it provided, but this was at the cost of the nutritional value that came from beer. Although in the 1840s, tea still seemed to be taken unsweetened, once sugar duties began to fall sweeter tea became the taste. Tea with sugar was a useful hunger killer and, for many women, may have been used as an alternative to solid meals on many a day, while the husband got whatever was nutritious or filling. In the 1870s, there was still criticism that tea played too large a part in the working man's diet. Such comments, perhaps as much as anything, reflected the sense among the better off that tea drinking was losing its status as a validation of rank that it had once had.

Until the early 1830s, there was a great deal of home brewing of beer, but the excise laws and the 100 per cent duty on malt were making the production of home-made beer more difficult. Even by 1812, the historian David MacPherson was writing that tea was cheaper than beer.[23] There were, however, plenty of drinking places – one pub to twenty-four families in Dundee in the 1840s – and there was no equivalent of the English Beer Act of 1830 in Scotland that allowed the buying of licences to brew and sell only beer. In Scotland licences always covered both beers and spirits. Grocers' shops often incorporated drinking places and change was sometimes taken in the shape of a glass of whisky.[24] Shopping, particularly when many shops were merely rooms in private houses, was always a very complex social interchange.

At the table, wood and pewter platters remained in use. A Skye minister reported that in some houses a communal square wooden dish and a shared horn spoon were not unknown.[25] But cheap crockery was being spread by travelling folk, exchanging dishes for rags – 'Piggmen', 'pigg-wives' or 'pig and raggers'.[26] In David Wilkie's painting of the fair at Pitlessie, which dates from 1804 (and is one of the few of his paintings that is likely to be an

Figure 2.1 Sir David Wilkie, Pitlessie Fair (1804). Reproduced by permission of the National Galleries of Scotland.

accurate contemporary depiction rather than a nostalgic look at some romantic past) there is a woman with a creel of crockery pictured at the fair.

For warmth there was the open fire. In most cottages, even in the
Highlands, the fire had by the end of the eighteenth century moved from the
middle of the house to the gable. There and elsewhere, thanks to the Carron
Iron Works, brass and steel grates were around, 'the pride of housewives,
the dread of chilly guests and the torment of housemaids' according to
one commentator in 1824.[27] Coal was replacing peat as the main fuel, with
many of the most accessible peat beds being worn out. In Aberdeenshire
and Banffshire, coal, transported from Sunderland, was cheaper than peat,
although in the Lothians there were complaints that coal was getting dearer.[28]
Coal necessitated grates to raise the fire above floor level, but presumably
created problems about lighting the fire and keeping it lit. After all, the
great thing about peat was that it would smoulder long enough and could be
easily be brought back to life. Phosphorous matches were not around commercially until the 1830s and it is difficult to know how widespread the wax
and sulphur spunks were. Friction matches did not appear until the 1860s.
Lighting a coal fire, without paper, with a flame ignited from a tinderbox can
never have been easy and keeping a damped down fire alight overnight was
difficult and expensive and made cleaning difficult.

For most people, lighting, such as it was, took the form of whale or fish
oil cruisies. In the Highlands, fish liver was left to liquefy before being used
in this way.[29] In some parts of Aberdeenshire and in the Highlands, long
splinters of resinous pine provided the lighting.[30] The better off would have
tallow candles, although these made little improvement in the actual light
provided and required regular trimming and snuffing.[31] From a modern
stance, it all seems greasy, filthy and smelly. However, by the end of the
1840s gas lighting was making its way into houses. Cullen in 1841 had gas
lighting in eighty of its houses and in Tain it was in 'almost all the respectable houses', while gas lighting was apparently in use more extensively in
Edinburgh than it was in London.[32] But it was still relatively expensive to
maintain and not particularly comfortable, making rooms hot and oppressive. In the warrens that some inner-city tenements became, little natural
light penetrated at any time of the day and the inhabitants must have had to
live with the meagre glow from the fire.

With the grate you could also get the iron pot-crane or 'swey'. Local
blacksmiths came up with a variety of ingenious items for use on the new
grates – things like trivets for drying oatcakes and variations on the ubiquitous girdle. The kettle became more common. Apparently, there were only
three kettles in the whole of Forres in 1750, while by the end of the century
there were 300.[33] The swey also allowed for larger pots to be used. It meant
that there could even be hot water for washing clothes.[34] But there was generally only room for a single pot in which what variety there was had to be
cooked: so herring would be placed on top of the boiling potatoes.

Ovens were largely the preserve of the very well-to-do or of bakers, but a pot oven was used. 'Meg Dods' describes the process: first the metal lid is heated and laid on the hearth, 'the pot is then turned upside down over it; turf embers are placed all around or over this little oven'. She was clearly assuming that peat was still around, and some kitchens seem to have continued to use peat on a flat hearth, while the coal grate was reserved for the best room. A variation of the oven, using a clay flowerpot, was still being used in Christian Watt's house on the Aberdeenshire coast in the 1860s.[35] By the 1840s, cooking ranges were making their appearance – again thanks to Carron – with the oven at one side, but the problem with these was that they used very large quantities of fuel and the ovens tended to heat very unevenly.[36] There were also enclosed stoves from Bonnybridge's Smith and Wellstood, but one difficulty with these, as with later closed ranges, was that they required hard steam coal that would not burn in open fire grates, so two kinds of coal had to be kept in the house.[37] Not surprisingly, given the difficulties, the criticism of many working-class women was that they avoided the trouble of cooking altogether. According to Margaret Maria Brewster in 1858, 'the wife of the labouring man has a shilling in her pocket and goes out shopping for a day's dinner; she buys a couple of bottles of beer, and a bit of butter, and some bread and cheese'. For half the price, she could get parings and vegetables to make a broth,[38] but her decision was probably a rational one, based on a realistic assessment of the costs and the difficulties of cooking on an open fire in a crowded room at home.

It was Thomas Carlyle who made the point that clothing was more about ornament than warmth. 'The first spiritual want of a barbarous man is Decoration; as indeed we shall see among the barbarous classes in civilised societies.' Veblen at the end of the nineteenth century was making a similar point: 'it is by no means an uncommon occurrence, in an inclement climate, for people to go ill-clad in order to appear well dressed'.[39] To Veblen, a lot of fashion was about emulating those regarded as social superiors. But not everyone would agree that that was a substantial motive force. Much of it, as Brewer and Porter point out, was about asserting one's own moral worth, of which emulation might well be a part but it was not the sole motivation, hence, the importance of alternatives to working clothes for public occasions, the visit to church, the friendly society meeting or trade-union parade, the temperance rally. The Sunday suit was becoming a necessity for the social standing of the working man, even if it spent most of the week in the pawnshop.

Dress and grooming could also be about sexual attraction, of course. In all societies concern with the coiffure is great. An account of the Highlands talks of girls using elm bark to give their hair a shine ready for the trip to church.[40] It is doubtful if there was much washing of hair – just comb and bran or starch powders were what were used in France. There is room for a study of the progression of the head covering, from the all pervasive mutch, which seems to have been favoured by married women in the Highlands,[41] to the bonnet with its ribbons and lace, which had reached Edinburgh by the 1820s, the cap popularised by Queen Victoria and the elaborate hat with exotic feathers and garish flowers.

The NSA has numerous critical comments on the dress of young women. In Gairloch it was suggested that 'when a girl dresses in her best attire, her very habitiments, in some instances would be sufficient to purchase a better dwelling house than that from which she has just issued'.[42] In Lesmahago, the style and manner of dress was 'rather expensive', with 'the servant girls dressing as gaily as the squire's daughter did thirty years ago'.[43] In Perthshire, straw bonnets and umbrellas were common for both church and market, and people 'were more solicitous about making a decent personal appearance in public, than enjoying the luxuries of good eating'.[44] Although the price of clothes was becoming cheaper,[45] many such girls and their families depended on hand-me-downs from their employer's family. There was also a huge business, both at home and by tailors, in renovating old clothes. Women were expected to learn the skills of re-footing stockings, dyeing dresses and altering skirts. As the advice of one household manual had it, 'a dress that can be turned should always be chosen'. But even among the less well-off, a great deal of clothes-making went out to dressmakers and tailors. In D. M. Moir's *Life of Mansie Wauch, Tailor in Dalkeith*, published in *Blackwoods* in the 1820s, the minister sends his old black coat 'to get docked in the tails down to a jacket'. The market in second-hand clothes was national. In the 1840s, Henry Mayhew found Scottish dealers in London buying left-off clothes to take back north.[46] Clothes tended to pass through a lot of different hands before they made it to 'Paddy's market' or went to the ragman.

One might ask whether Presbyterianism made a difference to Scottish fashions. Was there wariness about too much show? There is little evidence of this, although perhaps Scotland led the way in the general darkening of men's clothing and the reproving tones of many of the clergy at excessive display are apparent in the Statistical Accounts. Clothes for the ritual of burial were always important. An advertisement in the *Inverness Journal* of 1809 reads 'Mrs Fraser, next door to Fraser's hotel, has just got to hand from London, a variety of ready-made grave clothes, all sizes and prices.' Funerals and mourning tended to be an important but expensive business, involving yards of black drapes and becoming even more lavish in the Victorian era. There was a mortcloth to hire from the parish church – 6s. in the 1820s in Alva, a week's wages for a handloom weaver.[47] Ale, wine and whisky (often in prodigious quantities) had to be provided for mourners, before the body was 'lifted' and it often involved the purchase of new clothes for the family.[48] The widow was expected to move into black clothing for the rest of her life. The importance for families to provide a 'decent funeral' for a loved one remained into the twentieth century and payment of burial insurance often took precedence over other 'necessities'. It was an area where middle-class patterns were followed by people who could ill afford it, but where the standing of the deceased was presented for public judgement. According to the secretary of the Glasgow pawnbrokers in 1870, bereavement was often the cause of an individual's first visit to the pawnshop.[49] And, of course, the expense did not end there; there was the gravestone to be bought, where the phrase 'Erected by' was often more prominent that the name of the deceased.

Clothes, of course, got dirty very quickly and had to be washed. The straight streets of Edinburgh's new town were notorious for the clouds of dust that blew along them.[50] Probably cleanliness meant clean linen rather than a clean body. Georges Vigarello, in a study of concepts of cleanliness in France, sees a major shift in thinking about cleanliness in the last quarter of the eighteenth century and a growing awareness of stink.[51] In Scotland, this probably did not penetrate very far before the 1830s and 1840s and the spread of miasmatic theory by public health reformers. The occasional medical man *was* pressing for the removal of obstructions to the skin from dirt to allow it to breathe and exhale carbon dioxide, which was the general belief. But worries about the enfeebling effect of hot water seemed to persist. There was no Scottish published book with the word 'hygiene' in the title before the 1840s. However, a few of the NSA comment on the great improvements in cleanliness in respect of both people and houses.

Keeping clothes clean was no easy task. This often involved unpicking dresses before washing and then sewing them up again.[52] Presumably, petticoats – at least three – were worn in an attempt to keep the dress clean and were more easily washed. Drawers, essentially two leg tubes made of muslin or linen attached to a waist band were worn by most middle-class women by the 1840s. Ideally you needed large amounts of underwear, but then that created problems of storage. Expectations of cleanliness were heightening in the nineteenth century and this made the whole process of laundering much more troublesome and time-consuming. For women, there was the added issue of menstruation. No absorbent pads seemed to have been around during the century and women generally had to make do with pieces of rag, helped a little by the appearance of the safety pin from the 1850s. Little wonder that there was pressure for better water supplies, both more regular and cleaner. It may be that one attraction of the ubiquitous tartan shawl, whose popularity was increasing from the 1820s, was that as well as being functional it was a cover-all for shabby or dirty clothing and, at the same time, could be used coquettishly.

Men's clothes went through a substantial change in the early nineteenth century before settling down into a dull uniformity. Trousers replaced both breeches and the kilt, with doubled-tongued braces coming in from the 1820s.[53] By the 1840s, the coat, waistcoat and trousers, not necessarily matching, were the norm and mid-century saw a fad for bright waistcoats. Through to the 1850s, there was still a tendency towards light checked

trousers and colourful waistcoats, but as the century went on dark functional colours had become standard among the middle class, while working
men favoured moleskin or corduroy. Cotton underclothes were replacing
flannel. The big Kilmarnock bonnet was disappearing in favour of a variety
of headgear – again judging by the Wilkie painting. As women's dress
became more elaborate, men's became more simple.

Shoes were pretty primitive. From his days at school, Henry Cockburn
recalled his 'clumsy shoes made to be used on either foot, and each requiring to be used on alternative feet daily'.[54] Photographic evidence shows
that for the rest of the century, in both town and country, children cast off
their shoes at the earliest opportunity and went barefoot. There was a huge
number of shoemakers in most parts of the country and the quality must
have varied tremendously. An Elgin directory in the mid-1840s, for example,
had twenty-six shoemakers, compared with only ten tailors, and seventeen
bakers. At the same time, Inverness had something like thirty or forty. Shoes
were expensive and needed to be protected. A French visitor to Scotland in
1810 noted that he had 'seen some fine women, very well dressed, with white
muslin gowns, gloves and even a parasol, holding their shoes and stockings
in their hands, and walking bare-footed through the mire'[55] – which perhaps
confirms the argument that cleanliness was about clean white stockings not
clean feet.

Before the coming of the railway network, markets were mainly local
ones, but the development of toll roads and new bridges made the movement
of goods much easier. Carters fanned out from the towns into the rural areas
bringing groceries, cloth and hardware and taking back butter, cheese and
milk to sell. But goods were also coming from further afield. Smacks were
plying between Inverness and London, taking only ten to fourteen days, but
steamers made the biggest difference. The first steamers from Glasgow to
Inverness came in 1817, from Glasgow to Kyleakin in 1820. Elgin had regular
supplies from London landed at Burghead. A box of tea from London,
shipped on 29 December 1819, together with snuff from Glasgow, was delivered to a Fyvie merchant by the Turriff carrier on 15 January.[56]

Undoubtedly, dramatic changes were taking place. Most towns of any size
still had their weekly or twice-weekly markets and numerous fairs. Falkirk
had nine fairs in the 1830s not counting the trysts; Ayr had four; Mauchline
had seven plus an annual horse race. At such fairs, drapers and shoemakers had stands and 'almost everything needed for house, bed or back could
be had'.[57] But the fairs and markets were beginning to disappear. Christian
Watt recalled that in Aberdeenshire, as farms got bigger and more strangers
came to look for work, it 'was considered bad taste for a woman to be seen
at feeing markets', where once there had been stalls for wives and children.
More fixed shops were appearing and more goods were available. Stirling
had 'splendid shops' to match its 'elegant suburban villas', while in Beith the
number of shops meant that all sorts of cloth, groceries and meat could be

got 'as good as in Glasgow'.[58] Regional and national markets were developing. There was much more cash around and local tradesmen were adjusting to new market conditions. But it was not until after the 1840s that a real revolution in consumption took place in Scotland.

1850–1870s

The mid-century decades saw a sharp rise in the incomes of the middle classes in particular, and with that came great changes in the patterns of expenditure on food and drink and on household requirements generally. Consumers began to have a greater choice. Most had more than one set of clothes and, therefore, were in a position to choose between alternatives. With more household furnishings available, people could consciously choose what to purchase and what to display.

Christian Johnston in her *Cook and Housewife's Manual* had been trying to regain that sociability that had been so much part of eighteenth-century Edinburgh by persuading the better off to entertain at home. There is little doubt that, as Pierre Bourdieu pointed out, the knowledge of which foods to eat and which cutlery to use was becoming of increasing importance in revealing people's origins and, what he calls their '*habitus*', their internalised sense of their own social position.[59] How successful Christian Johnston was in persuading the middle ranks to entertain at home is questionable. There is some evidence that home entertaining was declining in these mid-century years and, as Olive and J. A. Banks pointed out, many of the middle class, because of the size of their families, were having to maintain appearance and all 'the paraphernalia of gentility' without having the actual means to support it. According to the *Scotsman* in 1849, three-quarters of the middle class had earnings of less than £400 per annum and only 10 per cent earned more than the £300 which was the standard of living at which most middle-class manuals aimed.[60] There was a caution among the middle classes about entertaining, lest it reveal the reality of their circumstances.[61] None the less, the internal display of a house in the dining room, the parlour or the drawing room was of great importance in revealing the taste, the economic standing and the moral worth of the host. Home was also supposed to be 'the haven of refuge from temptation, the calm resting place from labour and care, and the bright cheerful abode of comfort'.[62] For most of the urban working class this was hardly realistic. Robert Gray identified an often precarious labour aristocracy in mid-century Edinburgh struggling to maintain standards of respectability. The drinking customs of an older popular culture were being rejected by many as the temperance movement gained influence, but it was difficult to maintain standards in old tenements with their lack of privacy, their social mix and their often raucous close life.[63]

The mid-century decades saw changes in retailing in response to the needs of a growing, but often impecunious middle class. Furniture and drapery warehouses begin to appear in the cities, and the development of railways allowed relatively cheap travel to visit them. The press of the 1850s was full of advertisements for such warehouses as Stewart and McDonald's drapery and John Anderson's universal trading warehouse in Glasgow's Clyde Street, soon Anderson's Polytechnic. With flamboyant advertising and sales' gimmicks, these aimed at a rapid turnover of stock. Monthly or even three-monthly accounts, once the expectation of the well-to-do, and haggling over price gave way to cash payments. The increasingly lavish premises of the new retailing entrepreneurs not only tempted the purchaser, but taught those who merely came to gaze what they should aspire to. Such were the crowds who flocked on a Saturday to Wylie and Lochhead's new store in Glasgow's Buchanan Street in 1855, that tickets of admission had to be distributed.[64] Not surprisingly there were bitter complaints from small traders at the 'locust-like-eat-up-all warehouses in the city, devouring alike the Milliner, the Shoemaker, the Tailor, the Cabinetmaker and the Dressmaker's Trade'.[65]

Furniture and fittings by mid-century tended to be over-stuffed and overly ornate. Walter Scott's writings and Victorian enthusiasm for the Highlands encouraged the tartans, the antlers and the 'Monarch of the Glen' paintings identified with Scottish baronial style. Rooms were cluttered with furniture, ornaments and plants, a practice which having a servant to do the dusting made possible. Chimney pieces tended to be swathed in draperies, which must quickly have been covered in smuts from the fire. With the taxes on paper removed, wallpaper replaced the yellow, red, green or grey distemper of an earlier era, although that in turn brought its own problems. Stuck on with a paste of flour and water, the advice was that it should be taken off every few years to eradicate bugs and mould. In the 1870s, the advice was still that painted walls were better than papered ones.

In clothes, the new dyes, beginning with Perkins' 'mauvine' in 1856, brought a range of brighter colours. The new technology of steel-making allowed the whalebone or horsehair to be replaced by the steel cage and brought the crinoline to its heyday. Since the 1830s, waists had been becoming lower and skirts fuller. As one 'victim' recalled, for the everyday, they were hardly convenient: 'We were wedged together in carriages, with hoops billowing up to the roof; we scuttled crab-like through turnstiles; we were unable to pass in gangways'.[66] On the other hand, they did liberate women from the layers of heavy petticoats that had been used previously. The danger of actually falling over was real and with that came the even greater danger of exposing all, thanks to either being drawerless or wearing open-crotch ones.[67] Most women's underwear was made at home and Emma Hill Burton noted that her maid, Barbara's underwear was 'her glory', 'a maze of embroidery, emblematic in her mind of the inward refinements characteristic of a lady'.[68] From the Scottish point of view, one advantage was the boost that the décolletage of the crinoline gave to the Paisley shawl with its

Kashmiri motifs. By the 1870s, the all-round crinoline had been replaced by the hooped-out behind, pointing the way to the bustle in the 1880s. There was a reaction against such elaboration, and calls for dress reform, influenced by Amelia Bloomer from the United States. An advocate of reform even reached Inverness: 'Her appearance, however, in a short skirt, or kilt, and wide Turkish trousers, did not commend the innovation.'[69]

The American sewing machine, which had first appeared at the 1851 Exhibition, took off quickly and by the time of the Paris Exhibition of 1867 there were fourteen different makes on display. The new machines eased the lives of the countless dressmakers, shoemakers, sailmakers and harnessmakers around, but, thanks to the use of hire-purchase by the Singer Company and others, it also made dressmaking in the home more accessible. Dresses could be altered and lengthened relatively cheaply. Singer, from the mid-1850s, deliberately aimed at the family market, with carefully designed machines that could be folded away to look like side tables and to disguise the fact that they were for work in the home. From the 1870s, Singer were into mass production of machines at their Clydebank factory and were pioneering hire-purchase, with Glasgow and Edinburgh being amongst their largest markets.[70] The effect was probably to slow down the appearance of ready-made clothing for women. The coming of a cheap, local press also allowed information about fashions to percolate society. Most papers from the 1840s had regular accounts of the latest London and Paris fashions lifted from up-market journals. By the 1870s, the ubiquitous *People's Journal* and its stable-mate the *People's Friend* brought similar information to every corner of Scotland and advertising was becoming ever more pervasive.

The majority of people lived in houses of only one or two rooms and space, for all but the very rich, tended to be at a premium. It was a saleable commodity and lodgers were commonplace, with more than half the houses in central Scotland at the end of the century shared. Available space had also to fulfil a variety of functions. A description of even a relatively large Highland farmhouse kitchen in mid-century notes the clutter:

> a lofty ceiling of wood or cabers from which depended some dozens of hams, sides of bacon, and dried fish; whilst, interspersed among the above, and resting on cross spars, were kebbucks of cheese, and other winter stores, domestic utensils, implements of husbandry, fishing and the chase . . .[71]

The increasingly popular, multi-purpose kitchen dresser would be there, where things could be stored, plates could be displayed and the surface could be used for baking.[72]

Clothes were stored in kists rather than in wardrobes. In bigger houses, there would be presses, but these were often damp. As Robert Louis Stevenson and his parents found when they moved to Inverleith Terrace in 1853, the result was mildewed clothes.[73] Where space was available, the tendency was to use it for a parlour rather than an additional bedroom. While, for the wealthy, the dining room, with as large a sideboard as possible, was the room intended to impress, for the petite bourgeoisie and the respectable working class it was the parlour, generally just referred to as 'the room', the 'best room' or just 'ben the hoose'. Even the normal two-roomed house had a best room, often with the blinds drawn to most of the time to prevent the carpet fading.[74]

The parlour was the theatre of domestic events where the lady of the house could display her taste. It was what has been called a 'memory palace' sending messages to all who entered.[75] Here the most treasured possessions would be displayed, showing off family history, religious affiliation and aesthetic taste. There might also be displayed the evidence of a wife or daughter's skills in needlework on samplers or antimacassars.[76] Here there would be, perhaps, an eight-day, probably American, clock, a certificate of membership of some self-help body, a framed print from an offer in the *People's Journal* and even a small library of Burns or Scott. By the 1880s, a few ran to a piano or, in the aftermath of Moody and Sankey, a small harmonium, for display as much as use and probably bought on a three-year instalment plan. It was often too precious to use. Also, while in a middle-class home a piano might indicate an accomplished daughter, there was little marriage-market value in a piano-playing working-class daughter. In no part of the house was there much concern with comfort rather than appearance. Despite the admonitions of public moralists to the contrary, relaxation took place outside the home.

For the Stevensons, moving to the smarter Heriot Row, things were better, but there were still no bathrooms. The privy was at the end of the narrow garden and at night there was the chamber pot or a commode. In 1880, Robert Louis' Californian wife, Fanny, was astonished by the lack of plumbing in the house. A washstand in the bedroom, and the occasional hip bath filled by maids carrying buckets was all that was available.[77] In small villages, the dunghill that had to be carted away from time to time by the 'scaffie', was often alarmingly close to the back door.

It is almost impossible to appreciate fully the work involved in running a Victorian house, whether it fell to a number of servants or to the much more common single all-purpose maid or to the wife herself. Coal came in large lumps that had to be 'axed' to a reasonable size. In the tenements of Scottish cities it had to be carried up two or three storeys from an outside shed and the ashes carried down. Cast iron and steel grates had to be polished and blackened, while at the same time it was wise to try to ensure that the fire did not go out completely overnight because of the difficulty of relighting.[78] Candles had replaced oil cruisies in most houses, but they were expensive and left their own mess to be cleared up. By the 1870s, oil lamps or, as they were initially referred to, petroleum, kerosene or 'paraffine' lamps began to come in. According to an historian of lighting, these were 'simple, safe and easy to manage, almost odourless and pleasantly bright', but they did require pretty constant attention.[79] They were, however, cheap to use. *Cassells's Household Guide* of 1873 compared the cost of getting ten hours of light:[80]

Wax candle 7s. 2d. [36p]
Tallow candle 2s. 8d. [13p]
Sperm oil lamp 1s. 10d. [9p]
Coal gas lamp 4½d. [2p]
Petroleum oil 6d. [2½p]

Lamps gradually brought something of a minor revolution in the life style of most homes. Rooms probably became slightly differently arranged, as chairs were placed around the table to take advantage of the light, albeit still comparatively dim.[81]

But costs always put restraints on convenience. Despite the growing availability in the cities of gas cookers, which could be hired from the corporation, many of the working class clung to the old pattern of using the coal fire for cooking, because coal was substantially cheaper and for gas there was the need to invest in lighter pans.

Cleaning was a huge problem, but there was increased emphasis on the need for it. According to Mrs J. W. Laurie, whose domestic manual went through numerous editions, 'every day will have some spare hours in which washing, ironing and scrubbing can be done' and cleaning should be daily: 'weekly cleanings . . . are a sign of a slovenly housewife'.[82] Soap, taxed until 1853, came in large blocks and had to be cut into pieces by a wire. Cleaning materials needed to be specially prepared, so for brasses and stair rods the advice was 'pulverize some rotten stone, and when the powder is very fine, mix it with sweet oil'. Marble chimney pieces could be cleaned with a mixture of bullock's gall, turpentine, pipe clay and soap. Furniture could be polished with a mixture of linseed oil, vinegar, turpentine and spirits of salt. Fireplace blacking, according to one recipe, could involve the mixing of 'ivory black', treacle, set oil, sulphuric acid, water and vinegar. Not surprisingly, blacking was one of the first, labour-saving commercially produced substances to come on the market. Shoes and boots had to be cleaned with a mixture of white wax and turpentine.

Clothes washing was a huge problem, as is apparent from this advice on washing silk dresses:

> Mix six ounces of strained honey with four ounces of soft soap, then add to it a pint of gin or whisky. The dress must be entirely taken to pieces, then each piece must be spread flat on a table and brushed over by the mixture.[83]

The recipe for washing white clothes advised by Mrs Laurie involved cutting up ½ lb of soap and dissolving it in ½ gallon of boiling water, pouring another ½ gallon of boiling water over ½ lb of soda and yet a third ½ gallon of water over a ¼ lb of quicklime. It would then all be boiled together for

20 minutes and then placed in a jar to settle. Collars, wrist bands and the feet of stockings would be scrubbed before being placed in the wash boiler. That would be filled, the soda and lime mix strained into it and the whole thing boiled for half an hour to an hour. It was a task beyond the means of all but the largest house. One advantage was that the same soda and lime mix could be used to clean silver, brass, copper and tin! Laundry work was rarely confined to a single day. If flannel was washed on a Monday, then whites had to be done on a Tuesday and others on a Wednesday. There was then the heavy task of putting things through the mangle and the wringer, followed by heating up the flat iron in preparation for ironing. There was the odd patent like the 'dolly tub', a barrel in which clothes could be stirred and twisted, to try to ease the work of wash day. The grooved washboard from America appeared in the late 1870s. A visitor to Edinburgh in 1880 noted the ragged clothes attached to sticks hung from the windows of houses in the old town on a Saturday afternoon and was told that the men and children were probably in bed while their only clothes were dried.[84] And, of course, water had to be carried up from ground level. Few poorer tenements had running water. They might have sinks, but without water these soon became encrusted with dirt.[85] The difficult task of drying clothes generally meant that they aired in the kitchen/living room, adding to the general clutter.

Bedrooms were a particular problem, with a battle against fleas. Feather beds, it was advised, ought to be opened up every three years and debugged with a mixture of quicksilver and egg whites. Chaff or straw palliasses, common in the rural areas, had to be replaced annually. Carpets in bedrooms needed to be easily lifted every few months and the floors scrubbed with soap and sand. To a large extent this must have been a question of moving dust from one place to another, and it was not until 1878 that the first Bissell carpet sweepers were patented and decades before they became commonplace.[86] But again it was only the better off who would have bedrooms separate from a living room. In 1865, Glasgow had 31,732 houses at rentals of under £5 a week and often with more than one family sharing a single apartment.

Bugs were a particular hazard in wooden bedsteads and built-in box beds, and the coming of iron bedsteads in the mid-century was seen as a major breakthrough. But the box bed or the recess bed (generally not more than 4 feet wide), which had the value of giving an element of privacy, remained in Scottish tenements and in rural cottages well into the twentieth century. There was storage space beneath it, sometimes for what in Glasgow was called a hurley bed that could be pulled out at night. Spring mattresses to replace feather ones began to arrive in the 1870s, but wool and flock mattresses remained more common and even these were not cheap until well into the twentieth century. Early in the century, all-purpose plaids and shawls seem to have acted as bed covers, but inexpensive mass-produced blankets were becoming available, sold as a pair and generally having to be cut and hemmed.[87] The process of the annual washing of these required communal effort and fine judgements about the weather to ensure that the blankets could be washed *and dried* in the same day.[88]

The preparation of food was tedious. Sugar, coming in conical loaves had to be pounded, rolled and sifted. Vegetables had to be shopped for regularly. The, reputedly ever-popular, delicacy, sheep's head broth, required singeing, soaking, scraping, splitting to remove brains and tendons, followed by washing and blanching before boiling for at least five hours.[89]

The Great Exhibition encouraged developments in gardening, as with so many other things. Peter Lawson and Sons from Edinburgh exhibited and published catalogues, listing some 174 varieties of potato, as they attempted to revive interest after the famine years. Carrots were becoming more popular, although parsnips were only at an experimental stage. An Elgin gardener carried off first prize at the London Horticultural Society show in 1852 with ten varieties of dessert pears.[90] Many local horticultural societies began to appear in the 1850s and 1860s, and the Edinburgh Working Men's Flower Show was one of the key events for those who managed to escape from the tenements to one of the newer working men's cottages with gardens. But vegetable consumption beyond carrots, turnips and leeks remained stubbornly low.

Thomas and Jane Carlyle remembered baking their own bread at Craigenpuddock in the 1830s,[91] but this may already have been something of a dying art. According to one writer, baking bread at home was less common in Scotland than in England by the mid-century.[92] Despite the fact that baker's bread was often adulterated with potatoes, rice, alum and even plaster of Paris, and often produced in notoriously dirty cellars, it gained in popularity, and wheaten bread was penetrating even relatively remote areas.[93] Because of the lack of space and the sheer problem of cooking at an open fire, it is hardly surprising that many continued to purchase ready-cooked foods from street stalls. Domestic manuals continued to condemn wives for their 'fecklessness' and their 'failure to provide' their husbands with nourishing broth.

1880–1900

It is from the late 1870s and 1880s that patterns of consumption become recognisably modern and lifestyles developed that were to last through at least until the 1950s. People undoubtedly became cleaner. Glasgow got its first public baths and wash-house by the Green in 1878 and other 'steamies' followed. Soap production, with the soap now available in ready-cut tablets, increased strongly year on year from the late 1880s. There were many local firms, most moving out of candle production, ready to supply the market: Ogston and Sons in Aberdeen, Tennants in Glasgow, Taylors in Leith, Sims in Paisley. From 1894, Lever Brothers' 'Lifebuoy' soap, complete with advice on how to use it, began to outsell the others. It was, however, not until the early years of the next century that soap powder appeared. The new tenements being built usually had a wash-house in the yard where tenants could take turns of the wash-boiler.

The greatest changes were in eating habits. This was particularly important for Scotland where expenditure on food was proportionally higher than in England. Thanks to imports from the Americas and Australasia as well as Europe, foodstuffs became cheaper than they had been since the years of the Napoleonic wars. These also came in more labour-saving forms. Sugar cones gave way to ready-cut lumps and to caster sugar. Suet and jellies came in packets, gelatine in powder form and meats and fruit in tins. Bread became a major part of the working-class diet. The rather stodgy, dirty brown loaf had given way to the (not necessarily healthier) white loaf, thanks to the introduction of the roller mill, first used by Oscar Oerle in Glasgow in 1872 and pioneered for industrial production by Bilsland Brothers. Unlike in England, where the medieval assize of bread still regulated weight and price, it was easy for industrial baking to spread in Scotland and, by 1882, Bilslands were producing 17,000 loaves a week. Seebohm Rowntree's study of York at the turn of the century still found families baking bread, but there was no sign of this among Scottish families surveyed early in the new century. As Roy Campbell pointed out, the disappearance of payment in kind, once common in rural areas, had given people a freedom of choice on what to eat and the result was a decline in the standard of diet.[94] Bread had largely replaced oatmeal as the staple. In one Dundee case, half of food expenditure went on bread, often bought stale at the end of the week. Three and a half loaves could be had for 6d. (about £2.02 in 2008 money) on a Saturday night in Edinburgh.[95] But middle-class eating patterns were changing too. With more job opportunities available for girls, it was proving difficult to get young servants and almost impossible to get ones who were capable of, or willing to, bake bread.

Thanks to developments in refrigeration, cheaper meat from the Americas and Australasia was available. The cattle slaughter of the late 1860s, due to rinderpest disease, produced supply shortages and the New York company, T. C. Eastman, began to ship first live cattle and then chilled and then refrigerated meat to their Glasgow agent, James Bell and Sons. Slowly butchers' shops began to get cold storage, but most houses lacked adequate pantries for food storage and, even at the end of the century, there was still a late-night and end-of-week trade to sell off cheap cuts. The preservation of food in tins had been around for many decades and seems to have been particularly a Scottish development. Moir and Sons in Aberdeen preserving first salmon and then meat and chicken and vegetables since the 1820s, had developed what was known as the 'Aberdeen process' of preservation using boiling water and chloride of calcium, and others followed. But the market was mainly in the Empire, 'so that Scotchmen of every clime can be gastronomically reminded of the culinary delicacies of their native land'.[96] In the last quarter of the nineteenth century, tinned products began to spread to the domestic market and the trade was reversed with cheap tinned meat, like corned beef, coming from the Empire (formal and informal) to Britain, but the dietary surveys of the early twentieth century show no evidence of its being widely consumed.

More dairy produce was coming into the diet, pushing up the consumption of fats. Cheese from the United States or Canada, ham and bacon from Ayrshire, but also the less fatty kind from Denmark and Ireland, butter from Ireland, Denmark and the Empire. The cattle shortage of the late 1860s had led to a sharp rise in the price of butter and cheap substitutes began to appear. Coming first as 'butterine' it was standardised as 'margarine' by the Margarine Act of 1887. Although it was half the price of butter, it was slow to catch on and even in the early twentieth century many working-class families seem to have clung to the more expensive butter. Only two of the families surveyed in a study of diet among the Edinburgh labouring classes at the turn of the century bought margarine instead of butter and the average consumption of both butter and margarine among the families was no more than an ounce per day.[97]

Milk remained a fairly doubtful commodity until the end of the century and consumption among urban working-class families did not reach half a pint per week at the turn of the century.[98] The transporting of milk into the cities improved, with trains, better milk cans and improved cooling systems, but people, with some justification, remained suspicious. Farms tended to be pretty foul places and it took growing concern about tuberculosis to stir public health interest in what went on in them. Condensed milk in cans, and sweetened, tended to be more popular than fresh and was a staple in many of the multiples.

Tea, usually well-stewed by the fireside, continued to grow in popularity, especially as duties were steadily reduced. The spread of tearooms was socially important for different social classes. Starting in Aitken's Hotel in Argyle Street in 1884, by 1900 Miss Cranston had three tearooms in Buchanan Street, Argyle Street and Ingram Street in Glasgow and imitators in most towns. Here the lower middle-class could meet socially without the complications of inviting people to their home. But tea consumption at home also continued to rise. To accompany tea, biscuit production expanded. Crawfords moved into factory production in Edinburgh in 1860 with their 'Granola', MacFarlane Lang in Glasgow had their ' Victoria' in time for the jubilee in 1887, McVitie and Price the 'Digestive' and Gray, Dunn and Co. had its chocolate creams in the 1890s.

The Scots had long shown themselves to have a sweet tooth. The diary of the Dundee millwright, John Sturrock, in the 1860s is full of references to his visits to the sweetie stalls in the High Street.[99] Lord Boyd Orr, the pioneer nutritionist, writing in 1937, saw the fivefold increase in sugar consumption

Figure 2.2 *In the Scottish Highlands on a Huntley and Palmers biscuit card (1890).*
© *Mary Evans Picture Library.*

as 'the most striking change in the nation's diet during the last 100 years'.[100]
With the removal of the last duties on sugar in 1874 and the importing
of refined sugar, the jam industry expanded, overcoming the deep-seated
working-class suspicion of fruit.[101] From Paisley came James Robertson and
Sons' preserves, eventually breaking into national markets with its 'Golden
Shred' marmalade. From Dundee there was James Keiller and Sons, the
largest in the country by the 1860s, but there were soon many others such
as McLintocks in Glasgow, R. & W. Scott in Carluke. Jam or syrup was the
main accompaniment to the bread that featured in the tea or dinner menu of
most working-class families.

It was in the grocery and provision trade that the multiple shop developed
most rapidly and extensively. Thomas Lipton, selling Irish ham, butter and
eggs, had his first shop in Glasgow's Stobcross Street in 1871, but by 1880
he had branches in all the Scottish cities as well as in Paisley and Greenock
and was turning his attention to south of the border. Alexander Massey,
opening in 1872, also specialised in Irish and American produce, but confined his activities largely to Glasgow. Others like the Templeton Brothers
in Ayrshire, William Galbraith in Paisley and Andrew Cochrane in Glasgow
followed Lipton's model, but on a more localised scale. All of them gradually extended the range of what they sold over the next few decades. Most

were also selling tea, margarine and jam by the 1890s. But they focused on the demands of the better off working class and on things that either had a quick turnover or could be easily stored. Although Lipton's introduced wines and spirits to some of the stores in 1898, this was not a great success.[102] They seem to have been particularly successful, however, in bringing about more egg consumption. Eggs, many of them imported, seemed to feature in the working-class diet as never before, helped no doubt by the relative ease in cooking them.

The new multiples were large and impersonal and demanded cash payments. For the great bulk of the working class, the local corner shop was still vital because here the housewife could get credit if she was known to the shopkeeper as respectable and reliable. For many, the availability of credit to help balance expenditure and income was essential, not just on a weekly basis until the pay packet came in, but to carry a family through bad times. It kept people within the neighbourhood where they were known and being able to get credit was a sign of social advancement for many of the working class. For the skilled working class, the co-operative store had the attraction of providing a useful twice-yearly dividend on purchases. The fact of having a Co-op 'divi' was itself a sign of respectability and could assist with getting credit at the corner shop. The leadership of the Co-op set its face against sales on credit, but in most local societies the membership was determined that the practice should be allowed.

Cooking and washing became a little more convenient, with the development of sculleries separate from the living room, although only about half of the one- or two-roomed houses in Edinburgh had their own sink by 1917.[103] With the growing availability of paraffin and gas cookers, cooking could move also. But there was always a difficult balance to be struck between convenience and cost. The slot-machine payment for gas did not come until the early twentieth century and many still clung to the coal fire for cooking or, at best, had to make do with a single gas burner.

The conditions of cooking did little to improve health. It is important to remember that the Victorians were frequently in pain from indigestion, toothache and other ailments of all kinds. One necessity was access to patent medicines and these were legion. To take just one issue of the *Falkirk Herald*, as well as the long-established Holloway's pills and ointments to treat asthma, liver disease, rheumatism and dropsy, there were Dr De Roos' Pilulae Vitae or Vegetable Life Pills for 'removing all obstructions, headaches, depression of spirits, dimness of sight, nervousness, blotches, pimples and sallowness', Whelpton's Vegetable Purifying Pills, Dr Townsend's Sarsaparilla, 'the Blood Purifier', Keating's Worm Tablets, Rackham's Liver Pills, Beecham's Pills ('worth a guinea a box') and the Marston Remedy Company's 'Boon for Men', dealing with 'Nervous debility, lost Vigour and Exhausted Vitality'.[104] There was also Dr Rech's Female Pills ('No obstruction stands against them') and no doubt the prospect of yet another child in a large family encouraged many a woman to look for a means of avoiding it by resorting to such a potential abortifacient.

From the 1880s, there was cheaper ready-made clothing available and the wearing of second-hand became less acceptable. For the less well off, clothes tended to be bought by instalments, through clothing clubs or out of overtime money, from a wife's earnings or from the co-operative society dividend. Initially most ready-made was for men rather than women, who were still expected to dressmake at home. But the wholesalers, Stewart and MacDonald, began to produce ladies' and children's underwear in the 1880s and Fleming, Reid and Co.'s 'Scottish Wool and Hosiery' shops grew from their first in Greenock in 1881 to nearly 200 by the early twentieth century. 'Aunt Kate', who wrote a cooking and advice column in the *People's Journal*, a weekly paper that was selling to a quarter of a million homes throughout Scotland in the 1890s, advised that a simple outfit for a new bride was three sets of undergarments, two of which should be of flannel (probably combinations), an upper petticoat, two flannel bodices, two washing dresses for doing the housework, an afternoon gown, and a best one for Sundays and holidays, topped off with a bonnet, a hat and a jacket or cape.[105]

For men, the frock coat was largely confined to aristocrats and politicians by the end of the century and what eventually became known as the lounge suit began to catch on, although with the fashionable 3-inch high starched shirt collar, the look was not a comfortable one.[106] The Bohemian socialist, William Morris, had shocked Glasgow with his blue shirt on his visit in the 1880s, but coloured shirts were gradually making an appearance. Factory-made boots and shoes were available, and chains of shoe shops began to appear from the 1870s. Home-made shoes, even in the Highlands, were becoming a thing of the past. But shoes from a multiple were still expensive and many working-class women kept their skirts long, often dragging in the mud, rather than reveal their ill-fitting boots. The bowler hat, first appearing in the 1860s, by the end of the century had become part of the uniform of the lower middle class and the skilled working class, a particularly important status symbol in public parades for bodies like the Orange Order or the Free Colliers.

Ready-made furniture was also in much greater supply and the department stores in the cities and the catalogues sent out from them were educating women into what was seen as the ideal home lay out. Wylie and Lochhead in Glasgow, for example, began to display complete room settings from the 1870s, offering models for taste as well as an element of romantic fantasy to pull people into the store.[107] Chests of drawers became more widely available, replacing the all-purpose kist. Furniture stores were among the first to offer 'the new easy payment system'. The styles tended to replicate older ones, although there was a new, less-cluttered look in rooms being encouraged by the arts and crafts movement. But styles in furnishings were always slow to change.

For many of the working class, the Co-op was the best source of ready-made, just as it had been for good quality unadulterated food. The Scottish Co-operative Wholesale Society had a tailoring section in its new production site at Shieldhall in Glasgow in 1888, and shirt-making, underwear production and moleskin and serge clothes for working men were all being produced in the 1890s. A footwear factory was in successful production in 1885 and after the move to Shieldhall in 1888 the cabinet-making section developed into a huge supplier of a range of furniture.[108]

CONCLUSION

For the bulk of the population, the balancing of income and expenditure was a formidable task. Employment was often cyclical and seasonal. Ill-health and accidents at work frequently led to disruption of earnings and family size added to the burdens in many homes. The message that the working classes were the cause of their own misery was an ever-present one, with Scots seeming to play an inordinately large role in preaching on the need for individual self-reliance. One thinks of Samuel Smiles, with his highly successful moral tales in *Self Help* (1859) and *Thrift* (1875) and of Thomas Mackay and C. S. Loch, leading spokesmen for the intrusive and judgemental Charity Organisation Society, both products of Glenalmond School. They tended to assume that with less drink and a bit more effort the working class could save for family crises and old age. And, indeed, they did save, in friendly societies, savings clubs, trade unions and insurance companies, but it was almost impossible with irregular employment for many to maintain the necessary payments throughout a working life.

The burden of providing necessities predominantly fell on women. In the houses of the well-to-do, that burden fell on women servants, but most homes did not have servants and most of those that did had no more than one. It was women who had the huge task of battling against the ever-encroaching dirt and dust of the Victorian city. It was women who emptied the chamber pots and cleaned the privies. It was women who had to ensure that fires were lit, that food was cooked. It was women who had to shine the brasses and polish the furniture, essential for maintaining the outward appearance that was so important in signalling a family's place in the world. Although it seems to have been men who often chose the furniture, it was women who took the responsibility for the decoration and lay-out of rooms. And it was women who had to repair and make most clothes. It was women who among the less well off had to find the means to spread a meagre income over seven days or longer. It was women who had to balance the importunings of different creditors, to deal with or dodge the rent-man, the tallyman, the insurance collector. It was they who had to negotiate with the shopkeeper or the pawnbroker. It was they who daily had to present the public face so crucial to social standing.

Women of all social classes had the task of keeping house with all that that involved in revealing and asserting status. But consumption and house-keeping were also about providing sustenance, comfort and welcome for members of the family and for strangers and for maintaining the health of the breadwinner and the children. Vanessa Dickerson sums it up: 'To keep house was not only to cook, clean and nurse, but also to regulate and police, to draw, paint and write, to hold, own, save and consume.'[109]

Notes

1 C. Palmer, 'From Theory to Practice. Experiencing the Nation in Everyday Life', *Journal of Material Culture*, 3:2 (July 1998), 176, citing S. Pearce (ed.), *Experiencing Material Culture in the Western World* (Leicester, 1997).

2 For working-class saving in the late nineteenth century see P. Johnson, *Saving and Spending. The Working-Class Economy in Britain 1870–1939* (Oxford, 1985).

3 H. Mackay (ed.), *Consumption and Everyday Life* (Milton Keynes, 1997), p. 4.

4 I. Levitt and C. Smout, *The State of the Scottish Working Class in 1843* (Edinburgh, 1979), pp. 34–5.

5 A. Fenton, 'Place of Oatmeal in the Diet of Scottish Farm Servants in the Eighteenth and Nineteenth Centuries', in J. Szabadfalvi and Z. Ujváry (eds), *Studia Ethnographia et Folkloristica in Honorem Béla Gunda* (Debrecen, 1971), p. 97.

6 A. Somerville, *The Autobiography of a Working Man* (London, 1855), p. 117.

7 *Inverness Courier*, 20 August 1845.

8 Fenton, 'Place of Oatmeal', p. 94.

9 J. Barron, *The Northern Highlands in the Nineteenth Century* (Inverness, 1903), p. xxvii.

10 A. Gibson and T. C. Smout, 'From Meat to Meal. Changes in diet in Scotland', in C. Geissler and D. J. Oddy (eds), *Food, Diet and Economic Change Past and Present* (Leicester, 1993), p. 20.

11 W. Alexander, *Johnny Gibb of Gushetneuk* (Aberdeen, 1871; Turriff, 1979), pp. 48–51.

12 *Inverness Journal*, 25 July 1817.

13 D. Stevenson (ed.), *The Diary of A Canny Man 1818–1828. Adam Mackie Farmer, Merchant and Innkeeper in Fyvie compiled by William Mackie* (Aberdeen, 1991), p. 60.

14 New Statistical Account of Scotland [NSA] XII, *County of Aberdeen*, Aberdeen City, p. 101.

15 NSA VIII, *Dumbarton, Stirling, Clackmannan*, Larbert, p. 365.

16 *The Cook and Housewife's Manual; Containing the Most Approved Modern Receipts for making soups, gravies, sauces, ragouts, and made dishes; and for pies, puddings, pastries, pickles and preserves, also for baking, brewing, making home-made wines and cordials etc. by Mrs Margaret Dods of the Cleikum Inn, St Ronan's* (Edinburgh, 1826). Meg Dods was a character in Sir Walter Scott's novel, *St Ronan's Well* (1823).

17 NSA VI, *County of Lanark*, Hamilton, pp. 278–9.

18 J. Mackenzie, *Pigeon Holes of Memory. The Life and Times of Dr John Mackenzie (1803–1886)*, C. B. Shaw (ed.) (London, 1988), p. 44.

19 *Cook and Housewife's Manual* (1829 edn), p. 200.

20 *Cook and Housewife's Manual*, p. 141 (emphasis in original).

21 J. L. Story, *Early Reminiscences* (Glasgow, 1911), p. 27.

22 NSA X, *Perth*, p. 558.

23 Quoted in S. W. Mintz, 'The Changing Role of Food in the Study of Consumption', in J. Brewer and R. Porter (eds), *Consumption and the World of Goods* (London, 1993).

24 *Report of the Select Committee on Public Houses in Scotland*, Parliamentary Papers (PP), 1846 XV.

25 A. Ross, *Scottish Home Industries* (Inverness, 1895), p. 35.

26 A. Fenton, 'Pigs and Mugs', in A. Fenton and J. Myrdal (eds), *Food and Drink and Travelling Accessories. Essays in Honour of Gösta Berg* (Edinburgh, 1988), p. 41.

27 Quoted in A. Fenton, 'Hearth and Kitchen: the Scottish Example', in M. R. Schärer and A. Fenton (eds), *Food and Material Culture. Proceedings of the Fourth Symposium of the International Commission for Research into European Food History* (East Linton, 1998), p. 30.

28 NSA XII, *County of Aberdeen*, Udny, p. 137, Old Deer, p. 164; NSA XIII, *Counties of Banff Elgin and Nairn*, Banff, p. 62, Forglen, p. 94, Aberlour, p. 142, Fordyce, p. 995, Gamrie, p. 295, Cullen, p. 254, Boharm, p. 37, Elgin, p. 27.

29 H. Cheape, 'Pottery and Food Preparation, Storage and Transport in the Scottish Hebrides', in A. Fenton and E. Kisbain (eds), *Food in Change. Eating Habits from the Middle Ages to the present* (Edinburgh, 1986), p. 107.

30 NSA XII, *County of Aberdeen*, Huntly, p. 1047; Ross, *Scottish Home Industries*, p. 4.

31 W. T. O'Dea, *The Social History of Lighting* (London, 1958), p. 3.

32 NSA XIII, Cullen, p. 254; A. Fenton, 'Lighting', in Susan Storrier (ed.), *Scottish Life and Society, vol. 6: Scotland's Domestic Life* (Edinburgh, 2006), p. 76; J. C. Loudon, *Loudon's Encyclopaedia on Cottage, Farm and Villa Architecture and Furniture* (London, 1935), p. 1027.

33 According to a caption in Elgin Museum.

34 Fenton, 'Hearth and Kitchen', p. 57.

35 D. Fraser (ed.), *The Christian Watt Papers* (Edinburgh, 1983), p. 83.

36 E. Rice, *Domestic Economy* (London, 1879), p. 87.

37 F. Dye, *The Cooking Range: its Failings and Remedies* (London, 1888).

38 M. M. Brewster, *Household Economy. A Manual intended for Female Training Colleges and the Senior Classes in Girls' Schools* (Edinburgh, 1858), p. 20.

39 Both quoted in M. Carter, *Fashion Classics from Carlyle to Barthes* (Oxford, 2003), pp. 27, 46.

40 Shaw, *Pigeon Holes of Memory*, p. 318.

41 Mrs Gibb of Gushetneuk in Aberdeenshire was still wearing 'a very well-starched close "mutch"', in the 1840s, but the Gibbs were old-fashioned people. See Alexander, *Johnny Gibb of Gushetneuk*, p. 11.

42 Shaw, *Pigeon Holes of Memory*, p. 49.

43 NSA VI, *Lanark*, Lesmahago, p. 34; Dalziel, p. 463.

44 NSA X, *Perth*, Monzie, pp. 558, 276.

45 NSA X, Longforgan, p. 411.

46 B. Lemire, 'Consumerism in Pre-industrial and Early Industrial England: the Trade in Second-hand Clothes', *Journal of British Studies*, 27:1 (January 1988), 30.

47 W. Drysdale, *Alva in the Time of Our Grandfathers* (Alloa, 1886), p. 6.

48 J. Strathesk, *More Bits from Blinkbonny. A Tale of Scottish Village Life between 1831 and 1841* (Edinburgh, 1885), p. 242.

49 Johnson, *Saving and Spending*, p. 174.

50 Story, *Early Reminiscences*, pp. 231–2.

51 G. Vigarello, *Concepts of Cleanliness. Changing Attitudes in France since the Middle Ages* (Cambridge, 1988).

52 C. Walkley and V. Foster, *Crinolines and Crimping Irons. Victorian Clothes: How They were Cleaned and Cared For* (London, 1978).

53 L. Johnston *et al.*, *Nineteenth Century Fashion in Detail* (London, 2005).

54 H. Cockburn, *Memorials of His Time* (Edinburgh, 1856), p. 20.

55 *Inverness Journal*, 26 July 1816.

56 Stevenson, *Diary of a Canny Man*, p. 49.

57 Strathesk, *More Bits*, p. 111.

58 NSA VIII, *Dunbarton, Stirling, Clackmannan*, p. 414; NSA V, *Ayrshire*, p. 603.

59 P. Bourdieu, *Distinction: a Social Critique of the Judgement of Taste* (London, 1984).

60 E. Gordon and G. Nair, *Public Lives. Women, Family and Society in Victorian Britain* (New Haven, 2003), p. 15.

61 J. A. and O. Banks, *Feminism and Family Planning in Victorian England* (Liverpool, 1964); Anon., *The Home Book of Household Economy: or Hints to Persons of Moderate Income* (London, 1854), p. 8.

62 *The Home Book of Household Economy*, p. 1.

63 R. Q. Gray, *The Labour Aristocracy in Victorian Edinburgh* (Oxford, 1976), p. 98.

64 M. Moss and A. Turton, *A Legend of Retailing. House of Fraser* (London, 1989), pp. 26–36.

65 *Falkirk Herald*, 26 January 1865; for similar sentiments see also [Teaddy,] *Sir Colin Cut-up & Co. or As it is Now-a-Days* (London, 1857), preface.

66 L. B. Walford, *Recollections of a Scottish Novelist* (Waddesdon, 1984), pp. 68–9.

67 J. Fields, 'Erotic Modesty: (Ad)dressing Female Sexuality in Open and Closed Drawers, USA, 1800–1930', in B. Burman and C. Turbin (eds), *Material Strategies. Dress and Gender in Historical Perspective* (Oxford, 2003), p. 126.

68 E. H. Burton wrote a delightful account of a young woman trying to run a house without the help of servant, *Miss in the Kitchen or A Week's Misadventures in House Keeping* (Edinburgh, 1877), p. 4.

69 *Inverness Courier*, 18 December 1851.

70 A. Godley, 'Homeworking and the Sewing Machine in the British Clothing Industry 1850–1905', in B. Burman (ed.), *The Culture of Sewing Gender: Consumption and Home Dressmaking* (Oxford, 1999), pp. 257–63.

71 Ross, *Scottish Home Industries*, p. 3.
72 D. Jones, 'Living in One or Two Rooms in the Country', in A. Carruthers (ed.), *The Scottish Home* (Edinburgh, 1996), p. 46.
73 J. Pope-Hennessy, *Robert Louis Stevenson* (London, 1974), p. 32.
74 Carruthers, *Scottish Home*, p. 27.
75 K. C. Grier, 'The Decline of the Memory Palace: the Parlour after 1890', in J. H. Foy and T. J. Schlereth (eds), *American Home Life 1880–1930. A Social History of Spaces and Services* (Knoxville, 1992), p. 58.
76 Macassar was hair oil that became popular with men from the 1850s.
77 F. Young, 'RLS's Bathroom', in S. Mackay (ed.), *Scottish Victorian Interiors* (Edinburgh, 1986).
78 Burton, *Miss in the Kitchen*, p. 25.
79 O'Dea, *Social History of Lighting*, p. 23.
80 *Cassell's Household Guide: being a Complete Encyclopaedia of Domestic and Social Economy, and Forming A Guide to Every Department of Practical Life, vol. 2* (London, 1873), p. 204.
81 Foy and Schlereth, *American Home Life 1880–1930*, p. 36.
82 J. W. Laurie, *Home and its Duties; A Practical Manual of Domestic Economy for Schools and Families* (Edinburgh, 1870), pp. 13–4.
83 *The Home Book of Household Economy*, p. 37.
84 *Girl's Own Paper* (1880), quoted in Walkley and Foster, *Crinolines and Crimping Irons*, p. 63.
85 J. Begg, *Happy Homes for Working Men, and How to Get Them* (Edinburgh, 1866), p. 159.
86 K. Hudson, *Food, Clothes and Shelter. Twentieth-Century Industrial Archaeology* (London, 1978), p. 129.
87 N. Tarrant, 'The Bedroom', in Carruthers (ed.), *Scottish Home*, p. 195.
88 For a description of the process in a Highland village at the beginning of the twentieth century see J. MacDonald, *Rogart. The Story of a Sutherland Crofting Parish* (Skerray, 2002), pp. 135–6.
89 It was still there in the fourteenth edition of 'Meg Dods', in the 1870s.
90 G. B. Hill, *Footsteps of Dr Johnston (Scotland)* (London, 1890), p. 36.
91 T. Carlyle, *Reminiscences*, K. J. Fielding and I. Campbell (eds) (Oxford, 1997), p. 56.
92 Brewster, *Household Economy*, p. 26.
93 NSA X, *Perth*, Kenmore, p. 471.
94 R. H. Campbell, 'Diet in Scotland; An Example of Regional Variation', in T. C. Barker, J. C. McKenzie and J. Yudkin (eds), *Our Changing Fare. Two Hundred Years of British Food Habits* (London, 1966), p. 54.
95 Dundee Social Union, *Report on Housing and Industrial Conditions and Medical Inspection of School Children* (Dundee, 1905), p. 32; D. N. Paton, J. C. Dunlop and E. M. Inglis, *A Study of the Diet of the Labouring Classes in Edinburgh carried out under the auspices of the Town Council of the City of Edinburgh* (Edinburgh, 1902), p. 25.
96 G. P. Bevan (ed.), *British Manufacturing Industries* (London, 1876), p. 59.

97 Paton, Dunlop and Inglis, *Study of the Diet of the Labouring Classes in Edinburgh*, p. 34.

98 R. L. Cohen, *A History of Milk Prices* (Oxford, 1936), pp. 4–5; Paton, Dunlop and Inglis, *Study of the Diet of the Labouring Classes in Edinburgh*, p. 70.

99 C. A. Whatley (ed.), *The Diary of John Sturrock, Millwright, Dundee 1864–65* (East Linton, 1996).

100 S. W. Mintz, *Sweetness and Power. The Place of Sugar in Modern History* (New York, 1985), p. 146.

101 Mintz, *Sweetness and Power*, p. 126.

102 P. Mathias, *Retailing Revolution* (London, 1967), passim.

103 H. Clark, 'Living in One or Two Rooms in the City', in Carruthers (ed.), *Scottish Home*, p. 75.

104 *Falkirk Herald*, 14 July 1888.

105 [Helen Greig Souter], *Aunt Kate's Book of Personal and Household Information* (London, 1895), pp. 4–5.

106 C. Breward, *The Hidden Consumer: Masculinities, Fashion and City Life* (Manchester, 1999), p. 32; P. Bryde, *The Male Image. Men's Fashions in Britain 1300–1970* (London, 1979), p. 107.

107 T. Chapman and J. Hockey, *Ideal Homes? Social Change and Domestic Life* (London, 1999), p. 28; J. Kitchen, 'The Drawing Room', in Carruthers (ed.), *Scottish Home* p. 178.

108 J. Kinloch and J. Butt, *History of the Scottish Co-operative Wholesale Society* (Glasgow, 1981), ch. 6.

109 V. D. Dickerson, *Keeping the Victorian House. A Collection of Essays* (New York, 1995), p. xxix.

Chapter 3

Rituals, Transitions and Life Courses in an Era of Social Transformation

Andrew Blaikie

One doesn't abandon it all on a whim. The kirk, the kirkyard, my family, me, you – there's something much bigger than religion going on in all that. Much bigger.[1]

INTRODUCTION

Everyday life is distinguishable from other elements of popular culture because it is unconscious and repetitive.[2] Indeed, many behaviours are so routine as to be unexamined, both by researchers and by their subjects. By virtue of their profundity, life events do not fall into such a category: births and deaths cannot be considered mundane occurrences because they are the most significant moments in everyone's lives. As movements into and out of existence they are transitions involving 'transcendental speculation' about where we have come from and where we will go – they partake of the unknown.[3] Meanwhile, marriage, while frequently challenged or ignored, is symbolically crucial in Christian and other societies because it represents the socially sanctioned union required for the parenting of legitimate progeny; that is, it is the orderly means through which society reproduces itself. Paradoxically, however, the very ubiquity of these life events renders them commonplace. The same may be said about the various stages of the life course and, indeed, the points of transition within it – childhood, going to school, puberty, adolescence, starting and ending work, adulthood, bereavement, old age. While these processes provide the dramatic backdrop to individual experience, we accept their generality as markers of normality, the framework supporting ordinary being. At first sight, therefore, trying to understand everyday life in the past by means of an analysis of ritual appears to be perverse. By definition, rites of passage surrounding life events are set apart from the profane: they are sacred, occasional, exceptional, ceremonial, formal and rule-governed, whereas daily life is banal, informal, commonsensical. However, since the function of ritual is 'to regulate, maintain and transmit from one generation to another sentiments on which the constitution of the society depends' these customary observances clearly perform a major role in sustaining the social order.[4] If we are to comprehend continuities and discontinuities in the experience of everyday life, it is first necessary to appreciate how much or how little these foundations have shifted. It would, nevertheless, be ahistorical to compound the unwitting conformity of our subjects by adhering to an interpretive concept like the life cycle when referring to individuals, perceiving life as series of age-related stages determined simply by physical processes of maturation, decline and death, although the term remains applicable to groups like the family. Accordingly, the analysis works with a notion of the life course, which regards the ages and stages of life as socially constructed, thus flexible and open to change.[5]

Anyone setting out to investigate the relationships between everyday life, rites of passage and demography in the nineteenth century soon recognises the importance of the local parish. Prior to industrialisation, in an overwhelmingly Presbyterian country, the (Established) Kirk was by definition central to the affairs of every parish community, and it was certainly crucial in administering the rites of passage. Christenings, weddings and funerals were the preserve of the minister, the session clerk recording baptisms, marriages and burials, and elders assessing and addressing the welfare needs of impoverished, disabled and elderly individuals through the kirk session, a body which, as church court, also policed the morals of parishioners. Following the Disruption of 1843, whereby around two-fifths of parishioners in Scotland seceded from the Established Church to join the newly-formed Free Kirk, these functions were gradually secularised: after 1845, paupers became the concern of the Inspector of Poor and Parochial Board, while from 1855 the registrar of births, marriages and deaths took over from the session clerk. However, despite these changes in its framework, the administration and moral regulation of family concerns remained at the parish level, its officials playing a more or less intermittent role in everyone's lives.

At the same time, the period was distinguished by high levels of migration and mobility that were particularly disruptive of the collective mores of pre-industrial communities. Growing urbanisation and industrialisation, coupled with subsistence crises and depression in agriculture, are reflected in large-scale movements of population. The success and failure of institutional attempts to manage such social turbulence are evident both in the efforts of the churches to contain parishioners and in the growth of non-ecclesiastical forms of social regulation. Life-course rituals were caught up in this process through the secularisation of birth, marriage and death registration. However, recording these wholesale administrative changes gives no real sense of the ways in which the unprecedented upheavals of the period impinged upon individual lives. Instead, the researcher is immediately challenged by issues of scale: at what level is it meaningful to discuss changes in the rites and rituals that attended different life-course stages?

In recognising that personal experiences are affected by societal shifts as well as by community and family attitudes and practices, this chapter examines the relationship between underlying demographic processes and the properties of different life passages, with particular reference to courtship, marriage and childbearing. It also considers the significance of shifts in the character and duration of life-course stages. Subsequently, in relation to a single parish example, it explores shifts in the relationship between official and popular mentalities concerning the ritual regulation of sexual conduct. Throughout we are limited by the survival, availability and tractability of sources. As anthropologists, antiquarians and ethnologists will testify, the analysis of customs related to these rites, though fascinating, is so marked by local variations as to be of little value when attempting to assess (and concisely summarise) national patterns over the course of a century.[6] One is bound, therefore, either to seek generalities or to attempt case studies.

POPULATION PATTERNS AND STATUS PASSAGES

In providing a context for the understanding of changes in life-course patterns, it is logical to begin with demography. Between 1831 and 1911 the population doubled, although this pattern was inconsistent and demonstrated marked geographical contrasts. Scotland was 'a country with a very substantial regional variation within an overall pattern of low nuptiality and high emigration and marital fertility', depopulation being endemic in all rural areas except the north-east.[7] Both birth and death rates declined continuously and rather gently. However, these patterns disguise pronounced differences, with, for example, low natural increase in the North-west Highlands but high birth rates in mining and textile areas. Two million people emigrated between 1830 and 1914, although there were also substantial flows of immigrants, notably from Ireland, and of migrants from the Highlands to the cities.[8] To what extent can we get beneath these grand trends to the weave of daily life in any one place? For the historian in search of hard data, the initial prognosis is not good. Since 1552, baptisms, marriages and burials had been the official concern of the Established Kirk. However, because registers varied in their format and consistency between individual session clerks, parishes and periods, and many have not survived, or have survived only in patches, there is nothing like a national sample indicative of how vital events and weddings were recorded. Burial registers are particularly few and far between.[9] Furthermore, registering an event was effectively discouraged by the levying of a fee, while many non-conformists chose instead to have matters recorded in their own denominational registers. As in England, high levels of migration, and especially urbanisation, reduced the effectiveness of the church, with only around a third of events being captured in many urban districts.[10] However, in 1855 the machinery of Scottish local government shifted to a secular administration, ensuring civil registration of all births, marriages and deaths. Thereafter, the researcher is far better served, yet even these much improved and rather more comprehensive literal accounts of events in every family reveal little of the meaning and experience of these occurrences, save in their quantification. It is to other social science disciplines that we must turn.

The concept of rites of passage originates with the anthropologist Arnold van Gennep, who found a universal characteristic of all such rites in the threefold process of separation of the individual from his or her former status, followed by a period in transition, when he or she falls outside normal social requirements (such as having to work), and finally re-integration into society through incorporation in their new status.[11] Thus, for example, the confinement of an expectant mother indicates the separation stage of the birth process and the beginning of a transition phase, a time when, in the nineteenth century at least, she would be apart from the menfolk. However, it is the commonality of form that is distinctive and important rather than the specific content of any one ritual in any particular time or place. The rites of passage are associated particularly with features that mark boundaries and focus on liminality as the key feature of transition between stages, with, for instance, spaces in the home being allocated specific importance: the threshold over which a groom carried his new bride, symbolising their new status; doors and windows opened immediately after a death to allow the departing spirit to escape; both expectant mothers and laid-out corpses occupying the 'good room' of the house.[12] Overcrowding in single-end tenement flats forced compromises to such spatialisation; indeed, a feature of both childbirth and dying before the mid-twentieth century was that they were far more likely to have occurred at home and among family than in the hospitalised post-war environment.

The social patterning of different rites was later explored by sociologists Glaser and Strauss, who used the synonym 'status passage'. While each passage exhibits stage-like characteristics, they observed that several properties apply to life-course rituals. These are: desirability; inevitability; reversibility; repeatability; whether undergone alone, collectively, or in aggregate; awareness; communicability; voluntariness; the degree and nature of control; legitimation; clarity; whether open or disguised; the centrality of the event to the individual; and duration.[13] Transitions may be compared with one another on the basis of their common characteristics, as well as those they do not share. For example, marriage is collective, generally of central importance to the individual undergoing it, but also serially repeatable. Death, by contrast is neither reversible nor repeatable, but is central. Moreover, properties of the same transition may signify in different ways for the various parties involved – there could, say, be conflicts between a mother, her family and the kirk if a child were conceived out-of-wedlock; in this case, the properties of desirability and legitimation are relevant to a social understanding of the tensions surrounding the birth. Since the degree and nature of control of all these processes are historically variable, the comparison of properties allows some insight into how life-course transitions in the past might differ from contemporary experience.

Glaser and Strauss further point out that all transitions follow paths – 'trajectories' – that are characterised by an expected timetable to be pursued in a structured manner, while sharing a capacity to encompass significant others (other, that is, than the protagonist undergoing the passage). The nature of interaction will here depend upon the level and type of shared awareness. Thus, for example, when a patient is diagnosed with a terminal illness, the length of time before death will be estimated, stages of decline acknowledged and appropriate care and medication advised. If the patient and significant others are notified, then open awareness ensues, but if, say, the medical team refuses this information, or restricts communication to the patient alone, then closed or partial awareness respectively result. We would then wish to ask why it is that information might be withheld in one instance but divulged in another. Clearly, such variable properties, trajectories and awareness contexts have implications both for how status passages are experienced in different historical situations and upon how we might subsequently interpret them.

Population trends might appear to be only tenuously linked to everyday ritual. However, as will become apparent, the degree of direct influence people had over their lives is reflected in their demographic behaviour. As in any era, individuals and families came to terms with shifts in their material environment. It is debatable whether during the nineteenth century there was an increase in the extent to which they felt in control of their earthly destinies or, conversely, the speed and scale of industrial and social upheaval simply lessened the hold of local institutions, especially the kirk, over their behaviour. However, it is possible to assess relative probabilities by considering changes to the delicate balance between popular customs and institutionally imposed rituals.

COURTSHIP AND MARRIAGE

An important consideration in the analysis of rituals is that they are always socially managed. The issue of who controlled courtship is, therefore, critical in determining its nature. The timing of first conception in relation to marriage was related to courtship patterns, and these varied considerably by class, gender and region. For young middle-class women, meeting potential suitors was a matter of close chaperonage. Their courtship was strictly policed, involving accepted rules of open etiquette, and was not a performance undergone alone. Chastity was crucial, and ruin befell any girl who was known to have lost her virginity prior to marriage, not that the opportunity could have arisen other than very occasionally. Few were pregnant at marriage and illegitimacy was almost unknown among the bourgeoisie. Despite, or because of, this, awareness of the facts of life appears to have been somewhat lacking. Christopher Smout cites an engineering manager's daughter, born in 1889, who told an oral history interviewer that 'when I was expecting my first baby I didn't know whether it was going to come out of my tummy or where it was going to come out of . . . and I was 27½'.[14] By contrast, young men were expected to know what to do on their wedding night, and the Victorian double standard ensured a toleration of their pre-marital use of prostitutes in the getting of such wisdom.

Although the labour aristocracy aped such conventions in the cities, among the working classes courtship codes were quite different. While urban domestics were to a degree monitored by the 'no followers' rule and the threat of losing employment should they fall pregnant, the growing absence of supervision of female farm and domestic servants by the guidwife was heavily implicated in the rise of illegitimacy to high European levels in north-east and south-west Scotland. However, despite the largely unregulated sleeping arrangements for fisher lassies and hairst workers, this did not happen extensively elsewhere.[15] While the lack of parental or employer surveillance of young adults was claimed to be responsible for brides being with child at their weddings in many areas, both material and cultural factors militated against unmarried motherhood. It was frequently necessary (as it was for many in the middle class too) to delay marriage until a house was either affordable or available. In the east coast seatowns it was customary for the bride's father to build a house for the couple before they married, although judging by the high levels of 'antenuptial fornication' (pre-marital sex) and consequent pregnancy recorded, only just before the first child arrived.[16] Such 'betrothal licence' differs from the courtship conventions of the Northern Isles where 'bundling' practices, similar to those of Scandinavia, were common.[17] Here, it was normal for youths to visit girls late at night after they had been carding wool outdoors and to share their beds. Nevertheless, such midnight visiting did not produce much illegitimacy (ratios were generally below 5 per cent) and we might conclude that heavy petting was the limit of their adventure, although recent historical evidence from Shetland suggests that intercourse was more than possible.[18] Very different was the situation in the north-east countryside, where between a fifth and a quarter of all births were illegitimate, making having a bastard child a normal part of the life course for many women. In this region, sex before marriage had always been common, but until the 1830s couples had managed to find a house and marry. When tenancies became scarce because lairds wished to rid their estates of impoverished cottars who drained Poor Law resources, they continued time-honoured courtship traditions, which included sexual intercourse, but no longer married at the appropriate stage. To have done likewise in the crofting counties would have been impossible since there were simply insufficient resources to feed the extra mouths in a subsistence economy. But in the north-east, parents crucially came to the aid of unmarried daughters, taking in their children while they continued in service and sent back remittances to support their children.[19] Different again, were the islanders of Lewis and the immigrant Irish whose morality appears to have put very strong store by female chastity. It would be easy to presume that this was down to strong religious convictions, but if so why was illegitimacy very high in Catholic countries such as Austria and Portugal?[20] Arguably, a group immigrating to Scotland's cities because of famine carried with it the legacy of land hunger where the onset of marriage had long been attenuated and bearing a child only worsened one's poverty.

In the Highlands couples married late, the rate of marriage was depressed, and – despite high fertility levels – family size was limited. Crofters had to wait for fathers to die before they could obtain scarce land and begin their own families. By comparison, in industrial areas the timing of marriage was influenced by the trade cycle with many marriages in boom years and few during periods of slump. In the demographically buoyant urban Central Belt, areas of mining and heavy industry were characterised by relatively low age at marriage, high marriage rates and high fertility: 'although housing and working conditions were often appalling and employment in many occupations was very irregular, they were, nevertheless, probably the areas of the country where earnings for the mass of the workforce were highest'.[21] Thus, the growing industrial districts offset decline in the north and north-west. Meanwhile, marriage rates in rural areas were generally slightly below average.[22]

Until 1834, non-conformists had to undertake an irregular marriage in order to marry within their faith. Such liaisons accounted for perhaps one-third of the total, although this proportion clearly dwindled thereafter, accounting for just 0.18 per cent of all marriages by the 1860s.[23] But if, conversely, during both eighteenth and twentieth centuries, irregularity was far more common, this Victorian phase of apparent high conformity does not reflect any greater effectiveness in ecclesiastical regulation; nor, on the other hand, was official marriage being challenged by a rebellion of unrecorded non-marriage. Couples adjusted their courtship practice according to practicalities while steered in their behaviour by their peers. Over the century, mean ages at first marriage hardly changed, but such an average disguises a broad spectrum, with entry into marriage frequently delayed by constricted opportunities. Marriage patterns correspond closely to the state of the economy and, as in previous centuries, nuptiality was greatly influenced by a couple's perceived chances of establishing a viable nuclear family unit; that is, a home of their own, independent of parents and other kin. The character of courtship lent young women little control over their fertility, which was largely reliant upon the local mores prevalent among their generation. Peer group behaviour effectively legitimated illegitimacy in some areas and bridal pregnancy in others, while economic circumstances could enforce chastity or long delays in getting married in others. We have, in effect, a three-way interdependence between culture, economics and demography, and as Anderson points out, 'it was only very gradually that the Church was able to defeat a widespread view that entry into marriage was a lengthy and gradual process in which the public rites were just the symbolic endpoint'.[24] Morals other than those of the kirk were not only commonly accepted, but were themselves enshrined in ritual ceremonies, such as the Horseman's Word among ploughmen, a complex set of initiation rites combining the shift from youth to manhood with an apprenticeship in a particular field of labour and expectations regarding seduction ('skeel [skill] o' horse, skeel o' woman').[25] Contemporary commentators, meanwhile, being middle-class moralists, misread the circumstances, assuming 'immorality' among young-sters to be a function of modernisation corrupting traditional peasant virtue and prudence.[26]

CHILDBEARING, LIFE EXPECTANCY AND CHANGING FAMILY PATTERNS

The transitional processes surrounding precise life events may be quite prolonged: for instance, with birth, there is a nine-month gestation period following conception and a period of weaning after parturition, that may vary from months to several years. Beyond this there is the cultural frame-work in which the decision, or non-decision, to become pregnant is made, the social context and meaning attached to baptism and the experience, regulation and institutionalisation of infancy and childhood as stages of socialisation. In the nineteenth century, the desirability or otherwise of bearing a child depended largely upon economic factors. While from the 1870s the urban middle classes initiated a trend towards lower fertility in the interests of smaller, better resourced families, at the opposite end of the spectrum impoverished crofters were visited by subsistence crises that rendered each new child a liability.[27] This said, in rural areas like much of the north-east, it was commonly believed that each woman 'had her bit bairnie', in or outside wedlock, bearing her pre-ordained number of children in due course.[28] Indeed, beyond the effects of poor maternal nutrition and amenorrhoea, which affected women in times of severe economic hardship such as the 1840s in the Highlands and Islands, the inevitability of concep-tion was high, since awareness and usage of effective birth control methods, save abstinence, was low. In part, this was due to ignorance, and customary adages provide evidence of an earlier, yet surely outmoded set of beliefs. In 1929, one folklorist, writing about the north-east wrote that: 'Almost to our own day it was believed that if a male cat chanced to jump over food and emitted semen, the one who partook of the food conceived cats'.[29]

Once pregnant, the supposedly aversive properties of tansy, rue and pen-nyroyal were known in the countryside, although the incidence of miscar-riage and stillbirth are impossible to compute. Concealment and consequent non-registration are also unknown factors, although, as we shall see, the issue of who was aware of the impending birth and how was an important one.[30] We do know that infant mortality was high and did not begin to

decline until early in the next century. From 1860 to 1910 the proportion
of deaths of babies under 1 year old per thousand live births varied between
109 and 127, a stark comparison with contemporary proportions, which by
2006 stood at just 4.5 per thousand.[31] Many babies simply failed to thrive
and causes of death such as 'marasmus' (malnutrition) and infantile debility
were legion. Such circumstances were productive of – and, indeed, help to
explain – a greater fatalism than that which existed during the interwar years
of the twentieth century, by which time improved maternal and infant care
and the diffusion of contraceptive practices from the middle classes had
produced smaller and far more stable families.

Although suffocation and overlaying were far from rarely recorded on
death certificates, and cases of post-mortem examination sometimes entered
into, deliberate infanticide and abortion are unlikely to have ever been more
than minimal.[32] Certainly duration of the transition phase is a significant
property here, both as regards the acceptable length of confinement and the
period during which an infant was breastfed. The two were related in that by
today's standards, most mothers could not provide prolonged breastfeeding
(which would have reduced their fecundity and thus lengthened intervals
between each birth) since they had to work both within and beyond the
household. In some cases, unmarried mothers were known to have returned
to work within a day or two of giving birth, with often dire consequences for
their offspring who would then be bottle-fed or farmed out to wet nurses.[33]
Infant mortality rates for illegitimate children were everywhere higher than
for the legitimate.

In reconstituting families from old parish registers of baptisms one occasionally finds two sequential children being given the same name, the first
having died. The period of labour, birth and the immediate aftermath was
a hazardous, liminal phase, surrounded by superstition. Confined women
would stick needles in their bed or a Bible under the bolster to ward off the
fairies; mother's milk was protected by preventing lactating women from
sitting on the bed of a woman who was lying in.[34] Such popular customs co-
existed alongside the ritual processes of the Kirk. For instance, the discovery
of foundlings could invoke draconian measures to establish who the mother
was:

> Kirk sessions, knowing well the heavy additional burden which the upbringing
> of such a child involved, made the utmost endeavours to discover the unnatural
> mother . . . the chief method employed to trace the culprit was to put in operation
> the lacteal test . . . Intimation was made from the pulpit . . . that all unmarried
> women 'come to perfection' or between the ages of twelve and fifty or widows
> should assemble in the Church on a certain day and hour, and have their breasts
> drawn. Those who neglected this citation were summoned again. Frequently, in
> this residuum, the guilty party was found . . . The minister and elders on the occa-
> sion were accompanied by midwives, or alternatively, women of good repute.[35]

It was a popular belief that infants who died unbaptised would remain in permanent limbo. Thus, all parents, Kirk or non-conformist, were eager to have their children christened. Scottish infants tended to be baptised relatively quickly. For instance, at Rothiemay in Banffshire, 50 per cent of intervals between birth and baptism were of five days or less between 1801 and 1810, compared with only 3.6 per cent over twenty days. However, there are indications that expectations of life were becoming more positive, with just 6 per cent of intervals at five days or less by the 1840s and, by contrast, 58 per cent over twenty days.[36] Since acknowledgement of fatherhood and undergoing a diet of absolution were conditions of baptism, the process was often delayed in the case of illegitimate children.[37] And, symbolically, since more bastards died in infancy, longer birth–baptism intervals had the effect of increasing their chances of remaining in limbo. Nevertheless, after civil registration arrived in 1855 all births had to be registered within three weeks.

The great majority of births occurred in the home, and a sizeable proportion did not involve a doctor. This we know from the birth certificates where 'no medical attendant' is frequently noted. With baptism, the Scottish trend, like the English, was towards private celebration, although much might depend upon the minister in question. One authority notes: 'In the nineteenth century the Session had perhaps less than ever to do with Baptism, for this was now generally celebrated in private.' The Banff record of 1841 does not stand alone when it declares that 'public baptism has in this parish been discontinued for upwards of fifty years'. Only towards the close of the century did it become at all common again. Nearby Rothiemay was similar, with 94.5 per cent of christenings happening at home between 1751 and 1790. Yet once the Revd James Simmie began his incumbency in 1791, the trend altered markedly, with 51.9 per cent of baptisms during his time in office to 1827 being celebrated in public 'before the congregation'.[38] Such was the continuing hold of the local kirk, and, indeed, its local idiosyncrasies, over parish affairs.

In terms of the properties of status passage, dying is generally not desirable although nothing is more inevitable. Yet its probability clearly altered for the better: in the 1790s, overall life expectancy in Scotland varied between 36.19 in the western Lowlands and 48.46 in the north-east.[39] By 1871, mean female life expectancy at birth in Scotland was 42.1 years, whereas by 2004 it had risen to 79.4 years (for men it was 39.8 and 74.3, respectively).[40] As in every other era, people might only guess and fear as to their own destiny. However, as the statistics for infant mortality show, life was distinctly more precarious then in its early stages, while associated maternal mortality also made giving birth a far less secure prospect for the mother than today. Childhood was more prone to the onslaughts of infectious and contagious diseases, although rather less so after inoculation and vaccination had taken hold, while respiratory disease in particular killed many who worked in hazardous mines and factories and inhabited damp houses. Crisis mortality persisted, the cholera epidemic of 1832, for example, killed almost 10,000 (there were further epidemics in 1848, 1853 and 1866), although the demographic consequences of the 'Great Highland Famine' of the 1840s were seen more in destitution and consequent emigration than outright starvation.[41] As a consequence of higher mortality levels, the proportions surviving into what we now regard as old age were far lower. In 1810, only 20 per cent of the population reaching age forty-four had their father alive, whereas 65 per cent were in this position by the 1980s. And it was not until the interwar years of the twentieth century that more than half a cohort began to survive long enough to know all their grandchildren. Despite larger family size, higher mortality meant that adults did not have many more siblings alive in the Victorian era than we do now.[42]

With adult death rates only beginning a marked decline after 1870, and child mortality remaining high, it is unsurprising that burial customs were many. Funerals were especially important in 'allow[ing] the community to fall back on the security of established order at a time when the bereaved cannot possibly have the inner resources to organise anew the entire procedure from the moment of death to the last farewell of burial'.[43] Although elements of individualism crept into middle-class conventions with arrangements being handed over to undertakers, most funerals remained community events, especially in the more rural areas and in the Islands: neighbours still walked the coffin from the kirk to the graveyard in Uig, Skye in the 1970s. In the era of Queen Victoria's prolonged mourning for Albert, affluent families produced funeral cards for dead children, including poems and even photographs, while the respectable working class paid insurance to secure a 'decent' burial.[44] Pauper funerals, by contrast, were basic ceremonies, retaining the appropriate rites, but attended by few, if any, mourners and paid for by the parish.

Changes in marital fertility have also affected the family life cycle in significant ways. The age at first marriage for both sexes has not varied much over time. However, the pattern of childbearing within marriage has altered dramatically. In respect of rites of passage, this raises questions of the transmission of awareness of birth control techniques and the extent to which women were empowered by this, and of the legitimation of changing attitudes in local cultures as well as the relationship between customary behaviour and socio-economic circumstances. More fundamentally, the reduction in completed family size indicates a shift in the evaluation of children, from being regarded as an important household resource to being nurtured for their own potential. However, among working people in the nineteenth century, sons and daughters still contributed to the family economy, either directly through co-operative kin-based tasks related to crofting and fishing, as labour on the family farm, or as paid servants and industrial workers outside the home.[45] Today the mean family size is less than two.[46] By contrast, as

Figure 3.1   *Funeral party at the graveside of a child, with coffin ready to be lowered.*
© *Falkirk Museums. Licensor www.scran.ac.uk.*

recently as 1901, crofters' and miners' families averaged over seven children. Fishermen, farmers and agricultural labourers reached similar levels, while workers in heavy industry and shipbuilding averaged over six and textile workers just above five. Even among the professional groups, doctors, lawyers, teachers and ministers had a mean family size of around four. Nevertheless, the trend towards the two-child family was becoming evident by 1911 among physicians and surgeons.[47] They were the keenest, and most informed exponents of artificial contraception and their pattern of limitation was to become widespread. What was already apparent in the 1870s was that the wives of professional men were ceasing to bear children by their early thirties. As well as reducing family size, this had the important effect of concentrating births into the early years of marriage. Thus, for the vast majority of couples in the mid-twentieth century, 'the years of childbearing were few; on average, couples had their last child within seven years of marriage'.[48] This bunching had not been characteristic of the earlier regime, where there was little evidence of deliberate birth spacing and children appeared almost as frequently as their parents' fecundity allowed. Between the 1830s and the post-war years of the twentieth century, the combined effect of reduced family size and of clustering was a lowering of eleven years in the age at which a married woman bore her last child.[49]

Indeed, as Michael Anderson has demonstrated, what we think of as the 'modern' British life cycle emerged between 1939 and the 1970s. By then, the process by which most individuals moved through life-course transitions was a particularly rigid one of 'clearly demarcated stages through which most of the population passed within a relatively narrow band of ages'.[50] It was historically highly specific in terms of both timings and structure, and indicates the impact of medical intervention, both in prolonging lives and limiting births. By contrast, in the nineteenth century many events occurred later in life than they do today, although within a shorter overall lifespan in which the majority did not experience grandparenthood (certainly not great-grandparenthood), and where the long phase following the end of childcare but before the onset of old age simply did not exist. Because of the pronounced fall in the span over which certain life-course transitions normally occurred in the 'modern' period, those falling outwith fairly narrow expectations were liable to be stigmatised: a woman bearing a child in her late thirties was assumed to have fallen pregnant by mistake; some men who worked until they were seventy were accused of taking away younger men's jobs.[51] By contrast, it may be argued that during the nineteenth century, because these transitions were still widespread across the age spectrum, the potential for stigmatisation would have been lower: it is difficult to tell at what age people began work, especially when children performed many household and caring tasks, while there was little concept of retirement, let alone an abrupt transition to it. There was less sense in which events such as getting married, having a first child or finishing work were expected to happen at

closely specified points in the life course; rather, the absence of rigid timing
was coupled with greater uncertainty. While mid-twentieth-century orderli-
ness has since been disrupted by such phenomena as rising divorce levels, in
1850 premature death led to the dissolution of just as many marriages. Such
instability, especially in an age before the welfare state, led to greater reliance upon extended kin (although not necessarily to extended family households). Where this was most feasible, notably where people were beginning
to survive in numbers to grandparental age, it offered forms of cushioning
that facilitated, for example, the relative long-term stability of illegitimacy of
the north-east, a pattern which even became a normative mode of upbringing. Where it was least possible, as in the famine-hit north-west Highlands,
families either dissolved having been diluted by the emigration of young
adults or came to depend on subsistence relief.

Questions of control over the different processes of the life course were
crucial, from who regulated conception, and how effectively, to the ability to
limit the chances of dying. The diffusion of popular contraceptive methods,
public sanitation and improved medical diagnoses each had considerable
effects. But for present purposes, what becomes particularly interesting
as one moves into the twentieth century is the way in which a growing
command over these physical processes manifests itself in the often unprecedented choices made by individuals, couples and families in shaping their
own life courses.

Prior to this, legal constraints, such as the great difficulty of getting a
divorce, and practical necessities, such as living with lodgers, restricted
such opportunities. There remained huge inequalities according to region,
class and gender, and much must have still seemed a matter of providence.
Nevertheless, even among the relatively impoverished, cultural differences
were emerging that began to question certain age-old modes of conduct,
often for practical rather than idealistic reasons. These were triggered by the
wide-scale demographic changes of the period: mass transfer of population
from the rural areas to the cities, including the arrival of a sizeable proportion of Irish Catholics, prompted a decline in local ecclesiastical control;
vaccination, inoculation and advances in the knowledge and treatment of
a range of diseases increased life expectancy, slowly reducing the sense of
fatalism; while birth control methods were beginning to diffuse through the
class system. The coalescence of behaviours culminating in what, by the mid-
twentieth century, became the 'modern British life-cycle' saw an increased
rigidity in popular expectations about when, and with whom, key life-course
decisions and behaviours were appropriate. This reflected a shift in policing
of universal life rituals from formal ecclesiastic controls to everyday social
approval. As life for many became less precarious and more predictable the
pull of religious obligations diminished, while the effects of social stigma
became more pronounced. The latter were nevertheless variable according
to class and geography, with local popular cultures powerfully defining and

limiting world-views in an age before global mass media. Meanwhile, the kirk's social influence over everyday life persisted through a legacy of moral concern about family arrangements, social welfare and the sacredness of the rites of passage.

THE TRANSFORMATION OF RITUAL: KIRK SESSION DISCIPLINE

The relationships between demographic patterns, life-course transitions and everyday life are best observed at the micro-scale. Two methodological requirements flow from this: first, analyses have to be conducted at the level of local communities, which means that, secondly, the infrastructure of parish society has to be understood. It is probably true that making distinctions between Annalist and micro-historical approaches is less fruitful than demonstrating how the one can inform the other: in particular, it is from the dry, systematic and institutional records of parochial administration that one might learn most – albeit in coded, often unsatisfactory ways – about the lives of the people.[52] For this reason, the second part of this chapter discusses the transformation of ritual in a single community. Its focus is on what we can discover from kirk session records, particularly as they apply to the pattern of dealing with sexual behaviour. Ritual is involved at two levels. First, the Form of Process through which 'offenders' were managed was itself a ritual mechanism; it had been instituted by the Church of Scotland in 1707 and was an abbreviated directory of discipline which covered the due and legal execution of excommunication, repentance and absolution. Secondly, changes in the style and effectiveness of the system demonstrate a shift in how the rites of courtship, childbearing and marriage were negotiated by a group of individuals who were, for the most part, themselves undergoing the transition from youth to adulthood.

Following the Disruption in 1843, both the Church of Scotland and the Free Kirk sessions maintained oversight of parochial morality through a disciplinary structure policed by the elders. Thus, despite the shifts of mid-century, and even though much of the population was on the move, kirk sessions continued to act as church courts that, ostensibly at least, monitored the morals of their congregation.[53] We know that in some districts, particularly the cities, they found this well nigh impossible as the sheer bulk of people moving in and out of each parish defeated attempts at social control. Equally, in some God-fearing country districts they continued to succeed, although such places would have had little cause for concern anyway. However, in a turbulent religious period, few places remained unaffected by economic, social and demographic upheaval. Henderson remarks that:

> The nineteenth century saw the gradual and almost complete disappearance of
> Session discipline. Certain improvements in the standard of morals and education

and civilization had taken place. Positive exhortation to virtuous and reverent courses was being preferred to exposure of breaches of the moral and spiritual law . . . the Church had lost the authority it once exercised over all parishioners, Christian and unchristian alike, and this authority passed to the civil powers . . . Discipline became restricted almost entirely to sexual offences.[54]

The Banffshire farming parish of Rothiemay was in many ways typical of a medium-sized parish in the rural Lowlands in that the Victorian era saw a decline in the effectiveness, and by implication, perceived cultural importance of the session. It is, however, unusual in that its population was both relatively stable, despite a mass of localised mobility, and characterised by a high and rising level of illegitimacy. Because of the latter, we might expect the elders to have been increasingly busy in trying to eradicate what they regarded as a sinister species of immorality. What in fact occurred was a lessening of discipline as the century progressed. It is unlikely that this reduction in social control itself caused the broad upsurge in unmarried motherhood – for that we must turn to socio-economic factors (see p. 94) – but it was undoubtedly symptomatic of a widening gulf in mores between the official guardians of conduct and a sizeable part of the local populace, including most of its youth. To be sure, observing the activities of the kirk session does not provide information concerning any shift in the nature of courtship practices or the manner in which both baptism and marriage rites were conducted. What is does indicate, however, is an erosion of the ritual means by which the misdemeanours of errant individuals were rectified so as to ensure the symbolic maintenance of social solidarity, demonstrating, in effect, a measure of increased latitude in the social system.[55]

Since the early eighteenth century, the Presbyterian Form of Process had involved a system of elders reporting suspected 'offenders' and summoning them to appear before the session after service on a stated Sunday.[56] By its decree, only sins with visible, physical manifestations were specified for treatment, kirk sessions thus losing an earlier power over the inner souls of their parishioners and no longer now dealing with matters such as pride and jealousy.[57] By contrast, pregnancy provided tangible evidence of guilt. It is thus hardly surprising that fornicators came to dominate the minute books, albeit in lessening numbers, while women were disproportionately represented.[58] Offenders became so many 'cases' to be dealt with, a fact reflected in the mechanical format assumed by the minutes of discipline, and, as noted above, very few of these were now other than sexual in nature.

Unmarried persons found 'guilty' of having had sex, including those who later married ('antenuptial fornication'), suffered the lesser excommunication by which, as penitents, they lost communion privileges while submitting to a diet of discipline. Traditionally, this had consisted of public humiliation, offenders being clothed in sackcloth and made to sit on the 'cutty stool', or seat of repentance, in front of the full congregation, the number of appearances – usually three – being determined by the supposed severity of their offence. However, in 1804 the Presbytery of Strathbogie ordained that public rebuke be replaced by private appearances before the session in the vestry after the service.[59] The symbolic significance of 'immorality' was nevertheless maintained. In a neat demonstration of the official translation of morality into local practice, dispensations through the parish Poor Law system at this time remained reliant upon income from those fined by the session – the punishment of sinners paid for charity towards the deserving. During the 1830s, fines for fornication (£1 3s. 4d.), and, rather less frequently, adultery (£2 10s.), were considerable. Even antenuptial fornication accrued a penalty of 2s. 6d. per partner, with irregular proclamations of marriage banns charged at just over twice this sum. Yet in 1835, 'because it does not appear lawful', the Rothiemay session decided to end the system of fines for antenuptial fornication and, shortly after, for all offences.[60]

Despite such changes, for the remainder of the century the session minutes would initially suggest that good order prevailed. Page after page records that fornicators were 'cited to appear', 'compeared', were accused, and, 'craving absolution', had nevertheless 'to remain under church censure' until, having being 'solemnly rebuked and suitably admonished' and having 'professed penitence', 'they were 'absolved from scandal of their sin, and restored the privileges of the Church'. Yet this was no more than a customary record of proceedings, a façade, behind which lay a collapsing edifice, the ghostly enactment of an increasingly moribund morality play:

> One envisions a church court in which the elders, full of ire, berate their guilty cousins, the officials summoning up requisite gravitas to keep form while the deflowered maiden blushes wistfully. Unfortunately we can only imagine. Erving Goffman has noted that: 'When normals and stigmatised do in fact enter one another's immediate presence, especially when they attempt to sustain a joint conversational encounter, there occurs one of the primal scenes of sociology; for, in many cases, these moments will be the ones when the causes and effects of stigma must be directly confronted by both sides.' Of course, in Rothiemay the encounter would depart from this expectation in several important ways: firstly, elders and accused only represented 'normals' and 'stigmatised' in a formal sense; secondly, and relatedly, a session meeting, with its attendant ritual and scriptural language, was hardly a 'joint conversational encounter'; thirdly, such ceremonial guaranteed that 'the causes and effects of stigma', if not disguised by the process, were only confronted in an indirect manner.[61]

In 1827, the clerk noted the session's resolve 'to dismiss none from church censure upon his or her first appearance'.[62] But if those under penance were to be dealt with severely, they would come to represent no more than the pious or unlucky few. As illegitimacy ratios in the parish rose from 13.3 per cent in the 1830s to 25.8 per cent in the 1870s, so the number of cases dealt with by the Established Church fell from eight-two to just twenty-seven.[63]

While in the later 1820s there had been twice as many fornication cases dealt with as there were registered illegitimate births in the parish (at a time when the session clerk was also *de facto* the registrar), by the 1890s there were over three times as many registered illegitimate births in Rothiemay than fornication cases listed in the Established Church minutes. Even allowing for the fact that the Free Kirk by then had a comparable number of adherents, and extrapolating that it would have disciplined a similar (or slightly higher) proportion of miscreants, it is clear that as the century progressed kirk sessions in no wise kept pace with what by their standards was illicit sexual behaviour.[64] Close analysis of minute books shows that the frequency of meetings to enact discipline dwindled, while cases were increasingly dropped as offenders failed to appear.

It was necessary to undergo discipline before an infant could be baptised if the child had been born within nine months of marriage, and the data reveal that both partners satisfied in the great majority of instances. To this extent, the propriety of the ritual seems to have been sustained. Nevertheless, as illegitimacy increased, so the numbers of antenuptial cases plummeted (by some 60 per cent between the 1860s and 1870s). And here, where no marriages were involved, the growing ease with which young men came to evade all discipline is startling. In the 1770s three-quarters of men admitted paternity of bastards, but by 1850 only one-third did so.[65] Undoubtedly, this was generally because of the threat, and cost, of alimony. The session persisted in summoning the alleged offender, requiring him to re-appear several times. But as the century wore on, putative fathers increasingly failed to show at all. This growing absence of suspected offenders was reflected in two trends: increasingly paternity was acknowledged by letter, or men simply absconded. Most putative fathers were farm servants, whose frequent mobility required ministers to exchange written summons in order to enforce attendance when the men moved between districts. By mid-century, this tracking mechanism had been superseded by non-resident men pleading in writing. However, regardless of repeated summons, increasing numbers of fathers simply disappeared, their partners having lost all trace of their whereabouts. Meanwhile, remarks like 'who has absconded but admits his guilt' and 'has gone abroad, but a letter was produced which showed that he admitted the paternity' indicate that some fathers, while honest, or even concerned, had little regard for the views of the Church.[66] The mothers, rendered rather less mobile both by having (incipient) babes in arms and usually requiring either family or Poor Law support, were far more liable to local discipline. It was thus the women who underwent prolonged periods of penitence or who were referred to the presbytery for 'grave dealing' following repeat offences.[67] Yet latterly, as the scale and complexity of individual movements forced a decline in the coherence of parochial discipline, they too evaded anything that might be termed public discipline, or, at least, appearance before the elders. In line with many others, by 1895 the Rothiemay session had resolved that antenuptial fornicators should be admonished by the minister in private, and in 1902 the General Assembly decreed that the names of offenders everywhere be rendered illegible in the minutes once five years had elapsed.[68] After 1904, no written record of discipline appears in Rothiemay. Thus, in the space of seventy years, a mandatory system of public shaming for all parishioners had given way to a voluntary practice of private confessional taken up by a minority of church adherents.[69] The attendant shift in style from moral arbitration to counselling saw the effective collapse of a community ritual. As Boyd writes, in reference to Scotland as a whole, not only was discipline 'a dead letter for all practical purposes', but also 'with the virtual disappearance of the elders from the disciplinary scene there was little to show that such discipline represented the mind of the community'.[70]

RITUAL, BELONGING AND COMMUNITY

On the face of it, this outcome would seem to bear out the truism that rituals fail to survive when their social function declines. It is not the content but the form that matters, and quite clearly in this case the Form of Process became an anachronism no longer attuned to local society. This may have been an augury of twentieth-century secularisation, insofar as secularisation has been defined as 'the process whereby religious thinking, practices and institutions lose social significance'.[71] However, it did not mean that the demise of church discipline reflected any breakdown in community in a broader, regional sense, or in the customary means of affirming shared values.

Certainly, the failings of the kirk cannot simply be attributed to rising individualism. Mitchison and Leneman suggest that, in the early-modern period, it is 'unlikely that any sizeable part of the population regarded sexual intercourse as a normal prelude to marriage'.[72] By the same token, pre-marital customs such as handfasting or 'betrothal licence' would have been rare.[73] However, pre-marital sex is known to have been commonplace in north-east Scotland during the eighteenth century, and in Rothiemay nearly a third of brides were pregnant at marriage in the 1770s.[74] The protracted nineteenth-century rise in unmarried motherhood developed on the basis of such pre-existing and habitual, possibly 'fertility-testing', behaviour in that intending couples, who had already conceived, were unable to marry and set up home independently because affordable rented housing became scarce. Most 'delinquents' seen by the session were thus life-cycle servants in agriculture whose route from single late adolescence to married early adulthood had been barred by economic circumstances. The explanation for illegitimacy thus lies in structural factors and is not, as some theorists suggest, a function of modernisation promulgating more personalised, rather than communally-sanctioned fertility behaviour.[75]

A materialist rationale also explains the decline of sessional appearances by 'fornicators', in that from around 1840 the mobility of farm and domestic servants at this stage in the life course intensified as more entered the 'hire-house' and moved between farms, albeit within the region, on six-monthly contracts. As farming conditions deteriorated in the post-1870s depression, more also emigrated.[76] Alongside, rather than against this argument, con-temporary commentators derided the decline of 'kindly relations' between master and servant, blaming sexual licence upon the anonymous, and non-supervisory, social relations of production that superseded them. However, it would be wrong to assume, as did many Victorian moral reformers, that the 'low moral tone prevalent in the countryside' demarcated a deviant social group, whose attitudes and behaviour were wholly at odds with other elements of rural society. With illegitimacy ratios averaging over 20 per cent across a broad swathe of Banffshire and Aberdeenshire, unmarried motherhood was remarkable only by its normality, clearly affecting a much higher proportion of the population when family connections are taken into account. Indeed, of the twenty-four kirk elders ordained in the Established Kirk in Rothiemay between 1827 and 1894, twelve were in one way or another linked to 'immorality' within the parish: one had fathered a bastard while a young man, nine had sons and daughters who produced illegitimate offspring, four had siblings who had bastards, and one was disciplined for 'antenuptial fornication' while himself an elder.[77] Nearly all these men were small tenant farmers, socially typical of the locality, less hypocrites perhaps than victims of a common circumstance to which little stigma can have attached.[78]

This, of course, points to a cultural corollary. The changing methods by which communities sought to deal with morality bear comparison with Ruth Benedict's distinction between shame cultures, which are ritu-ally policed through external sanctions on individual behaviour, and guilt cultures that rely on their members internalising norms of right and wrong within their own consciences.[79] Against the confessional form of the Catholic Church elsewhere in Europe – a guilt culture where the spiritual sin was confronted but, arguably, its social stigma left intact – it may plau-sibly be contended that public shaming acted to eradicate the social stain through ritual absolution. By this logic, the Form of Process ushered in a culture that purged not only the sin, but also its social stigma. However, as the public nature of discipline diminished in the later nineteenth century to be supplanted by private dealing, there was no return to a guilt culture since the inquisitorial mechanisms of the pre-eighteenth century Reformers were no longer deployed. An interview with the minister sufficed and any disap-proval was 'expressed in private and personal ways, not with authority'.[80] Although it may be posited that 'as a mechanism for social control, public shaming requires a cohesive congregational culture where all people know one another well and continually live and move within daily sight of each other', its demise in a period of greater individual mobility neither reflected nor heralded social anomie.[81] Nor can it simply be explained by reference to growing individualism, whether evident from declining religiosity or the privatisation of belief.

In large measure, life-course rituals are habitual and unquestioned. However, at a time when the institution empowered to conduct ceremonies appeared to be losing its authority, it is debatable whether the Kirk (or kirks) remained the arbiter of mores within the local world, at least in some otherwise unremarkable localities. The kirk session, like the law, might commonly have been regarded in several different lights: as something magisterial and distant (unlikely where the composition of the eldership was as above); as a game with rules to be manipulated; or as an arbitrary force to be challenged.[82] It was there to be negotiated with or ignored, not just obeyed. In this sense, what survived of older rituals after the nineteenth century was largely dependent upon what was popularly acceptable. And this, in turn, was a matter of accommodating everyday culture to the realities of social and economic change.

In some respects, the law remained unquestioned. For example, irregular marriages (those not conducted by a minister of the church) accounted for just 1 per cent of the Scottish total in 1875, and it was not until 1939 that the Marriage (Scotland) Act introduced civil marriage in the office of a registrar.[83] Throughout the nineteenth century, most people made automatic recourse to their minister or priest to perform christenings, weddings and funerals – as many do over a century later – but a failure to toe the line of observance required of religious adherents may be seen in the socio-sexual behaviour of some parishioners. What is remarkable is not so much their disregard for chastity, as an unwillingness to undergo the time-honoured process associated with their ritual punishment and re-incorporation into the community. For some, at least, the kirk into which they had been baptised, through which they might be married and almost certainly by which they would be buried no longer entirely determined the morality of their private activities. How they conducted themselves was perhaps more a matter of choice than before – and, in this sense, people did demonstrate greater individualism – but this was nevertheless complemented by a strong need for belonging. It was a matter of considerable import that one's entrance into the world and exit from it be duly recognised and recorded: Mark this for posterity – here, in this community, I was born and here – in this or another place – I died.

The wider lesson to be drawn from our example is, therefore, that life-course rituals do indeed celebrate profound, if sometimes unconscious, social solidarities, but that the character of such solidarities, while often reflected in ecclesiastical ceremonies, cannot be ascertained from within the religious sphere.[84] Against the decline of disciplinary ritual may be set the continuance of christenings, weddings and funerals presided over by the Church until the present day. Whatever the reason for their survival, these customs serve to bind individuals to a communally sanctioned moral order. Relatively stable areas, like Rothiemay, were perhaps slow to change, but even in the late-Victorian city it may be argued that 'although the majority of the working-class population attended church infrequently or not at all, there was a continuing strong belief in church 'connection'.[85] Whilst this was scarcely a satisfactory situation from the standpoint of the Church, it was recognised by churchmen that even this tenuous attachment had important stabilising effects on society.'[86] The nineteenth century shows the significance of the shift from a near universal system of social control by the Kirk to a fractured system of governance where the inspector of poor and registrar of births, marriages and deaths took over some functions, while after the Disruption religious adherence became a matter of 'connection' to one of two or more congregations within a parish. In coming to terms with this, people adapted the pretexts and usages of an older, more perdurable moral economy as they made their necessary life transitions. Some may have feared that damnation would result from disbelief, others perhaps felt a private bond while disliking the social constraints or pretensions of organised religion; but almost all conformed to tradition in recording, or, rather, having recorded for them, the bare but essential facts of their lives.

Notes

1 J. Robertson, *The Testament of Gideon Mack* (London, 2007), p. 227.

2 M. de Certeau, *The Practice of Everyday Life*, trans. Steven Rendall (Berkeley, 1984).

3 R. G. deVries, 'Birth and Death: Social Construction at the Poles of Existence', *Social Forces* 59 (1981), 1074–93.

4 A. R. Radcliffe-Brown, 'Religion and Society', in L. Schneider (ed.), *Religion, Culture and Society* (New York, 1964), p. 64.

5 A. Bryman *et al.*, *Rethinking the Life Cycle* (Basingstoke, 1987), pp. 2–3; T. K. Hareven, *Family Time and Industrial Time* (Cambridge, 1982), p. 6 notes: 'The life course approach is concerned with the movement of individuals over their own lives and through historical time and with the relationship of family members to each other.'

6 For a diverse collection of traditions surrounding rites of passage in Scotland, including much oral testimony, see M. Bennett, *Scottish Customs: From the Cradle to the Grave* (Edinburgh, 1992). Among contemporary observers, see particularly Revd W. Gregor, *Notes on the Folk-lore of the North-East of Scotland* (London, 1881) and Revd J. Napier, *Folk Lore: or, Superstitious Beliefs in the West of Scotland within this Century* (Paisley, 1879).

7 M. Anderson and D. Morse, 'High Fertility, High Emigration, Low Nuptiality: Adjustment Processes in Scotland's Demographic Experience, 1861–1914', *Population Studies*, 47:I (1993), 25.

8 M. Anderson and D. Morse, 'The People', in W. H. Fraser and R. J. Morris (eds), *People and Society in Scotland, Vol. 2* (Edinburgh, 1990), pp. 13, 15.

9 M. W. Flinn (ed.), *Scottish Population History* (Cambridge, 1977) provides comprehensive analysis.

10 D. Levine, *Family Formation in an Age of Nascent Capitalism* (New York, 1977), p. 158; A. Blaikie, *Illegitimacy, Sex and Society: Northeast Scotland, 1750–1900* (Oxford, 1993), p. 73. Non-conformity had a severe effect on registration in England but was much less significant in Scotland. For example, the *Old Statistical Account, Vol. 19* (Edinburgh, 1797), p. 390 records 94.8 per cent of Rothiemay inhabitants as belonging to the Established Church.

11 A. van Gennep, *The Rites of Passage* (Chicago, 1960).

12 G. J. West, 'Custom', in S. Storrier (ed.), *Scottish Life and Society, Vol. 6: Scotland's Domestic Life* (Edinburgh, 2006), pp. 563, 565, 567–9.

13 B. Glaser and A. L. Strauss, *Status Passage* (London, 1971), pp. 3–6. Although sociologists assume that status passages are regular, scheduled and prescribed, these properties 'can be absent or present only in some degree in some types of status passage', p. 3.

14 T. C. Smout, 'Aspects of Sexual Behaviour in Nineteenth-century Scotland', in A. A. MacLaren (ed.), *Social Class in Scotland: Past and Present* (Edinburgh, 1976), p. 56.

15 Smout, 'Aspects', pp. 56–78, discusses contemporary literature from around the country.

16 J. Gerrard, *The Rural Labourers of the North of Scotland: Their Medical Relief and House Accommodation as they affect Pauperism and Illegitimacy* (Banff, 1862); 'An Old Fisherman' [G. Green], *Gordonhaven: Sketches of Fisher Life in the North* (Edinburgh, 1887), p. 74.

17 P. Laslett, 'The Bastardy Prone Sub-Society', in P. Laslett, K. Oosterveen and R. M. Smith (eds), *Bastardy and its Comparative History* (London, 1980), pp. 217–40.

18 L. Abrams, *Myth and Materiality in a Woman's World: Shetland, 1800–2000* (Manchester, 2005), pp. 154–90.

19 A. Blaikie, 'A Kind of Loving: Illegitimacy, Grandparents and the Rural Economy of Northeast Scotland, 1750–1900', *Scottish Economic and Social History*, 14 (1994), 41–57.

20 Smout, 'Aspects', pp. 73–8.

21 Anderson and Morse, 'High Fertility', pp. 335–6.

22 Flinn, *Scottish Population History*, p. 327.

23 T. C. Smout, 'Scottish Marriage, Regular and Irregular, 1500–1940', in R. B. Outhwaite (ed.), *Marriage and Society: Studies in the Social History of Marriage* (London, 1981), pp. 221–2. In the 1855–70 period only one marriage per thousand was irregular.

24 M. Anderson, 'New Insights into the History of the Family in Britain', *Refresh*, 9 (1989), 4.

25 N. Roy [A. D. Russell], *The Horseman's Word* (London, 1895), frontis.; I. Carter, *Farm Life in Northeast Scotland, 1840–1914* (Edinburgh, 1979), p. 155; J. R. Allan, *Farmer's Boy* (London, 1935), p. 113, discussing hierarchy among male farm servants, remarks that 'the etiquette of the bothy' was such that the foreman 'had the right to make the first pass at the kitchen maid'.

26 K. M. Boyd, *Scottish Church Attitudes to Sex, Marriage and the Family, 1850–1914* (Edinburgh, 1980); Blaikie, *Illegitimacy*, pp. 32–65.

27 D. Kemmer, 'The Marital Fertility of Edinburgh Professions in the later Nineteenth Century', unpublished Ph.D. thesis, University of Edinburgh, 1989.

28 G. Seton, 'Illegitimacy in the Parish of Marnoch', *Proceedings of the Royal Society of Edinburgh*, 5 March 1888, p. 232.

29 J. M. McPherson, *Primitive Beliefs in the North-East of Scotland* (London, 1929), p. 113.

30 Although the high incidence of *registered* illegitimate births indicates that these parents conformed to the normal requirements for recording a birth.

31 B. R. Mitchell and P. Deane, *Abstract of British Historical Statistics and Annual Abstract of Statistics*, cited in R. Mitchison, *British Population Change since 1860* (London, 1977), p. 50; NHS Scotland, *Scottish Perinatal and Infant Mortality and Morbidity Report*, 2006 (Edinburgh, 2007), p. 3, table 1.

32 A. Blaikie, 'Infant Survival Chances, Unmarried Motherhood and Domestic Arrangements in Rural Scotland, 1845–1945', *Local Population Studies*, 60 (1998), 39–40.

33 T. Ferguson, *Scottish Social Welfare, 1864–1914* (Edinburgh, 1958), pp. 260–1, notes a doctor's claim in 1876 that 'refusal to afford outdoor relief in such cases led almost invariably to the death of the children, from inattention and starvation', it being impossible 'to induce the mothers to go to the poorhouse, and the children are farmed out with the too-well-known sad result of baby-farming'.

34 West, 'Custom', p. 564. When the baby arrived, it was hanselled (welcomed with a gift), often by placing a silver coin in the pram or cradle. This was supposed to bring luck and, insofar as the custom persisted into the later twentieth century in many areas, became more a legacy of past fears than a reminder of continuing vulnerability.

35 McPherson, *Primitive Beliefs*, pp. 120–1. This practice was still extant in the early nineteenth century. Since 'howdies' [midwives] gave practical help at both births and deaths – where they would dress corpses – they were viewed with particular suspicion by both churchmen and doctors since they presented a popular challenge to the authority of religion and, latterly, medical science.

36 Blaikie, *Illegitimacy*, p. 72. English studies suggest considerably longer intervals, although the deleterious impact of non-conformity on registration efficiency was a more significant factor there. For example, in nineteenth-century Shepshed, Leicestershire about one child in seven was over one year old when baptised (Levine, *Family Formation*, p. 159, n.10). Higher levels of mobility resulting from industrialisation also resulted in delayed baptism. A woman in confinement was believed to be heathen, hence her first visit to church following a birth – known as the kirking – acted as a ritual reincorporation. Bennett, *Scottish Customs*, pp. 28–32 and 54–6 provides evidence of regional variations in customs supposed to protect newborn children who, without the benefit of this sacrament, were often considered prone to being carried off or turned into changelings by fairies.

37 A. A. MacLaren, *Religion and Social Class: the Disruption Years in Aberdeen* (London, 1974), p. 128.

38 Blaikie, *Illegitimacy*, p. 72. G. D. Henderson, *The Scottish Ruling Elder* (London, 1935), p. 254.

39 Flinn, *Scottish Population History*, p. 270.
40 Anderson and Morse, 'The People', p. 30; Registrar General for Scotland, *Scotland's Population 2005* (Edinburgh, 2006).
41 T. M. Devine, *The Great Highland Famine: Hunger, Emigration and the Scottish Highlands in the Nineteenth century* (Edinburgh, 1988).
42 Anderson, 'New Insights', p. 2.
43 Bennett, *Scottish Customs*, p. 175.
44 Bennett, *Scottish Customs*, pp. 224–6; Anderson and Morse, 'The People', pp. 16–17.
45 S. R. Baillie, 'The Structure of Population in Fishing Communities of North-East Scotland', unpublished Ph.D. thesis, University of Aberdeen, 1984; Carter, *Farm Life*, pp. 92–4.
46 Economic and Social Research Council, *The Demographic Trends in Scotland: a Shrinking and Ageing Population* (Swindon, 2005), p. 9. In 1934 completed family size was 2.63; by 2004 it was 1.6.
47 Anderson and Morse, 'The People', p. 40.
48 Anderson, 'Modern Life Cycle', p. 69.
49 Anderson, 'New insights', p. 2.
50 Anderson, 'Modern Life Cycle', p. 69.
51 Anderson, 'Modern Life Cycle', p. 86.
52 As Segalen points out for the French peasantry, we must be careful to distinguish proverbial discourse and symbolic acts from everyday life. See M. Segalen, *Love and Power in the Peasant Family: Rural France in the Nineteenth Century* (Oxford, 1983).
53 Minority persuasions such as Roman Catholics and the United Presbyterian Church had their own means of disciplining adherents.
54 Henderson, *Scottish Ruling Elder*, p. 241.
55 For a detailed discussion that places declining sessional activity within the context of Presbyterian discipline in Scotland and Northern Ireland see: A. Blaikie and P. Gray, 'Archives of Abuse and Discontent? Presbyterianism and Sexual Behaviour during the Eighteenth and Nineteenth Centuries', in L. Kennedy and R. J. Morris (eds), *Order and Disorder: Scotland and Ireland, 1600–2001* (Edinburgh, 2005), pp. 61–84.
56 I. M. Clark, *A History of Church Discipline in Scotland* (Aberdeen, 1929) provides detailed analysis.
57 Henderson, *Scottish Ruling Elder*, pp. 242–5.
58 R. Mitchison and L. Leneman, *Sexuality and Social Control: Scotland, 1660–1780* (Oxford, 1989), p. 136, comment: 'it appears a very constant pattern in the eighteenth century that the allegation of fornication was not made until a woman was visibly pregnant, usually in the sixth or seventh month'.
59 Public rebuke had died out almost everywhere by 1850, although some Free Kirk sessions persisted with the practice until much later (Henderson, *Scottish Ruling Elder*, p. 245).
60 Rothiemay Kirk Session Minute Book [KSMB] 8 February 1829, 13 September 1829, 16 May 1830, 16 July 1837, 5 October 1828, 14 June 1835. In 1837 the General Assembly passed an act 'forbidding the raising of money for the poor

from people under discipline' (Henderson, *Scottish Ruling Elder*, p. 243). For the sake of clarity, the remaining discussion focuses on the fortunes of the kirk session alone. However, a significant element in its declining influence was the transfer in 1845 of poor relief arrangements to the Parochial Boards, who thereafter became responsible for deciding whether and how to support illegitimate children. As with the kirk sessions, their records indicate individuals caught between official and popular frames of reference in their negotiations with authority. See A. Blaikie, 'Accounting for Poverty: Conflicting Constructions of Family Survival in Scotland, 1855–1925', *Journal of Historical Sociology*, 18:3 (2005), 202–26.

61 Blaikie, *Illegitimacy*, pp. 225–6.

62 Rothiemay KSMB, 9 September 1827. In Rothiemay, no minutes exist between 1751 and 1827. The timing of this absence reflects a pattern that was common across Scotland.

63 The minute books of Rothiemay Free Church cannot be traced. However, as analysis of both denominations in an adjacent parish reveals, its disciplinary apparatus was identical and its pattern of coverage, including decline, was very similar.

64 For detailed coverage of these rates of capture see Blaikie, *Illegitimacy*, pp. 185–210.

65 Mitchison and Leneman, *Sexuality*, pp. 238, 203.

66 Rothiemay KSMB, 20 January 1833, 13 September 1835, 31 December 1837, 4 May 1873, 1 September 1890.

67 Rothiemay KSMB, 10 June 1860, 13 August 1894, 17 February 1900.

68 Henderson, *Scottish Ruling Elder*, pp. 246–7; Rothiemay KSMB 4 August 1895; Clark, *Church Discipline*, p. 166. The Act of the General Assembly 1902 (VIII) acknowledged that the Form of Process had fallen into desuetude, attempting to replace it with a series of amendments that recognised the private nature of dealings.

69 Henderson, *Scottish Ruling Elder*, p. 232, suggests that this also affected the role of the elder: 'In the latter part of the century there is abundant testimony that though the duties of the Scottish elder were not in detail what they had once been, the emphasis had come to be laid more upon the spiritual function and less upon the merely administrative'.

70 Boyd, *Scottish Church Attitudes*, p. 158.

71 B. Wilson, *Religion in Secular Society* (London, 1966), p. xiv.

72 Mitchison and Leneman, *Sexuality*, p. 182.

73 Handfasting involved a ceremony of joining hands and exchanging consents to be married at a later date. However, the commonly held belief that this was a trial marriage lasting for a year and a day has been discredited, see: A. E. Anton, '"Handfasting" in Scotland', *Scottish Historical Review*, 37 (1958), 89–102. On the distinctions between regular and irregular marriage, see Mitchison and Leneman, *Sexuality*, pp. 79–133, and Smout, 'Scottish Marriage'.

74 W. Alexander, *Notes and Sketches Illustrative of Northern Rural Life in the Eighteenth Century* (Edinburgh, 1877), p. 213; Blaikie, *Illegitimacy*, p. 103.

75 Cf. E. Shorter, 'Female Emancipation, Birth Control and Fertility in European History', *American Historical Review*, 78 (1973), 605–40.

76 T. M. Devine, 'Scottish Farm Labour in the Era of Agricultural Depression', in T. M. Devine (ed.), *Farm Servants and Labour in Lowland Scotland, 1770–1914* (Edinburgh, 1985), pp. 243–55; M. Harper, *Emigration from North-East Scotland*, 2 vols (Aberdeen, 1988).

77 Blaikie, *Illegitimacy*, pp. 206–8. Interestingly, the proportion of elders linked to 'immorality' did not increase over time, with six of the ten elders ordained in 1832 variously connected as against just six of the fourteen ordained in 1845, 1875 and 1894. Nothing is known of the exploits of the eldership before this period since no session minutes exist for Rothiemay between and 1737 and 1827, although Revd William Duff, who was the minister from 1765 until 1786 was recorded as 'a natural son of William Duff of Braco', 1st Earl of Fife (H. Scott, *Fasti Ecclesiae Scoticanae*, 2nd edn (Edinburgh, 1926), p. 332).

78 The class composition of the eldership was rather different in the cities, where most were affluent businessmen, thus established as a social as well as spiritual elite. See the biographies listed in MacLaren, *Religion*, pp. 221–55.

79 R. Benedict, *The Chrysanthemum and the Sword: Patterns of Japanese Culture* (New Haven, 1946).

80 L. Leneman and R. Mitchison, *Sin in the City: Sexuality and Social Control in Urban Scotland, 1660–1780* (Edinburgh, 1998), p. 160.

81 Blaikie and Gray, 'Archives', p. 84.

82 See P. Ewick, *The Common Place of Law: Stories from Everyday Life* (Chicago, 1998). Following de Certeau, *Everyday Life*, it is useful to distinguish between the strategies of local institutions and structures, such as the kirks, Poor Law and employers, and the tactics used by individuals to modify their position within strategically defined environments. The different ways of evading sessional discipline would represent one such tactic.

83 D. W. R. Brand, 'The Marriage Law of Scotland', *Quis Custodiet?*, 25 (1969), 178.

84 C. G. Brown, *The Death of Christian Britain* (London, 2000), contends that cultural predisposition overrides attendance figures as an indicator of religiosity. The significance of ceremony or custom is not straightforwardly amenable to quantification either, although the healthy survival of some life-course rituals was, and is dependent upon their normative status within the community.

85 While the extent of church attendance may be deduced, albeit imperfectly, from church statistics, the extent to which individuals believed in 'connection' with the kirk is difficult to assess. As may be expected, the churches demonstrated persistent concern over the non-church-going behaviour of the working classes and adopted several strategies to capture and retain the young or to woo the lapsed masses – Sunday schools, young communicants classes, walking or cycling clubs, picnic outings – a factor exploited by 'defaulters' who 'shopped around' different denominations for more sympathetic treatment. See Blaikie, *Illegitimacy*, pp. 198–200.

86 MacLaren, *Religion*, p. 144, who also notes on p. 128: 'A request for the sacraments of marriage or baptism led to a moral enquiry by the session, which must have inhibited many from seeking more than this basic connection with a church.'

Chapter 4

Beliefs and Religions

Stewart J. Brown

Nearly all nineteenth-century Scots believed themselves to be Christian, and the large majority professed to be Reformed, or Calvinist, in their beliefs. At the beginning of the century, probably between 80 per cent and 90 per cent of the population adhered to the Presbyterian Church of Scotland, or the Church by law established. Of those who worshipped outside the established Church, the large majority belonged to one of a half dozen Presbyterian secession denominations, which all shared essentially the same system of theology and patterns of worship as the Church of Scotland, but which had broken away as a result of ecclesiastical conflicts, largely concerning church–state relations. There were smaller bodies of Scottish Baptists and Congregationalists, and these were also mainly Calvinist in their beliefs. To be sure, not everyone shared the dominant Calvinism. There were small numbers of Scottish Episcopalians, Wesleyan Methodists and Roman Catholics, a tiny number of Jews and some non-believers (who for the most part kept a low profile). However, the overwhelming majority of Scots were, at least nominally, Presbyterian and Calvinist. Presbyterianism was closely connected with the traditional communal culture of Scotland; Presbyterian religious practices, including the Lord's Supper, baptism, marriages, Sunday services, family worship, pastoral visiting and disciplinary procedures, were vital in shaping communities as well as individual lives. Many social services, including poor relief and primary education, were located in the parishes of the national Presbyterian Church of Scotland.

During the course of the nineteenth century, massive social changes transformed Scotland, and in the process they put an end to much of the traditional communal Presbyterian culture. Rapid industrialisation brought large-scale movements of population and the expansion of towns and cities, where the Presbyterian parish system broke down under the sheer weight of numbers. Government became more centralised, democratic and secular, and the role of the parish church in social welfare and education declined. As traditional communal structures broke down, class divisions increasingly defined social identities and relationships. The influence of modern science and technology became more pronounced. Individuals became less willing to submit to the authority of the churches in matters of sexual behaviour or personal morality. Until recently, historians were generally agreed that these social changes brought with them a significant decline of religious belief. The changes ushered in a 'Victorian crisis of faith', a rejection of religion by the working class and an inexorable advance of secularisation at all levels of society. Secularisation was viewed as an inevitable consequence of nineteenth-century modernisation.

This consensus, however, has been shattered in recent decades by the seminal research of a group of social historians and sociologists of religion in modern Britain, including Hugh McLeod, Mark Smith, Jeffrey Cox, Robin Gill and especially Callum Brown.[1] Their work has demonstrated convincingly that industrial capitalism, urbanisation and internal migration did not necessarily usher in a decline of religious belief in nineteenth-century Scotland. On the contrary, many of those moving into the new urban districts clung all the more firmly to religious faith, which helped them in their everyday lives to retain a sense of identity and of continuity with the past (see, in this context, Chapter 9). In urban churches, they found a sense of belonging and mutual support in an often threatening and anonymous environment. The waning of Presbyterian dominance in the more liberal political environment opened the way for the emergence and growth of other Christian denominations and faith groups. Many church leaders embraced the entrepreneurial attitudes of the market-place – conducting missions, building hundreds of new churches, making services more attractive and church interiors more welcoming, developing church-based social activities, adapting the message of their faith, and in short marketing their religion. Scotland became more religiously pluralistic, and religion remained central to the lives of most nineteenth-century Scots. This chapter will explore the role of religion in the everyday lives of Scottish people. It will begin with the dominant Presbyterian and Calvinist tradition, and then explore other traditions and the diversification of the nineteenth-century Scottish religious landscape.

PRESBYTERIAN AND REFORMED BELIEFS

The dominant Reformed or Calvinist system of belief received its fullest expression in the Westminster Confession of Faith, a systematic expression of doctrine that was adopted by the Church of Scotland in 1647 as its subordinate standard of faith – subordinate, that is, to the authority of Scripture. The Westminster Confession defined orthodox belief within the established Church of Scotland, and also within the several Scottish Presbyterian denominations that were outside the established Church. Until the last decades of the nineteenth century, all Presbyterian ministers took an oath at their ordination to preach in accordance with the Confession. Most Scots were first exposed to the Confession as children, when they had Calvinist doctrine drilled into them through repetition of the Shorter Catechism, a compendium of brief questions and answers based on the Confession, which was taught in parish schools and denominational schools (until the Scottish Education Act of 1872, the Presbyterian Churches controlled most primary education in Scotland) and also in church-based Presbyterian Sunday schools that became increasingly widespread in Scotland from the 1830s. In one telling anecdote, the American revivalist, Dwight L. Moody, asked a children's meeting in 1874, rhetorically, 'what is prayer'. He was dumbfounded as hundreds of children responded in unison that 'Prayer is an offering up of our desires unto God, for things agreeable to His will, in the name of Christ, with confession of our sins, and thankful acknowledge-ment of His mercies'. For Moody had inadvertently asked a question from the Shorter Catechism.[2] The Westminster Confession informed the sermons that church-goers heard Sunday after Sunday, and the admonitions they heard when parish ministers visited their homes. Calvinism also informed the dog-eared Puritan and Covenanting devotional works that, together with the Bible, were the only reading material in many homes. While there is no way of knowing how much of the Westminster Confession defined the private beliefs of individual worshippers, it is safe to assume that, in its essentials, its influence was profound and pervasive.

According to the Westminster Confession, human nature was totally depraved as a result of the original sin of Adam, the first man, who had disobeyed God's command and brought about the fall of all humankind. Through Adam's fall and the sin of the first father, no one was pleasing in the eyes of God; all were steeped in sin, selfishness and wickedness, which corrupted even the good deeds they might occasionally perform. All were deserving of damnation and eternal torment by God's righteous judgement. None the less, God had elected to save some souls from perdition. He had done so entirely out of his own grace and mercy, and not because of any merit on the part of those he saved. By his eternal decrees, God had predes-tined from before all time some souls for eternal salvation and others for eternal damnation; the eternal fate of each person had been decided before he or she was born. When Christ had died on the Cross, he had not died for the sins of all humankind, but only to redeem the elect. Those whom God had elected to eternal salvation, meanwhile, he would never abandon. They might backslide and succumb to the temptations of the flesh. But if chosen, they were forever among the elect and would in the fullness of time know eternal happiness in heaven.

This was a faith that could inspire profound fear and insecurity. There was to be eternal torment for the non-elect and the hell's horrors were often vividly portrayed in sermons. Many anguished over the question: am I among the saved or the damned? There was no certain way of knowing, and the Westminster Confession made it clear that persons in this world could not be assured of their salvation.

However, the Calvinist faith, with its overriding emphasis on God's majesty and absolute sovereignty, also had its consolations. God had ordained all things by his eternal decrees; nothing happened in the world that he had not directly willed. Those he elected were saved by his grace, regardless of their human shortcomings, and those he elected would be sustained in their faith. God had a purpose for each person, this purpose involved his divine glory, and individuals should trust in him. If they feared God and trusted in his purpose for their lives, they need fear nothing else in this world. Many found comfort in this uncompromising faith, and strength in the face of danger, adversity and death. Nor was it all gloom. The beauty of the natural world, the happiness individuals experienced among family and friends, the kindness they encountered from others in their daily life, the special talents possessed by some individuals – all were gifts from God, and signs of his goodness.

But despite these consolations, many were uneasy with Westminster Calvinism. As the nineteenth century progressed, this unease grew, and Scottish popular belief in the harsher aspects of Calvinism – in predestination, limited atonement and eternal punishment – began to wane. This resulted in part from new notions of social progress, and more humane, sentimental social attitudes (reflected in the anti-slavery movement, campaigns for child welfare and efforts to reduce the number of hangings). The late 1820s and early 1830s witnessed new developments in Scottish theological thought, associated with the layman and author, Thomas Erskine of Linlathen, and the Church of Scotland ministers, John MacLeod Campbell, Edward Irving and Alexander Scott. These thinkers rejected the Calvinist doctrines of limited atonement. They insisted that Christ had died for the sins of all people and those who had faith in Christ could have a personal assurance of their salvation. MacLeod Campbell, Irving, Scott and several others were deposed from the ministry in a series of heresy trials that shook the Church in the early 1830s. None the less, their teachings of God as a loving father who sought, through Christ's sacrifice, the salvation of all humanity found fertile ground, and by mid-century began to be heard from the pulpits. It was not that ministers openly criticised the doctrines of predestination, limited atonement and eternal punishment (they were, after all, bound by their ordination vows to teach in accordance with these doctrines); rather, they directed their sermons more and more to the love of God, the unconditional offer of divine grace to sinners and the harmony of the natural creation. An emphasis on Christ's earthly life and moral example – that is, on the incarnation of God and what it meant for humankind – also became increasingly prominent in the last decades of the century.[3] The dominant ethos became one of evangelicalism, a warm, activist faith, with a passionate conviction that Christians were called to proclaim the gospel to all in the hope that all could be saved.

'The continuous earnest struggle of Scotch thought', observed a writer in the *Contemporary Review* of 1872, 'to escape from the harsher points of the [Westminster] Confessional theology has been nowhere without result'.[4] As belief in the harsher points of Calvinism waned, the larger Presbyterian denominations eased the terms of subscription to the Westminster Confession by new ministers. The United Presbyterian Church adopted a declaratory act in 1879, the Free Church adopted a similar declaratory act in 1892 and the Church of Scotland altered its formula of subscription in 1910. These acts made it possible for new ministers to declare at their ordinations that the Westminster Confession conveyed the essentials of the Faith, without having to state which doctrines they viewed as essential and which they did not. It was clear that many new ministers no longer viewed limited atonement, predestination or eternal punishment as essential to their Faith. Probably most late Victorian Scots were happy that their preachers increasingly 'buried the dry bones of Calvinism'.[5] At the same time, there was also a feeling that with their focus on Christian action in this world and growing silence on questions of predestination and hell, late nineteenth-century Presbyterian preachers were neglecting what was one of the most pressing questions for many people – that is, what happens when we die? 'The Church', observed the Church of Scotland minister, Norman Maclean, early in the twentieth century, 'gives no answer to the question, "Where are our Dead?"'.[6]

WORSHIP

The regular expression of faith was Sunday worship. As the nineteenth century opened, worship in the large majority of Scottish churches was defined by the Westminster Directory, which had been adopted by the Church of Scotland in 1647 and continued to define worship in both the established Church and the other Presbyterian denominations. Services included the congregational singing of Psalms, the reading of passages of Scripture, long, extempore prayers given by the minister (which could last from twenty to forty minutes), the recitation of the Lord's Prayer, a sermon and a benediction. Early in the century, churches would generally have two services, in the morning and the afternoon, while some also had an evening service. However, as the century went on, the afternoon and evening services became rare, except in the larger towns and cities. The centrepiece of all Presbyterian services was the sermon. At the beginning of the century, sermons were long, normally an hour or more in length. Some preachers gave their sermons in series, progressing through a book of the Bible passage by passage on consecutive Sundays; each series could take a year or more to complete. Sermons were usually given extempore, as most congregations disliked and distrusted 'read' sermons: they believed their preachers should be directly inspired by the Holy Spirit. However, in the more fashionable urban churches, preachers were increasingly reading their sermons from prepared texts. For while extempore sermons could be profoundly moving, they could also often ramble on, with repetitions, tired phrases, and theological jargon that polite middle-class town congregations could find irksome.[7]

Early nineteenth-century church interiors were generally simple and austere, with white-washed or grey stone walls, plain glass windows, stiff-backed pews, a prominent, high pulpit, and often a long communion table, which was normally placed against a side wall during regular services. As the century opened, congregations sat while singing the Psalms and stood for prayer. This was reversed in most churches later in the century, much to the consternation of traditionalists. There was no instrumental music in early nineteenth-century Scottish Presbyterian services. Several gifted Church of Scotland ministers had produced metrical paraphrases of the Psalms in the eighteenth century; these were of great poetic power, although they were never officially adopted by the Church.[8] In the singing of Psalms, a precentor would first sing a line, which would then be repeated by the congregation, in a process known as 'lining'.

Seating on the pews in most Presbyterian churches was rented out, with the proceeds helping to pay for the minister's stipend (or salary) and the upkeep of the church. The level of pew rents varied, depending on the location within the church, the popularity of the minister and the general demand for seats. Rents were generally paid quarterly, and families would normally rent a section of pew. While most churches provided a number of free seats for the poor, these were usually located in inconvenient places – in dark corners or behind pillars – and there was a stigma attached to occupying them. Pew rents ensured that the outside social hierarchy was continued within the church – with the seating of families determined largely according to their wealth. And while skilled working-class families would often take pride in renting their family pew, as a sign of their independence and respectability, the poorer members of society were discouraged by pew rents from regular church attendance.[9]

In the second half of the century, there were significant changes in Presbyterian worship, reflecting influences from England and the Continent, and the desire of middle- and upper-class worshippers for more decorous and seemly services. The reforms were led by a number of liberal Presbyterian ministers, and most famously Robert Lee of Greyfriars Church, Edinburgh. In 1865, the reformers formed the Church Service Society to promote improved orders of service, the beautification of church interiors and restorations of church buildings. In 1867, this Society issued the first of several editions of the *Euchologion, or Book of Prayers*, which offered ministers a choice of a number of liturgies drawn from different Christian traditions. Services grew more formal, as ministers began to follow printed orders of service. Sermons became shorter, until by the end of the century they averaged about thirty minutes; by now, most ministers were reading their sermons or speaking from notes. During the century, the precentor-led singing of Psalms became gradually replaced by the congregational singing of hymns, or songs of praise, many of them with lively melodies and sentimental themes. The singing of hymns was first introduced in the United Presbyterian Church during the 1850s, and then became general in the Church of Scotland and the Free Church during the 1870s. The Church of Scotland adopted the *Scottish Hymnal*, with some 200 hymns, in 1870, while a Free Church hymnbook was published in 1882.

The first organs in Presbyterian churches were introduced in 1807 and 1829, but these proved to be short-lived experiments, immediately condemned by the church courts and most worshippers. Some United Presbyterian churches again began introducing organs again after 1856, but it was not until 1866, after a bitter struggle in the Church courts involving Robert Lee's Greyfriars Church, that organs were allowed in the Church of Scotland, and not until 1883 that organs were permitted in the Free Church.[10] But worshippers liked organ music and an 'organ movement' commenced in the 1870s, with more and more Presbyterian churches introducing organs; during the last decades of the century, churches also began employing music directors and introducing trained choirs in Sunday worship. In 1904, the General Assembly of the Church of Scotland conducted a survey of praise. Of a total of 1,414 congregations, 1,249 responded to the survey. Of these, 1,096, or 88 per cent, reported having an organ, and 1,050, or 84 per cent, had a choir.[11] Church decoration was growing more elaborate. From the 1840s, Scotland embraced the gothic revival in church building, with new churches having towering spires, pointed arches and tall columns. This was in a sense surprising, given Presbyterian disdain for medieval superstitions, and it reflected the influence of English and Continental styles among the Scottish middle and upper classes.[12] Stained-glass windows were introduced in Glasgow Cathedral in 1854 and in Greyfriars Church in Edinburgh a few years later. The final decades of the century witnessed some major church restorations, including Paisley Abbey and Dunkeld and Dunblane Cathedrals; these promoted a sense of continuity with Scotland's pre-Reformation beliefs and worship. The restored St Giles' Church in Edinburgh became a national abbey for Scotland, and from 1883 Scottish regimental battle flags were hung in the nave.[13] The more seemly church services, polished sermons, music and impressive church interiors made the churches more attractive to the polite tastes of the middle-class members who contributed most to the financial support of the churches. However, grand churches could also have the effect of making working-class Christians feel less comfortable and welcome at Presbyterian Sunday services.

The Presbyterian denominations did not mark or celebrate the traditional holidays of the Christian year – including Easter and Christmas. They regarded these holidays as either pagan survivals or Roman Catholic innovations, and shunned them as idolatrous or frivolous. However, the observance of the Sunday Sabbath, as a day set aside for congregational worship, prayer, devotional reading, and private prayer, was very strict. The Sabbath, it was believed, had been ordained by God for religious observance, and to neglect it was to dishonour God and risk divine wrath. Pious literature was full of stories of people being struck down by death or illness for the sin of breaking the Sabbath by playing frivolous games, fishing or getting drunk. For much of the century, public parks, museums, art galleries, public houses and restaurants were closed on Sunday. Families were expected to stay indoors when they were not walking solemnly to and from church; it was a time for religious reading and reflection, and for many it was an ordeal to be dreaded. Some families would not even cook on the Sabbath, eating cold meals prepared the night before. Church elders would often patrol the streets, looking for evidence of Sabbath levity. Describing the Glasgow streets on a Sunday in 1819, the author, J. G. Lockhart, observed that 'they are all as deserted and still . . . as if they belonged to a City of the Dead. Not a sound was heard from end to end'.[14] Nor had this changed much later in the century. The son of a small Glasgow businessman described the Sabbath in the 1870s as a 'dismal ordeal for the younger generation' when 'all newspapers and books of a secular character were carefully put out of sight', the family dressed in solemn black, attended both morning and afternoon services, and, if the weather were good, 'had a sedate walk to a Cemetery'.[15] There was a loosening of this strict Sabbatarianism in the final decades of the century, as some public parks, museums and galleries introduced limited Sunday openings, in part to allow working-class families to enjoy these facilities on what was often their one day of rest.

For much of the century, it was common for respectable middle-class families to hold regular family worship, normally on a Sunday, but sometimes on weekday evenings as well. These services generally consisted of the father or mother reading a passage of Scripture, leading a prayer, and the family singing a Psalm. Household servants normally joined the family for such devotions. In working-class families, it was normally the mother who took responsibility for the family's religion, saying prayers with the children before bedtime, telling children stories from the Bible or Christian history, and seeing to it that they attended Sabbath school, even if the family did not regularly attend church. Through bible stories, the geography of the Holy Land – the Sea of Galilee, the River Jordan, the towns and villages – would have been more familiar to many Scots than the geography of their native land, especially with the spread, after mid-century, of pious illustrated magazines, such as *The Christian Herald*, *Good Words*, or *The Penny Illustrated*, produced for Sunday family reading.[16] Bible reading at home could inculcate social reform commitments. As Donald Meek has observed, poor crofters in the Highlands and Islands often found comfort in the stories of the Hebrews being liberated from pharaoh's bondage and led to the Promised Land.[17] In the urban areas, many working-class reformers found inspiration in accounts of social justice in the Old Testament prophets or the social teachings of Jesus.

COMMUNION SERVICES

Scottish Presbyterianism recognised only two sacraments (that is, solemn ceremonies instituted by Christ for his Church) – the Lord's supper (or holy communion) and baptism. In most Presbyterian churches, the Lord's Supper, commemorating Jesus' last supper with his disciples on the night before he was put to death, was celebrated only once or twice a year.[18] But it was a significant event for the congregation. For weeks in advance, the minister and congregation prayed together to be worthy of receiving the sacrament. In the days before the sacrament, hundreds or even thousands might arrive in the parish from surrounding districts to join in the sacrament, and neighbouring ministers would come to assist the parish minister. The Thursday or Friday before the sacrament was a day of fasting and meditation on the Lord's sacrifice. It was also a time in which to confess secret sins and seek reconciliation with neighbours; for it was seen as important that the whole community try to purify itself for the event. In Highland parishes, Friday was normally the day of the 'question time' when people would put questions of a spiritual nature to the more mature laymen, while youths were expected to sit quietly and learn from the elders. Saturday was given over to catechising, with the minister questioning those intending to take the sacrament, and issuing communion tokens to those deemed eligible by their theological knowledge, morals and manners. Early on Sunday, the minister would deliver a solemn admonition against persons taking the sacrament while in an unworthy state – the so-called 'fencing of the tables'. Those taking the sacrament would then be brought forward in small groups of twelve or fifteen, and be seated around the communion table, while a minister served them the bread and wine; it was an effort to re-enact Christ's last supper. While the groups were being served, the assisting ministers would preach in succession to the waiting crowds – sometimes in the church, and sometimes, depending on the numbers attending, outdoors in a 'preaching tent' (or small enclosure that covered the preacher). On the Monday following the communion, there was normally a service of thanksgiving.

These sacramental occasions could arouse profound emotions. In the 'fencing of the tables', ministers often issued horrifying condemnations of the unworthy who took the sacrament; they were eating and drinking their own damnation, while their sin might also bring down divine wrath on the whole community. At the same time, ministers would insist that for a worthy Christian not to take the sacrament was to spurn Christ's sacrifice and trample under foot the covenant of grace purchased by his blood. Confronted by these alternatives, it is hardly surprising that many believers were terrified, and before the sacrament there were often all-night prayer meetings with much anguished soul-searching. In some parishes, especially in the Highlands, thousands might attend the sacramental occasion, but only a couple dozen actually come forward to take the sacrament. The events, however, were not without their lighter side, and not all felt fear and trembling. Many attended these communion gatherings largely as an opportunity to socialise with folk from neighbouring parishes, catch up on gossip and farm lore, open casks of ale and, for younger people, flirt and look for potential marriage partners. These were 'holy fairs', and local workers took the fast days as holidays from work and might attend several communions each year at neighbouring parishes.

In the Highlands and Islands, the sacramental occasions contributed to the formation of a distinctive group of laymen, known simply as the 'Men' (to emphasise their distinction from the clergy).[19] These were older men, respected for their biblical knowledge, pious lives and intense spirituality. The 'Men' played the leading role in the Friday 'question meetings', when they would be called on them to answer questions concerning spiritual life or offer testimony on matters of the faith. In the nineteenth century, the 'Men' cultivated a distinctive appearance, wearing a long cloak, letting their hair grow down over their shoulders and tying a coloured scarf around their heads.[20] The relations of the 'Men' and ministers were often mutually supportive, but tensions could emerge. As Steve Bruce has noted, Highland folk often preferred the 'supernaturalist Calvinist evangelicalism' of the 'Men' over the sermons of their ministers and would consult the 'Men' about everyday religious and moral concerns.[21] Further, the 'Men' could sometimes be openly critical of their parish ministers. As a result, some Highland ministers developed a deep dislike for the 'Men', viewing them as representing 'the power of fanaticism and superstition' and exercising a local 'spiritual tyranny'.[22]

As the nineteenth century progressed, the sacramental occasions became less prominent. The fast days and the large gatherings at sacramental occasions came under increasing criticism by employers, who objected to labourers taking the time off from work. The gatherings could also be seen as raucous and crude by polite congregations. In towns and cities, churches began dispensing with the communion table, and instead served the elements to members of the congregation while they were seated in the pews. This practice was first introduced in St John's parish in Glasgow in 1824, and despite being condemned by the General Assembly in 1825 and 1826, the practice spread during the following decades. Churches began getting rid of their unwieldy communion tables – until by the end of the century, the tables survived in only a minority of mainly rural parishes.[23] In parts of the Highlands the sacramental occasions continued to draw thousands throughout the century, but in the industrial and commercial Lowlands, congregations were by mid-century holding smaller, more frequent communion services, with the elements served to people in the pews and without the days of formal preparation.[24]

RITES OF PASSAGE: BAPTISM, MARRIAGE, FUNERALS

Apart from the Lord's supper, the only sacrament recognised in Scottish Presbyterianism was baptism (the rite of admission into the Church). The Presbyterian churches practised infant baptism; that is, people were normally baptised before they had any conscious belief. According to the Westminster Directory, baptism was to take place in front of the congregation during a time of regular worship, and as soon as possible after the child's birth. By the early nineteenth century, however, public baptisms had become rare, and most baptisms took place in private homes with only the minister and family members present. Here, the example had been set during the late seventeenth and eighteenth centuries by wealthier families, who viewed a private baptism as more decorous. Private baptisms could also spare couples public scrutiny if a first child were born too soon after marriage. The sacrament of baptism did not have the urgency in Scottish Presbyterianism that it had in some other Christian denominations, as official doctrine had it that death before baptism would have no effect on a child's eternal fate.

Marriage was not a sacrament in the Reformed faith, though marriage services were led and witnessed by the ministers. According to the Westminster Directory, marriages were to be witnessed publicly, after the 'banns' or formal notice given at three regular Sunday services in the parish church. The marriage was then to be celebrated by a short service led by the minister before several witnesses in the parish church. However, during the nineteenth century, a decreasing number of marriages were celebrated in churches, and ministers instead went to private homes or rented halls to lead the short worship service. As with baptisms, the example here had been set by the wealthier classes and then became general, until by the end of the nineteenth century, church weddings were unusual.[25]

The Westminster Directory was insistent that there be no special religious services or prayers for the dead. The seventeenth-century framers of the Directory had feared that funeral services would promote the delusion that prayers for the dead could influence their eternal fate, which the framers believed God had predestined through his unchanging decrees. According to the Directory, the body was to be moved from the house to the place of burial in a seemly manner. The minister might be present at the graveside when the body was interred, but only to ensure proper decorum and not to lead a service of prayer or worship. For prominent public figures, ministers sometimes preached special sermons with some words of eulogy at the regular Sunday service, and these were frequently published. But there was no funeral service as such.

As the nineteenth century opened, it was traditional for the friends and neighbours of the deceased to hold a watch over the body in a private home, with the family providing food and alcoholic drink to the watchers. This not infrequently led to some watchers becoming intoxicated. To guard against this, ministers were often invited to join the mourners at the watch and in the procession to the burial place. Frequently, the ministers would be asked to say some words of comfort and offer a prayer for the mourners. The custom gradually developed of having a brief service of prayer and scripture reading both at the home and at the graveside. But many mourners wanted more than this. In 1867, the Church Service Society's *Euchologion, or Book of Prayers*, included a suggested order of service for funerals, which some ministers adopted; however, it was not until 1897 that the Church of Scotland gave official sanction to funeral services.[26]

Despite this ambivalence regarding funeral services, Scottish funeral processions were public events. Most churches owned elaborately woven mortcloths to cover the coffins; these cloths were rented out for funeral processions. In urban areas, the funeral procession of a prominent public figure, such as Thomas Chalmers, could involve hundreds of mourners, and would wind through the city, with shops closed and the streets lined with onlookers. In rural areas, funeral processions from dwellings to churchyards could involve lengthy journeys over mountains, rivers and moors. A large number of mourners might take part, with the coffin bearers relieving one another during the journey as it was considered disrespectful or even (a survival of pagan beliefs) ill-omened, to let the coffin touch the ground, except when it was placed on special resting cairns which existed along many rural tracks for this purpose. When Kythé Mackenzie died after childbirth in Gairloch in 1834, her husband's prominent Highland family organised a funeral procession of 500 men to carry her coffin over 130 miles across Scotland for burial in her family plot in the churchyard at Beauly. At every resting cairn where the coffin was allowed to rest for the night, each man in the procession left a stone in commemoration of her final journey.[27] Funeral processions were frequent sights on the rural roads and tracks.

DISCIPLINE

A defining aspect of the Reformed tradition in Scotland was the system of discipline. Presbyterians sought to impose a strict morality upon all the inhabitants of Scotland, so that the commonwealth would reflect God's glory. All people were expected to obey God's laws in this world and, when they transgressed, to confess their sins openly and do public penance as an example to others.[28]

The system of discipline in Scottish Presbyterianism had replaced the system of penances in the medieval Roman Church – the system by which individuals had confessed their sins privately to a priest, were assigned acts of penance and were absolved from the penalties of their sin upon showing true contrition and duly performing the penance. In the Presbyterian system, responsibility for Christian discipline was shifted from the priest to the kirk session, a body made up of the minister and several elders from the congregation. Elders were to be selected on the basis of their piety, judgement and learning, and they were ordained to their office for life. The number of elders in the different congregations varied, but most congregations had several elders, and there were an estimated 20,000 Scottish Presbyterian elders in the 1870s.[29]

The elders were expected to police the morals of a parish or congregation. When they discovered evidence of wrong-doing – such as extra-marital sex, drunkenness, brawling, profanity, libellous language, Sabbath-breaking, or shady business practices – they were to summon the suspects to appear before the kirk session, which acted as a court of religious law. If after the trial, the kirk session found a person guilty, he or she would be admonished and assigned a penance which was to be performed openly before the congregation, as a public sign of contrition. Penances normally involved standing before the congregation (sometimes dressed in sackcloth), or sitting in a prominent place in church during a given number of Sunday services. Once a wrong-doer had confessed and duly performed the assigned penance, he or she would be absolved in the eyes of the Church. In theory, the absolved sinner would also be reconciled with the community, though this was not always the case. Public penance could in truth be extremely traumatic for inhabitants of traditional communities, where shame was deeply felt by individuals and their families and where memories were long. Some women chose to kill their illegitimate new-born babies, or themselves, rather than 'stand the session' and endure the humiliation of public penance and the permanent alienation from the community that too often followed.

In the early nineteenth century, influenced by the growth of evangelicalism, kirk session discipline was revitalised in many Presbyterian churches. Peter Hillis has directed attention to a broad range of offences subject to Presbyterian discipline in mid-nineteenth-century Glasgow, including drunkenness, brawling and dishonest business practices, as well as sexual offences.[30] For many Scots, kirk session discipline was linked with the mid-Victorian emphases on self-help, individual respectability and moral improvement.

However, during the latter part of the century, a reaction set in and the place of kirk session discipline in communities waned. In late Victorian Scotland, more and more church members began viewing Presbyterian discipline as oppressive and unnecessary, a theme examined in attitudes to unmarried sex and illegitimate births by Andrew Blaikie. In part, this reflected a growing privatisation of religion in Scotland's liberal, urban society. Many Presbyterians were coming to view religion as a personal matter rather than as a communal responsibility, and – with the waning Calvinism – to perceive of God as a loving father rather than a stern law-giver. Surely, these individuals believed, a loving God would forgive human failings – the working man drinking too much after his hard labour, the businessman emulating the sharp practices of his competitors, the unwed woman succumbing to the promises of her lover – without requiring the probing eyes of middle-class male elders or public humiliation before gossiping neighbours. When accused of infractions, many individuals were likely to leave the congregation and join another church, or even cease attending church altogether, rather than 'stand the session'. From the 1870s onwards, discipline became largely restricted to unwed mothers, who wished to have their children baptised or be considered of 'reformed character' in order to qualify for charitable relief. But late Victorian male elders, influenced by modern novels about wronged women and by the new psychology, were growing uncomfortable about pressing these women to reveal the names of their sexual partners or confess the nature of their sexual activity. The elders were no longer confident that they were doing the Lord's work in scrutinising private sexual behaviour. There was also a sense that Presbyterian discipline was having little effect on Scotland's high illegitimacy rates. 'The end of all discipline', observed a Church of Scotland General Assembly report in 1896, 'is to mark the condemnation of sin, and . . . to evoke "the godly sorrow which worketh repentance"'. 'It is obvious', the report added, 'that this end is not being adequately accomplished.'[31] In 1902, the Church of Scotland enacted a new set of procedures, by which ministers were empowered to act in the name of the kirk session and meet privately with suspected wrong-doers, and seek to counsel rather than chastise them.[32] Other Presbyterian denominations were moving in the same direction and towards a more private religion, and in the new century the admonishments by kirk sessions and public penances largely ceased.

THE GROWTH OF CHRISTIAN PLURALISM

Although Scotland was overwhelmingly Presbyterian throughout the nineteenth century, Scottish Presbyterians were by no means united; on the contrary, they showed a remarkable capacity for division and ecclesiastical strife. There had been several Presbyterian denominations in Scotland at the beginning of the century, but by the middle of the century, as a result of church unions, there were three major Presbyterian denominations. These included the Church of Scotland, which remained the Church by law established in Scotland. There was the United Presbyterian Church, which believed that there should be a strict separation of church and state. Finally, there was the Free Church. This had been formed at the Disruption of 1843, when nearly half the membership of the Church of Scotland had seceded, in an act of protest against what they viewed as efforts by the state to control and manipulate the religious functions of the Church. The Free Church believed there should be a proper connection of church and state, but they believed that the existing British state and established Church were corrupt and ungodly. According to the Census of Religious Worship conducted by the state in 1851, about 85 per cent of those attending church in Scotland

Figure 4.1   The Black Stool (The Stool of Repentance), *black ink and watercolour, by David Allen (1795). By the early nineteenth century, nearly all cases of kirk session discipline involved unmarried mothers. Here a young mother undergoes the ordeal of public penance before the congregation. Reproduced by permission of the National Galleries of Scotland.*

Figure 4.2   Tent Preaching, Islay, *ink and watercolour, by John Francis Campbell (1821–85) (no date). Outdoor preaching was an integral part of the distinctive communal Scottish Presbyterian celebration of the Lord's Supper. Reproduced by permission of the National Galleries of Scotland.*

Figure 4.3 Examination of Doon School by the Church of Scotland Presbytery, *drawing, by Jemima Blackburn (née Wedderburn) (1839). For most of the century, local presbyteries were required to visit parish schools and examine the children on their knowledge, including their knowledge of the Westminster Confession. Reproduced by permission of the National Galleries of Scotland.*

Figure 4.4 Presbyterian Catechising, *oil on canvas, by John Phillip (1847). Local presbyteries regularly visited and examined congregations on their religious knowledge, their morals and their manner of living. Reproduced by permission of the National Galleries of Scotland.*

were Presbyterian. Approximately 32 per cent of these churchgoers attended the established Church of Scotland, about 32 per cent attended the Free Church, and about 19 per cent attended the United Presbyterian Church. There was also a small denomination of Reformed Presbyterians, representing about 2 per cent of the churchgoers.[33]

All these Presbyterians shared essentially the same theology, worship and church organisation, although they differed in their views on the proper relationship of church and state. Outsiders could find the divisions between the Presbyterian denominations difficult to understand, but for the Scottish Presbyterians their disagreements were very real and deeply rooted in historical memories and contested interpretations of Scotland's often violent religious past. Across Scotland, there were rival Church of Scotland, Free Church and United Presbyterian churches, often standing in close proximity to one another. In many areas, this rivalry resulted in an over-supply of church accommodation relative to population – as each denomination sought to out-do its rivals by building larger and grander churches, with higher steeples, more resplendent interiors and more pews – meant to attract worshippers. Many of these grand churches, however, remained half-empty, while their congregations struggled with onerous building debts and maintenance costs.[34] In the mid-1870s, the Free Church and the United Presbyterian Church became allies in a political campaign to disestablish the Church of Scotland and end its connection with the state. This campaign, which would prove ultimately unsuccessful, was hard fought throughout the rest of the century and further embittered Presbyterian relations in Scotland.

The nineteenth century witnessed a revival of the Roman Catholic Church in Scotland. As the century began, the number of Roman Catholics was small, reduced to a remnant by centuries of persecution. There were an estimated 30,000 Catholics, living mainly in the north-east or in the western Highlands and Islands.[35] The legal persecution ended when Parliament passed Catholic relief acts in 1793 and 1829, but Scotland's Catholic community remained small and kept a low profile. This began to change, however, from the 1830s as Scotland's industrialisation generated a heavy demand for labour – and drew a growing number of Irish economic migrants, who came mainly to Glasgow and the west, or to the jute manufactures of Dundee. This migration became a flood during and after the great Irish famine of 1846–51. Most of these Irish migrants were Roman Catholics and they brought their faith and their priests with them. The post-famine arrivals were often haunted by the memories of starvation and humiliation, and their Catholic faith was vital to their identity and self-respect as they confronted their new, often unwelcoming surroundings. Their Catholicism was shaped by what the historian, Emmet Larkin, has described as a 'devotional revolution', in which many responded to the famine trauma by warmly embracing a theologically conservative, institutional faith, including an emphasis on devotional aids and practices – rosary beads, crucifixes, holy pictures, fasting, keeping of the holy days, devotion to the Virgin Mary, pilgrimages, invocation of the Saints, veneration of the Pope.[36] Homes included crucifixes or prints of Christ's sacred heart or the Virgin on the walls. Catholics in Scotland formed inward-looking communities, which struggled amid their poverty to educate their children in Catholic schools, support their priests and build new churches, maintain Catholic social welfare organisations and cultural associations, pursue political programmes (centred on Irish home rule), and, from the 1870s, support Catholic football teams. Unlike most Protestant churches, Catholic churches remained open during the week for private devotion and prayer, while working-class Catholics felt welcome in their working clothes. By 1850, there were an estimated 150,000 Catholics in Scotland, by 1878, 332,000, and by 1901, 433,000: by now they represented some 10 per cent of the total Scottish population.[37]

The Roman Catholic Irish migrants encountered hostility from Scots who feared the competition for jobs, felt the migrants were depressing wages and hated the migrants' faith. The Catholic migrants, moreover, arrived with bitter memories of sectarian strife in Ireland and often harboured a deep hatred of Protestantism. They preferred to keep apart from their Scottish Protestant neighbours. Both Protestants and Catholics often believed the 'others' were not only enemies of the true faith, but were probably damned for all eternity. There were bitter sectarian tensions in the west of Scotland and sporadic violence. Some Presbyterian ministers – for example, the Evangelical Free Church minister, Dugald MacColl of Glasgow – felt called by God to convert the Catholics, but their efforts, as in the case of MacColl's outdoor preaching in Catholic neighbourhoods in 1860, could lead to riots.[38] Nor did the Scottish–Irish hostility exist solely between Protestants and Catholics. There were also ethnic tensions between the small number of Scottish Catholics and the Irish Catholic migrants, with the former regarding the migrants as overly militant, and the migrants viewing Scottish Catholics as sleek and accommodating. Despite these tensions, however, the Roman Catholics in Scotland were bedding down by the end of the century, with growing numbers of Roman Catholic churches, schools, priests and nuns, and the children and grandchildren of Irish migrants viewing themselves increasingly as Scots.

The economic migrations associated with industrialisation also contributed to the revival of the Scottish Episcopal Church. This Church had experienced severe persecution in the eighteenth century because of its association with Jacobitism, and Episcopalian numbers had fallen to several thousand by the time they were emancipated from their civil disabilities in 1792. Older Episcopalians perceived themselves as an elect body of true believers, preserved by God against the dominant Presbyterianism, holding fast to traditional forms of worship, as represented by their liturgy, sacraments and historic episcopate. From the 1830s, a combination of economic migration and legal emancipation brought a significant increase in their numbers

– to some 44,000 by 1851 and 116,000 by 1900.[39] A large proportion of the nineteenth-century Irish migrants to Scotland – some 20 to 25 per cent – were Irish Protestants, and of these the majority were Irish Episcopalians, who settled largely in the west of Scotland. The number of Episcopalians in the diocese of Glasgow and Galloway grew from about 400 in 1800 to over 55,000 by 1923. These migrants tended to be evangelical and strongly anti-Catholic in their piety.[40] There was also a significant migration into Scotland of English Episcopalians, mainly from the north of England. Many of these English migrants, and a significant portion of upper- and middle-class Scottish Episcopalians, were affected by the Oxford Movement and embraced high views of the authority of the visible Church, the sacraments and the importance of ritual. The grandeur and rich interior decoration of St Mary's Cathedral, erected in the West End of Edinburgh in the 1870s, reflected the growing confidence among these high Episcopalians – while the missions to the poor led by Bishop A. P. Forbes in Dundee or the Revd James Donald D'Orsey in Glasgow, testified to their social commitment.

In addition to the Roman Catholics and Episcopalians, there was also a steady growth of non-Presbyterian Protestant denominations. These included Congregationalists (who held a Calvinist theology but believed in the independence of each congregation), Baptists (with a belief that only adults should be baptised), Wesleyan Methodists (who believed in the freedom of the individual will and human potential to achieve spiritual perfection), Unitarians (with their emphasis on the oneness of God), Brethren (evangelicals who rejected the notion of a separate, ordained clergy) and Quakers (with their emphasis on the inspiration of the Holy Spirit). Adherents of these denominations were generally independent-minded, individualistic and committed, prepared to place themselves outside the dominant Presbyterianism and generally liberal in their politics. And there were a number of smaller, independent mission churches, such as Carrubber's Close mission in Edinburgh, which often had no affiliation to any denomination, welcomed worshippers in their working clothes, dispensed with pew rents and proclaimed a simple gospel of salvation through faith in Christ, conveyed in everyday language and punctuated with rousing gospel songs. After 1880, Scotland also experienced a significant immigration of Jews, largely poor, Yiddish-speaking Jews from the Baltic provinces of the Russian empire. This was part of the large-scale migration of Jews from the Russian empire and Eastern Europe westwards, to escape waves of murderous pogroms from 1881 onwards and growing economic hardship. The newcomers were often traumatised and disoriented, and encountered hostility and persecution in the deprived districts in which they were forced to settle. As with the post-famine Irish Catholic migrants, Jews found in their historic faith a sense of communal identity, self-respect and mutual support that was vital in adapting to their new environment.[41] There were some 10,000 Jews in Glasgow by 1900, about 1,500 Jews in Edinburgh and smaller Jewish communities in other towns.

REVIVALISM

Within Christianity, there is a belief that God occasionally sends forth His Spirit to inspire revivals of the faith. A revival might take the form of extraordinary events occurring within a single congregation or a small district over a course of days or weeks. Or a revival might affect a larger region or even a whole nation, and continue for months or even years. Revivals often included emotional meetings, an immediate sense of approaching death and judgement, and mass conversions to a vital, heart-felt religion. They sometimes occurred at times of communal stress, for instance, economic downturns that left many feeling vulnerable. Revivals were by their nature of a limited duration. While its effects on a community might prove lasting, each revival had a beginning, a climax and an end.

Scotland experienced a number of revivals during the course of the nineteenth century. In the early decades, revivals were mainly rural affairs. There were local revivals in the Highlands that were associated with powerful Gaelic-speaking preachers and with the anxieties surrounding the introduction of commercial agriculture and the Highland Clearances. These included revivals in Breadalbane, Perthshire, in 1800–4, in Arran in 1812, in Ardeonig, on Loch Tay in 1817 and on the Isle of Lewis in 1823. These revivals helped to spread an evangelical Presbyterianism across the Highlands and Islands.[42]

Later, there were also urban revivals. In 1839, amid a downturn in the economy and the intensifying conflict between church and state that would culminate in the Disruption of the Church of Scotland, a revival began in Dundee, then spread to Kilsyth and across the Lowlands, with hundreds of converts and highly emotional meetings. A further, mainly urban-based revival occurred between 1858 and 1862. It was inspired by a major revival movement in the United States, and it included impassioned lay preaching by both men and women. It also introduced a new phenomenon in Scotland – the professional revivalist preacher (such as the American, Charles Grandison Finney, who came to Edinburgh in 1859). Revivalist preachers employed well-honed methods of mass evangelism, including protracted prayer meetings, special seating for those anxious about their souls, direct, highly emotional preaching and the use of gospel songs to heighten feeling.

Perhaps the most famous revival swept through Lowland Scotland in 1873–4. It was led by two American professional revivalists, Dwight L. Moody, a fast-talking, intense layman with only five years of schooling, who preached a simple gospel message in everyday language, and his partner, Ira D. Sankey, who sang lively, sentimental gospel songs in a deep baritone voice, accompanied by a harmonium or small portable organ. These two revivalists showed little interest in Scotland's historic denominational divisions, or in its traditions of a learned ministry, but their meetings attracted crowds of thousands. Moody encouraged his followers to 'buttonhole', or grab strangers by the buttonholes in their coat lapels, get up close and personal, and ask them if they were saved. Sankey's gospel songs, with lively tunes drawn from a burgeoning American popular music industry, became well loved and promoted the spread of music in churches. The methods of these professional revivalists were opposed by some, especially conservative Calvinists in the Highlands and Islands, who believed that mass revival methods sentimentalised religion and spread the delusion that conversions could be manufactured.[43] The Moody and Sankey movement none the less claimed thousands of converts, especially among the young, and saw the spread of mission halls, street preaching, 'buttonholing' and gospel singing.

THE SOCIAL GOSPEL

The final decades of the nineteenth century brought the spread of a different set of religious beliefs – which emphasised not reward or punishment in an afterlife, but rather the coming of a future moral order in this world that would be based on co-operation, benevolence and social justice, and that would mark the culmination of human history. Some came to believe that industrial society was moving inexorably towards the socialist classless society, in which the means of production, distribution and exchange would be owned in common, and the wealth generated by modern industry and agriculture would be shared equally and ensure fulfilling lives for all. These socialist idealists focused their faith on social change in this world, rather than heaven or hell in the afterlife. From the 1880s, Scottish towns and cities became home to local branches of socialist societies – the Social Democratic Federation, the Scottish Land and Labour League, the Scottish Labour Party or the Fabian Society. As Stephen Yeo has argued, there emerged what can be described as a religion of socialism, which echoed many beliefs and practices associated with evangelical Christianity – including charismatic preaching, emotional conversions, missionary zeal to spread the good news, choirs and the singing of socialist hymns, commitment to sacrifice for the cause and, from the 1890s, the formation of Labour churches and socialist Sunday schools.[44] According to Michael McCabe, early socialist activists in places like Airdrie in central Scotland behaved very much like evangelical Christians and, indeed, can be seen as part of the mission culture and free marketplace in religion.[45]

Some socialists rejected any belief in God and denounced Christianity as a mere prop of a corrupt capitalist order that was destined to be swept away by the tide of historical progress. But other early Scottish socialists, among them Keir Hardie and Ramsay MacDonald, professed a Christian faith. They placed emphasis on Jesus as a working man, who opposed the established order of the day, denounced the corruptions of wealth, championed the common folk and called for fundamental social reform. Within the Scottish churches, moreover, an articulate minority of ministers and prominent lay members embraced from the 1880s what was known as Christian Socialism.

For them, the Old Testament prophets and the New Testament Christ had taught that this world should reflect God's justice and compassion, and that social responsibility must be a religious duty. The Christian Socialists were rather vague about specific economic and political reform programmes. They were, however, openly critical of the social inequality and misery resulting from competitive industrial capitalism, and they proclaimed that Christians had a duty to work for co-operation among employers and labourers, and for increased state efforts to improve housing, education, sanitation and social welfare.

Such Christian social engagement was not new. From the 1820s, many churches had provided services aimed at helping the poor to improve their lives – including bleaching greens, laundry facilities, savings banks, Sunday schools and reading rooms. Some, including the Presbyterian pastors, Thomas Chalmers, Norman MacLeod and William Ross, maintained that churches should take a leading role in community-building, and work to unite the social classes. The number of church-based social services and activities greatly expanded after about 1880, to include charitable societies, clothing societies, soup kitchens, football teams, boxing clubs, boys' brigades, choirs, mothers' meetings, literary societies, Women's Guilds, rambling clubs, young men's and young women's meetings, games rooms, sewing circles, temperance societies, and nursery schools – while more and more churches built adjoining halls to accommodate these activities.[46] This reflected the growing amount of leisure time for many people, as working hours were reduced through labour legislation; churches endeavoured to provide healthy and improving uses for this free time, in competition with pubs and betting shops. As the century closed, many churches were functioning largely as social centres, while ministers, especially in the urban districts, were often hard-pressed to oversee the varied social activities, as well as provide pastoral care, religious instruction and meaningful sermons. Some traditionalists feared that the churches were becoming overly concerned with social criticism, social work and leisure activities at the expense of the worship of God, spiritual growth and the afterlife.

By the last decades of the nineteenth century, Scotland was home to a great diversity of religious denominations. As the country became less religiously homogeneous, Scots increasingly found their beliefs challenged by growing numbers of 'others', who were often their neighbours, their workmates, or even (as a result of marriages or conversions) members of their own family. Many held to their religious beliefs as defining their identity and humanity in a rapidly changing and increasingly anonymous urban-industrial society; this was perhaps most pronounced among urban Irish Catholic or Jewish migrants, but it was no less true of Gaelic-speaking Highland Free Church Presbyterians coming into the cities. In an urbanising Scotland, churches competed with each other for members in what began to resemble a free marketplace in religion. Late nineteenth-century Scotland was home to a vigorous evangelical culture, what Callum Brown has termed a 'salvation economy'.[47] In this marketplace of beliefs, people increasingly chose to attend a particular church, not necessarily because their parents or grandparents had adhered to that faith community, but because they themselves were personally attracted by the personality or preaching of a particular minister, or because they were comfortable with the liturgy or architecture, were drawn to the young peoples' meetings, sports teams, or reading groups, or felt welcomed by the members of the congregation.[48]

Many, to be sure, did not attend church regularly. The Census of Religious Worship conducted in 1851 suggested that only about 35 per cent of the Scottish adult population attended church on the census Sunday. But these statistics were very imperfect, with large numbers of churches declining to make any return and many providing only rough estimates of attendance. And it is certainly not the case that those not attending church were without Christian belief. There were many reasons for irregular church attendance. Many did not attend regularly because they lacked the proper Sunday clothes, or could not afford to pay pew rents, or disliked what they viewed as a certain snobbery among church goers, or were servants, or were elderly or infirm or did not view regular church attendance as necessary for the believer. Some have argued that the nineteenth century was a time of church decline in Scotland. However, recent work by Callum Brown and others has indicated that, roused by the prevalent Victorian evangelical culture and 'salvation economy', nineteenth-century church attendances held up well and may have increased. 'Despite the tremendous population growth of the nineteenth century', Brown has observed of Scotland, 'church membership was growing faster – probably more than doubling between 1830 and 1914 – and doing so during the height of industrialisation and urban growth.'[49]

NON-CHRISTIAN BELIEFS

Although nineteenth-century Scotland had been predominantly Christian for over a thousand years, many beliefs persisted that were not Christian and that were probably far older than the Christian faith. These included belief in spirits, premonitions, healing wells and various forms of magic. While such beliefs were found throughout most of nineteenth-century Scotland, they were especially prevalent in the more remote Highlands and Islands, where the influences of scientific thought were less prevalent and where communities often felt vulnerable and powerless in the face of economic and technological changes coming from outside. Such beliefs could provide people with a sense that they could be empowered by spiritual forces that only they appreciated or understood, and the beliefs survived, sometimes against and sometimes alongside the powerful influence of nineteenth-century evangelical Christianity.

SPIRITS

For some Scots, the world was inhabited not solely by the visible beings of the natural world, but also by beings who were not normally visible to the human eye, and who were more spiritual than physical. They were no less real for all that. Among such spiritual beings were the earth spirits or fairy folk, an ancient, almost forgotten race of social beings who lived within the earth, sometimes in mounds, who resembled humans in many respects, and who could communicate with people.[50] The earth spirits normally moved about imperceptibly, but they did occasionally appear in a bodily form. They also existed in a different dimension of time. Stories were told of persons who might come across a gathering of earth spirits in an evening, join in their dancing and drinking through the night, and then return in the morning to discover that scores of years had passed, their homes had mouldered away, their families and friends had long since died – while they themselves soon withered and turned to dust in the light of day.[51] The earth spirits had the power to assist those they favoured, but they could also exercise malign influence. They could, for example, cause cows not to give milk, kill cattle mysteriously (with an invisible fairy dart), or steal away children or nursing mothers, sometimes leaving a changeling, or double, in place of the real child or mother. They could also fill a person's senses with delusions and hallucinations, leading them on wild ramblings for days or months on end, until the person, who was 'away with the fairies', either perished or was released from the spell, often by a sudden shock.

There was also a widespread belief in Scotland that each individual possessed a spiritual double, a mirror image of the true self in all respects, but existing in another dimension, or spiritual realm. This other, or second self, was normally invisible. However, very occasionally people would catch a sight of their own double, usually when they were alone and distressed, and the effect would be eerie and un-nerving. Such a vision could also be ill-omened, as it might be a premonition of the person's death. Sometimes people would see another person's double, which might also be a sign of that person's imminent or recent death. The existence of the second self or double formed a main theme in James Hogg's powerful novel, *The Private Memoirs and Confessions of a Justified Sinner* (1824).

SECOND SIGHT

Some people were believed to possess an involuntary faculty or gift of 'second sight'. This was, properly speaking, a faculty of *double* sight, or the ability both to see the material world and to have glimpses into the spiritual realm.[52] And because the spiritual realm existed outside the natural laws of time and space, those with second sight could sometimes see future or past events, or they could see concurrent events occurring far away. They could also occasionally see the spiritual double, or the second self, of a person. The faculty of second sight was said to be hereditary. It was also believed to be more a curse than a blessing – giving the gifted person often horrifying visions: of the funeral procession of a loved one or of a mutilated or drowned corpse after an accident. People who claimed the powers of second sight were often shunned by their neighbours – both because of fear of what they might see, and because of distrust of their visions (and there were impostors). Sometimes these visions of future events could serve as warnings: if persons changed their behaviour they might avert the events portrayed in the vision. But more often the visions were of future events that could not be altered or averted. In such cases foreknowledge of a death or accident could only heighten the sense of tragedy, as the inevitable chain of events occurred despite all human efforts. Not all visions, however, related to death or misfortune. Those with second sight could sometimes foresee future marriage partners, good fortune or long lives.

Those with second sight did not personally prosper as a result of their visions. Often they could not decipher a vision, which might be of an event that had occurred in the far past or some distant region. Certain animals were believed to possess second sight and thus to see spirits. They included dogs, which would often howl at the moment of a death, or horses, which could become agitated in the presence of a funeral or burial.

WITCHCRAFT, HEALING WELLS AND THE EVIL EYE

Belief in witchcraft and magic survived, with some persons credited with possessing special powers over the natural world. Witches or magi were believed to possess the ability, through means of incantations and rituals, to cause illness or death, sink ships, destroy livestock or crops, or drive fish away from fishing grounds. Others, however, used their powers to benefit people. Many cures were rooted in occult beliefs and practices. For example, the skull of a woman who had committed suicide, when filled with water from a healing well, was believed to cure epilepsy, an illness that was all too common in the Highlands.[53]

Healing wells, rooted in recognition of the life-giving powers of water, remained important in nineteenth-century folk beliefs. The waters of such wells were believed to possess healing properties, especially with regard to certain diseases and when drunk on certain days or at certain hours of the day. Sometimes a piece of the afflicted person's clothing was dipped in the well, held to the injured or diseased part of the body and then fixed to the branch of a nearby tree or shrub, so as not to touch the ground. Those partaking of the waters would leave a small gift, such as a coin or an oatcake, as a mark of respect. Healing wells had probably been venerated long before the coming of Christianity; during the medieval period they often became associated with the name of a particular saint and were places of Christian pilgrimage. Despite the efforts of the post-Reformation Church to suppress pilgrimages, many people with afflictions continued to make their way to healing wells, leaving their small gifts and bits of cloth.[54]

The evil eye was believed to be a power possessed by some individuals, by which their mere glance could, under certain circumstances, cause illness, disfigurement or death. The effects caused by the evil eye were often unintentional: they might result from a momentary lapse into envy or malice. Those credited with possessing the evil eye were often older women, or persons with two different coloured eyes. As it was generally the prettiest children or the best livestock that were likely to attract the envious glance of the evil eye, special precautions were often taken to protect them. An attractive child might be deliberately ill-dressed – with a shabby coat turned inside out or buttons wrongly done up – so as not to draw an envious look. A sprig of rowan might be tied around the neck of a cow, or the ears and horns of livestock smeared with tar or they might be sprinkled with urine.[55]

FOLKLORE, SPIRITUALITY AND THE CHURCHES

The latter part of the nineteenth century saw systematic efforts on the part of folklorists to collect and publish descriptions of these non-Christian beliefs. Such work was promoted by the Folklore Society in Britain, which had been founded in 1878. The attitudes of the Scottish clergy to these folk beliefs varied greatly. Some ministers were profoundly hostile to the beliefs, viewing them as superstitious, idolatrous and even diabolical. But other ministers became amateur folklorists, helping to collect and publish accounts of popular beliefs. They included such pioneering nineteenth-century folklorists as the Revd John Gregorson Campbell, Free Church minister of Tiree and Coll, and the Revd James McDougall, Church of Scotland minister of Duror. Some ministers – including Dr John Kennedy, the highly respected Free Church minister of Dingwall – believed that such supernatural phenomena as second sight were manifestations of God and part of the divine order.[56] Indeed, some of the Highland Presbyterian 'Men' were said to have the gift of second sight.[57] It was also widely believed that St Columba, the great sixth-century evangelist of Scotland, had possessed second sight.[58]

The late nineteenth-century Glasgow-based author and poet, William Sharp, who sometimes wrote under the name 'Fiona MacLeod', was one of those who took an active role in preserving Highland folk beliefs; for him, these were expressions of an ancient but fading Celtic wisdom. Sharp had connections with Irish authors, including W. B. Yeats and Augusta, Lady Gregory, who were, at this time, promoting similar notions of a 'Celtic Twilight' in Ireland. There was also a significant Scottish interest in spiritualism, or the communication with the spirits of the dead through mediums. The spiritualist movement reached Britain in the early 1850s from the United States and quickly gained a following, especially in urban districts and among the working classes; it offered, for many, proof that there was an afterlife and that relationships in this world would continue into the next. Glasgow alone had some 250 practising spiritualists and mediums in 1880, while Scotland produced some celebrated nineteenth-century mediums, among them Daniel Dunglas Home.[59] The last years of the century saw a small number of Scots exploring still other belief systems, including theosophy, eastern religions and esoteric magic.

CONCLUSION

Nineteenth-century Scottish beliefs and religious practices were diverse. Most nineteenth-century Scots sought answers to the perennial questions of the meaning of life and death within the framework of the Calvinist belief system. But that system, as we have seen, underwent a sea-change during the course of the nineteenth century and many key points faded away entirely. There was a shift away from belief in limited atonement, total depravity, predestination and eternal punishment, and towards the love of God, the moral example of Christ and human flourishing in this world. People agonised less over whether they were among the saved or the damned, and focused more on how their Christian faith could help them, as individuals, to lead more fulfilling lives or how God might help bring them through illness or adversity. Reformed religion became less law-bound and more humane, less rooted in dogmas and more in feeling and sentiment. The traditional communal aspects of Presbyterianism – communion seasons, kirk session discipline – waned, and in many ways religion became more private, more a matter of individual conscience and taste. But this privatisation of religion should not be exaggerated. For there were also new forms of communal expression of the faith, including the many charitable societies, youth clubs, choirs, reading groups and temperance societies, which met in churches and church halls and helped to keep the churches at the centre of community life. For many in the rapidly growing towns and cities, including Catholic migrants from Ireland, Presbyterian migrants from the Highlands and Jewish migrants from Eastern Europe, religion provided communal identity and mutual support in an unfamiliar environment.

The competition among both the various Presbyterian denominations and the growing number of non-Presbyterian denominations gave nineteenth-century Scottish religion a dynamic character. Different churches competed for members within a free marketplace for religion. This competition promoted aggressive home missionary activity, especially in the cities, and also efforts to make worship more appealing. This competitive atmosphere, combined with evangelical commitments and the new methods of mass revivalism, helped ensure that Christianity remained a vibrant part of Scottish everyday life. The religious divisions, to be sure, had their negative effects, not least in the sectarian animosities between

Protestants and Catholics that darkened much social life, especially in the west of Scotland. But whether liberal or strict, tolerant or bigoted, expansive or inward-looking, religious beliefs and practices were important to individual lives throughout the nineteenth century. These included not only Christian teachings, but also beliefs in premonitions, spirits and communications with the dead. It was true that ministers and commentators expressed concern about the number of people, especially among the working classes, who did not attend church. None the less, most of these non-attenders did apparently retain their Christian faith, and most had some connection with a church. The real decline in religious belief and practice in Scotland would not come until the next century.

Notes

1 For the changing interpretations of the timing of secularisation, see C. G. Brown, *The Death of Christian Britain* (London, 2001), pp. 16–34; S. Bruce (ed.), *Religion and Modernization: Sociologists and Historians Debate the Secularization Thesis* (Oxford, 1992).

2 A. L. Drummond and J. Bulloch, *The Church in Late Victorian Scotland 1874–1900* (Edinburgh, 1978), p. 15.

3 A. C. Cheyne, *The Transforming of the Kirk: Victorian Scotland's Religious Revolution* (Edinburgh, 1983), pp. 60–85.

4 Cheyne, *Transforming of the Kirk*, p. 71.

5 N. Maclean, *Set Free* (London, 1949), p. 108.

6 Quoted in T. C. Smout, *A Century of the Scottish People 1830–1950* (London, 1986), p. 195.

7 T. Leishman, 'The Ritual of the Church', in R. H. Story (ed.), *The Church of Scotland, Past and Present*, vol. 5 (London, 1890–2), pp. 420–1; R. Lee, *The Reform of the Church of Scotland in Worship, Government, and Doctrine* (Edinburgh, 1866), pp. 1–83.

8 W. D. Maxwell, *A History of Worship in the Church of Scotland* (Oxford, 1955), pp. 164–7.

9 C. G. Brown, 'The Costs of Pew Renting: Church Management, Church-going and Social Class in Nineteenth-Century Glasgow', *Journal of Ecclesiastical History*, 38 (1987), pp. 347–61; C. G. Brown, *Religion and Society in Scotland since 1707* (Edinburgh, 1997), pp. 76–7, 99–100, 111–13.

10 J. R. Fleming, *A History of the Church in Scotland 1843–1874* (Edinburgh, 1927), pp. 117–19, 202–10.

11 A. K. Robertson, 'The Revival of Church Worship in the Church of Scotland', unpublished Ph.D. thesis, University of Edinburgh, 1956, pp. 212–14.

12 G. Stamp, 'The Victorian Kirk', in C. Brooks and A. Saint (eds), *The Victorian Church: Architecture and Society* (Manchester, 1995), pp. 98–117.

13 N. Maclean, *The Life of James Cameron Lees* (Glasgow, 1922), pp. 184–232.

14 Quoted in A. C. Cheyne, *Scottish Piety* (Edinburgh, 2007), p. 81.

15 Quoted in Smout, *A Century of the Scottish People*, p. 183.

16 A point explored in the English context in E. Bar-Yosef, *The Holy Land in English Culture 1799–1917* (Oxford, 2005), pp. 105–36; see also Brown, *Death of Christian Britain*, p. 141.

17 D. Meek, 'The Bible and Social Change in the Nineteenth-Century Highlands', in D. F. Wright (ed.), *The Bible in Scottish Life and Literature* (Edinburgh, 1988), 179–91.

18 For the Scottish sacramental occasions, see L. E. Schmidt, *Holy Fairs: Scottish Communions and American Revivals in the Early Modern Period* (Princeton, 1989) and H. Cheape, 'The Communion Season', *Records of the Scottish Church History Society*, 27 (1997), 305–16.

19 D. M. M. Paton, 'The Myth and Reality of the "Men": Leadership and Spirituality in the Northern Highlands, 1800–1850', *Records of the Scottish Church History Society*, 31 (2001), 97–144.

20 J. Kennedy, *The Days of the Fathers in Ross-shire*, 2nd edn (Inverness, 1897), pp. 85–120.

21 S. Bruce, 'Social Change and Collective Behaviour: the Revival in Eighteenth-century Ross-Shire', *British Journal of Sociology*, 34:4 (December 1983), 567–8.

22 Maclean, *Life of James Cameron Lees*, pp. 60–7; P. C. Simpson, *The Life of Principal Rainy*, 2 vols (London, 1909), vol. 1, p. 444.

23 H. Sefton, 'Occasions in the Reformed Church', in C. MacLean and K. Veitch (eds), *Scottish Life and Society: a Compendium of Scottish Ethnology: Religion* (Edinburgh, 2006), p. 471.

24 G. B. Burnet, *The Holy Communion in the Reformed Church of Scotland 1560–1960* (Edinburgh, 1960), pp. 277–91.

25 Sefton, 'Occasions in the Reformed Church', pp. 474–6; K. M. Boyd, *Scottish Church Attitudes to Sex, Marriage and the Family 1850–1914* (Edinburgh, 1980), pp. 46–69.

26 Leishman, 'The Ritual of the Church', pp. 413–15; Sefton, 'Occasions in the Reformed Church', pp. 477–8.

27 J. Mackenzie, *Pigeon Holes of Memory: the Life and Times of Dr John Mackenzie (1803–1886)*, C. B. Shaw (ed.) (London, 1988), pp. 205–10.

28 For the system of kirk session discipline, see I. M. Clark, *A History of Church Discipline in Scotland* (Aberdeen, 1929), pp. 85–186; G. D. Henderson, *The Scottish Ruling Elder* (London, 1935), pp. 100–45; A. Edgar, 'The Discipline of the Church of Scotland', in Story (ed.), *The Church of Scotland*, pp. 427–556.

29 I. H. Murray, *A Scottish Christian Heritage* (Edinburgh, 2006), p. 341.

30 P. Hillis, *The Barony of Glasgow: a Window onto Church and People in Nineteenth-century Scotland* (Edinburgh, 2007), pp. 129–40.

31 'Report of the Commission on the Religious Condition of the People', (1896), quoted in Boyd, *Scottish Church Attitudes*, p. 118.

32 S. J. Brown, 'No More "Standing the Session": Gender and the End of Corporate Discipline in the Church of Scotland, c.1890–1930', in R. N. Swanson (ed.), *Gender and Christian Religion. Studies in Church History, vol. 34* (Woodbridge, 1998), pp. 447–60.

33 Brown, *Religion and Society*, p. 45.

34 R. Gill, *The Myth of the Empty Church* (London, 1993), p. 72.

35 J. McCaffrey, 'Roman Catholics in Scotland in the Nineteenth and Twentieth Centuries', *Records of the Scottish Church History Society*, 21 (1983), 275.

36 E. Larkin, 'The Devotional Revolution in Ireland, 1850–75', *American Historical Review*, 77 (June 1972), 625–52.

37 Larkin, 'The Devotional Revolution in Ireland', p. 276.

38 D. MacColl, *Among the Masses; or, Work in the Wynds* (London, 1867), pp. 320–7.

39 R. Strong, *Episcopalianism in Nineteenth-Century Scotland* (Oxford, 2002), p. 29.

40 I. Meredith, 'Irish Protestant Migrants in the Scottish Episcopal Diocese of Glasgow and Galloway, 1817–1929', unpublished Ph.D. thesis, University of Durham, 2007, pp. 101–31.

41 T. M. Devine, *The Scottish Nation 1700–2000* (London, 1999), pp. 518–22; K. E. Collins (ed.), *Aspects of Scottish Jewry* (Glasgow, 1987).

42 D. Meek, 'Gaelic Bible, Revival and Mission: the Spiritual Rebirth of the Nineteenth-century Highlands', in J. Kirk (ed.), *The Church in the Highlands* (Edinburgh, 1998), pp. 114–32.

43 K. R. Ross, 'Calvinists in Controversy: John Kennedy, Horatius Bonar and the Moody Mission of 1873–74', *Scottish Bulletin of Evangelical Theology*, 9 (1991), 51–63.

44 S. Yeo, 'A New Life: the Religion of Socialism in Britain, 1883–1896', *History Workshop: A Journal of Socialist Historians*, 4 (Autumn 1977), 5–56.

45 M. A. McCabe, 'A Question of Culture? Evangelicalism and the Failure of Socialist Revivalism in Airdrie, c.1890–1914', *Records of the Scottish Church History Society*, 29 (1999), 107–18.

46 Brown, *Religion and Society*, pp. 105–6.

47 Brown, *Death of Christian Britain*, pp. 35–57.

48 This is explored during the late nineteenth century in C. G. Brown and J. D. Stephenson, '"Sprouting Wings?" Women and Religion in Scotland, c. 1890–1950', in E. Breitenbach and E. Gordon (eds), *Out of Bounds: Women in Scotland in the Nineteenth and Twentieth Centuries* (Edinburgh, 1992).

49 C. G. Brown, 'Religion, Class and Church Growth', in W. H. Fraser and R. J. Morris (eds), *People and Society in Scotland, vol II, 1830–1914* (Edinburgh, 1990), 313.

50 J. G. Campbell, *The Gaelic Otherworld: John Gregorson Campbell's Superstitions of the Highlands and Islands of Scotland (1900) and Witchcraft and Second Sight in the Highlands and Islands (1902)*, R. Black (ed.) (Edinburgh, 2005), pp. 1–81; J. M. McPherson, *Primitive Beliefs in the North-east of Scotland* (London, 1929), pp. 96–107.

51 Campbell, *Gaelic Otherworld*, pp. 33–5.

52 J. MacInnes, 'The Seer in Gaelic Tradition', and E. Watt, 'Some Personal Experiences of the Second Sight', in H. E. Davidson (ed.), *The Seer in Celtic and Other Traditions* (Edinburgh, 1989), pp. 10–36; A. Ross, *The Folklore of the Scottish Highlands* (London, 1976), pp. 33–62; Campbell, *Gaelic Otherworld*, pp. 240–70.

53 Ross, *Folklore of the Scottish Highlands*, pp. 80–3; Campbell, *Gaelic Otherworld*, pp. 153–8, 172–233; McPherson, *Primitive Beliefs*, pp. 147–262.

54 Campbell, *Gaelic Otherworld*, pp. 228–9; McPherson, *Primitive Beliefs*, pp. 37–60.

55 Campbell, *Gaelic Otherworld*, pp. 201–5; Ross, *Folklore of the Scottish Highlands*, pp. 84–91; R. C. MacLagan, *The Evil Eye in the Western Highlands* (London, 1902).

56 D. Davis, 'Contexts of Ambivalence: the Folklorist Activities of Nineteenth-century Scottish Highland Ministers', *Folklore*, 103 (1992), 207–21.

57 Paton, 'Myth and Reality', p. 104.

58 J. MacQueen, 'The Saint as Seer: Adomnan's Account of Columba', in Davidson, (ed.), *The Seer in Celtic and Other Traditions*, pp. 37–51.

59 S. J. Sutcliffe, 'Alternative Beliefs and Practices', in MacLean and Veitch (eds), *Scottish Life and Society: a Compendium of Scottish Ethnology: Religion*, p. 318.

Chapter 5

Movement, Transport and Tourism

Alastair Durie

Travelling for health and pleasure, as well as for business, is so different now.
William Alexander, *Johnny Gibb of Gushetneuk* (1870).

INTRODUCTION

The journalist and author William Alexander was born in 1826 into a world of foot, horse and water travel. By 1870, when the novel *Johnny Gibb of Gushetneuk* was published, as he recognised, it was a much-changed world from his childhood, one in which he could travel further and faster than his father could ever have managed, and at no more cost. A key element was the coming of the railways to and throughout his own part of Scotland, to Aberdeen itself in 1850, to the county town of Elgin in 1852, to communities great and small from the market town of Old Meldrum in 1856 to the fishing port of Peterhead in 1862. He may well have seen the Royal Train en route to Ballater on the Deeside line which opened in 1866. He had certainly witnessed the end of the canal boats on the Inverurie to Aberdeen canal, the collapse of coaching services, except in the tourist season, the end of the long strings of carriers' carts which had once carried goods to market, and had become aware of the ease with which the Atlantic was being crossed. It was a world which was both shrinking in distance and time, and also expanding in terms of news and of communication, thanks to the telegram and the letter post, later the postcard and then the telephone. All parts of Scotland, save perhaps the Isles, were reachable in a scheduled day, the Continent in a few more hours, and America, to which so many of his folk were bound or had already gone, in a week or so. Yet, of course, more change was to come; the arrival of the bicycle from the 1870s and then right at the end of the century, the motor car which with its dust and noise was to so upset the quiet country roads and their sluggish horse-drawn traffic. The bigger towns were already snarling up, with private and commercial vehicles battling with trams and other traffic. The degree of change varied from area to area, and was more visible – and audible – in the urban and industrial areas than the rural, where traffic was still quite light. A survey taken in the second week of April 1894 during daylight hours at the Drip Bridge west of Stirling on the Callander road showed no more than ten vehicles an hour during the week, fewer on the Saturday, and only a handful on the Sunday. There were still constraints: the seasons and weather exercised a degree of restraint on travel, as did the Sabbath. Chopin, writing in October 1848 from Keir House in Perthshire, was not alone in his lament over the dullness of the Scottish Sunday: 'no post, no railway, no carriage (even for a drive); not a boat, not even a dog to whistle to'.[1] That was to change also, in no small degree due to the conversion of the day of rest into a day of pleasure taken in and through travel.

There used to be a fashion for calling this period one of transport revolution, and certainly there is some weight to this assessment, when the situation, on both land and water, at the beginning of the nineteenth century is compared with that at the end. The roads system had been improved and everywhere the sledge and the packhorse alike had gone, displaced by the cart, the trap and the stagecoach. The coming of the steamship had altered sea, coastal and inland water travel out of recognition, providing regular services. The railways shifted goods and people around and beyond Scotland, not without noise and confusion at peak times, but benefiting both those areas to which people travelled and those from which they came. Railways were tied to timetables, though specials could add a degree of flexibility. The bicycle, the safety rather than the cumbersome penny-farthing, introduced a degree of personal freedom for many in society. And then there was the coming of the motor car which brought with it speed and danger to drivers, passengers and the general public alike. On the horizon – or above the ground – were the first flights, more a spectacle than anything else, but attracting attention. Transport changes caught everyone's attention, although not necessarily with enthusiasm, and transport was on the agenda for public discussion throughout the period. It was a subject talked about in business and government circles, within communities, by the haves and the hopeful. There were schemes constantly being brought forward, only a proportion of which (perhaps fortunately) ever came to term. There were ideas for new canals, the Mid-Scotland schemes of the 1840s and again in the 1890s, even for rural tramways (in Argyll),[2] and, of course, for railway lines here and there, sometimes if only to spite a rival company, and not really to anyone's benefit.

FORMS OF TRANSPORT CHANGE

As there is an extensive literature on the ways in which transport changed, this section is no more than a summary and broad chronology of what happened when.[3] The first step forward in the nineteenth century was the coming of the steamship, of particular significance to coastal and island communities. The early paddle steamers may have been small and slow, but they held out the prospect of travel on the water, breaking away from the shackles of wind and, around the coast, of tide; although weather and night work continued to be limiting factors for a while. This innovation, pioneered on and around the Clyde in the 1810s, was taken up with enthusiasm round the coast of Scotland, up the estuaries, on inland waters and across to Ireland or down to England. Leaving Glasgow in September 1822, Dorothy Wordsworth was struck by the 'labouring of smoke in the harbour from so many steam-boats'.[4] By the 1830s, three dozen steamers were operating in and around the Clyde estuary,[5] with Rothesay alone having six scheduled sailings a day from the Broomielaw- and others were to be found at work on the Forth and the Tay. Passengers of all classes benefited (Wordsworth saw 'grimly attired' mechanics and peasants, as well as women), as did freight; and by the 1850s live cattle no longer had to walk their way south; droving was killed by steamer shipment to the south. Steamships were to transform sea travel for business and for leisure: down the Clyde, or up the Forth, to the Western and Northern Isles and then beyond, to the Isle of Man or Ireland. From the 1850s, the transatlantic crossing was cut from a month at best under sail to ten days at worst under steam, to the benefit of emigrants and travellers alike.

Another presence, often underrated, on the transport scene in the first part of the nineteenth century were the canals with their track boats. In 1809, 15,877 passengers took the sedate passage boat service on the Forth & Clyde between Glasgow to Falkirk's Loch 16, where they were met by the Edinburgh stagecoach. This business built up, and canals came to carry appreciable numbers of passengers as well as coal and other commodities: the main four Lowland canals (Forth & Clyde, Union, Monkland and the Crinan) carried 376,224 passengers in 1836. The Paisley claimed an aston- ishing 423,186 that year, and the Inverurie and Caledonian canals would have made a further substantial contribution.[6] As Paterson concludes, 'the canals certainly kept Scots on the move'.[7] Others made their way to Glasgow by river boat. John Poynter, a Glasgow merchant who owned a mill at Greenock, travelled there and back on average twice a week in 1835-6, gener- ally taking two and half hours for the trip, but was frequently delayed by fog, or on occasion by running aground.[8]

What, of course, was to take away the passenger business from the Lowland canals was the coming of the railways. The stagecoaches were equally adversely affected, and the opening of a railway service was usually sufficient to produce an immediate collapse of stagecoach operations: the Edinburgh and Glasgow stagecoach companies went out of business over- night when the Edinburgh & Glasgow Railway opened in February 1842. The great coaching inns (and their stables) fell silent. Many country routes lost most of their traffic; after the railway line to Inverness came into use, which shortened the time to Perth to four hours instead of a long day, trav- ellers reported that there was grass growing over the main road north of Perth. Coaching services survived only for the sightseer and excursion party: as an Argyllshire land factor observed in November 1881, 'A tourist coach pays best in the most outlandish place.'[9] Turnpike trusts ran into financial difficulty and their roads were taken over by the county authorities: the toll gates in Aberdeenshire, for example, were taken down in 1865. The canals tried, and with some success, to hold back the challenge of the railways by cutting their fares, but it was a losing cause, and the passage boats of the Lowland canals were withdrawn forever in 1848. Speed and time increasingly trumped cost (and indeed comfort) as far as consumers were concerned. Freight kept some waterways in use, but not the Inverurie canal, which was taken over in 1853 by the Great North of Scotland Railway Company, a process hastened by the railway contractors breaching the wall of the canal, leaving a number of boats stranded. The lower section from Kittybrewster to Aberdeen harbour, with its bridges still chaffed by years of tow ropes, was converted into the Waterloo branch line, its station on the site of the canal basin.[10]

The coming of the railway was a jerky process, left as it was to the initiatives of private enterprise, rather than built to any state blueprint. Competition, rather than coherence, dictated the system, which explains why some localities were over provided with services. The small village of Dolphinton found itself with not one but two stations, each as solitary as a graveyard. The system had started with the early coal lines mainly in and around Glasgow and Edinburgh, with an outlying cluster around Dundee in the 1830s (built to a different gauge).[11] These were followed by the burst of construction in the 1840s which saw the regional become linked to the national, the push north to Inverness, which was reached indirectly by Aberdeen in the 1850s and directly from Perth in 1863, and so on. The last great project, though there were some light railways yet to come, was the West Highland in the 1890s, a 'latter day railway mania', as one of the promoters acknowledged.[12]

The actual process of construction involved discussion and dispute, from which the lawyers reaped a rich harvest, over land to be acquired and in the cities involved the demolition of buildings, some slum, some historic. And the workforce of navvies, some local or Highland, others Irish or English, disrupted everyday life for the communities in the locality of their works. Brawls, fights and riot were common, especially on pay day. The *Montrose Standard* reported 'a barbarous and fatal attack of the Railway Navvies on Stonehaven' in January 1848,[13] provoked, it was said, by the local shop owners who had put up prices to exploit their presence. Twenty locals were injured and one subsequently died of his injuries, and only military assistance from Aberdeen enabled the situation to be brought under control. The railway itself had an immense impact on the environment, on what people saw – the bridges, viaducts, cuttings and embankments. There was the sound and noise, and in the towns the concentrated smoke and soot. But once the lines came into operation, the railway station became the focus of movement in town and countryside alike. The suburban stations were busiest at either end of the working day, the port terminals during the shipping season, the Highland stations during the shooting season, and the pierhead stations during the tourist and excursion season. Away from the summer, many of the coastal and rural stations had much less traffic, save for lightly used passenger services, the weekly coal train and whatever freight, fish or cattle, say, that there might be.

The railways shouldered aside the canals and the roads, but while the passenger coach and the fly boat were no more, the carting and carrying business realigned itself on the railway siding, the coal yard and the goods shed. Coach services linked with the stations, while those with the means had the independence of their own horse, or their own trap or carriage. From mid-century, the railways dominated the movement of people, as we shall explore below, for some to their work, for many to their sport and leisure, for nearly all to their holidays. Yet, in their turn, the position of the railways was itself to be challenged, gently at first, and then with increasing strength, by new forms of transport. In the towns from 1870 onwards, there were the horse-drawn trams (later electric), another presence on already busy streets, growing ever more congested with private carriages, taxis, goods vans and delivery carts and the occasional steam lorry. By the early 1880s, the Glasgow system, the largest in Scotland, was carrying over 25 million passengers a year.[14] Many of the middle and professional classes came in from the expanding suburbs by train, and, thanks to cheap workmen's fares, some workers continued to commute by rail: from Aberdeen out to the paper and textile mills at Stoneywood, or from the east end of Glasgow to Paisley's thread works. Every working day found no fewer than fourteen early morning 'specials' arriving at the Singer works at Clydebank, a workforce drawn from all round Glasgow and beyond from Airdrie and Balloch. But these services were exceptional: mostly the tram systems, regular and cheap, won. Their operations hurt suburban railway revenues and caused closures; the virtually complete Paisley & Barrhead District line of the Caledonian was never opened to passengers. There was also the arrival of the bicycle, not the boneshaker nor the heavy penny-farthing which only the young, strong and fit (and male) could manoeuvre, but the safety bicycle of the 1880s. This gave a better and an easier ride, assisted by pneumatic tyres, and one that became available, if perhaps only second-hand, by the turn of the century for work or pleasure to a growing number of middle-class and artisan users, many of whom were women and girls. By the mid-1890s, there may have been as many as 150,000 cyclists in Scotland.[15]

If cyclists made the crowded streets of the cities even more contested territory, they also enlivened the countryside. Country inns benefited from their custom. 'Wheelmen' remarked Sir Andrew Geikie in 1905, 'appear to be drouthy cronies'.[16] But there was the other side: the dust thrown up by passing machines was not welcomed by householders. Regulations were passed to regulate speed and behaviour. And for their part, cyclists complained about the calibre of road surfaces, which led to so many punctures, accidents and even fatalities. A twenty-five-year-old police constable, on

IF YOU'RE RUN DOWN,
COME TO PITLOCHRY

Figure 5.1 *'If you're run down' (original postcard, Cynicus, c. 1905, author's collection). Early motorists were a hazard to all around, including themselves, as there was no driving test. Pitlochry was a nightmare for its locals during the summer months because of the many touring cars heading north, or coming back.*

his first cycling holiday was killed at Torphins in May 1899 when he lost control on a downhill slope.[17] E. R. Shipton of the Cyclists' Touring Club sent a circular to the County Clerks in Scotland in September 1897 about the damage done to his members' pneumatic tyres by hedge clippings left on the highway.[18] All of these issues were to be repeated in a much higher gear with the arrival of the motor car. The first in Scotland, a Panhard plus one barrel of 'essence petroleum',[19] was imported to Leith in October 1895. Despite difficulties and opposition from the authorities, automobilism soon became an enthusiasm among the moneyed and leisured classes, and a necessity for professionals liable to be called out at short notice: some manufacturers described their two-seaters as 'doctors' cars'. By June 1905, there were 2,382 motor cars registered in Scotland, and a further 2,156 motor cycles.[20] In his evidence in November of that year to the Royal Commission on Motor Traffic, the Secretary to the Scottish Automobile Club commented that:

> Already a large number of medical men use motor vehicles, commercial firms use them for conveying their travellers and samplers from place to place: market gardeners, carriers, storekeepers, warehousemen and provision merchants use them in increasing numbers.

The first motor bus services had appeared, such as that started in May 1904 between Braemar and Ballater by the Great North of Scotland Railway Company, but the numbers were small until after the war. The problems that the rise of motor traffic caused were many, not least to the unwary bystander or householder, and their livestock, or to horse-drawn traffic, and there was a considerable degree of resentment over the imperious motorist. But motoring was another significant element in the increasing mobility, and its arrival was felt by, for example, the railways which began to lose the traffic of the better off to the touring car. Adding to the woe caused by the loss of first-class fares – typically more than double that for third-class travel[21] – was the associated disappearance of revenue for luggage, servants and horses.

THE IMPACT ON THE WORLD OF WORK

The extent to which people were affected in their working lives by the changes in transport varied from region to region and over time. But no activity and nowhere was unaffected, though not necessarily to the same extent. There was still the daily trudge for many a child to school, or farm-hand to the hoeing field, and plenty of work for shoemakers and boot menders. There was the occasional move of workers and their families to new pastures. The feeing market or hiring fair, part business and part pleasure, with its stalls, refreshment tents and shows, was oftimes followed by a shift – possessions and all – to a new farm,[22] usually within the same locality, but not necessarily so. Whereas in mainland Scotland, the railway was central to greater mobility, in the Western and Northern Isles, it was the coming of the steamer which so altered life, and the ship became naturalised as a highway for a range of travellers, better off and working class, into and from the area.[23] Out went sheep and shepherds, fish and fishermen (and girls), in came tourists and sportsmen. The transport industry itself directly created a vast range of jobs: over 26,000 in the railways alone, according to the 1891 census, for drivers and stokers (6,003), guards (2,001), porters and servants (10,357), clerks, pointsmen, crossing keepers, stationmasters and so on.[24] People could progress through the ranks: John McIntosh, a tenant farmer's son rose over thirty years (despite losing a hand in an accident) from a workshop position to become manager of the Caledonian in 1895.[25] There were more opportunities in the railway hotels, as at Turnberry or Cruden Bay, on the station library and newspaper stalls, or refreshment rooms. And then there were the beneficiaries, including that overlooked and unglamorous occupation, the commercial traveller.

Better transport, by sea and by land, meant more opportunity to respond to short-term or temporary work, for seasonal workers from the Highlands or Ireland to go to the Lowland harvest (until the reaper arrived), or navvying or industrial work. In the 1840s, the chemical complex at St Rollox was using seasonal migrants from Tiree. Highlander labourers at the Glasgow gasworks in the winter (when demand was high) became deck hands in the Clyde herring fisheries during the summer.[26] Some went to England, and there were even previously unthought-of opportunities abroad for the longer distance seasonal worker. By the 1870s and 1880s, several hundred granite workers from Aberdeen were crossing each spring to America for work there, some of whom returned home in the winter, to cross again the next year.[27]

The fishing industry is a good and representative example of the many ways in which better transport assisted development; the fast fish train from Buckie, or Aberdeen or Mallaig was profitable to both the railway companies and the fishing crews. The fishwife, travelling on a concession ticket with her creel, was a familiar figure at many inland stations.[28] And then there were the movements of the many fish girls required for the gutting and packing, following the herring fleet, who might be switched at very short notice, depending on where the landings were. The Sladden family on a Hebridean tour in August 1911 found themselves forced to change boats at Kyle of Lochalsh as the *Chieftain* on which they had been travelling was diverted back to Stornoway from whence they had just come. They were told that:

> several hundred fish women were on their way back by rail from some other fish centre and were urgently wanted at Stornoway and the weather being rough it was necessary to employ a powerful seaworthy vessel. Having seen the enormous quantity of herring brought into Stornoway yesterday I can quite understand it required hundreds of women to deal with them.[29]

Neither the comfort nor the pace of third-class rail accommodation should be exaggerated (it was not until 1884 that the Great North of Scotland Railway Company actually got round to putting cushioning in all its carriages),[30] but for many it did provide a way to travel. There were, however, still others, as there had always been, to be found on the road, through poverty or choice: chapmen, pedlars and small dealers. On the Crinan boat for Greenock, Dorothy Wordsworth observed an old man with a huge hamper of chickens which he had gathered for resale from house to house, 'a perfect tramper grown over with hair'.[31] Not all of these were as welcome as this man was, 'all fun and rags'. Better communications, the minister of the parish of Strath in Skye observed in April 1840, had introduced into the country a variety of vagrants 'such as gypsies, rag-men, vendors of crockery, tinsmiths, egg-dealers and old clothes men'. In mainland Inverness-shire, the Revd John Grant complained that the road to Aberdeen was 'peculiarly infested by impostors pretending to be shipwrecked sailors, clerks and school masters whose health has failed, and vagrants with forged or outdated passes'.[32] Tinkers long had a bad reputation. There has survived a fascinating social document, the returns for 1882 of the Brechin Model Lodging-house[33] that shows the mix of those who sought accommodation there, many of whom were on the road. Over 5,500 people stayed, two-thirds of whom were Irish, though there were 759 English, forty-two Americans and four 'negroes'. While the largest occupation groups were those of labourer (900), licensed pedlar (710) and cattle drover (578), there were an extraordinary number of itinerant musicians. There were singers (386), brass band instrument players, most or all of whom were German (105), plus Italian organ grinders, concertina players, fiddlers, flute players and pipers. Rather surprisingly, except perhaps to Grant above, there were twenty schoolmasters. Among the miscellaneous were a dozen quack doctors, four sleight-of-hand men, two Punch and Judy men and two clergymen. Was it choice or necessity that put the last there?

THE IMPACT ON LEISURE

Some years ago, Jack Simmons offered a speculative but very intriguing calculation. The number of passenger journeys being undertaken by railway in Great Britain appears to have been about four per person in the mid-1830s; by the year 1910, the four had become 120.[34] Some of this was due simply to the increased coverage, but much of the growth was due to people travelling much more often, for work and business, for leisure and pleasure. Britain had become a much more mobile society. New flows and destinations emerged: traditional patterns faded or were taken over. The annual trip from the rural hinterland to the wells and sea bathing at Macduff in the 1830s which William Alexander described,[35] was then (and had been for some time past) undertaken by common cart. Fifty years later, it was the train that took people to the seaside, or in the west of Scotland, the river steamers: as James Caldwell put it in 1890 'The cheap steamers are the working man's highway to the sea air'.[36] The scale of the exodus by river during the Glasgow Fair was without parallel in Britain, or indeed in Europe. The cheap steamers from the Broomielaw were packed, almost regardless of the weather, though it did help when the sun shone. In 1883, the first steamer for Rothesay, fully loaded with 700 passengers, could leave at 6.20 am on the Saturday, to be followed before noon by another nineteen – a total of some 14,000–15,000 people.[37] Others went to the coast by train. Travel for pleasure and for leisure was not a new phenomenon in Scotland, but it was to expand very greatly in the nineteenth century, fed by rising incomes and more free time. It might be a day trip, a visit to the town for the opening of a new building, a big religious or political meeting or to gape at a celebrity. Or longer, perhaps for a visit or to the coast for the day or weekend, or if possessed of the means, for a month. It could be as an individual, or as a family, or in a group from work, or organisation (church, temperance or masonic, say) or a locality. But people travelled as the fancy took them, as well as for special occasions. Travel became part of life, a built-in part of everyday experience. There was the holiday which became more and more a time away for all sections of society – and the honeymoon away from home, lengthy for some, a few hours only for others. At Eyemouth on 14 October 1881, the parish minister performed a marriage, a pre-dawn wedding for a cooper and his bride, a simple ceremony of a few minutes. After the community *creeling*, they and their best man took a horse trap carriage to Burnmouth station, where they caught a train for a day trip to Edinburgh. The best man missed his day's fishing, and in the terrible storm, his replacement drowned.[38]

The taste for travel was fanned by the transport industry, which quickly recognised the potential for profit in day trips. It was an idea quickly promoted in Scotland by the steamboat companies. Dr Lucas of Stirling noted in his diary[39] on Friday, 6 August 1814 that the steam boat went to Alloa 'with above fifty passengers in her to attend the Burgher Sacrament and returned again with them in the evening'. John Galt's *Mr. Thomas Duffle* was but one of many Glasgow citizens who took an 'adventure for health and pleasure' down the River Clyde to Greenock. Where the steamboat proprietors led, the railway companies were to follow, with the unlikely Glasgow & Garnkirk, essentially a coal line, the first in Scotland. The 8-mile route, which linked the city to the Monklands coalfield, was to pioneer rail excursions in the early 1830s. Some were in the summer evenings, others on Saturdays, and even Sunday trips were offered, advertised (in order to avoid the wrath of the Sabbatarian lobby) as an opportunity for the people of Airdrie to attend divine worship in Glasgow. While it did offer a special train with first-class coaches for the genteel, some of its trips were geared to a more proletarian clientele: 'nine pence for the closed carriages and sixpence for the open'. The Glasgow Fair Holiday week of 1832 saw a doubling of the number of outings on offer to seven a day, and to judge from the receipts from the 1,250 who travelled out from Glasgow and back, many were taking advantage of the cheaper fares. What is clear is that for many of the passengers it was the *experience* of travelling that was the attraction as much as, or more than, the destination. The same sense of thrill about the railway comes across in a letter from an east of Scotland girl to her cousin, dated 28 May 1832. She was travelling in an extraordinarily diverse company, with what she called a 'promiscuous mixture' of young lassies, ladies and crones, dandies, parsons, farmers, merchants, weavers, and ploughmen. Her letter begins 'you can't think how delighted I was last week with the ride from Dundee to Newtyle in the Railway Coach'.[40]

Excursionism went on to become big business for the railway and the steamship companies.[41] Excursions and excursionists were often labelled rowdy, or worse. While they boosted takings for the transport industry and local shopkeepers, respectable visitors and middle-class residents tended to be very resentful of the working-class hordes bent on a good time who arrived in their resort communities at the weekend. One North Berwick letter writer to his local paper complained bitterly in July 1873 that 'Saturday after Saturday there are poured into the streets excursion parties, the members of which have no other idea of passing a holiday than by swilling strong drink'.[42] And the Clyde steamer services on Sundays after the passage of the Forbes Mackenzie Act of 1853, which had created the bona fide traveller, were notorious. Works outings had a poor reputation for behaviour. Henry Underhill, a solicitor from Wolverhampton, came across a large and noisy party of excursionists on a day trip from Elgin on the Loch Ness steamer in August 1868, with a large and very bad brass band, not a few of whom 'had imbibed pretty freely'.[43] Early in the same tour, he and his nephews had met a landowner at Oban very disgruntled because the Glasgow Fair 'had latterly been held, and many excursionists [had] invaded his place committing all manner of damage'. The Saturday evening of the Glasgow Fair was reckoned at many resorts to be the roughest night of any holiday period.

Yet any stereotype of the badly behaved working-class excursion is unfair. Many of them were organised by exceedingly respectable organisations: Sunday schools and churches, temperance organisations and the like. And they passed off without any offence. The local newspaper, after yet another pleasure party from Kirkcaldy – 300 strong – had spent a day in and around Stirling in July 1850, commented that it could bear willing testimony to the excellent order maintained by this respectable party, and indeed 'on all occasions by our Fife friends'.[44] Another example of this was a very large excursion of some 1,760 Roman Catholics, men, women and children from Edinburgh to Peebles on 1 August 1868. They processed, walked to Neidpath castle, danced and amused themselves, and when the time came, formed into an orderly column to return to the station where the special trains were waiting. The local newspaper was full of praise for their behaviour: there were a few troublemakers whose time in the public house led to a brawl or two, but the seven priests who accompanied the party had otherwise enforced admirable restraint. What a contrast it was to the Edinburgh bakers and their families whose visit to the burgh three years previously was still vividly remembered, and obviously not with warmth.[45]

Nor were their social betters, the mannered and the moneyed, necessarily all that much better in their behaviour. Not all were as carefully conducted as Thomas Cook's parties, although even he had some embarrassment over an incident in 1861, when allegedly an eagle was shot on his orders, intended as a centrepiece for a museum display.[46] Indeed, vandalism predated the working-class day tripper. An American visitor was appalled in the early 1830s to see the destruction wrought by some tourists burning tar barrels in order to see the interior of the Spar cave on Skye.[47] At Lincluden, the local landowner complained to Lord Cockburn in September 1844 about the damage to that historic building 'from the mischief of tourists and Dumfries picnickers'.[48] Somehow the behaviour of all groups tended to slip when away from home territory. In the 1880s, Gertrude Martineau observed, with horror the damage that was done by coach parties in the Cairngorms near Aviemore:

> . . . as the carriages passed under the trees the people laid hold of the boughs and tore them off and flung them on the road; they threw stones at the squirrels and screamed to each other across the loch.[49]

One person's freedom is another's provocation, and this was to be true of cycling, a significant form of movement which has been overshadowed by the motor car. By the 1880s, there were an increasing number of clubs, with meets, races and runs, usually held on a Saturday afternoon. Country roads, grass-grown in many places, 'woke up from their long sleep after the abandonment of coaching', said one Borders guidebook.[50] While some riders undertook long-distance holiday tours, many riders just went out for pleasure during summer evenings or at weekends, even on Sunday. Bands of young men were to be seen at the Clyde resorts and elsewhere, meeting on the Sabbath morning during the summer season with their bicycles, bent on an excursion for the day. This last did arouse strong feelings in the clergy, or some of them, who were not satisfied with the practice of going to church in the forenoon, and then cycling in the afternoon.[51] The Revd Menzies Ferguson, addressing a special cycle church parade in June 1896, saw nothing wrong in cycling to church or using the cycle to visit elderly relatives instead of taking a horse or walking a distance on foot. What he questioned was spending the Lord's day in the useless errand of covering long distances and scorching down quiet country roads 'to the danger and alarm of quiet people'.[52] The number of cycling accidents on a Sunday proved God's disapproval, remarked another, less tolerant, minister grimly.

When cyclists rode was one issue; how they rode another. The cyclist had a rough ride from the popular press in the early 1890s because of the number of accidents to pedestrians. In April 1897, a young lady, talking with a friend at the foot of Morningside Road in Edinburgh, was run down and

Figure 5.2 *'The Cyclist as he is too often regarded'* (The Scottish Cyclist, 14, *September 1893, author's collection). The speed and lack of courtesy shown by cyclists made them much resented. They were supposed to ring their bells, but . . .*

fatally injured by a nineteen-year-old youth, who was subsequently charged with furious cycling.[53] It was the pace and the lack of advance warning that confused the unwary. But the cycling – bicycle, tricycle or tandem – was a liberating experience. There was no train or coach or steamer timetable to which the cyclist was tied; trips could be impromptu fun. The pleasure is well caught in this poem:[54]

> They are bicycle men! I hear their bells ringing
> Stand clear of the roadway and look at them coming
> So lightly, so smoothly, along they come sailing
> On the wings of the wind, so easy so pleasing.
> In boating there's pleasure and pleasure in yachting
> In walking there's leisure and leisure in driving
> The big lord loves hunting, the masher loves riding
> But I love the joys and enjoyments of cycling.

Cycling began as a male preserve, mostly for the better off, but it was to change as machines became cheaper or could be hired. That it could be enjoyed by the poorest city clerk, the apprentice mechanic or the struggling student was an assertion made in 1906; it 'is rapidly becoming universal among all classes but the very poorest'.[55] Or, indeed, by growing numbers of females over whose participation there had been some initial misgivings. Ladies should sit at the back of a tandem, was one view, because they were too excitable to sit at the front, but the lady cyclist had become a familiar figure in town and country alike by the later 1890s.

Motoring arrived in Scotland, and made even more impact on life. Unlike cycling, the car, and to some extent even the motor cycle, were enthusiasms only for the well-off landed and professional classes. Although a few coach-men may have been converted into chauffeurs, the ordinary folk suffered the motor car rather than benefiting from it. The motor bus was to redress the balance for them, but not in any number until after the First World War, although by 1911 some firms, such as Hendersons of Stirling, were offer-ing summer evening motor tours. The motorist was too often a danger to bystanders, to horse-drawn traffic and, indeed, to himself and his passengers. There was no driving test to be sat, and experience came dear. Accidents and crashes, injuries and even deaths were all too common. The local courts found themselves with a spate of motoring cases involving reckless driving, excessive speed or scorching and so on. It was very different from the kind of roads' business which had come before them half a century before: driving with a single rein, or an ill-loaded cart or one with no name. Nor would any householder any longer be fined for his pig 'digging up the road'.[56] The touring car caused particular offence, chewing up the roads, throwing up mud and dust and generally lording it over the populace. Two touring cyclists from Paisley spoke for many when they cursed the motor traffic on the road between Perth and Inverness: 'the motors were innumerable and intolerable. What with the stink of their petrol, the bray of their hooters, the pother of their dust, and the illimitable lordliness of their occupants, they added appreciably to the terrors of life.'[57] Motoring did bring business to country inns, particularly those at a distance from cities or country railway station: one such, according to the Secretary of the Scottish Automobile Club in November 1905, which had gone days with not a customer, was (now) receiving eighty by motor a week.[58] But what also was becoming apparent was that the motorist trade tended to arrive and then move on; they toured and hotels could not, as they once had done, rely on people booking in for a minimum of a week.

THE COMING OF THE TOURIST

One striking difference for many Scottish communities, rural and coastal, over the nineteenth century was in the numbers of visitors and tourists whom each spring and summer brought, many Scots, some English and Irish, a few American or European. There were those on tour, the sporting tourist up for the season, professional people and their families spending the summer at a country or seaside home, the respectable for their stay at a spa or a hydro, the student reading party, the rambler and the naturalist, the weekender and the picnicker. From June onwards, there was the arrival at many places of new faces, to a cottage on Speyside, or on a croft at Lochearnhead or lodgings at Rothesay. Some booked rooms in the many new hotels which were springing up, or rented parlours, others crammed up in rooms from which the family members had been exiled to a garden shed.

People took what they could in peak season: the small sporting inn at St

Figure 5.3 'The Height of the Season at Prestwick' (print from original postcard, Cynicus, c. 1905, author's collection). During the summer, and especially during the Glasgow Fair or the Edinburgh Trades weeks, all resorts were packed to overflowing.

Mary's with sleeping accommodation normally only for a dozen or so could somehow fit in three times that number. The redoubtable innkeeper, Tibbie Shiel, explained to a newspaper journalist 'That's only about the twalt o' August when the shooters come up amang the hills. After all the beds are filled they just lie on the floor or onygate.'[59] Of course, once September was past, visitors became few and far between until the next spring. Four summer months only was the tourist season for Oban's seventeen hotels in the early 1880s: outwith that period, 'they practically do nothing'.[60] Many Highland hotels closed between October and May, with only a skeleton staff retained.

For most, the stranger in their midst, arrived by steamer, train or carriage, was a visitor for pleasure and leisure, sport and scenery, to be welcomed rather than worried over, as they were bringing income for the locals. Clearly, their money made some visitors more welcome than others: the landlord of the New Inn at Inveraray turned away Dorothy Wordsworth and her companion in September 1822 after a rapid glance, having thought 'that we were not likely to be profitable guests'.[61] Tourist spending on travel, accommodation, on food, sport and amusement, on guides and services, on clothing and souvenirs, became a significant factor. It benefited, though not equally, all layers of society, from the sporting estates to the crofters who let out their homes during the summer, from the hoteliers to the lodging landlady, from the gamekeeper to the city guide, the coach proprietor or boat hirer. It was felt not just in the big tourist centres, such as Oban, a town which was described in the 1880s as 'existing for tourists', but even in the more remote areas. The children of Iona offered pebbles, the St Kildans socks and seabirds, eagerly 'holding out their hands for whatever was presented to them'.[62] It might only have been the spending of pennies, given to boys caddying for visitors at the local golf course as at Eyemouth, or a tip for carrying luggage, or summer wages in selling lemonade or serving in the hotels. Typical in the 1870s of the casual earners by tourism was a somewhat battered old soldier. Known as *Rams Shackles*, he used to wait for the arrival of the Trossachs coaches at the Lanrick brae where it was customary for the passengers to get off in order to lighten the load for the horses. His placing of the dismounting ladders earned him 'a stream of copper', which once the season was over, he proceeded to use in an extended carouse.[63]

Transport made tourism for the many, as opposed to the intrepid travelling of the few, possible. People travelled more, to places for pleasure. The annual trip or holiday, if perhaps only for a weekend, was now expected. In James Lumsden's turn of the century poem, an Edinburgh working-class family argue in July over where they should go for a jaunt. The little lad, Alfie, fascinated by Rob Roy, fancies somewhere in the Highlands, the wife campaigns for the Fife seaside resort of Aberdour (a week's rest by the sea would 'health restore and gie us power the winter's cauld to dree'). Strapped for cash, the husband offers only a walk to Leith Links, which is greeted with derision. They settle on a day at Hawthornden and Roslin.[64] There were those in the slums or in remote or rural areas who were not part of this new pattern of life, but the general picture was one in which people of all ages and classes came from industrial and urban areas to resorts and destinations which would never have been in consideration for their parents, unless wealthy. The better off had more choice; for them there might be the south coast of England or the Continent, or a Cook's tour to Palestine or Egypt. Some of their household, a nurse or governess, a maid or coachman, might also be taken along. Those of modest means could look to the many Scottish resorts within a morning's travel, or in increasing number to Blackpool and other popular English seaside destinations. The Isle of Man was also within range, though one Scots girl found it expensive: 'this is the place for a holiday. You can fairly go through the money here. If you look at a tramway horse they charge you 2d. If you wink it is 3d.'[65] But even the poorest had some chance of a trip away to a beach, or a city or country park, thanks to churches and philanthropic enterprise, by way of the Sunday school outing or some other sponsored venture, such as a hospital boys' trip. Some communities benefited as visitor destinations, others participated only by being the starting point. A few were both, such as Stirling or Edinburgh. A measure of the recognition of the commonness of the tourist or visitor is the way in which the old term 'stranger' dropped out of everyday language. That was the term that, for example, Dr Lucas used in the early nineteenth century of visitors to Stirling: 'the town is full of strangers mostly on their travells [sic] to different parts for the sake of health or viewing the country'.[66] But a hundred years later, the tourist was no longer a stranger. The species was now familiar, not alien. Indeed, in some places where families had returned year after year, they were merely 'summer residenters', known and welcome.

THE IMPACT ON SPORT

One aspect of leisure which greatly changed with, and in part because of, better transport was sport. As Tranter has argued, the revolution in the extent and nature of sporting activity in Victorian Britain owed much to the coming of the railways and other forms of improved transport.[67] While some sports, such as horse racing and football, were transformed in terms of geographical range and levels of participation either as players or spectators, few sports entirely escaped the influence of transport improvements. Better transport allowed for competition over a much wider area, and underpinned the takeoff of the touring team, the travelling player or fan. Sport was not a new phenomenon, if usually only occasional, loosely organised and local, but some events were capable of attracting large crowds even before the coming of the railways. The races at Leith and Musselburgh had long drawn a mix of spectators from all classes, but the biggest gathering was for those held at Paisley, said to rival some of the top English tracks in terms of its crowds.

One English race official estimated the crowd in 1837 – four years before the Glasgow & Paisley Railway opened – at over 110,000.[68] Horseracing particularly benefited from the railways which not only brought to the courses at Ayr, Hamilton and Lanark large numbers of spectators, jockeys, owners, officials for the day, but also horses from a distance equally fresh. Yet the first English horses at Paisley were recorded in 1834 – before the railway.

Other sports were to benefit in slightly different ways. Shooting, the pursuit of grouse, was already by the turn of the century an enthusiasm for young English upper-class males. Steamships greatly expanded the numbers from the south. According to Catherine Sinclair, in the 1830s during August, parties of English sportsmen were disembarking at Dundee and Aberdeen to shoot their way across the moors in the (misguided) belief that such sport was free and that no one would stop them.[69] But the railways made the north a sporting playground for the rich, and the Highland lines were never busier than on the eve of the Glorious Twelfth when stations such as Perth and Inverness became a pandemonium of men, luggage, dogs, and later families. Golf catered for a much wider constituency, and during the later nineteenth century, the railway did much to assist its growing popularity.[70] Golf also made money for the railway companies, and they invested in great railway hotels, with their golf courses attached, at Cruden Bay, Turnberry and last of all, Gleneagles. They ran golfers' specials to a circle of golf courses in range for the city businessman after work in the summer, or on Saturdays. Some country courses had their own private halt, and at Luffness on the Aberlady & Gullane line (known as the Golfers' Line) it was standard practice for passengers to ring down to Gullane station to make sure that the train stopped for them on its way back to Edinburgh.[71] With curling it was less the movement of the players and spectators but the heavy stones which required carting. The railway allowed curling to expand from the parish or local match to grand matches between north and south. Significantly, when in 1852 the Royal Caledonian Curling Club[72] took a lease of Carsebreck loch near Blackford in Perthshire as a place to hold a national bonspiel, Curling Pond Halt on the Scottish Central railway was given sidings where the wagons carrying the stones could be unloaded. The rise of association football in the late nineteenth century owed much to the way that the railway network allowed the development of leagues with away fixtures at some distance, to which teams and their supporters could travel on Saturday afternoons. Home matches could be reached on foot or by tram, but the train expanded the range for teams to compete. There were occasional problems: Hibs had to start a league match against Motherwell in October 1893 with nine men because two of their team had missed their train in Edinburgh – but football fixtures became national and, indeed, international. Glasgow Rangers had not only played in the English FA Cup, but reached the semi-final in 1886. Sport made many a man happy, if not perhaps their wives or family. Football gave meaning to the working week. 'Football', as Murray says, 'could now be added to alcohol, and religion as one of man's great comforters [and] in Glasgow the more fanatical could enjoy all three at the same time.'[73] The summer holiday, the Glasgow Fair or the Trades might be the highpoint of the year for the working-class family, and for the women. But for the working-class urban male it was the weekly football. And while the internationals drew very large numbers – 50,000 for Scotland v. England at Celtic Park in 1898[74] – it was the many smaller games and their crowds that underlined the game's popularity.

CONCLUSION: THE EXPERIENCE OF TRAVEL

By the turn of the nineteenth century, everyday life in Scotland had been transformed by changes in travel. It seemed likely that people travelled far more, whether for work, for pleasure or for leisure. Horizons broadened. An engineer from Lasswade (near Edinburgh) took his family in the summer of 1851 to the Great Exhibition in London, a 'country of which I had seen nothing and knew almost as little'.[75] People did know much more about other parts. And transport made its presence felt and heard. To the noise of the motor car and the cycle, the sound of bicycle bells and car horns, the smell of petrol, and the sight of smoke from the train, the soot, dust and mud that traffic threw up, a new sound was audible in the skies just before the First World War.

Figure 5.4 'How to get around'. An unusual, but very well-equipped, motorcycle combination sets out for a day's excursion from a hydropathic hotel. By permission of West Lothian Libraries, Byson family album.

Before this, there had been balloons and even gliders. But the last few years before the First World War were to bring a new sight, the aeroplane, with Scotland's first aviation meeting held at Lanark in the second week of August 1910. Fifteen garage sheds were erected, and large numbers of spectators came. Military airports at Montrose attracted spectators as did private and exhibition flights. People started to become aware of what might be above them: on arrival at Tibbie Shiel's fishing inn at St Mary's Loch in July 1911 a group wrote that they were expecting to be met by 'Cody with his biplane'. Cody was one of the competitors in the Daily Mail's great London to Stirling and back Air Race. It was yet another indication of how very different the world had become from that at the beginning of the nineteenth century or even that of *Johnny Gibb* in 1870. Scott Moncrieff Penney, the editor of the remodelled eighth edition of *Murray's Handbook for Travellers*, spoke in his introduction of the way in which through railways, steamers and road conveyances a 'perfect revolution'[76] had been effected in Scotland in favour of the tourist. This was no more than the truth. But it was not just the tourist that benefited, it was also travellers of all kinds, and travel of every sort, longer and short distance, for work or pleasure, in city and in countryside.

Notes

1   E. L. Voynich (ed.), *Chopin's Letters* (New York, 1971), p. 385.
2   D. Anderson, *Argyllshire's Needs and How to Meet Them* (Dunoon, 1910).
3   A good standard account is still H. J. Dyos and D. H. Aldcroft, *British Transport. An Economic Survey from the Seventeenth century to the Twentieth* (Leicester, 1971). For Scotland, see A. Gordon, *To Move With The Times. The Story of Transport and Travel in Scotland* (Aberdeen, 1968).
4   E. De Selincourt (ed.), *Dorothy Wordsworth, Journal of my Second Tour in Scotland* (London, 1941), p. 351.
5   A. J. S. Paterson, *The Golden Years of the Clyde Steamers* (Newton Abbot, 1969), 16.
6   According to the *Prospectus of the Stirling Canal* (Glasgow, 1835; reprinted 1983), the Paisley canal, with twelve services a day, carried 7,176 passengers a week in 1835, as against 1,508 a week in 1831. The Stirling canal to Castlecary was projected to carry 120,000 passengers annually.
7   L. Paterson, *From Sea to Sea, A History of the Scottish Lowland and Highland Canals* (Glasgow, 2006), p. 50.
8   C. J. A. Robertson, *The Origins of the Scottish Railway System, 1722–1844* (Edinburgh, 1983), p. 143.
9   Argyll and Bute Archives, Lochgilphead, BO 43.4, Evidence to the Oban Road Trustees, p. 244: 'The wheel traffic on the roads is chiefly during the months of July, August, and September . . . in connection with the tourist traffic.'
10 H. A. Vallance, *The Great North of Scotland Railway* (Nairn, 1989), pp. 24–8.

11 Robertson, *Origins*, p. 125. See also L. James, *A Chronology of the Construction of Britain's Railways, 1778–1855* (London, 1983).

12 J. McGregor, *The West Highland Railway. Plans, Politics and People* (Edinburgh, 2005), p. 17.

13 J. J. Waterman, *The Coming of the Railway to Aberdeen in the 1840s* (Aberdeen, 1976), p. 17. See also J. E. Handley, *The Navvy in Scotland* (Cork, 1970), especially ch. VIII, 'Quarrels'.

14 J. R. Hume, 'Transport and Towns in Victorian Scotland', in G. Gordon and B. Dicks (eds), *Scottish Urban History* (Aberdeen, 1983), pp. 202–5.

15 This is on the assumption that the numbers in Scotland were broadly in line with those elsewhere in Britain, estimated at over 1.5 million in the mid-1890s. See D. Rubinstein, 'Cycling in the 1890s', *Victorian Studies*, (Autumn 1977), 51.

16 Sir A. Geikie, *Scottish Reminiscences* (Glasgow, 1905), p. 310.

17 *Aberdeen Journal*, 12 May 1899.

18 Argyll and Bute Archives, CO 2/1/56: *Road Trustees File*.

19 The actual bill of lading is reproduced in Royal Scottish Automobile Club, *Gang Warily. The Jubilee History of the Royal Scottish Automobile Club* (Glasgow, 1949), p. 1. See also R. Grieves, *Scotland's Motoring Century* (Paisley, 1999), p. 3.

20 A. J. Durie, 'The Impact of Motor Traffic on the Roads System of Central Scotland', *Scottish Economic and Social History*, 17:2 (1997), 94.

21 According to Baddeley's handbook, in 1912, the tourist ticket by the Caledonian from London to Inverness was first class 146s. 11d. and 60s. third class.

22 M. Robson, 'The Borders Farm Worker', in T. M. Devine (ed.), *Farm Servants and labour in Lowland Scotland 1770–1914* (Edinburgh, 1984), p. 80 cites a description of the July fair at St Boswells with tents and stalls covering the ground, with linen, hardware, toys, crockery shoes and books for sale.

23 N. S. Robins and D. E. Meek, *The Kingdom of MacBrayne* (Edinburgh, 2006), p. 24.

24 The comparable figure in the census figures in 1891 for the category of 'Roads', was 42,000, of which coachmen (13,149) and carters (26,491) were the main elements.

25 J. Thomas and D. Turnock, *A Regional History of the Railways of Great Britain, Vol. 15: The North of Scotland* (Newton Abbot, 1989), p. 17.

26 T. M. Devine, *Clanship to Crofters' War* (Manchester 1994), pp. 136–8.

27 M. Harper, *Emigration from North-East Scotland, Vol. 1: Willing Exiles* (Aberdeen, 1988), p. 255.

28 A. O'Dell, *Railways and Geography in N.E. Scotland* (Aberdeen, 1985), fig. 12, 'Fish traffic and concession tickets for fisherwomen, 1881–1887', p. 33.

29 Worcester Record Office, BA 9520/705/1037: The Sladden papers, *Diary of a Trip aboard the Chieftain from Oban to Stornoway and back*, August 1911.

30 O'Dell, *Railways*, p. 34.

31 Selincourt, *Dorothy Wordsworth*, p. 377.

32 Gordon, *Move with the Times*, p. 53.

33 D. H. Edward, *Pocket History and Guide to Brechin and District* (Brechin, 1890), pp. 209–10.

34 J. Simmons, *The Victorian Railway* (New York, 1991), p. 317. Simmons also gives figures for the number of letters delivered: 231,000 in the 1840s rising to 2,940,000 in 1910–13, and for telegrams sent: 9,244 in 1870–1 to 81,626 in 1908–13.

35 W. Alexander, *Johnny Gibb of Gushetneuk* (Aberdeen, 1871), p. 9.

36 Paterson, *Golden Years*, p. 69.

37 Paterson, *Golden Years*, p. 144.

38 P. Aitchison, *Black Friday. The Eyemouth Fishing Disaster of 1881* (Edinburgh, 2006), p. 89.

39 Stirling Archives, PD 16/4/2, *Diary of Dr Lucas*.

40 C. Tennant, *The Radical Laird, A Biography of George Kinloch* (Kinneton, 1970), p. 227.

41 This draws on A. J. Durie, 'Tourism and the Railways in Scotland: the Victorian and Edwardian Experience', in A. V. B. Evans and J. V. Gough (eds), *The Impact of the Railway on Society in Britain* (Aldershot, 2003).

42 *The Haddingtonshire Courier and East Lothian Advertiser*, 18 July 1873.

43 Glasgow University Library, Special Collections, Dougan MS 109: *Henry Underhill Tour in Scotland, 1868*.

44 *Stirling Observer*, 16 July 1857.

45 J. Duncan, 'The Peebles Railway', unpublished Ph.D. thesis, The Open University, 2004; appendix 7, 'Peebles and the Excursionists', pp. 349–53.

46 P. Brendon, *Thomas Cook, 150 Years of Popular Tourism* (London, 1991), pp. 75–6.

47 See also Geikie, *Reminiscences*, p. 407: 'The spar cave . . . a couple of generations of Sassenach tourists aided by the hammers, candles and torches of ignorant Celts [have] defaced the place beyond belief.'

48 Lord Cockburn, *Circuit Journeys* (Hawick, 1983), p. 157.

49 Cited in R. A. Lambert, *Contested Mountains. Nature, Development and Environment in the Cairngorms Region of Scotland 1880–1980* (Cambridge, 2001), p. 24.

50 E. Simpson, *Going on Holiday* (Edinburgh, 1997), p. 64.

51 *The Scottish Cyclist*, vol. 2, p. 20 November 1889, p. 672, 'Sunday Riding'.

52 *The Stirling Observer*, 24 June 1896. Owing to a wet morning only some thirty cyclists from the Scottish Central Cycling Club attended.

53 *The Scottish Cyclist*, vol. X, 7 April 1897, p. 300.

54 'On Cyclists', in *Caledonian Notes and Jottings. The Magazine of the Caledonian Insurance Company*, 3 (1894–6), 292.

55 *The Scottish Cyclist*, vol. XIX, 11 July 1906, p. 499.

56 Argyllshire and Bute Archives: *'List of Offenders against the Road Act brought before the Justices of the Peace, year ending 1 February 1845'*.

57 W. A. Mursell, *Two on a Tour* (Paisley, 1909), p. 37.

58 *Report of the Royal Commission on Motor Cars* (1906), p. 6.

59 *The Scotsman*, 29 July 1878, cited in M. J. H. Robson, *Tibbie Shiel* (Ovenshank, 1986), p. 13.

60 *Argyll Roads*, p. 13.

61 Selincourt, *Dorothy Wordsworth*, p. 369.

62 Robins and Meek, *MacBrayne*, p. 76.

63 J. MacDonald, *Character Sketches of Old Callander* (Callander, 1901; reprinted 2006), p. 99.

64 J. Lumsden, *Edinburgh Poems and Songs* (Edinburgh, 1899) cited in *Days Out, Night Out, Edinburgh People and Leisure* (Edinburgh, n.d.), p. 4.

65 Postcard, sent on 22 July 1914, with view of the Port Jack Bathing Creek, Onchan, IOM, to Miss Jean Gibson at Millbrae, from 3 Switzerland Terrace, Douglas (author's collection).

66 Lucas, *Diary*, 6 September 1814.

67 N. Tranter, *Sport, Economy and Society in Britain 1750–1914* (Cambridge, 1998), pp. 32–3.

68 J. Burnett, *Riot, Revelry and Sport in Lowland Scotland* (East Linton, 2000), p. 114.

69 A. Durie, '"Unconscious Benefactors": Grouse shooting in Scotland, 1780–1914', *International Journal of the History of Sport*, 15:3 (December 1998), 57–8.

70 D. Hamilton, *Golf: Scotland's game* (Kilmacolm, 1998), pp. 120–1.

71 A. M. Hajducki, *The North Berwick and Gullane Branch Lines* (Oxford, 1992), p. 83.

72 D. B. Smith, 'Curling', in G. Jarvie and J. Burnett (eds), *Sport, Scotland and the Scots* (East Linton, 2000), p. 76.

73 B. Murray, *Football. A History of the World Game* (Aldershot, 1994), p. 29.

74 S. Berry and H. Whyte, eds, *Glasgow Observed* (Edinburgh, 1987); *The Glasgow Observer*, 8 April 1898; 'from noon an unbroken procession of vehicles . . . the snorting crowd-dispersing motor-car to the harmless necessary growler. Lumbering char-a-bancs, ancient 'buses, festive four in hands, decayed broughams, flag-bedizened brakes . . . moved and mixed in the tortuous vehicular current'.

75 J. A. Auerbach, *The Great Exhibition of 1851: A Nation on Display* (New Haven, 1999), p. 63.

76 J. Murray, *Handbook for Travellers in Scotland*, S. M. Penney (ed.), 8th edn, remodelled (Edinburgh, 1903), p. xv.

Chapter 6

Work, Leisure and Time in the Nineteenth Century

Trevor Griffiths

INTRODUCTION: THE PARAMETERS OF CHANGE

Work and leisure are such central and familiar aspects of life, that to begin with problems of definition may seem an unnecessary complication. Yet a brief consideration of what is understood by both terms may assist in establishing the parameters of the ensuing discussion and in identifying the contributions of an everyday perspective to an understanding of both. The historiography of work has long been dominated by questions surrounding the wage bargain and employment relationships. While class was regarded as the principal driver of historical change, such a perspective appeared unproblematic. More recently, however, the exploration of other sources of identity, in particular gender, have pointed up the degree to which society remained dependent on a sizeable body of unpaid, largely female labour. Incorporation of such forms of work into our analysis assists not merely in establishing a more balanced approach to questions of gender, but also in raising questions about the relationship between work and leisure in a period of significant social and economic change. For Hugh Cunningham, writing in the *Cambridge Social History of Britain*, the link was clear: leisure was seen as 'the time which is left over after work and other obligations have been completed'.[1] If this interpretation assists in locating leisure as a central aspect of everyday experience, it also gives rise to problems. The notion of work as a period of a fixed and defined duration captures the lot of many but by no means all workers across the nineteenth century, while the identification of leisure with time might be thought to miss its vital characteristics. If taken in the round, free time would encompass periods of rest, which contemporaries were clear was emphatically not leisure. For many Victorians, leisure gained legitimacy through action, through which the individual was reinvigorated and re-created, rendering him or her better able to pursue the more important task of work. Historians have, to a degree, followed suit in seeing leisure as a series of activities through which social meanings are constructed. Here, however, attention is directed less at the activities themselves but at the wider forces giving rise to and sustaining them. Peter Borsay's study thus emphasises leisure's capacity to act as a symbol of the relationships and ideas underlying a particular society.[2] This was most forcefully expressed through the more public manifestations of leisure, the games and pastimes which, while not everyday in the strict and literal sense of the term, were carriers of the rituals and practices by which society came to be understood by those within it.[3] At no point was this more apparent than during periods of marked social, economic and cultural change, such as the nineteenth century.

Over the 100 years or so that saw Scotland transformed from a predominantly rural country to an overwhelmingly urban society, in which almost half the population lived in towns with populations of 20,000 or more each, both work and leisure were subject to fundamental change.[4] In terms of paid work, key developments affected time, technology and organisation. Workers in agriculture and domestic industry lacked a fixed sense of routine, the length of the working day and the intensity with which they worked being determined by the immediate task at hand. The advent, from the late-eighteenth century, of more centralised forms of production, dependent on the application of machine technology or the subdivision of work into a series of simplified, repetitive tasks, necessitated a more regular and regulated work regime. Working hours became fixed and punctuality highly prized as industry came to function around new time–work disciplines driven by the clock.[5] Previously unconsidered fragments of time became subject to precise measurement and, in a system in which time was increasingly equated with money, acquired a particular value. In addition to the growing emphasis on regularity, the nature of work also underwent significant change. Skills rounded over the course of prolonged apprenticeships were replaced by tasks that were repeatable and which could be performed with only limited experience. From one perspective, therefore, the history of work in the nineteenth century is one of the progressive marginalisation of skill in the face of new mechanical and management techniques, reducing much labour to the status of semi-skilled machine tenders.[6]

This, it must be stressed, was the outcome not merely of impersonal economic forces, but of a deliberate project of cultural and political reform. Taking its inspiration from a powerful fusion of evangelical religion and political economy, this aimed at a wholesale reformation of popular behaviour and attitudes, whereby the irregularity of pre-industrial work patterns would be replaced by a diligent and dedicated approach to work. By instilling more regular work habits, a change would also be effected in workers' conception of time, a preoccupation with the immediate and the short term giving way to an ability and increasingly a readiness to plan ahead. Thrift and foresight would come to characterise a more 'rational' workforce.[7]

This ideal extended to workers' use of free time. Established leisure pursuits, linked to an established, seasonal calendar, were increasingly seen to be out of step with the requirements of the new industrial order. Often lacking a fixed duration, such events were deemed wasteful of time, while their pursuit in open or public spaces gave rise to concern over the maintenance of social order.[8] As significantly, their pursuit legitimised the relaxation of 'normal' standards of behaviour by which established measures of social distinction were held temporarily in abeyance and, not infrequently, violence was sanctioned.[9] Indeed, in more extreme cases, the infliction of harm on a fellow human or, more often, an animal, appeared an event's sole raison d'étre. It is difficult to discern an alternative rationale for such practices as the Haddington 'cat race', the 'goose race' at St Andrews, or the bull baitings which took place in areas such as Leslie in Fife at the start of the period.[10] While the eventual suppression of such events reflected in part an increasing sensibility towards the sufferings of animal kind, it was also informed by concern over the potentially brutalising effects of such sports on participants and spectators. Where physical harm occurred, action was often immediate. Magistrates at Cullen in Banffshire thus moved in the 1830s to prohibit the local variant of bowls, which involved projecting a cannon ball across the links in the fewest throws, following the death of a man.[11] Yet it did not require such extreme events to produce suppression. Broader economic changes themselves sufficed. At Kelso, it was reported that formerly popular sports were no more 'by reason of the long hours which a tradesman must work in order to provide the means of subsistence, [as a result of which] there is a want of time, even when there is no lack of disposition, for these manly and healthful recreations'.[12] Elsewhere, such developments sufficed to extinguish long-established events, such as the games played on Fastern's E'en (Shrove Tuesday) at Kilmarnock.[13] In some historical accounts, the outcome of this trend was a recreational vacuum, filled after mid-century by a range of activities more fitted to the demands of an increasingly urbanised, industrial economy.[14] Chief among these were newly-codified sports, in particular football, firmly established by the end of the period as the leading passion of the average working-class male Scot. Its growth coincided with decades in which a sustained improvement in living standards, along with a reduction in working hours, widened access to leisure on a regular basis for large sections of the population. It was a game that exemplified the bounded nature of modern leisure, in terms of the time it consumed, the spaces it occupied and the manner in which play was conducted according to set rules. It also slotted perfectly into the Saturday half-day holiday secured by most workers from the 1870s.[15] That decade proved key to the sport's growth. In its early years, matches involving Edinburgh's leading clubs were still played on open ground, on the Meadows. By 1880, however, Hibernian had a permanent ground of their own at Easter Road, elevated to the status of 'The Holy Ground' by some supporters, while Hearts had entered on a more prosaic lease for the use of grounds at Powderhall.[16] There, as elsewhere, spectators witnessed a game conducted according to set rules, whereby aggression was contained and duly channelled in the wider interests of the team. In this way, the individual skill of the player was married to the co-operative endeavour of the eleven, so that football in particular and sport in general provided, for many, a perfect model for the conduct of a modern industrial society, whether at work or play.

The nineteenth century may thus be presented as marking the gateway between a 'traditional' ordering of time, work and leisure, and one that was more recognisably 'modern'. Yet this is a view which historians, with their inherent mistrust of such simple formulations, have come to question. In the case of work, emphasis has increasingly been placed on the gradual and uneven pace of technological and organisational change. The innovations of the classical period of the Industrial Revolution had relevance for but a few advanced sectors.[17] Even in the most 'modern' of manufactures, textiles, technological change was, for many decades, confined to particular fibres (mechanical techniques were more readily applicable to the production of cotton than to that of linen) and processes. Hand-loom weaving thus continued for several decades after spinning had been effectively mechanised.[18] Across most of industry, for much of the century, technological change was substantially unknown, so that work remained hand-based and centred on small workplaces, lacking a centralised power source. By mid-century, at which point agriculture and domestic service remained the largest single sources of paid employment, barely a third of industrial workers were engaged in occupations that could be designated 'modern'. The most marked expansion in the application of steam power to industry thus came in the final quarter of the century. Only from that point did the machine become the mainstay of industrial work.[19] Yet even this conveys an imperfect impression of the degree of change. Labour historians have sought to capture the impact of technological and organisational innovation through a close examination of the work process, adopting the perspective if not the language of the everyday. This indicates that the impact of change was often, in practice, mitigated, and that workers, even in the most advanced sectors, retained some control over their work routine. So, over the period the punitive exercise of managerial authority to instil discipline in a new, often young labour force, gave way to a more indirect approach. By 1833, the factory commissioners found that corporal punishment was not extensively exercised in Scottish works.[20] Furthermore, recruitment to and discipline within the workplace was frequently delegated to members of the workforce, be they family members or near neighbours. By thus subcontracting authority to groups of adult workers, an alternative was found to more formal, bureaucratic modes of supervision. At its most extreme, control of the work process as a whole was contracted out. Across Ayrshire in the 1890s, subcontractors assumed responsibility for working sections of local coal mines, overseeing the recruitment and pay of the miners under their charge.[21] More generally, management was primarily exercised via the pay packet. Piece-rate payments, by linking the wage directly to levels of output, was thought to offer the most effective means of guaranteeing consistency of effort. Yet the result was to allow workers some discretion over the pace at which they

worked, so that they quickly came to appreciate the level of production liable
to ensure a living wage. The more zealous, intent on achieving higher levels
of output for individual gain, were discouraged, as this was likely to herald
a downward revision in wage rates. The ability to pursue what came more
generally to be known as 'ca' canny' tactics indicates that, for all the spread
of new technologies and organisational forms, task-based working patterns
were never wholly supplanted.[22] The clock exercised a contingent tyranny
at best. Finally, studies of work practices suggest that 'skill' remained a
central feature of nineteenth-century industry. From Edinburgh printers
to Lanarkshire miners, 'skill' was less the rounded understanding of a specific production sequence, but more the experience and knowledge gained
through work on a particular machine or place of work. A familiarity with
each, acquired over time, enabled high levels of production to be achieved
without compromising safety. Furthermore, production, even in 'modern'
sectors, such as engineering, remained substantially bespoke, allowing experienced workers discretion over the setting machinery and the pace at which
it operated.[23] All in all, if work had changed, this had not obliterated all signs
of 'traditional' practice. The uneven pace of industrialisation allowed pre-
industrial norms to thrive through the nineteenth century and beyond.

These threads of continuity have also impressed historians of leisure. As
change in the workplace proved faltering, so 'traditional' leisure practices
were not easily expunged. Neil Tranter's work on the two series of Statistical
Accounts from the 1790s and 1830s indicates that recreational cultures
flourished most obviously in precisely those areas of Scotland undergoing industrialisation and urbanisation. While in part this involved novel
developments, such as the emergence early in the nineteenth century of the
playing of cricket in places such as Dundee and Montrose, it also indicates
the capacity of more established pastimes to continue to prosper. Despite
attempts by local magistrates to prohibit cock-fighting in Glasgow, a new
pit was opened in the city centre in 1835, the same year that Parliament first
passed legislation to prohibit the pursuit of what were increasingly seen as
'cruel' animal sports. What is more, construction of the pit was funded
through the thoroughly modern medium of joint-stock finance.[24] In smaller
population centres, dependence on elite patronage rendered local practices
more vulnerable to change, particularly as ideas of 'progress' associated with
the Reformation of Manners encouraged the rejection of certain animal
sports as unwelcome survivals of a 'rough' recreational culture. By the 1830s,
opposition from local lairds had led to the suppression of cock-fighting in
Canonbie, Dumfries and Lammingtoune, Lanarkshire.[25] As these examples
suggest, the survival of such practices depended on a sufficient concentration
of wealth to finance them. A favourable demographic balance was, as Tranter
notes, also critical. The support of the young, the most physically active
groups as a rule, could offset a more general decline in the games culture. So,
at Kelso, where 'nothing of the nature of sport is to be seen among the people

at large', the only exceptions to that observation were provided by games of football and quoits among apprentices.[26] Where conditions allowed, there-fore, popular culture was capable of displaying a marked resilience.

In place of a narrative marked by discontinuities and a wholesale dis-placement of 'traditional' by 'modern' leisure activities, a picture emerges in which the two co-existed and often overlapped. This could be observed in a variety of settings. Bob Morris has noted the tendency of middle-class voluntary organisations, ostensibly concerned to promote ideas of sober, rational improvement, to adopt more popular and spectacular forms of entertainment to get their messages across.[27] In the same spirit, theatres offered their audiences the classics, albeit often in bowdlerised form. Few could match the efforts of David Prince Miller, who presented Glasgow theatre-goers in the 1840s with 'Richard III' in twenty minutes, enabling him to stage twenty-seven performances in one day.[28] If the 1843 Theatre Act established some distinction between popular and 'legitimate' theatre, other forms of entertainment continued to embody aspects of the rough and the respectable. Phrenology, embraced early in the century as a scientific means of divining characteristics and aptitudes from the shape of the head, in later decades became a fairground sideshow in which cranial peculiarities were used to predict an individual's future.[29] Nowhere was the mix more evident than at the fairs, popular gatherings at set points in the calendar, which, in the early part of the period at least, combined economic and recreational functions. In the early 1840s, Dundee's First Fair offered the spectacle of a 'wonderfully large pig' jumping through a hoop, and the exhibition of the 'Ichaboe Mummy', a body preserved in guano and recently uncovered on the coast of Africa. Two decades later little had altered, so that a revivalist preacher could find himself competing for attention with a performer whose speciality was reported to be skinning live rats with his teeth prior to biting off their heads. The latter act, which had already proved too strong even for Glaswegian stomachs, was ended prematurely on the intervention of the local police.[30] If this suggests a greater culture of regulation, rendering the fairground and other places of amusement more 'polite', the degree of change should not be over-stated. The variety theatres and music halls that sprang up across urban Scotland in the second half of the century offered bills that carried strong echoes of older forms of entertainment. Animal acts thus continued to abound into the twentieth century, although their partici-pants were no longer required to die for their art. Rather, they were called on to display a variety of skills, from the musical (Professor Duncan's Dog Orchestra) to the intellectual (Harry Edson and his 'Human-Brained' Dog, 'Doc', and Pilau the Thought-Reading Dog among others).[31] Alongside such wonders, the spirit of the 'freak show' was evoked by the representation of morbid obesity as a matter of public amusement, a familiar concept to habit-ués of modern-day reality television. In 1906, Bostock and Wombwell's Menagerie at the Scottish Zoo and Hippodrome in Glasgow engaged Charlie

Dunbar, 'The Clydebank Fat Boy', who, aged five and a half years, weighed in at 10 stone 12 lbs.[32] The following year, visitors to A. E. Pickard's Museum on the Trongate were able to place him in perspective by viewing 'America's Champion Fat Girl', trumpeted as '40 stone 7 lb of Youth and Beauty. A Sight Never to be Forgotten'.[33] At other times, the display of the exotic still carried a veneer of intellectual respectability. The appearance of pygmies from central Africa at Glasgow's Hippodrome in November 1905 generated, as newspaper notices acknowledged, a broader anthropological interest, although the liberal use of exclamation marks in the accompanying copy conveys the fact that they functioned primarily as entertainment: 'The Most Curious People ever seen! The Talk of Europe!! The Missing Link between Anthropoid Apes and Man!!!'[34] Potential spectators were reassured by a subsequent review of their first night in Glasgow, which reported that the pygmies spoke 'very good English'.[35] New technology was also employed in ways that married enhancement and amusement. A variety of performers thus explored the educational and entertainment potential of electricity, perhaps none more flamboyantly than the self-styled 'Doctor' Walford Bodie, 'M.D.', who through the act 'The Electrocuted Man' sought to expose the cruelty, as he saw it, of the latest means for execution in the United States.[36]

In thus incorporating elements of the popular and the polite, music halls and variety theatres reflected the everyday world around them. The culture of the skilled, male working class, although it promoted the values of thrift was also, particularly early in the century, infused with alcohol. It was also the skilled worker whose attendance at football matches in later decades gave rise to concern over the extreme, often violent emotions expressed.[37] So, the categories often employed to structure narratives of nineteenth-century society, 'traditional' and 'modern', 'rough' and 'respectable', proved in practice to be highly permeable. Where changes occurred in work and leisure patterns, their precise pace and nature varied according to particular circumstances. Individual experiences could vary markedly from any pre-supposed 'norm'. For example, the ba' game played each year in the streets of Kirkwall between those born up town (the 'Uppies') and those born down town (the 'Doonies') pursued an idiosyncratic course over the century. Prior to 1800, the contest was staged in a defined space, on the Kirk green. From that point, it moved into the streets of the town, but even then continued to be played according to strict rules, which required the ball to be kept on the floor. Only from mid-century did the game evolve fully into its 'modern' form as a mass scrummage.[38] The Kirkwall Ba' Game's transition from the 'traditional' to the 'modern' thus followed a route directly contrary to that observed more generally in favour of greater regulation in terms of time, space and the rules governing play.

It is impossible in a work of this length to capture all or even most instances of local variation. Indeed, if this were to be attempted, the result

Figure 6.1 *Displaying the Exotic: Bostock & Wombell's Royal No. 1 Menagerie, 1905.*
© *South Lanarkshire Libraries and Community Learning. Licensor www.scran.ac.uk.*

would resemble a descriptive catalogue, in which the meaning and consequences of the patterns being observed would remain obscure. Here, the 'everyday', with its emphasis on the rhythms, routines and relationships that shaped social experiences may offer some illumination. In the ensuing discussion, this point is pursued by examining the theme of time. Conceptions of time altered significantly over the century, as the clock rendered it more precisely measurable, down to previously unconsidered units such as minutes and seconds. Yet older conceptions of time, based on the workings of natural rather than human agency, such as the seasons, retained their utility for both work and leisure. The relationship between these different, often overlapping, sequences of time has much to tell us about change over the period. The year was central to work and leisure at the start of the century: employment was often shaped by annual contracts, while the major festivities which defined the leisure calendar were scheduled according to the seasons. Over time, the impact of the changes wrought by industrial capital and related movements for moral reform would be felt at the level of the week and the day. A more regular work experience had its concomitant in a reordering of leisure time around the weekend, with the Sabbath at its heart, while attempts to encourage consistency of effort and diligence at work centred on changing the nature of the working day. For all this, however, we must also note the experience of those sections of society unaffected directly by such changes. For women, in particular, the manner in which their time was constructed provides the clearest evidence for the consolidation of gender differences within Victorian Scotland.

TIME AND THE WORKER: THE YEAR

For large groups of Scottish workers at the start of the period, the seasons had an immediate practical significance. In a number of leading sectors, labour was engaged on annual or six-monthly contracts. In agriculture, such arrangements applied throughout the century. Scotland's balanced system of cultivation ensured that seasonal variations in activity were less marked than south of the border. What is more, the long-term and accelerating trend for those most economically active to migrate out of rural areas meant that labour was often in short supply. In such circumstances, extended employment contracts maintained their value by guaranteeing the availability of manpower over a longer period.[39] In other trades, however, a change to shorter contracts was quickly apparent. Following the abolition of serfdom, most Scottish coal-miners were employed for annual terms. Yet, as early as the third decade of the century, a shift in favour of fortnightly contracts was noted in western parts of the coalfield.[40] Over time, the trend towards shorter periods of notice was maintained. Although the fortnight remained the norm across Fife and Clackmannanshire, further west daily contracts were in place by the 1850s. Here, a sizeable in-migration of labour from Ireland and surrounding rural areas created the conditions of manpower surplus that sustained short-term employment relationships. The result was a highly mobile workforce, among whom a sense of attachment to either the form of work or the place was thought to be limited. The 1891 Census thus found that, among Blantyre miners, barely 10 per cent were residing in the parish in which they had been born. Even then, mobility was not a universal characteristic. Further east, observers noted a more stable and settled workforce.[41] Nevertheless, the tendency in mining, as in most industries across nineteenth-century Scotland, was towards short employment contracts capable of being terminated with the minimum of notice.

Yet the year continued to exert a powerful influence over the work experience. Many trades, in addition to being subject to longer-term shifts in the economic cycle, experienced marked seasonal fluctuations in activity. Work in the building trade flourished, when broader economic circumstances allowed, in the long daylight hours and drier weather of summer. As the nights drew in, the converse applied. By the end of the century, it was observed that an average working week of 51 hours over most of the year could be reduced to 39.5 hours during December and January.[42] Edinburgh coopers experienced some slack in the spring months, while Glasgow's dock workers were driven to seek alternative berths in local shipyards and foundries as shipping volumes fell off in the winter.[43] Scotland's miners also experienced seasonal variations in activity, although these differed between eastern counties, where dependence on export markets limited demand during winter months, and further west, where production for local domestic and industrial use slackened off over the summer.[44] The comparative immunity of textile trades to short-term fluctuations produced, in the view of some, a stable labour force, among whom habits of thrift and regularity appeared to have taken deep root. In his evidence to the Royal Commission on Labour in 1892, Charles James Wilson, the President of the South of Scotland Chamber of Commerce, noted the 'constancy' of Hawick's textile workers, whose propensity for improvement was evident in the 'rational' and temperate use of their free time. In this case, short contracts had not produced a short-term outlook.[45]

The greater flexibility in nineteenth-century labour markets reduced the need for formal systems of recruitment in most trades. Across urban, industrial Scotland, jobs were secured, for the most part, through personal connections, primarily based on friends, family or neighbours. This also served to ensure that such mobility as did occur tended to be short distance and operated within existing social networks. In the countryside, by contrast, recruitment was conducted through the more formal agency of the hiring fair. Here, workers, whose twelve- or six-monthly contracts terminated simultaneously, gathered in local market centres to advertise their availability for work and came into contact with prospective employers. The

Note of absentees at start of work after Holidays	1900				1901 (2 days)			4th July (Queen Victoria Funeral 2/2/00)
	New Year	10 A.M	Spring Holiday	Summer Holidays	Autumn Holiday	New Year Holidays	10 A.M	
South Weaving	137	35	30	53	38	204	43	4
North	54	17.52	9	25	9	97	30	1
Weft Winding	36	8	12	20	18	55	22	1
Warp	29	3	13	9	18	48	8	-
Dressing	15	-	1	2	2	10	4	1
Warping	3	1	-	2	=	1	-	-
Fulling House	9	1	-	2	2	9	2	-
Yarn	1	1	-	-	=	2	-	-
Mechanics	1	1	-	2	7	3	1	-
Cloth Room	3	1	1	-	1	2	-	-
Drawing	23	6	1	5	2	19	3	-
Tenters	2	2	-	2	2	1	1	-
Oilers	3	1	-	1	-	1	=	-
Cleaners	4	1	-	1	4	5	2	-
	310 (6 A.M)	78 (10 AM)	67	124	103 (6 A.M)	457	116 (10 A.M)	7

Figure 6.2　Time, work discipline in action. Notebook listing the number of absentees after various holidays, Baxter Bros & Co. Ltd, 1895–1957. © Archive Services, University of Dundee. Licensor www.scran.ac.uk.

fair was part of an invariable annual sequence of gatherings at which labour was one of a number of commodities being traded. In the parish of Kelton, in Kirkcudbrightshire in the 1830s, seven fairs were held each year between February and November, three of which were concerned with dealing in horses and labour. By that date, most had transferred to Castle Douglas, where 'the multiplicity of places of entertainment' and the availability of banking facilities rendered it a more productive setting for transacting the business of the fair.[46] As this suggests, the fairs involved more than commodity dealings. They were also occasions at which a transient but intense concentration of spending power, workers having received payment at the end of their previous term, generated much expenditure for pleasure. In 1860, Moffat's October hiring fair also included 'stalls, shooting-galleries, merry-go-rounds, etc'.[47] As fairs provided unusual opportunities to spend among people who, it was believed, lacked the moral perspective to use their money appropriately, the fairs became, unsurprisingly, a focus for moral concern through the period. The introduction of a fair at Yester, in Haddingtonshire, for the hiring of shearers towards the end of the Napoleonic wars was deemed to have been:

a great inconvenience to the parish; as the shearers to the number of 500, flock to Gifford *on Sabbath*; and not only wait to be hired, but profane the Lord's day by drunken and disorderly conduct.[48]

In other ways also, the hiring fair offended against the 'rational' sensibilities of the age. The presence of young women in need of work gave rise to particular concern. Obliged to stand on open display, 'like so many cattle or pigs', they were subject to the gaze of 'every licentious blackguard – the chaff of our working population'.[49] By mid-century, the hiring fair was seen by some as an occasion for the encouragement of improvident and debauched behaviour, in which the only people to prosper were, as the Biggar minister, Dunlop, had it, the publican, the pickpocket and the police.[50] One correspondent to *The Scotsman* in 1859 went further, in seeking to establish a correlation between the holding of fairs and the incidence of illegitimate births.[51] Some sought to defend the fairs, claiming that they enabled a close supervision to be maintained over prospective farm servants, and that they broadened the outlook of the young by giving them experience of places beyond the immediate locality.[52] For the most part, however, the critical voice tended to prevail. Alternatives to the fair were proposed, including cheap excursions, while at Biggar in 1862, a more 'rational' range of refreshments than that offered in local pubs was provided, in the form of 'the largest possible cup of tea and the largest possible slice of bread at the smallest possible charge', all served up to the tunes of Dr Guthrie's Ragged School Band from Edinburgh.[53] Yet while agricultural labour remained in such short supply the fairs retained their economic utility, and although alternative methods of recruitment were introduced, including registration offices at Mid-Calder from the 1850s, only a fundamental change in rural labour markets was likely to render the hiring fair redundant. An influx of Irish migrants offered some relief and, at Linton in 1851, resulted in the suspension of the local fair.[54] However, renewed out-migration from rural areas ensured that the annual ritual of the hiring fair remained a central feature of Scottish agriculture throughout the remainder of the period.[55]

If, in the face of much opposition, the hiring fair retained much of its original purpose, the tendency over time was for the 'pleasure' function of the fair to assume greater importance, particularly as new methods of trading diverted business along alternative channels. So, Glasgow Fair was last used for dealing in livestock around 1820. From that point, it assumed the character of a popular holiday, initially centred locally on Glasgow Green, but latterly taking in excursions out of the city. On Fair Saturday in 1873, an estimated 23,000 were carried by steamer from the Broomielaw to resorts along the Firth of Clyde, while others sought their pleasures further afield, in places such as Perth, Crieff and Aberdeen.[56] Industry now accommodated the holiday mood by suspending operations at the Fair. By the 1880s, iron works in Lanarkshire ceased operations for up to ten days, which also allowed repairs to be effected.[57] Glasgow Fair's growth signalled a significant recasting of the local holiday calendar. Celebrations to mark the Feast of St Mungo on 13 January, which consumed twenty days at the start of the period, was confined by mid-century to a more 'rational' and acceptable two days.[58] More generally, however, it is the durability of the fair as an occasion for collective celebration across Scotland that impresses. Many provided the occasion for organised, public forms of leisure. So, race meetings held in Paisley and Irvine coincided with local fairs held on St James' Day and Marymass, respectively, while that at Newton-on-Ayr was run at the Kipper Fair, marking the end of the salmon fishing season.[59] Taken together, the fairs constituted a network which helped to sustain the business of itinerant traders and entertainers. Through to the end of the century and beyond, travelling showmen continued to traverse Scotland on circuits determined by the calendar of local festivities. The Green family of Glasgow, in addition to operating their Carnival site on the Gallowgate, maintained a number of touring fairground shows, including one, let to Peter Swallow, which described a regular itinerary across northern England and southern Scotland. Returns were often variable. The Saturday of the Abbeyhill Carnival in Edinburgh in January 1905 yielded Swallow a mere 17s. 6d., but he remained confident that fairs in Girvan and Maybole in April would pay well.[60] The Greens maintained the travelling shows until 1914, when the death of one of his sons persuaded George Green to concentrate his activities on a variety of fixed venues, including a growing circuit of picture houses across west-central Scotland.[61] Many of the leading figures behind the emergence of the most popular mass leisure form of the first half of the twentieth century, the cinema, could trace their origins back to the fairground and the travelling show. These included 'President' Kemp at Saltcoats, Arthur Henderson in Dundee, the Poole family in Edinburgh and Alfred Palmer in Lesmahagow.[62] For some time then, the leisure experience of the twentieth century continued to bear the imprint of an older, annual entertainment culture.

The events which helped to shape the festive calendar carried wider meanings. However much they varied in outward form, they were symbolic of the identities and associations that informed the society in which they operated. Ideas of locality were thus emphasised, transcending other points of division based on status. The vertical ties uniting rich and poor in a 'community' were given prominence over the horizontal allegiances characteristic of a class-based society. The idea was most forcefully expressed through what Ronald Hutton has come to call 'Rites of Hospitality and Charity'. Most evident at the height of winter, when lack of daylight hours curtailed work opportunities and resources more generally were scarce, these involved the poor seeking the assistance of the wealthy of the area in the form of food or money ('hogmanay'). Help was sought as a right and served as a reminder to the elite of their dependence on the labours of the poor, and the degree to which neither group could exist without the other.[63] The new social order, constructed around the precepts of industrial capital and evangelical religion, had little time for such notions, elevating in their place ideals of temperance and self-reliance. Yet, for some, such values threatened to create a society riven by class division and vulnerable to conflict and disorder. A remedy was sought in older festive forms, which would reinvigorate the ties of 'community', while at the same time reinforcing an appropriate sense of hierarchy. At its most extreme, this took the form of the 13th Earl of Eglinton's self-conscious re-creation of an imagined medieval past in his Tournament of 1839.[64] A more lasting product of this exercise in Tory paternalism was the network of Gymnastic Games that came to extend across Lowland and Highland Scotland as the century progressed. The prototype for these gatherings was provided by the St Ronan's Border Games at Innerleithen, inaugurated in 1827 by the Ettrick shepherd, James Hogg. Here, 'community' was celebrated by means of a series of athletic contests for local people, while at the end of the day a more exclusive version of the idea was marked by the withdrawal of the 'quality' to a local hostelry for dinner.[65] The model was taken up elsewhere from the 1830s, such as at Haddington, where the East Lothian Tyneside Games were held under the patronage of the Marquis of Tweeddale, and at Dalkeith, where proceedings concluded in a gathering in the Cross Keys Inn to drink the health of, among others, the Duke of Buccleuch, the Marquis of Lothian and the Earl of Dalhousie.[66] By mid-century, the games were widespread and drew on varied forms of patronage; those at Musselburgh in the 1850s were overseen by the Chief Magistrates of the town. If the presence here, and elsewhere, of 'crack' professional athletes worked to undermine somewhat simple notions of community based around locality, the idea was sustained by reserving certain events for residents of the immediate parish. The 'Favourites Race' at Leith's Gymnastic Games fulfilled a similar function.[67]

Over time, the content of the Games and the ideas they were intended to embody changed. From the beginning, competition had encompassed a variety of sports, from basic track and field athletics to more rarified events, such as the sack- and blindfold-races held at East Lothian in 1835.[68] Events could also be shaped to reflect local circumstances. The Luss Highland Gathering in 1889, for example, offered prizes for the best hand-knitted hose and socks, one of the few occasions on which female participation was openly encouraged. Equally, among the 'sports' that graced the Horticultural Show at Ecclefechan in 1890 was a competition in which participants were required to pick up and place in a basket twenty-five potatoes, taking one at a time and completing the task in the shortest time. The Show also boasted more recognisably 'modern' events, such as the five-a-side football competition, won by the self-styled 'Duffers of Lockerbie'.[69] As the programmes varied, so the nature of the 'community' the Games sought to embody became more diverse over time. By mid-century, sport had become associated with ideas of social and moral improvement. As patron of Edinburgh's Gymnastic

Games, the Sheriff of Midlothian enlarged upon the wider virtues of the sports in opening the Games of 1851:

> I do not look on them merely as healthful recreations for the body – they are active, inspiriting, invigorating exercise for both body and mind . . . and they fall to be identified with any large and proper system of sanitary education for the people . . . They mature the judgment as well as ripen the muscles. It is not the mere weight of arm; it is the cool judgment – the clear eye – the sagacious understanding – the husbanding and proper use of strength that gain victory.[70]

For employers anxious to promote peaceful industrial relations and to encourage stability and loyalty within their workforce, such ideas had a more immediate utility. This may help to account for the inauguration from the early 1860s of games associated with the Arnieston and Vogrie Collieries. By 1869, when some 4,000 spectators were in attendance, the event was overseen by the pit's underground manager, replicating workplace hierarchies on the field of play.[71] Yet the Games model was sufficiently flexible to recommend it to other groups. Among skilled workers, the ideal of physical, intellectual and moral improvement had a powerful appeal. Friendly Societies, which embodied the pursuit of progress through collective effort, incorporated sporting competition into their annual calendar of events. In 1888, the Games of the Thistle of Portobello Lodge of the Order of Ancient Free Gardeners were held in Joppa Park and were preceded by a procession through local streets, headed by pipe and brass bands, a clear demonstration of the movement's civic importance.[72] A comparable statement was made two years later by the Edinburgh district of the Ancient Order of Foresters in processing to the grounds at Ardmillan Terrace from the capital's legal and administrative centre at Parliament Square.[73] Here, the 'community' being celebrated was one based around feelings of class, indicating the potential of the Games, while they persisted as a feature of the annual calendar to express new and varied sources of social identity over time. What this suggests is that, rather than marking a straightforward transition from a society based on the vertical ties of community to one structured around the loyalties of class, various forms of identity co-existed and, to a degree, overlapped.

TIME AND THE WORKER: THE RISE OF THE WEEKEND?

The relative importance of each identity is more precisely caught by shifting our focus to centre on the shorter spans of the week and the day. It was at these points that attempts deliberately to instil habits of regularity and discipline in the pursuit both of work and leisure were rendered most explicit. For many observers, particularly at the start of the century, workers' mental horizons remained bounded by the short term. They appeared incapable of responding to monetary incentives by increasing effort, justifying, for some, the payment of wages that barely rose above subsistence levels. Both symptom and cause of this outlook was the intermittent work schedule followed by many, so that leisure opportunities arose at uneven and unpredictable intervals. The uncertainties of work meant that incomes could fluctuate from week to week. Among Dundee's hand weavers in the later 1830s, the variation could be as much as 50 per cent, so that 'Saturday afternoon, Monday, and often Tuesday, are considered holidays, or rather idle days, during which little, if any, work is done'.[74] The timing of events in the recreational calendar accommodated this mutability. Fairs, more often than not, were scheduled for early in the week, with those at Dalkeith, Bathgate and Tranent, for example, falling between Tuesday and Thursday.[75] Gymnastic Games, even when not tied to local fairs, were also held on week days. Although the precise date might vary, those at Leith were scheduled for Tuesday or Friday.[76] Even events organised at comparatively short notice observed this pattern. Prize fights, such as that held in 1829 in central Scotland between two pugilists named Robinson, operated outside the law. Held slightly away from major population centres, in this case between Edinburgh and Glasgow, so as to minimise the potential for interference, while enabling large numbers to attend and so maximise the take through gambling, the fight, like many others at this point, was held on a Tuesday.[77] The capacity of such events thus to disrupt work routines was merely one of the features which rendered them anathema to rational recreationists. As a result, from mid-century, determined efforts were mounted to confine organised leisure opportunities to a fixed and predictable part of the week. Saturday-night concerts were instituted by members of the Total Abstinence Society in Aberdeen from the 1840s, and by the Abstainers' Union in Glasgow during the following decade.[78] If the evidence for assessing the impact of such initiatives is, at present, incomplete, a preliminary survey suggests that, in terms of popular behaviour and attitudes, change was faltering and uneven.

'Shadow' noted a tendency among certain Glaswegians to feel 'Mondayish' in the late 1850s.[79] If the greater regularity of work in later decades operated to check such propensities, for many the week retained its flexible character. Among Scotland's coal miners, in particular, the survival of the fortnightly pay allowed some discretion over the days worked. In evidence before the Royal Commission on Labour in 1892, Robert Smillie of the Larkhall Miners' Association described the custom for miners to work only five of the six days available during the week. Some sought to argue that this practice varied with economic circumstances. For Keir Hardie, a downturn in trade was the most likely guarantee of consistent attendance at the coal face.[80] The tendency for effort to vary as finances ebbed and flowed was also noted by J. S. Dixon of the Lanarkshire Coalmasters' Association before the Select Committee on the Miners' Eight Hour Day in 1907: 'It is more a question of wages than anything else. The miner does not think anything about the gross output of the country or the good of the colliery. If he makes money he will spend it, and he generally takes an idle day to do that.'[81] Others saw the propensity to play days as a customary practice, unrelated to shifts in family circumstances, although even then it was observed that 'the higher the wage is the less coal is put out'.[82] It is possible to see in this evidence of the survival of a popular political economy based on the belief that, through the limitation of output, fluctuations in employment would be evened out and a more regular income flow achieved. Such a view had informed calls for reduced working hours in the third quarter of the century and the achievement of the 8-hour day in the eastern part of the coalfield was seen to have encouraged more regular attendance than was observed further west.[83]

If the enduring flexibility of the work routine suggests a continuity in outlook, the detail of the miners' method of playing points to a slightly different conclusion. Although voluntary absenteeism on Mondays was reported, the days most likely to be taken off were thought to be Thursdays and, increasingly, Saturdays. Even where 'Mondayish' tendencies remained evident, miners were observed to attach increasing importance to Saturday as a free day.[84] From mid-century, moral reformers had promoted Saturday as a point in the week when leisure might be encouraged, in part out of a belief that free time on that day, appropriately used, would better prepare families for the Sabbath. From the 1860s, commercial interests came to see the weekend as a likely source of profit. Reduced hours of work, initially for textile factory workers, but extending to Edinburgh stonemasons in 1861 and most workers over the following decades, considerably extended opportunities for leisure, particularly through the institution of a half-day's holiday on the Saturday.[85] The third quarter of the century thus witnessed the emergence of new dedicated recreational venues. The Royal Patent Gymnasium, proclaimed as 'The New Wonder of Edinburgh', opened on ground opposite Royal Crescent and Fettes Row in 1864.[86] It sought to justify its billing by offering aquatic and aeronautic novelties, along with more regular pedestrian (athletic) meetings. These were scheduled for times likely to attract the maximum number of spectators. So, in contrast to the all-day spectacles of the Gymnastic Games, meets at the Royal Patent Gymnasium commenced late on Saturday afternoons and continued through to the early evening.[87] The popularity of such gatherings (a crowd of 10,000 being reported at one meeting in September 1869) tested the Gymnasium's capacity to such a degree that larger grounds were developed at nearby Powderhall.[88] By the end of the nineteenth century, then, the tendency for popular recreation to centre on the weekend was well established, so that the notion of Saturday as a play day was firmly set, even among groups such as Lanarkshire's miners, who were not otherwise noted for their devotion to habits of regularity.

Yet if the week increasingly became configured in a manner of which moral reformers could approve, this did not imply a broader acceptance of the ideals they were concerned to promote. The reform project was itself subject to acute points of difference. Across the second half of the century, an ongoing debate concerned the range of activities deemed appropriate to the Sabbath. In the eyes of many, the closure of public houses on Sundays had created a void that required filling by a range of constructive pursuits. Proposals to that end frequently encountered determined Sabbatarian opposition. If this sufficed to block moves to open Edinburgh's Botanic Gardens on Sundays in 1863, it could not prevent a progressive encroachment on strict interpretations of the Sabbath, particularly across the central belt. In 1898, the Edinburgh Sunday Society was formed with the intention of providing 'for the people on Sundays sacred and classical music, lectures on interesting subjects in science, literature, history, and art, and generally to promote the rational observance of the Sunday'.[89] In Glasgow, by the end of the century, sacred concerts were incorporating novel forms of entertainment and instruction, such as moving pictures. The films shown, as part of the Sunday entertainment at the Wellington Rooms included scenes from the Oberammergau Passion Play and footage of the contemporary Holy Land, oddly juxtaposed with views of the war in South Africa, all to the accompaniment of 'Appropriate songs'.[90] Further reflecting the increasing scope for latitude on the Sabbath, Sunday pleasure steamers had, by 1900, re-commenced business on the Firth of Clyde. Their activities provoked unease in the affected resorts, to the extent that, at Dunoon, proposals for a physical obstacle of barbed wire to prevent landings were being floated. Even here, however, opinion was divided, one councillor regarding what he called 'the barbed wire atrocity as more in keeping with the pre-Reformation days, when they burned witches'.[91] Despite the efforts of the Sabbatarians, the scope of activities deemed legitimate on the Sabbath was clearly widening by the start of the twentieth century. In order to gain ground, the cause of moral reform was constantly having to compromise.

TIME AND THE WORKER: THE DAY

A more insistent challenge to its ideals was posed by the nature of the working day itself. Here, attempts to instil time-work disciplines by means of the clock enjoyed fitful success at best. The mechanical measurement of time was most consistently applied in industries relying on a centralised place of work, enabling close supervision to be maintained. In the textile trades, clear limits to the working day were observed from early in the century. In the 1830s, these extended from 5.45 am to 8 pm, Saturdays aside, while by the last decade of the century, the typical working day in a Dundee jute mill ran from 6 am to 6 pm (1 pm on Saturdays) with two set breaks for meals at 9 am and 2 pm.[92] The importance of commencing work on time, when machinery was in operation, called forth a series of fines specifically to encourage punctuality. In one eleven-month period in Dundee in the early 1890s, these sufficed to raise £11 15s. 1d., equivalent to some 2,000 instances of late attendance.[93] Even in the mills, however, the notion of a fixed working period proved to be difficult to sustain. The maintenance of machinery often required engineers to work overtime, indicating that even in 'modern' sectors of industry, the notion of task-based work had not been entirely eliminated. Around mid-century, the Dundee millwright, John Sturrock, described through his journal the lengthy and often highly variable hours required to complete particular jobs. In one week in April 1865, his working day ended at times varying between 6.30 pm and midnight.[94] In the iron and steel trades also, the complexity of equipment elevated the task in hand above the dictates of the clock. Blast furnace men were thus observed to put in additional hours to complete particular jobs.[95] It was, however, underground that the obstacles faced in imposing new time-work disciplines were most obvious. Close supervision was impracticable where workers were dispersed across many workings, so that mine owners turned to the wage packet as the best guarantor of consistent effort. This still allowed face workers in particular great discretion over the duration and intensity of their working day. They were thus able to choose when to take meal breaks, observed at the work place, and the point at which the working day ended. In Fife, where, by the 1890s, the working of coal commenced at 6 am, operations usually ceased early in the afternoon, around 2.15 pm. Further west, where longer shifts prevailed, men were observed to leave the pit at various points through the day.[96] The readiness with which they did this points to a view of the day determined less by time (the clock) than by a level of output (the task). As Keir Hardie explained to the Royal Commission on Labour:

> In every district in the west of Scotland there is an understood number of tons or hundredweights which constitute a day's work. It is called the 'master's darg'. It is accepted by the employers and the workmen as representing a fair day's work for that particular seam of coal.[97]

Everyday practices within the workplace thus served to blunt the force of a capitalist ethos eager to equate time with money. Popular attitudes were not amended in the light of financial incentives. In one respect, however, an important change had come about: for most workers, work and leisure time had become quantitatively and qualitatively distinct.

For their wives, however, the experience was somewhat different. Most had been engaged in paid work outside the home while young, helping to boost the household income while helping to satisfy the early industrial economy's insistent demand for labour. Yet this phase of life, during which the individual, while earning on their own account, remained comparatively free of family responsibilities, represented for most women a brief interlude. Over the century as a whole, the trend was to limit formal participation in paid work outside the home after marriage. By a process of official prohibition, as with the outlawing of work underground from the 1840s, and the emergence of new notions of 'respectability', which placed stress on the central role of the male breadwinner, married women became increasingly tied to the home.[98] A more highly gendered notion of the working day resulted, in which the obvious distinctions between work and leisure experienced by most of those employed beyond the home broke down. For many women, the day lacked such formal boundaries, but rather was punctuated by the insistent, yet intermittent, requirement to fulfil household chores, interspersed with periods when duties were less pressing. If these interludes were the nearest that most women came to experiencing 'leisure time', they were often filled by activities vital to maintaining the fabric of the household, such as the mending of clothes or shopping for the next day's meal. By its very nature, such a use of time leaves few written records, but oral testimony gleaned from later generations of women suggest an outlook that recognised no simple dichotomy between work and leisure and in which the very idea of 'leisure' was open to question.[99] More than anything, the female experience provides clear evidence for the survival into the twentieth century of pre-industrial modes of behaviour and points up the degree to which change over the first century or so of industrialisation was complex and varied, coloured by factors such as age and gender, as well as by region and occupation.

CONCLUSION

An everyday perspective thus points up areas of both continuity and change over the nineteenth century. In that period, developments in both work and leisure were real and profound. By 1900, time spent at work, whether over the span of a single day or a whole career, was characterised by greater intensity and brevity. Although important exceptions remained in evidence, in agriculture, domestic service and retailing, working hours were increasingly regulated by law and collective agreement. At the same time, the more insistent demands of machine-based production also operated to foreshorten careers, many passing the peak of their earning capacity by their fifties. A future of low-paid work or dependence awaited, the origins of that problem of pauperism among the elderly that exercised policy makers over the later part of the period. The greater regularity of work that came with more benign economic conditions in the later decades of the period thus came at a price. For some, the cost was cultural as well as material. Within the workplace, the perception developed that work lacked the creativity likely to engage the labour force. As a result, many sought the individuality and self-expression denied them at work in their free time. The sense of release at the end of the working day, given visible expression in the factory-gate films that were a popular feature of early cinema shows, encouraged, so many believed, an unreasonable desire for physical and emotional gratification in leisure pursuits, which came to embody all the violent and competitive instincts held in check while at work.[100]

Yet this critique of working-class culture, while it was influential, also missed much. Although workers undoubtedly valued their free time, there is also abundant evidence that they found real satisfaction and a sense of self-worth in their work. Nineteenth-century industry continued to draw on the skill and discretion of workers. Knowledge of a particular process or place of work provided the basis for a continued sense of occupational pride and solidarity, which for some carried over into the uses they made of their free time. As was the case with John Sturrock, many skilled workers used their time away from work to augment their knowledge and hone further their understanding of their trade. Hobbies thus reflected an enduring continuity between the worlds of work and leisure.[101] For most industrial workers, however, these areas of life remained discrete. Lacking the compulsion and constraints of the workplace, time away from work offered the potential for self-expression and the assertion of collective identities. As reflected in the public leisure forms of the period, these gave expression to various versions of 'community', based around locality, occupation, religion and class, initially through occasional events such as the Gymnastic Games but latterly on a more regular and national basis through organised sport such as football. A multiplicity of identities and loyalties was thus sustained. So, while both work and leisure acted as carriers of change across the nineteenth century, they also continued to bear the imprint of older patterns of thought and behaviour, suggesting that rather than a clear and unambiguous transition to a more class-based society, early industrial Scotland was a society in which the 'traditional' and the 'modern' continued to co-exist.

Notes

1 H. Cunningham, 'Leisure and Culture', in F. M. L. Thompson (ed.), *The Cambridge Social History of Britain, 1750–1950. Vol. 2: People and their Environment* (Cambridge, 1990), p. 279.

2 P. Borsay, *A History of Leisure: the British Experience since 1500* (Basingstoke, 2006), p. 6.

3 P. A. Adler, P. Adler and A. Fontana, 'Everyday Life Sociology', *Annual Review of Sociology*, 13 (1987), 218–22.

4 R. J. Morris, 'Urbanisation and Scotland', in W. H. Fraser and R. J. Morris (eds), *People and Society in Scotland. II. 1830–1914* (Edinburgh, 1990), p. 74.

5 A classic statement of this view of early industrial work is in E. P. Thompson, 'Time, Work-Discipline and Industrial Capitalism', *Past and Present*, 38 (December 1967), 56–97.

6 E. J. Hobsbawm, 'The Formation of British Working-Class Culture', and 'The Making of the Working Class, 1870–1914', in his *Worlds of Labour: Further Studies in the History of Labour* (London, 1984), pp. 176–213; M. Savage and A. Miles, *The Remaking of the British Working Class, 1840–1940* (London, 1994), pp. 48–55.

7 P. Bailey, '"A Mingled Mass of Perfectly Legitimate Pleasures": the Victorian Middle Class and the Problem of Leisure', *Victorian Studies*, 21 (1977–8), 7–28; I.

Bradley, *The Call to Seriousness. The Evangelical Impact on the Victorians* (London, 1976); B. Harrison, 'Religion and Recreation in Nineteenth-Century England', *Past and Present*, 38 (December 1967), 98–125.

8 R. W. Malcolmson, *Popular Recreations in English Society, 1700–1850* (Cambridge, 1973), chs 6–7; N. Tranter, *Sport, Economy and Society in Britain, 1750–1914* (Cambridge, 1998), ch. 2; R. Holt, *Sport and the British. A Modern History* (Oxford, 1989), ch. 1; J. G. Rule, 'Methodism, Popular Beliefs and Village Culture in Cornwall, 1800–50', in R. D. Storch (ed.), *Popular Culture and Custom in Nineteenth-century England* (1982), pp. 48–70.

9 See George Owen's description of the game of 'knappan', as played in Pembrokeshire early in the seventeenth century, N. Elias and E. Dunning, *Quest for Excitement: Sport and Leisure in the Civilizing Process* (Oxford, 1993), pp. 228–9.

10 J. Burnett, *Sporting Scotland* (Edinburgh, 1995), p. 30; New Statistical Accounts [NSA] IX, *County of Fife*, Leslie, p. 115.

11 NSA XIII, *County of Banffshire*, Cullen, p. 332.

12 NSA III, *County of Roxburghshire*, Kelso, p. 325.

13 NSA V, *County of Ayrshire*, Kilmarnock, p. 544.

14 This sequence is set out most fully in Malcolmson, *Popular Recreations in English Society*, pp. 170–1.

15 E. H. Hunt, *British Labour History, 1815–1914* (London, 1981), ch. 3; M. A. Bienefeld, *Working Hours in British Industry: An Economic History* (London, 1972).

16 A. Lugton, *The Making of Hibernian* (Edinburgh, 1999), pp. 45–6; A. Mackie, *The Hearts: the Story of the Heart of Midlothian F.C.* (London, 1959), p. 51; D. Speed, B. Smith, and G. Blackwood (eds), *The Heart of Midlothian Football Club: A Pictorial History, 1874–1984* (Edinburgh, 1984), p. 6.

17 P. Temin, 'Two Views of the British Industrial Revolution', *Journal of Economic History*, 57 (1997), 63–82; N. Crafts and C. Harley, 'Output Growth and the British Industrial Revolution: A Restatement of the Crafts–Harley View', *Economic History Review*, 2nd ser., XLV (1992), 703–30; although see also, M. Berg and P. Hudson, 'Rehabilitating the Industrial Revolution', *Economic History Review*, 2nd ser., XLV (1992), 24–50.

18 W. W. Knox, *Industrial Nation: Work, Culture and Society in Scotland, 1800–Present* (Edinburgh, 1999), p. 35; D. Bremner, *The Industries of Scotland: Their Rise, Progress and Present Condition* (Newton Abbot, 1969 edn), p. 258; J. H. Clapham, *An Economic History of Modern Britain: The Early Railway Age, 1820–1850* (Cambridge, 1939), pp. 145–6.

19 Hobsbawm, 'The Making of the Working Class', p. 196; Hunt, *British Labour History*, p. 29; J. H. Treble, 'The Occupied Male Labour Force' and E. Gordon, 'Women's Spheres', in Fraser and Morris, (eds), *People and Society in Scotland* pp. 166–72, 206–9.

20 Parliamentary Papers (PP), 1833 XX (450), pp. 6, 8; S. Pollard, *The Genesis of Modern Management: A Study of the Industrial Revolution in Great Britain* (Cambridge, 1965), pp. 181–92.

21 PP, 1892 XXXVI, Part I (6795-IV), qq. 12645, 12680–1.

22 A. B. Campbell, *The Lanarkshire Miners: A Social History of their Trade Unions, 1775–1874* (Edinburgh, 1974), pp. 137–41, 265–7; PP, 1892 XXXVI, Part I (6795-IV), q. 10165; W. Lazonick, 'Employment Relations in Manufacturing and International Competition', in R. Floud and D. N. McCloskey (eds), *The Economic History of Britain since 1700*, 2nd edn (Cambridge, 1994), vol. 2, pp. 90–116.

23 R. Q. Gray, *The Labour Aristocracy in Victorian Edinburgh* (Oxford, 1976), pp. 33–6; PP, 1907 XV (3428), qq. 1286–9; S. Pollard, *Britain's Prime and Britain's Decline: the British Economy, 1870–1914* (London, 1989), pp. 19–25.

24 N. L. Tranter, 'Popular Sports and the Industrial Revolution in Scotland: the Evidence of the Statistical Accounts', *International Journal of the History of Sport*, 4 (1987), 21–38; NSA XI, *County of Forfar*, Dundee, p. 20, Montrose, p. 279; VI, *County of Lanark*, Glasgow, p. 211.

25 NSA IV, *County of Dumfries*, Canonbie, pp. 491–2; VI, *County of Lanark*, Wandell and Lammingtoune, p. 823.

26 NSA III, *County of Roxburgh*, Kelso, p. 325.

27 R. J. Morris, 'Leisure, Entertainment and the Associational Culture of British Towns, 1800–1900', unpublished paper, 1996; R. J. Morris, 'Clubs, Societies and Associations', in F. M. L. Thompson (ed.), *The Cambridge Social History of Britain, 1750–1950. Vol. 3: Social Agencies and Institutions* (Cambridge, 1990), pp. 395–443.

28 E. King, 'Popular Culture in Glasgow', in R. A. Cage (ed.), *The Working Class in Glasgow, 1750–1914* (Beckenham, 1987), pp. 153–4.

29 Edinburgh's Phrenological Society was especially noted and its collection provided the basis of those of societies elsewhere in Britain, see *Manchester as it is: or, Notices of the Institutions, Manufactures, Commerce, Railways, etc. of the Metropolis of Manufactures* (Manchester, 1971 reprint), p. 115.

30 I. McGraw, *The Fairs of Dundee*, Abertay Historical Society, No. 34 (Dundee, 1994), pp. 55–7, 59.

31 *Evening Times*, 5 November 1900, p. 9, for Duncan's Dog Orchestra ('The Most Intelligent troupe of Collie Dogs before the Public',) at the Italian Circus; 6 April 1903, p. 8 for 'Doc's' appearance at the Tivoli and Queen's; 18 June 1906, p. 8, for Pilau at the Glasgow Empire.

32 *Evening Times*, 14 March 1906, p. 7.

33 *Evening Times*, 26 January 1907, p. 8; J. Bowers, *Stan Laurel and Other Stars of the Panopticon: The Story of the Britannia Music Hall* (Edinburgh, 2007), pp. 112–17.

34 *Evening Times*, 13 November 1905, p. 8.

35 *Evening Times*, 14 November 1905, p. 8; two years earlier, the appearance at the Zoo Hippodrome of forty-four women warriors from Dahomey had similarly combined the exotic and the familiar, their performance of native music concluding with the singing of 'Goodbye Dolly Gray', 17 February 1903, p. 6.

36 *Evening Times*, 18 March 1901, p. 6; R. Jay, *Learned Pigs & Fireproof Women: a history of unique, eccentric & amazing Entertainers* (London, 1987), ch. 9.

37 Gray, *The Labour Aristocracy*, 100–2; N. L. Tranter, 'The Cappielow Riot and the Composition and Behaviour of Soccer Crowds in Late Victorian Scotland', *International Journal of the History of Sport*, 12 (1995), 125–40; J. Hutchinson, *The Football Industry: The Early Years of the Professional Game* (Glasgow, 1982), pp. 66–7.

38 J. Robertson, *Uppies and Doonies: The Story of the Kirkwall Ba' Game* (Aberdeen, 1967), pp. 114–15.

39 R. Anthony, *Herds and Hinds: farm labour in Lowland Scotland, 1900–1939* (East Linton, 1997), pp. 56–7; T. M. Devine, 'The Transformation of Agriculture: Cultivation and Clearance', in T. M. Devine, C. H. Lee and G. C. Peden (eds), *The Transformation of Scotland: The Economy since 1700* (Edinburgh, 2005), p. 83.

40 Campbell, *Lanarkshire Miners*, p. 34.

41 A. Campbell, *The Scottish Miners, 1874–1939: Vol. One: Industry, Work and Community* (Aldershot, 2000), pp. 87, 197; PP, 1892 XXXVI, Part I (6795-IV), qq. 13164, 13210; PP, 1892 XXXIV (6708-IV), qq. 3890–2.

42 PP, 1892 XXXVI, Part II (6795-VI), qq. 17865–6.

43 PP, 1892 XXXVI, Part II (6795-VI), q. 20453; PP, 1892 XXXVI, Part II (6795-V), q. 12879.

44 PP, 1907 XV (3428), qq.729–30, 1095–7, 3547.

45 PP, 1892 XXXV (6708-VI), qq. 7595–8, 7616, 7682–5.

46 NSA IV, *County of Kirkcudbright*, Kelton, p. 177.

47 *The Scotsman*, 29 October 1860, p. 2.

48 NSA II, *County of Haddington*, Yester, p. 172 (emphasis in original).

49 *The Scotsman*, 25 October 1862, p. 8; 20 October 1858, p. 1.

50 *The Scotsman*, 7 February 1862, p. 4.

51 *The Scotsman*, 22 March 1859, p. 4, letter by 'A Friend'.

52 *The Scotsman*, 11 October 1860, p. 4, reporting a discussion at the quarterly meeting of Galashiels Farmers' Club; 26 April 1877, p. 2, letter by 'J. M.'.

53 *The Scotsman*, 7 February 1862, p. 4.

54 *The Scotsman*, 12 March, 2; p. 10 September 1851, p. 3.

55 Anthony, *Herds and Hinds*, pp. 184–91, for fairs in the early twentieth century.

56 King, 'Popular Culture in Glasgow', p. 157; *The Scotsman*, 21 July 1873, p. 3.

57 *The Scotsman*, 14 July 1883, p. 6.

58 King, 'Popular Culture', p. 157.

59 J. Burnett, *Riot, Revelry and Rout: Sport in Lowland Scotland before 1860* (East Linton, 2000), pp. 111–24; J. Burnett, 'The Kipper Fair and the Cadgers' Races at Newton-on-Ayr', *Review of Scottish Culture*, 9 (1995–6), 36.

60 Scottish Screen Archive, Green Family, 5/8/26, Agreement between George Green and Peter Swallow, 14 January 1892; 5/8/28, Correspondence, Peter Swallow to George Green, 15 January, 3 March 1905.

61 J. McBain, 'Green's of Glasgow: "We Want 'U' In"', *Film Studies*, 10 (Spring 2007), 54–7; Scottish Screen Archive, Cuttings on George Green, 5/8/75, cutting from *The World's Fair*, 4 July 1914.

62 Scottish Screen Archive, George Kemp Ltd, 5/18/3, extracts from Merry Go Round; 8/47, transcript of interview with George Kemp, 28 June 1983;

Poole Family Collection, 5/4/1, '100 Years of Showmanship. Poole's 1837–1937'; Miscellaneous Film Material, 5/7/257, note on Henderson; Palmers of Lesmahagow, 5/7/345, cutting, n.d.

63 R. Hutton, *The Stations of the Sun: A History of the Ritual Year in Britain* (Oxford, 1996), pp. 65–6.

64 Burnett, *Riot, Revelry and Rout*, ch. 8; I. Anstruther, *The Knight and the Umbrella: an Account of the Eglinton Tournament, 1839* (Gloucester, 1986 edn).

65 Burnett, *Riot, Revelry and Rout*, 184–9; NSA III, *County of Peebles*, Innerleithen, p. 31; G. Jarvie, *Highland Games: The Making of the Myth* (Edinburgh, 1991).

66 *The Scotsman*, 2 July 1836, p. 1 (Haddington); 7 July 1838, p. 3 (Dalkeith).

67 *The Scotsman*, 16 August 1851, p. 3 (Musselburgh); 6 September 1860, p. 2 (Leith).

68 *The Scotsman*, 17 October 1835, p. 3.

69 *The Scotsman*, 6 July 1889, p. 1 (Luss); 18 August 1890, p. 4 (Ecclefechan).

70 *The Scotsman*, 9 August 1851, p. 4.

71 *The Scotsman*, 16 August 1869, p. 7.

72 *The Scotsman*, 16 July 1888, p. 4.

73 *The Scotsman*, 18 August 1890, p. 4.

74 PP, 1839, XLII (159), p. 187.

75 NSA I, *County of Edinburgh*, Dalkeith, p. 532; II, *County of Linlithgow*, Bathgate, p. 167; II, *County of Haddington*, Tranent, p. 303.

76 *The Scotsman*, 5 July 1845, p. 2; 25 July 1846, p. 3; 30 August 1848, p. 3; 11 July 1849, p. 1.

77 King, 'Popular Culture', p. 152; D. Brailsford, *Sport, Time and Society: the British at Play* (London, 1991), p. 7; D. Brailsford, *Bareknuckles: A Social History of Prizefighting* (Cambridge, 1988), ch. 2.

78 I. Maver, 'Leisure and Culture: the Nineteenth Century', in W. H. Fraser and C. H. Lee (eds), *Aberdeen, 1800–2000: a new history* (East Linton, 2000), pp. 402–3; King, 'Popular Culture', pp. 163–4.

79 [Shadow], *Glasgow, 1858: Shadow's Midnight Scenes and Social Photographs* (Glasgow, 1976 reprint), pp. 37–8.

80 PP, 1892 XXXVI, Part I (6795-IV), qq. 9830, 12450–1.

81 PP, 1907 XV (3428), q. 830.

82 PP, 1907 XV (3428), qq.1090, 1339.

83 I. MacDougall (ed.), *The Minutes of Edinburgh Trades Council, 1859–1873* (Edinburgh, 1968), p. 246; see above, n. 41.

84 PP, 1907 XV (3428), qq. 2973, 3013.

85 D. A. Reid, 'The Decline of Saint Monday, 1768–1876', *Past and Present*, 71 (May 1976), 76–101; PP, 1892 XXXVI, Part II (6795-VI), qq. 17954–7; Gray, *Labour Aristocracy*, p. 149.

86 *The Scotsman*, 13 June 1864, p. 2; 12 August 1865, p. 1.

87 *The Scotsman*, 7 October 1865, p. 1, for a demonstration of 'Cox's Patent Wreck Escape'; 1 April 1868, p. 4, for an illuminated balloon ascent; 16 August 1869, p. 7, for a meeting held between 4 and 8.30 p.m.

88 *The Scotsman*, 13 September 1869, p. 7; 30 December 1869, p. 6.

89 *The Scotsman*, 6 April 1898, p. 11; J. Wigley, *The Rise and Fall of the Victorian Sunday* (Manchester, 1980), pp. 200–1.

90 *Evening Times*, 12 March 1900, p. 6.

91 *Evening Times*, 11 July 1901, p. 2.

92 PP, 1833, XX (450), p. 4, 8; PP, 1892 XXXV (6708-VI), q. 10793.

93 PP, 1892 XXXV (6708-VI), q. 10798.

94 PP, 1892 XXXV, qq. 10803–5; C. A. Whatley (ed.), *The Diary of John Sturrock, Millwright, Dundee, 1864–65* (East Linton, 1996), p. 61.

95 PP, 1892 XXXVI, Part I (6795-IV), q. 14272.

96 PP, 1892 XXXIV (6708-IV), q. 3732; XXXVI, Part I (6795-IV), qq. 9826–7; PP, 1907 XV (3506), qq. 758, 1127.

97 PP, 1892 XXXVI, Part I (6795-IV), q. 12787.

98 A.V. John, *By the Sweat of their Brow: Women Workers in Victorian Coal Mines* (London, 1980), ch. 2; PP, 1842 XVI, 399, for action by the Duke of Buccleuch to prohibit female work underground.

99 J. Faley, *Up Oor Close: Memories of Domestic Life in Glasgow Tenements, 1910–1945* (Wendlebury, 1990); H. Clark and E. Carnegie, *She Was Aye Workin': Memories of Tenement Women in Edinburgh and Glasgow* (Oxford, 2003); C. Langhamer, *Women's Leisure in England, 1920–60* (Manchester, 2000), Part I.

100 T. Gunning, 'Pictures of Crowd Splendor: the Mitchell and Kenyon Factory Gate Films', in V. Toulmin, P. Russell and S. Popple (eds), *The Lost World of Mitchell and Kenyon: Edwardian Britain on Film* (London, 2004), pp. 49–58; V. Toulmin, *Electric Edwardians: The Story of the Mitchell & Kenyon Collection* (London, 2006), ch. 7.

101 Whatley, *Diary of John Sturrock*, pp. 13, 97, 99. Sturrock took the *English Mechanic*, which he valued as 'a weekly record of mechanical invention and scientific and industrial progress'; R. I. McKibbin, 'Work and Hobbies in Britain, 1880–1950', in J. M. Winter (ed.), *The Working Class in Modern British History: Essays in Honour of Henry Pelling* (Cambridge, 1983), pp. 127–146; reprinted in R. I. McKibbin, *The Ideologies of Class. Social Relations in Britain, 1880–1950* (Oxford, 1990), pp. 139–66.

Chapter 7

Crime, Protest and Policing in Nineteenth-Century Scotland

W. W. J. Knox and A. McKinlay

Christopher Whatley, in his introduction to *The Diary of John Sturrock*, a Victorian engineer, drew our attention to two incidents that occurred in Dundee within the space of twelve years of each other. The first concerned the social pandemonium surrounding the birthday celebrations for Queen Victoria in 1853, which led to the sacking of the town hall and the breaking of every window in the city's High Street by drunken crowds. The second proved to be a very different social occasion: one characterised by order and sobriety. In 1865, Sturrock and his friends, along with thousands of other citizens, enjoyed a performance of the Artillery Band in the city's Baxter Park without a 'hint of the disorder that coloured earlier celebrations of this event'.[1] The experience of Dundee was by no means unique. In the small town of Arbroath, the riotous behaviour of the crowd on the monarch's birthday in the late 1850s was put down by the magistrates and severe sentences handed out to the ringleaders 'which entirely broke the back of this annual carnival, so that its observance is now a thing of the past'.[2] Thus, by the mid-1860s it would appear that the turbulent socio-political culture of the eighteenth century and the first half of the nineteenth century had given way to a more stable social order. From that point onwards there was a decline in these disorderly public celebrations, which often culminated in full-scale riots, but also a fall in the incidence of theft and violence throughout Scotland and the rest of Britain.

The process of transition has its roots in the late eighteenth century, with the commitment of the middle classes to non-physical and rational forms of protest that relied upon 'the use of knowledge, printed information and statistical data, in the formation of rationally argued and published calls for change in the name of progress'.[3] The 'disorderly' community of the urban and rural poor were provided with textbook and model forms of behaviour in pursuit of political goals. However, until the last throes of Chartism, the lower orders generally declined to follow the lead provided for them by their social superiors, and numerous accounts of riot and disorder are available in any social history of the period. But with the failure of the 1848 Chartist protests, an acceptance of the liberal/capitalist framework of society brought a marked change in the working classes' political conduct. The Reform

Acts of 1867–8 gave the vote to the respectable working man, making pos-sible a degree of engagement with the political system from the previously unenfranchised. Under the impact of sharply rising improvements in the standard of living, leisure patterns also began to change, moving away from the rough culture associated with illegal sports, such as dog fighting, drink and the public house, and more towards the private spheres of family and church. Sport was promoted as alternatives to the rough culture, and between 1880 and 1883 skilled workers and the middle classes made up over 80 per cent of cricketers in Scotland, whereas football, athletics and quoit-ing drew players from an almost exclusively skilled background.[4] Economic growth and improved transportation saw the most common form of riot in the eighteenth and nineteenth centuries – the food riot – disappear, with the last recorded major incident taking place in north-east Scotland in 1847.[5] The growing commitment to the values associated with respectability signifi-cantly influenced the emerging labour movement in Scotland. Trade union meetings began to take place in coffee houses rather than pubs, and political protest appeared similarly respectable, replicating the methods and organi-sation that Stana Nenadic delineated in middle-class politics earlier in the century.[6] The unrespectable still existed but they posed little threat to law and order, steeped as they were in drink and depravity.

Thus presented, the transformation of social behaviour is almost an endorsement of the kind of Whig historiography so well captured in Sir Leon Radzinowicz's monumental *A History of the English Criminal Law*. However, much of the case for progress is based on the manipulation of criminal statistics; a notoriously swampy and dangerous area for the histo-rian.[7] Crucially, the available data fails to answer some of the basic questions central to the concept of transformation: first, was there an actual transition to a more orderly society taking place mid-century?; secondly, if there was, how was this achieved?; and, thirdly, how far has an historical focus on the question of the ordering of society obscured continuing traditions of popular protest and the vibrancy of the rough culture?

The work of Christopher Whatley on eighteenth-century Scotland, and E. P. Thompson, George Rude and Eric Hobsbawm and others on England,[8] has done much to dismiss the once dominant negative view of the crowd in action popularised through the work of the French social psychologist, Gustav Le Bon.[9] Le Bon could see in crowd formation and action only dis-organisation, irrationality and violence. In contrast, Marxist historians, like Thompson, saw disciplined groups of people engaging in purposeful action towards the achievement of specific objectives. If there was crowd violence, it was usually visited on property rather than persons. Rude calculated that of the twenty major disturbances that occurred in Britain between the Porteous Riot of 1736 in Edinburgh and the Chartist demonstrations in 1848 only twelve people were killed by the crowd, whereas the courts ordered 118 people to be hanged and soldiers shot a further 630.[10] In Scotland, only one man died as a result of crowd activity, and he probably died of a heart attack.[11] Riots and 'social' crimes were principally engaged in by working people, who were driven by hunger or other pressures from the growing commercial and industrial economy into defending their 'rights': the moral economy of the poor in confrontation with the new market values and the ascendancy of property. Even in rural areas, where conflict was more easily contained by the landlords and the law, protest developed an 'underground aspect', as sabotage and acts of defiance such as, 'stealing wood, pulling down dykes . . . refusal to obey orders', poaching and sheep stealing took place 'under the cover of darkness'.[12] Whatley in particular sees these instances of protest, overt or covert, as not only posing a challenge to the quiescence thesis of Tom Devine, Christopher Smout and other Scottish historians[13], but also as evidence of an emerging oppositional culture in the eighteenth century towards 'the old dialectic' of deference based loosely on economic position. The activities, objectives and values of the crowd pointed towards the birth of a class society.[14]

Thus, before 1850 crowd action and criminal behaviour are invested by historians with significance and a complex array of socio-political meanings. They also seem part of the everyday: crime embedded in the community and the privations of an increasingly disinherited and exploited people providing the social basis of protest. In the second half of the nineteenth century, these activities are interpreted by historians in a wholly different manner. Marxists, such as Rude and Thompson, who viewed riots taking place prior to 1850 as part of a radical collective challenge to property on behalf of the nascent working class, dismiss them in the post-1850 decades as 'backward' belches of the lumpen proletariat.[15] Karl Marx himself, in *The Eighteenth Brumaire of Louis Bonaparte*, spoke of the lumpen proletariat as 'vagabonds, discharged soldiers, discharged jailbirds, escaped galley slaves, swindlers, mountebanks, lazzaroni, pickpockets, tricksters, gamblers, maquereaus (procurers), brothel keepers, porters, literati, organ-grinders, rag pickers, knife grinders, tinkers, beggars – in short, the whole, disintegrated mass'.[16] Thus, for the left, the metamorphosis of the mob into the people can be achieved only by drawing a distinction between the productive and the unproductive, which paradoxically supported the authorities in their attempt to criminalise protest as mob activity and hence depoliticise it.[17] Similarly, Victor Gatrell in his hugely influential essay on the policeman-state, in the *Cambridge Social History of Britain* (1990), argues that since most crime was of a decidedly petty nature in the late nineteenth century it tells us nothing of any socio-political significance and certainly cannot be interpreted as evidence of class and class conflict.[18]

Such views on the transitional nature of Scottish/British society are open to question. First, if an ordered society had been achieved by mid-century then why do we have continuing concerns expressed by the middle classes regarding the masses and in particular the urban poor?[19] Secondly, how far was it simply the case that disorder in the second half of the nineteenth century was less to do with the pursuit of abstract political ideas, such as liberty, fraternity and egality, and social tensions released by hunger, than with issues connected with territory and how, and by whom, it was occupied? The everyday relationship to crime and protest was changing. For if the food riot, closely followed by political protest, was the most common source of disorder in the pre-1850 period, then it was sectarianism in the later period that accounted for most of the disturbances, particularly during the summer marching season. As Mark Harrison argues, Rude and others may have demolished the irrationalism thesis of Le Bon, but in the process they have entrenched the 'protesting crowd' as the dominant image of historians, when in other periods and places it was far from radical.[20] Moreover, as Alberto Melucci argues, the idea of systemic conflict as an explanation of collective protest should be jettisoned in favour of an approach to disorder that analyses each incidence of this behaviour as unique, one in which the actors 'organise their behaviour, produce meanings and actively establish relationships'.[21] He comes to this realisation on the basis that those involved in protest are unstable, inasmuch as they come together from different backgrounds to protest against some grievance in the social system and then dissolve and perhaps may not take part in this level of activism again in their lives.[22] Thirdly, to what extent was order simply a bourgeois construct which bore little relation to the lives of most working people in cities, where the pre-industrial rough culture continued to co-exist with the respectable? After all, as we will see, the creation of a stable society could be achieved only by a series of heavy-handed assaults through legislation by the policeman-state on the morals of the urban masses.

In many peoples' everyday lives, the idea of survival still predominated, such was the level of poverty and despair in a pre-welfare society, hence the continued need to operate within the illegal economy. However, with the creation of state-defined criminal sub-cultures, the purpose of which was to divorce crime and criminals from the social milieu within which they operated, this became increasingly difficult. Everyday concerns regarding the distribution of wealth and power also continued to shape protest, but mainly in the areas of industry and politics; otherwise communities were involved in struggles against each other. Thus, as we shall see, the whole relationship of the everyday to crime and protest was evolving over the course of the nineteenth century, eventually leading to their estrangement from embedded communities to individual acts of illegality.

CRIME IN NINETEENTH-CENTURY SCOTLAND

E. P. Thompson, in detailing the survival strategies of the rural poor in eighteenth-century England, remarked that 'if this is a criminal sub-culture' then 'the whole of plebeian England falls within the category'.[23] What the state defined as criminal was considered by the rural poor, the casual town labourers, destitute women and children as legitimate and necessary to survival. Criminal activity was, therefore, something that evolved from the community, which condoned it and in some ways protected those involved. And these attitudes were dominant in the early decades of the nineteenth century. As far as the ruling class was concerned the combination of a rapidly growing army of urban poor, along with a massive increase in political protest, especially during the Chartist period of agitation in the late 1830s and early 1840s, the criminal or 'dangerous' classes and the working classes were one and the same thing.[24] What might have been tolerated in terms of criminal activity in the eighteenth century was increasingly viewed as a threat to the hegemony of those above. The emphasis on order became synonymous with the defence of property.[25] Interestingly, ruling elites in Paris took a similar view to that of the British authorities'. It was an unquestioned assumption that those who were 'most likely to participate in revolution were also those most likely to indulge in crime'.[26] Draconian sentencing policies reflected the general fear among the propertied elite of the dangerous classes. A group of eight young men who robbed drunken crowds at the Tron in Edinburgh during the Hogmanay celebrations in 1811–12 saw four of their number hanged, two transported and two imprisoned for fourteen years.[27] Margaret Canovan was sentenced to seven years' transportation for stealing a coat from the Sheriff Clerk's Office by the Glasgow Court of the Justiciary in April 1833; Mary Hendry was given the same sentence for stealing a black silk gown; and Daniel Stirrat was transported for life for 'uttering a forged note in a public house in Calton'.[28] Of course, for those involved in political activities the sentences for sedition generally resulted in long periods of transportation and for some execution.

Thus, we have two parallel processes at work in the first few decades of the nineteenth century.[29] The first was the mob and the criminal as a moral disorder and comprehensible only in moral, perhaps theological terms. Such omnipresent disorder could be quelled only by occasional, spectacular demonstrations of power. The second began from the premise that the social was knowable and malleable. Systems of inspection, codifying and analysing specific populations, whether they be immoral women, workers or the poor, made their taming, if not their rehabilitation, possible.[30] We can see this logic in the moral geographies of cities divided by societies of theological cartographers and urban missionaries, most strikingly in the work of Thomas Chalmers in the St John's parish of Glasgow in the 1820s, or in the plans that theorised factories, not just as sites of production, but also as institutions for the improvement of character and orderly societies.[31] As Mary Poovey put it: '

According to [Adam] Smith, the living conditions of 'the great body of people' would improve along with the wealth of the nation, but in order to ensure that the

EXECUTION of the notorious WILLIAM BURKE the murderer, who supplied Dr KNOX with subjects.

Figure 7.1 *Sir Walter Scott is hidden amongst the 20,000 crowd that came to witness the execution of William Burke on 28 January 1829, and upwards of 24,000 people are estimated to have viewed the convicted murderer's remains. © Edinburgh City Libraries. Licensor www.scran.ac.uk.*

poor would contribute to this wealth . . . they had to be treated differently: their education and their morality had to be overseen; their neighbourhoods and their bodies had to be inspected.[32]

Early examples of this concern for control of the 'disaffected' were the instructions of the Glasgow Police Commission to the 'Watch' to 'sweep the main streets thoroughly in preparation for Sunday church services' and to summon and condemn publicans who opened their premises on a Sunday. Tom Devine says that in 1819 twenty men were appointed to 'range the streets and lanes' on the Sabbath and Saturday nights 'to apprehend idle and disorderly persons', and a further fourteen were employed specifically to report any house open for the sale of spirits.[33] Public begging was prohibited in 1811 and the police were empowered to arrest any beggars or vagrants from that point onwards.[34]

The second half of the nineteenth century witnessed the fusion of these processes as law-breaking became confined to a socio-legal constructed criminal class, alien and distinct from the law-abiding working-class majority. The criminal classes were made to appear delinquent and to live outside society with their own deviant values and codes of behaviour. The language of police and prison authorities in describing criminals is highly instructive in this process. Sir Evelyn Ruggles-Brise, chairman of the English Prison

View of the Hall of the Grand Inquisition.

Figure 7.2 *Caricature of Glasgow's Commissioners of Police, 1825.* © *Glasgow University Library. Licensor www.scran.ac.uk.*

Commission, saw 'offenders as defective', while Colonel A. B. McHardy, chairman of the Scottish Prison Commission, described prisoners as 'stragglers who fell away from an army on the march', and who robbed because they were 'lazy or merely loved the excitement of crime'.[35] As Michel Foucault points out, the middle-class authorities attempted to impose a highly specific spin on the 'common perception of delinquents to present them as close by, everywhere present and everywhere to be feared'; a strategy that made 'acceptable the system of juridical and police supervision of that portion of society'.[36] Victor Gatrell underscores this when he states that, by the end of the nineteenth century, 'experts . . . had no doubt that men turned to crime because of physical and mental as well as moral degenerativeness'.[37] The growth of criminology as a science in the second half of the nineteenth century also strengthened the view that criminal behaviour was hereditary. James Bruce Thompson, resident surgeon at Perth Prison, in an influential article written in 1870, stated that crime was a hereditary 'disorder of the mind' and that criminals were 'marked by a singular stupid and insensate look'.[38] The press and the emergence of crime fiction did much to aid this process of marginalisation. Criminal or delinquent behaviour, as Emile Durkheim pointed out, was an major factor in the integration of society: 'the offender draws the community together in indignation, thereby fostering social unity and helping the community to define and affirm a common morality and identity'.[39]

However, the creation of a consensus on values depended to a large extent on the ability of the economic system to deliver an increase in the general well-being of the majority; something of which it seemed incapable in the first half of the nineteenth century, and only fitfully in the second half. Despite rising standards of living in the post-1850 period, much of Scotland's population remained in poverty and squalor. Although there is no equivalent of the work of Charles Booth and Seebohm Rowntree,[40] their estimation that one-third of the populations of London and York, respectively, were in poverty would apply equally to cities such as Glasgow and Dundee, and the numbers would be swollen in times of economic depression. In a pre-welfare society, survival continued to mean depending at times on embracing 'skills which the authorities and investigators would . . . describe as "criminal" or "illegal"'.[41] Crime, such as did exist, was concerned with the theft of food, clothing and drink.[42] Most Victorian prisoners in English jails were poor and socially powerless; they included vagrants, suspicious characters, the drunk and incapable and some genuine burglars or thieves. Generally, they were convicted on little evidence, 'often, other than police testimony as to character. These then became the "criminal class"; and ideological stereotypes'.[43] As Archibald Alison, Sheriff of Lanarkshire, stated: 'it is from the lowest class that nine-tenths of the crime and nearly all the professional crime, which is felt as so great an evil, flows'.[44]

But what kind of 'crimes' did people commit, and what influence did age, gender and place exert on their illegal activities? Ian Donnachie found that crime in the period from 1805 to 1850 was 'overwhelmingly male', with males outnumbering females by a ratio of three to one; moreover, the vast majority of criminals were under thirty years of age, with two-fifths of all crime committed by teenagers.[45] Most came from the ranks of the low paid and the casually employed: labourers, colliers, spinners, weavers and carters. Female criminals were most often domestic servants or had some connection with the textile trades. The connection between these different occupational groups of people was poverty.[46] That reflected itself in the pattern of offences, which increasingly, in the first half of the nineteenth century, comprised crimes against property rather than those against the person. In 1810, 55 per cent of all offences in Scotland were against property, with 28 per cent against the person; the remainder were of an undefined public nature. By 1850 property offences accounted for 79 per cent of the total, while crimes against the person fell to 15 per cent, and those of a public nature sharply declined to only 6 per cent.[47] Clive Emsley found a broadly similar pattern in

Table 7.1   Scottish Criminal Statistics by Offence (1900).

Offences	Numbers	Percentage of total
Malicious mischief	5,700	3.3
Drunkenness	44,000	24.7
Breach of the peace	64,000	35.9
Assault on wives	4,000	2.4
Cruelty to children	600	0.4
Theft	13,000	7.5
Minor statutory offences (poaching, truancy)	46,000	25.8
Total	178,000	100.00

Source: A. B. McHardy, 'The Economics of Crime', Juridical Review, XIV (1902), 48.

England with steep increases in theft but, in sharp contrast to Scotland, also in assault until the 1840s.[48]

In the second half of the nineteenth century, because of the more thorough organisation of the police in Scotland and the availability of summary modes of prosecution, the number of court prosecutions grew from 142,346 in 1877 to 178,000 at the end of the century.[49] If we breakdown this data by category of offence, a preoccupation with order and respectability had come to form the main thrust of prosecution policies in Scotland, as the table above shows.

By 1900, the most common cause of crime was drunkenness and the category of breach of the peace, while crimes against property only accounted for 7.5 per cent of the total.[50] Indeed, 58 per cent of the prison population in Scotland in 1904 were there for drunkenness and/or breach of the peace;[51] the latter being a category of no significance in the first part of the century, was used in the later part as a catch-all category to deal with any act that 'disturbed the sensibilities of Victorian Scotland'.[52] This was similar to the English experience. One study showed that of the 2,308 persons in 100,000 tried in police courts in England in 1896, 609 were tried for drink offences, 221 for offences against the Education Acts and 108 for offences against the Vagrancy Acts.[53] Under pressure from temperance societies, the government introduced the Inebriates Act in 1898 which allowed for the incarceration of habitual drunkards. This legislation also reflected changing attitudes towards alcohol misuse. Hamish Fraser shows that in Glasgow during the late 1860s and 1870s, some 45,000–64,000 drunks were apprehended by the police, with two-thirds of them being discharged by the duty officer the following morning. After 1875, the authorities were concerned to charge those arrested for being drunk and disorderly.[54] Drink was also viewed as a direct contributor to other crimes. A study of the case histories of 280 prisoners in Scottish jails in 1902 showed that in 228 instances, 81.4 per cent, drink was the primary cause of their descent into crime. Colonel McHardy, of the

Scottish Prison Commission, believed that if 'intemperance could be cured the prison population would collapse'.[55]

However, while the profile of crime was changing it was still largely a male affair, with young men in the age group eighteen to twenty-five being the most active. In 1907, there were 61,339 committals in Scotland; of these 18,397, or 30 per cent, were female, which was consistent with the data presented by Ian Donnachie for the first half of the century. The only divergence was in the rate of re-offending among women, which was considered 'large' with more women than men having over 'twenty convictions'.[56] Of course, there were crimes specific to gender. Prostitution was exclusively female. It was estimated that in Glasgow in 1849 there were 211 brothels in the city occupied by 538 prostitutes with another 500 women soliciting on the streets. Ten years later, official statistics confirmed these figures. The Police Act of 1866 did much to reduce the numbers of brothels and prostitutes in the city with an all-out assault against the vice trade by the authorities, which led to 293 arrests in 1870 and 337 in 1871, before a peak was reached in 1875 with 1,839 arrests.[57]

The causes of crime were thus seen by most of the middle classes and criminologists as biological or psychological rather than socio-economic, with as we have seen alcohol being the most prominent, but other factors such as idleness, ethnicity (the Catholic Irish were viewed as more criminally-orientated), lack of education and parental neglect were also highlighted. When investigated, these views are shown to be somewhat problematic. Alistair Goldsmith's research has demonstrated that far from being uneducated some 75 per cent of those in custody in Glasgow's jails before 1850 had some degree of literacy.[58] As to the Irish, we do not possess any runs of statistics to test the widespread popular belief in Victorian Scotland in their inherent criminality, but if we take the data for admissions to reformatory schools of young boys and girls in 1880 as an indication of the sectarian propensity to commit crime, it would seem that out of 270 boys 66, or 24.4 per cent, were Roman Catholic, and of 58 girls admitted 29, or 50 per cent, were Roman Catholic; another study of the Scottish prison population estimated that one-third of prisoners were of Irish origin.[59] Research carried out on England points to the fact that the Irish were over-represented in the statistics of crime, but whether that was a result of their ethnicity or their poverty is open to question. Most criminals were from the poorest sections of society and the Irish community was noted for its poverty and squalid living conditions. But it could also be argued that they found themselves disproportionately represented in the criminal statistics as lifestyle casualties of the middle-class mission to alter social behaviour profoundly with the crackdown on drunkenness and other forms of anti-social behaviour after 1850. The English evidence shows that 'Irish criminality was highly concentrated in the often related categories of drunkenness, disorderly behaviour and assault . . . and to a lesser extent petty crime and vagrancy'.[60] However, regardless of their authenticity, these constructed beliefs were comforting to the well off since over the nineteenth century 'most commentators and experts went out their way to deny any relationship between low wages, poverty and the bulk of crime'; although it was indisputable that criminal activity was more intense in periods of economic crises.[61] In Glasgow, petty theft peaked in 1867–8 and 1906–7, years of widespread unemployment.[62] Clive Emsley also noted a coincidence in England of economic depression and political unrest with peaks of committals.[63] The link between low wages, poverty and crime was further demonstrated by the occupational profile of the Scottish prison population in 1898. A total of 1,944 male prisoners were classed as unskilled labourers far exceeding the next main category of 103 workers in the rougher iron trades, such as riveting, and 93 coalminers.[64]

For the nineteenth century, it is clear that most crime was petty in nature and, to a large extent, harmless. The criminalisation of everyday life was part of an assault by middle-class authorities on the morals and values of the working class, especially that part which was most vulnerable, the low paid, the casual labourer, the vagrant and the prostitute. They comprised people living on the margins of society; the surplus population; the 'outcast' groups. They were forced through cyclical and casual unemployment to survive in the 'illegal economies of the cities', and, because of their alienation, refused to subscribe to the holy grail of respectability.[65] Drink was not only a means of escape, but also one of the more obvious ways the poor, the unrespectable, had of flouting the moralising of the middle classes and their agents of coercion – the police.

PUBLIC ORDER

But the challenge to social order and the consensus of values was also expressed in full-scale public disorders, and these were fairly continuous throughout second half of the nineteenth century. Generally speaking, protest gave voice to everyday identities based on class, gender, religion and territory, but equally it also showed how complex, contradictory and competitive these voices could be. Sectarian riots in the main took the form of intra-class skirmishes between rival immigrant Irish Catholic and Protestant communities. However, while the participants were working class, unlike the eighteenth and early nineteenth centuries, these disturbances were less obviously to do with class relations, as witnessed in the King's Birthday or Food Riots, and more to do with issues concerning identity. From these 'conflicts over boundaries, ownership and meaning of places' separate identities were preserved and nurtured.[66] The conflicts over questions of identity clashed with the desire of an increasingly anxious ruling class for social order. From an early date, the authorities were active in suppressing sectarian conflicts as part of a wider campaign against radical activity and no Orange marches took place in Glasgow between 1822 and 1840, although serious disturbances occurred in rural areas such as Newton Stewart, Dumfries and Dalkeith, as well as in small industrial towns such as Airdrie and Port Glasgow in this period.[67] The main catalyst in these earlier disturbances was the strained relations between nomadic Irish navvies and the local population and these continued after 1850. Although the navvy had a rather bad press in Victorian Scotland, most of the clashes were provoked by locals under the leadership of itinerant Protestant preachers. In Greenock in August 1851 a riot was provoked by itinerant preacher, John Orr's lecture on popery. Crowds gathered and a mêlée broke out between townspeople and the navvies, which led to the virtual demolition of the Catholic Church and obliged the priests to flee to Rothesay.[68] Another riot took place in South Queensferry in 1864 between navvies and townspeople, again provoked by missionaries from the Carubber's Close Mission in Edinburgh. Order was restored only by the intervention of a company of Royal Marines.[69] Such disturbances often lasted several days, sometimes weeks. The report of the Glasgow magistrates into the August disturbances in Greenock illustrates how small disputes could escalate and engulf whole communities in major sectarian conflict:

> Terrific yells and shouts shaded into fistfights and then armed attacks; indiscriminate violence became more targeted and was used as a cover for theft. As the mob developed its own nightly routines Catholic inhabitants and their families are kept in a state of uncertainty and continual terror. The lawless excess of the well organised mob outflanked and overwhelmed the local police.[70]

But as the century wore on, the riots took place between settled communities rather than with peripatetic labourers. The touchstone for the disturbances was parading during the summer Orange marching season. The Glorious Twelfth parades, which commemorated the Protestant 'victory' at the Battle of the Boyne in 1690, often ended in local civil wars. On the surface, the parades were expressions of Protestant affection for the Union and the Crown; in other words, celebrations of their history and traditions. But as Neil Jarman and Elaine McFarland point out, there was also a darker side to them: 'parades were a means of marking territory, of showing local party strength and solidarity with neighbours',[71] designed to maintain political and territorial ascendancy over other communities. As one Irish historian put it: 'Where you could walk you were dominant and the other things followed'.[72]

The growing intensity of these religious conflicts became increasingly worrying to the authorities as Home Office papers show. Patrick Fraser, Sheriff of Renfrewshire, wrote to the Home Secretary in July 1873, asking for powers to prevent the 12 July Orange processions 'which provoked fierce assaults by irritated Irishmen . . . These encounters ended in bloodshed.'[73] The law was powerless to prevent a procession of sectarian loyalties 'even [one] armed with revolvers . . . without check'.[74] Replicating earlier geographical patterns, most of these confrontations took place in rural/mining areas and small towns, where boundaries were more static, and communities more clearly identified and less easily controlled. A Home Rule demonstration of 3,000 Irish Catholics in Coatbridge was attacked by a mob of Orangemen which led to rioting over two days in August 1883. *The Times* reported that 'upwards of fifty apprehensions [were] . . . made' and 'many persons were injured by stones and otherwise'.[75] A violent clash between Catholics and Protestants took place in Blantyre in February 1887 and resulted in military intervention and the arrest of fifty-one people, including several women. The rioting spread to Coatbridge and, after much stone-throwing and window breaking, the 4th Hussars were sent in to restore order. It appeared that the whole district was under military siege as armed soldiers and mounted constabulary were sent to Hamilton and Denny.[76]

In the large cities where, over time, spatial ordering had transformed unregulated neutral spaces into highly defined and regulated grids based on class, gender and ethnicity, people were more easily controlled by the police.[77] This, however, was no guarantee of order and violent clashes between the rival communities occurred from time to time. In 1875, Catholics celebrating the centenary of Daniel O'Connell's birth in the Partick area of Glasgow were attacked by hundreds of Orangemen and the fighting which ensued lasted for several days.[78] Glasgow was again the scene of violent disturbances in 1898 for the 'first time in over a decade, as returning [Orange] processionists deviated . . . and 'trespassed' into a Catholic residential area'.[79] Even in cities such as Dundee where sectarian tensions were less fierce, St. Patrick's Day or the Twelfth of July split the people into two factions the 'Blues' and the 'Greens'. As one observer noted, on these occasions 'In every back green, alley, and playground pitched battles were the order of the day.'[80]

The sectarian conflicts were also transferred to the sporting arenas. Football matches were subjected to pitch invasions in which rival fans fought each other and the police. The fighting was not simply confined to the 'Old Firm', but also involved lesser clubs in major confrontations. The riot between crowd and police at the match between Greenock Morton (Protestant) and Port Glasgow (Irish Catholic), left thirty-two policemen injured, three of them seriously, and resulted in the arrest after investigation of forty-three spectators. It was the most serious disturbance to occur at a football match in Scotland outside the infamous riot of April 1909 at the end of the Scottish Cup final replay between Rangers and Celtic.[81] Relations between the Glasgow clubs and their supporters had been tense for some time and matches were persistently abandoned by officials following pitch invasions. The first major one occurred in 1896, and an even more violent one occurred in 1902, which led the *Scottish Referee* to claim it was 'the most disgraceful exhibition that has ever been witnessed in a Scottish football arena'.[82] In the first few months of 1905 there were two more pitch invasions, but they were trivial compared with the 1909 cup final replay. During the full-scale riot that followed, when the officials refused to agree to extra time, pitch battles were fought between supporters of both camps, using knives, stones, bottles and pieces of wood, and police and firemen, leaving fifty policemen injured and another sixty unspecified casualties.[83]

Another product of the sport/religion connection was the thriving gang culture in Glasgow, which was motivated by 'religious intolerance'. In 1900 there were several gangs active in the city such as the Hi Hi in the north, the Ping Pong in the east and the San Toy, the Tim Malloy and the Village Boys in the south. Each gang had around 100 plus members, aged between sixteen and twenty, although the Redskins in the east end had some female members. They fought each other with knuckle dusters and pokers, and when not engaged in sectarian fighting frightened shopkeepers and publicans into paying protection money.[84]

The sectarian disorders were primarily aimed at making and maintaining ethnic and religious identities; however, industrial disturbances posed more immediate class concerns for the authorities and employers and as such were similarly stamped on. Michel Foucault has noted that workers' actions in France were regularly accused of 'being animated . . . by mere criminals' and that 'verdicts were often more severe against workers than thieves'.[85] In a more contemporary reference, Ian MacGregor, Chairman of the National Coal Board, during the 1984–5 miners' strike, referred to the striking miners as the 'howling mob', the 'rabble' and the 'rag tag mob of the militant left'.[86] The terminology of the pre-industrial world remained of value to the authorities in isolating and stigmatising perceived threats to private property. Those challenging the hegemony of property could be depicted as 'the other', that is, as groups outside of society whose behaviour and values were not only criminal but alien. The rhetoric was always backed by force. In April 1856, a strike by around 30,000 miners in the west of Scotland led to the mobilisation of special constables, the militia and pensioners as well as regular troops. According to Home Office figures, the amalgamated forces of coercion which were actively engaged in putting down the strike amounted to 513 in Stirlingshire, 3,077 in Lanarkshire, 921 in Ayrshire and 526 in Renfrewshire.[87] The creation of overwhelming force was seen as the best way of containing such challenges. The shrewd, ruthless and experienced Sheriff Archibald Alison of Lanarkshire was able to state with some satisfaction that a much larger strike action two years later was checked by the fact that the 'local authorities had a much larger force to meet it than on any former occasion . . . there were two regiments of militia . . . and . . . a rural police force under very efficient direction, consisting of 130 men . . . [as well as] Two troops of yeomanry'.[88] This did little to stem the tide of industrial rioting and violence in mining districts in Scotland. Alan Campbell recorded over fifty disturbances in Scottish mining districts between 1893 and 1919, which included attacks on managers' houses, fighting with police, looting of shops and beating and stoning blacklegs.[89] One incident in Slamannan might be seen as representative of the clashes investigated by Campbell. In 1878, in response to eviction orders a miners' brass band marched around the district whipping up a crowd, which under the cover of darkness proceeded to stone three policemen and the colliery manager, before breaking into one of the owners' homes and wrecking one of the rooms.[90]

Industrial protests were not confined to mining areas, although to be fair miners were responsible for most of this form of rioting in the second half of the nineteenth century. Women, mainly in textile centres, where the hours were long and the pay low, also took part in industrial riots. Of course, women had traditionally been as prepared to riot as men; in fact, they were more effective as protestors, as the authorities were less likely to attack them and they were also less likely to be prosecuted.[91] Drawing on this tradition of negotiation by riot, the largely defenceless, non-unionised women workers in nineteenth-century Scotland protested about their conditions of work and pay in ways that would have been entirely recognisable to their ancestors a century before engaged in Food Riots, opposing the Militia Acts of 1797 and fighting naval press gangs. An example from Paisley in October 1907 illustrates the general strategies and tactics of unorganised females taking part in industrial action. The strike was ignited by the introduction of new machinery which threatened to reduce piece-rate payments in the thread mill. On the morning of 2 October, 400 block polishers proceeded to create industrial mayhem. The *Glasgow Herald* described the scene as follows:

> [the polishers] armed themselves with spoolwood sticks and smashed a large number of windows in the department . . . the management . . . deemed it necessary to summon extra police . . . ejection was effected although not without considerable trouble.[92]

On being driven from the mills, the girls occupied the surrounding lanes and running battles took place between them and the police. The mobilisation of protest among the Paisley mill girls, and the spontaneous anarchic form it took, was criticised by the press as being irresponsible and 'unspeakably ridiculous'.[93] However, their behaviour was in line with other women workers in textile trades. Eleanor Gordon, in her study of the Dundee jute industry, found evidence of similar actions, such as parading through the streets of the town, barracking employers, assaults on workers refusing to obey the call to strike and so on.[94] Although this behaviour was at odds with the normally sober and respectable protest of skilled male trade unionists, she sees it as simply a transportation of female leisure into the sphere of industrial conflict: 'it was a flight from work, a collective expression of defiance'. At the same time, the so-called 'disgraceful' actions of the striking women were a rejection of male notions of acceptable feminine behaviour and of men's ability to control them.[95]

Women were also at the forefront of gender struggles over what constituted a woman's place in society in the nineteenth and early twentieth centuries. Although the First Reform Act of 1832 and the repeal of the Corn Laws in 1846 had satisfied middle-class ambitions, and, therefore, pretty much put an end to their engagement with extra-parliamentary activity, fear of economic and political emasculation formed the basis of male opposition to any educational and political reforms designed to reduce the democratic deficit in Victorian and Edwardian Britain. The first major public articulation of the deeply ingrained misogyny within the middle classes occurred in November 1870, and was a reaction to the admittance of women into the medical faculty of the University of Edinburgh. The riot that took place at Surgeons' Hall in Edinburgh was the culmination of a sustained campaign of harassment and bullying against the women that included obscenities being shouted at them in the streets, slamming doors in their faces, sending them dirty letters and so on. In a vain attempt to prevent the women sitting the anatomy examination, 200 male undergraduates, with the blessing of some members of staff of the university, on 18 November blocked the entrance to the Royal College of Surgeons. As the leader of the women, Sophia Jex-Blake put it:

> We walked straight up to the gates . . . [which] were slammed in our faces by a number of young men, who stood within, smoking and passing about bottles of whisky, while they abused us in the foulest possible language.[96]

After some jostling, the university janitors managed to obtain access to the anatomical classroom for the women, who by this time were mud-splattered and the examination proceeded. The actions of the male students brought nationwide condemnation, although it did little to further the cause of the women, who had to wait until 1892 before the doors of the universities were open to them.

In the Surgeons' Hall Riot the women were depicted as victims of male prejudice and harassment, and undoubtedly this won them much sympathy as their actions did not challenge male definitions of femininity, as it appeared that they were still in need of protection. However, in the campaign for the franchise later in the century they were active, independent agents. Challenging male perceptions of their gender on a whole series of levels, the militant wing of the women's suffrage movement, the Suffragettes, embarked between 1906 and 1913 on a sustained campaign of civil disobedience that bordered on social terrorism. Under the leadership of the Women's Social and Political Union (WSPU), the militants used violent methods, such as throwing stones, breaking windows, chaining themselves to railings, setting fire to pillar boxes, in order to raise public awareness of their campaign. In Scotland, the WSPU did not adopt militant tactics until 1913. Having done so, there occurred a wave of terrorist attacks, dubbed by the *Glasgow Herald* as the 'Scottish outrages'. Glasgow's pillar boxes were set alight, the mansion house of Farrington Hall in Dundee was fire-bombed, causing damage estimated at £10,000, and even in the near dormitory town of St Andrews there were several arson attacks, most notably on Leuchars railway station.[97] As the campaign intensified, especially after the passing of the Cat and Mouse Act in April 1913, increasing numbers of middle-class women were arrested and imprisoned. The direct action culminated in June 1913 when Emily Davidson died trying to stop the King's horse in the Epsom Derby. This was one act of defiance too much for the British public and the militant struggle lost ground among women generally.

The disorder provoked by struggles over gender issues in the second half of the nineteenth century was due mainly to economic and political factors; however, another source of tumult lay in the town and gown relations in the university cities of Scotland. This relationship is very much under-researched, but from the fragmentary evidence that has so far been uncovered it concerned perceptions of territory and its usage. An early example was that which occurred in Edinburgh in January 1838. The riot which ensued began as a harmless snowball fight between students and tradesmen, but quickly took a more sinister turn as townspeople and police battled with the former. Snowballs with stones secreted in them led to the 'breaking of an immense number of panes of glass'. A police and townspeople attempt to storm the university quadrangle in the South Bridge was the signal for hand-to-hand fighting, using sticks and batons which saw some of the participants 'severely wounded'. Events were brought under control when the Lord Provost ordered a detachment of the 79th Regiment armed with muskets and bayonets to storm the College.[98] The riotous events led to the arrest and prosecution of five students and in the trial that followed it became clear that tensions between town and gown in Edinburgh had been festering for some time. When the snowball fight escalated, the students felt that the police and magistracy had no civil jurisdiction within the university quadrangle and battled to keep the former, as well as the angry crowd, out, hence the cry 'to turn them out'. But there was also clearly a political aspect to the events, as the language of the crowd makes clear. According to one witness, Mr Hutchison, surgeon, epithets such as 'd-d puppies, Tory blackguards, and the like' were shouted at the students.[99] The age old resentment of privilege was an important factor in motivating the crowd, while the defence of territory became the main reason behind the actions of the students. The judiciary found in favour of the students, as it was felt that they had been the subject of provocation and acts of violence.

While middle-class men had achieved the 'de-legitimisation of earlier forms of community protest such as riot',[100] by dissociating themselves from such activities, the same was not true of those family members who remained outside constitutional frameworks. The marginalisation of youth and gender issues saw bursts of unlawful protest which were outward signs of deeper feelings of frustration with deference and misogyny.

POLICING

The policing of society is a relatively recent institutional innovation. Prior to the founding of Scotland's and Britain's first police force in Glasgow in 1800, crime and disorder were the responsibility of a number of mainly voluntary agencies, ranging from night and day watchmen, yeomanry, special constables and, of course, in more serious situations, the army itself. These agencies continued to be used well into the first half of the nineteenth century until they were gradually replaced by a permanent body of trained professionals. They were largely ineffective in dealing with crime, but enjoyed more success in putting down riots and rebellions. The following description of 'policing' in the small burgh of Arbroath provides some clues as to the ineffectiveness of such agencies in combating crime. In the 1830s, the burgh had two guardians of the peace, who 'perambulated the streets by night, and three by day. They had no distinctive dress, wearing their own corduroy breeks and tam o'shanters . . . there were two hodden gray overcoats . . . set apart for the use of the nightwatchmen'.[101] Similarly, special constables given their embeddedness in local communities were viewed as unreliable by the authorities. Archibald Alison, referring to a riot between Catholics and Protestants in Airdrie in 1834, remarked that 'though the blow struck was successful . . . it afforded a demonstration of how dangerous it is to suppress even the most outrageous violence in one part of the population by the aid of another'.[102] More reliable in suppressing riots and other disorders were the Yeomanry, who were composed of wealthy landlords and substantial tenant farmers. It was this voluntary force and the army that were the main vehicles for the suppression of strikes and political activities, particularly during the Chartist years of the late 1830s and early 1840s.

Alison was always ready to use martial law as a visible display of the potency of sovereign power, but he recognised that sporadic demonstrations of authority were risky, inefficient and inadequate to the demands of an industrial society. Far better was to have a permanent police force able to enforce urban and industrial discipline continuously, while developing efficient systems to understand and counter disturbance. He was concerned that in the county of Lanark 'beyond the bounds of Glasgow there was not a single policeman, nor in the suburbs of the city', where the main manufactories were located. Here, there was 'either no police at all, or a very inefficient one . . . Thus, in those localities where the danger was greatest, there was . . . no protective force.'[103] Indeed, the Glasgow suburbs of Gorbals, Calton and Anderston had only fifteen to twenty officers each to police around 30, 000–40,000 inhabitants.[104] But despite the urgency of the situation many burghs were reluctant to establish such institutions. Even in Glasgow, the merchant elite in the eighteenth century was concerned at the transfer, at their expense, of new powers to 'burgh authorities over whom they had no democratic check'.[105] What galvanised opinion behind the creation of a police force in Glasgow and other urban areas was the 'heightened fears of popular disorder', and in the countryside one might add vagrancy.[106] Tom Devine's work on the formation of the Glasgow police shows that the 'machinations of the disaffected' had become so menacing that the Police Commission attempted to establish 'regiments' for the protection of 'the lives and property of the community'.[107] From Glasgow's initiative in 1800 there followed a series of parliamentary bills in the period 1833 to 1847 aimed at the creation of a 'General System of Police' in Scottish burghs. However, it was clear from Alison's writings that the police were there largely to impose order rather than prevent crime. In his plans for the reorganisation of the police in Glasgow and the rest of Lanarkshire he stated that the main purpose was not only:

> to deter the greater part of housebreakers [but with] the power of a formidable police force of 100 to or 150 men to my part within the district where a strike had occurred, or violence to new hands was threatened, [which] would effectively coerce the designs of the trade unions, and, by depriving them of their grand engine – intimidation – materially abridge their duration and prevent their atrocities.[108]

The holy grail of a mobile centralised police force was still someway off as burghs only slowly adopted the legislation. Outside the main centres of population, only twelve out of 183 burghs empowered to do so had set up a police force by 1847. However, with the last throes of Chartist activity in 1848 there was a rush to join the club. By 1852, sixty-seven burghs were maintaining a police force in Scotland. The total number of police in that year was 1,370 with 80 in Aberdeen, 318 in Edinburgh, 613 in Glasgow and 66 in Dundee. The rest of the burghs generally had two or three policemen, and there were 500 for the whole of rural Scotland.[109] By the end of the century Scotland had a police force of around 5,000, costing £477,000 annually.[110]

After 1850 there was a distinct shift in the remit of the police; less to do with the maintenance of the social order, and more to do with the enforcement of moral behaviour. As part of the assault by the middles classes in the wake of Chartism on the morals and values of the working class[111] the police were afforded a key missionary role in this project. This mission involved the criminalisation of behaviour deemed unacceptable to the middle classes and extended to all aspects of economic and social life. Indeed, the attempts to regulate social conduct in the second half of the nineteenth century accounted for the only real growth in recorded criminal behaviour, as indictable offences fell. Time-sanctioned customs and popular practices were condemned and criminalised and people were subjected to an increased degree of surveillance and control compared with the earlier part of the century. As the middle class did not see why anyone should be in the street, local bylaws were used by burgh authorities to regulate street life and that regulation gradually imposed a 'regulation of its own'.[112] Recreational pastimes which had traditionally colonised urban spaces were outlawed and workers were encouraged to use the park, with, as Mark Billinge points out, its liturgical symmetry of space, lines and pitches; it 'mirrored the discipline of the rules of the games it sought to contain . . . [and provided] a pretext on which to clear . . . less organised activity out of . . . the street'.[113] These concerns were reflected in the Glasgow Police Act of 1892 which clearly stated that a fine of 40s. or fourteen days' imprisonment was to be imposed on 'Every person who pulls or rings any door-bell, or knocks for the purpose of begging' and that 'Every person who throws a snowball, stone or other missile, or flies a kite, or makes use of any slide, or throws on the foot pavement any orange skin' would be liable to the same penalty.[114] There were also sanctions against playing football, cricket or any other sport, making one liable to a fine of 20s. for each offence. Gambling was especially singled out for action. The same Act fixed a penalty of 40s. for any two or more persons assembled together for the purpose 'of engaging in lotteries, betting or gaming'.[115] There were also bylaws against bathing in the River Clyde, shaking a carpet between 8 am and noon, and licences were needed from a magistrate to allow someone to open a shooting gallery, dancing saloon, nine-pin alley and so on.

By these means the police were able to colonise the streets and enter the previously dark and rough parts of the cities and towns, setting up their new stations and establishing regular patrols.[116] Thus, naughty children, employees taking perks, obstreperous drunks, bad neighbours, street sellers, bookies, illegal drinking dens, increasingly found themselves objects of state intervention and control.[117] As two observers noted in 1911:

> In every direction, inside his own home, as well as out, the working-man's habits and convenience are interfered with . . . Whether or no he comes into collision with them is more a matter of good fortune than of law-abidingness . . . a working man may easily render himself liable to arrest . . . without in the least doing what is wrong in his eyes or in the eyes of his neighbours.[118]

Thus, the everyday was in the process of being criminalised and with each new piece of legislation more offences were added (for example the Education Act of 1872 which made attendance at school compulsory, created the truant) which only increased resentment among those affected by assaults on social activities. Interference by the authorities in the welfare of children was particularly resented. As Linda Mahood points out, 'What was seen by working-class parents as proper initiative and responsibility – for instance, when a son sold a newspaper or a daughter sang outside a bar for pennies – was evidence of neglect, cruelty or immorality' to the middle class.[119] Another area of contention were the powers to 'move-on', that is, to break up small groups of working men gathered in the streets and order them 'to go about their business'.[120] From 1816 in Glasgow, police constables were empowered to disperse anyone or anything 'causing a crowd of idle people to collect on the street'.[121] Transgressions of space were also punished. Those deemed to be in the wrong place, that is, women in male enclaves, poor people in rich areas, prostitutes at society weddings were arrested or stigmatised in some way.[122]

However, regardless of the level of resentment such interference provoked among workers and their families, it has been argued by some historians that it was sufficiently potent as a strategy to make even the lower classes feel as if the police were necessary and legitimate. As *The Times* put it in the early 1900s:

> In many a back street he [the policeman] not only stands for law and order; he is the true handy-man of the streets, the best friend of a mass of people who have no other counsellor or protector.[123]

Although there are recorded instances of anti-police riots in England earlier in the century,[124] by the 1890s the fact that most prosecutions were on behalf of working-class people who had been victims of theft or violence only served to emphasise the level of consent from those members of society who had most to fear from police interference. Paul Gordon's study of Scotland concurs with this view when he claims that worker confidence in the police was achieved by 'patrolling working-class areas where . . . they came to be seen as offering some form of protection to individual members of the working class'.[125]

However, while levels of crime and violence did decline in the second half of the century, this was by no means indicative of a wider legitimacy of the police within working-class communities. Research in this area of Scottish social history remains thin, which makes it difficult to arrive at any firm conclusions on the relationship between the working class and the police. Also it has to be remembered that although the police had established themselves in working-class communities, indeed, some were expected to live in the areas they policed,[126] there was still a tradition of self-regulation. Community justice was still dispensed to wife beaters who went to excess, to men who interfered with children and to others whose behaviour was deemed overly anti-social. However, in spite of these qualifications, there existed different perceptions of the role of the police in England and Scotland. While the police in England had the appearance of an occupying uniformed force from the outset, the Scottish police had a welfare role as well as overseeing the maintenance of law and order. The police had responsibility for hygiene and sanitation, as well as lighting and street cleaning. Indeed, some of the more enlightened reforms in these areas, such as the supply of clean drinking water, came in the form of Police Acts.[127] Thus, the dual nature of the police role may have reduced somewhat the potential for tensions and hostilities in Scotland. The growing professionalism of the police also did much to defuse tensions. The new police that emerged in the third and fourth decades of the nineteenth century were poorly trained. Stanley Palmer describes the new force in England as a badly paid, 'rough bunch', with a reputation for drunkenness and assault against men and women.[128] A study of the Glasgow police shows that description applied equally north of the border. In the first five and a half months of 1847, seventy-one men were dismissed for being drunk on duty, twenty for being 'worn out and unfit for duty', and four for assaulting prisoners.[129] Edinburgh's police in 1838 were described by Patrick Robertson, lawyer, as the 'disgrace of this metropolis – the most expensive . . . in Europe; and . . . the most inefficient and brutal'.[130] Gradually improved standards of conduct and greater efficiency in the prevention and detection of crime went some way to bolstering the standing of this previously motley, uneducated and ill-disciplined force in working-class areas.

But, in spite of increasing professionalism, there exists some evidence, admittedly fragmentary, which calls into question the rather Whiggish interpretation of the process of legitimisation, and rather points to an ongoing state of hostility between some groups of the population and the police from 1850 onwards. The anonymous commentator, 'Shadow', complained in 1858 that the police force has 'been assuming more a military than a civil power . . . Its members are everyday becoming more separate from the people, and their sympathies alienated.'[131] William Small, secretary of the Lanarkshire miners' trade union, protested in 1887 that the 'annoyance and aggravation of the police has become intolerable, they have abandoned themselves to tyranny, coercion and club law that human nature cannot tolerate and certainly will resent'.[132] A contemporary study of municipal government in Glasgow in the first decade of the twentieth century, pointed out that the 'lower . . . we descend in the social scale the greater will be found the popular antagonism to the police, till in the shady circles verging towards the regions of filth, vice and crime the very name 'police' is hated as much as it is feared'.[133] In England, David Jones claimed that there was a high level of violence aimed at the police until the 1870s, while Victor Gatrell has stated that a 'large minority' of the population never entertained any doubt 'that the policeman and the law were their enemies'.[134] To support this claim he cited the *Morning Advertiser*'s report that, in 1903, 20 per cent of London's Metropolitan Force had been assaulted in the course of their duties.[135] The language of resentment so prevalent in working-class areas would also suggest more of an 'armed truce' than legitimacy. The police were seen by workers in the north of England as parasites and known as 'blue bottles', 'blue drones', 'black locusts',[136] and similar labels were used in urban Scotland to vocalise opposition to the morals and values they were seeking to impose on a reluctant working class.

CONCLUSION

The gradual extension of the franchise and the irregular rises in the standard of living in the last three decades of the nineteenth century were no guarantees of social peace, as the majority of Scots were excluded from any material and political improvements: all women and a large minority of men remained unenfranchised and it was only the middle classes and the skilled male working class that experienced material gains. The excluded were able to express their economic and political frustrations only by

extra-parliamentary means. Riot and disorder were still considered legitimate forms of popular expression among the dispossessed and powerless,
although it is undoubtedly true that the nature of these events changed in the
course of the century. Radicalism and/or hunger ceased to be major factors
in promoting unrest, rather it became an issue connected with identity and
territory. Disorder of this kind was not aimed at overturning the economic
and political foundations of liberal capitalism, as in the case of the women's
suffrage campaign, it was about winning a place at the table, and in the sectarian conflicts it involved marginal groups trying to establish the supremacy
of their culture and symbols over others. There was also the day-to-day disorder of the rougher side of working-class culture, and although there was
a vigorous and committed campaign to domesticate this in the second half
of the nineteenth century, there were limits imposed on its success by the
widespread poverty and squalor that depended in various ways on the illegal
or criminal to survive. Norbert Elias, whose study of the growth of civilised
society has been hugely influential among historians of crime, particularly
violent crime, had to admit that it was difficult to apply his theory to some
elements of the working class, who 'live more fully in accordance with their
own manners and customs'.[137] He was only echoing an earlier observation by
Leslie Stephen, who stated that:

> We have amongst us large masses of population who have escaped the enervat-
> ing polish of civilisation. To them we may still look occasionally for vigorous
> passions and decided actions. They have the rude energy along with the brutal
> propensities of a more animal existence.[138]

The taming of these 'vigorous passions' involved the imposition of coercive
power in previously unregulated domains and sparked tensions and confrontation. As Gatrell points out, legal statutes did not eradicate unacceptable
social behaviour but it did 'delineate the physical arenas' in which it could
take place.[139] In the light of alternative sources of evidence, the 'transition
to order' thesis would appear to rest on rather ill-defined Whiggish ideas
concerning progress and stability and as such constitutes a barrier to a fuller
understanding of the role of unsocial behaviour and attempts to control it in
Victorian Scotland. Society did not become more stable after 1850, the difference lay in the groups involved in disorder and the means available to contain
it.

Notes

1 C. A. Whatley (ed.), *The Diary of John Sturrock, Millwright, Dundee 1864–65* (East
   Linton, 1996), pp. 20, 60.
2 J. M. McBain, *Arbroath: Past and Present* (Arbroath, 1887), pp. 104–6.
3 S. Nenadic, 'Political Reform and the "Ordering" of Middle-Class Protest', in

T. M. Devine (ed.),*Conflict and Stability in Scottish Society, 1700–1850*, (Edinburgh, 1990), p. 76.

4 W. W. J. Knox, *Industrial Nation: Work, Culture and Society in Scotland, 1800–Present* (Edinburgh, 1999), pp. 94–103; N. Tranter, 'The Social and Occupational Structure of Organised Sport in Central Scotland, during the Nineteenth Century', *International Journal of the History of Sport*, 4 (1987), 303–10.

5 E. Richards, 'The Last Scottish Food Riots', *Past and Present*, 6 (1982), 59.

6 W. H. Fraser, 'The Glasgow Cotton Spinners 1837', in J. Butt and J. T. Ward (eds), *Scottish Themes*, (Edinburgh, 1976), p. 97.

7 See I. Donnachie, 'The Darker Side: A Speculative Survey of Scottish Crime during the First Half of the Nineteenth Century', *Scottish Economic and Social History*, 15 (1995), 5–24, for Scotland and V. A. C. Gatrell, 'The Decline of Theft and Violence in Edwardian England', in V. A. C. Gatrell, B. Lenman and G. Parker (eds), *Crime and the Law: The Social History of Crime in Western Europe since 1500* (London, 1980), pp. 238–338, for England.

8 C. A. Whatley, *Scottish Society, 1707–1830: beyond Jacobitism towards Industrialisation* (Manchester, 2000); J. Bohstedt, *Riots and Community Politics in England and Wales 1790–1810* (Cambridge, MA, 1983); E. Canetti, *Crowds and Power*, trans. Carol Stewart (London, 1973); M. Harrison, *Crowds and History: Mass Phenomenon in English Towns, 1790–1835* (Cambridge, 1988); G. Rude, *The Crowds in History: A Study of Popular Disturbances in England and France 1730–1848* (New York, 1964); G. Rude, 'The Changing Face of the Crowd', in H. J. Kaye (ed.),*The Face of the Crowd: Studies in Revolution, Ideology and Popular Protest. Selected Essays of George Rude* (New York, 1988), pp. 56–7; E. P. Thompson, *The Making of the English Working Class* (London, 1963); J. Stevenson, *Popular Disturbances in England 1700–1870* (London, 1979); R. Quinault and J. Stevenson, *Popular Protest and Public Order* (New York, 1975).

9 G. Le Bon, *The Crowd: A Study of the Popular Mind* (New York, 2002 edn).

10 Cited in K. Logue, *Popular Disturbances in Scotland, 1780–1815* (Edinburgh, 1979) p. 211.

11 Logue, *Popular Disturbances*, p. 211.

12 C. A. Whatley, 'An Uninflammable People?', in I. Donnachie and C. A. Whatley (eds), *The Manufacture of Scottish History* (Edinburgh, 1992), pp. 57–8; Whatley, *Scottish Society*, pp. 156–7.

13 T. M. Devine, 'The Failure of Radical Reform in Scotland in the late Eighteenth Century: the Social and Economic Context', in Devine (ed.), *Conflict and Stability*, pp. 51–64; T. C. Smout, *A History of the Scottish People, 1560–1830* (London, 1969), pp. 223, 227–9, 442–5.

14 Whatley, *Scottish Society*, p. 152.

15 Harrison, *Crowds and History*, pp. 17–18.

16 K. Marx and F. Engels, *Selected Works* (London, 1968), p. 138.

17 P. Hayes, *The People and the Mob: The Ideology of Civil Conflict in Modern Europe* (West Port, 1992), p. 15; L. Farmer, *Criminal Law, Tradition and Legal Order: Crime and the Genius of Scots Law, 1747 to the Present* (Cambridge, 1997), p. 112.

18 V. A. C. Gatrell, 'Crime, Authority and the Policeman-State', in F. M. L. Thompson (ed.), *Cambridge Social History of Britain, 1750–1950, Vol 3: Social Agencies and Institutions*, (Cambridge, 1990), p. 305.

19 Harrison, *Crowds and History*, p. 23.

20 Harrison, *Crowds and History*, p. 11–12.

21 C. Melucci, *Nomads of the Present: Social Movements and Individual Needs in Contemporary Society* (London, 1989), p. 36.

22 Melucci, *Nomads*, p. 61.

23 E. P. Thompson quoted in S. Hall *et al.*, *Policing the Crisis: Mugging, the State and Law and Order* (London, 1986 edn), pp. 188–9.

24 J. Davis, 'The London Garrotting Panic of 1862: A Moral Panic and the Creation of a Criminal Class in mid-Victorian England', in Gatrell, Lenman and Parker (eds), *Crime and the Law*, p. 202.

25 Gatrell, 'Policeman-State', pp. 248, 254.

26 R. Tombs, 'Crime and the Security of the State: The 'Dangerous Classes' and Insurrection in Nineteenth-century Paris', in Gatrell, Lenman and Parker (eds), *Crime and the Law*, p. 214.

27 W. H. Fraser, 'Patterns of Protest', in T. M. Devine and R. Mitchison (eds), *People and Society in Scotland, Vol. 1: 1760–1830*, (Edinburgh, 1988), p. 279.

28 *Glasgow: Trials & Sentences* (Broadsheet, April 1833).

29 M. Poovey, *Making a Social Body: British Cultural Formation 1830–1864* (Chicago, 1995); M. Foucault, *Society Must be Defended: Lectures at the College de France, 1975–76* (New York, 2003).

30 D. Garland, *Punishment and Modern Society: A Study in Social Theory* (Oxford, 1990).

31 S. J. Brown, *Thomas Chalmers and the Godly Commonwealth* (Oxford, 1982); A. Ure, *The Cotton Manufacture of Great Britain*, 2 vols (London, 1836).

32 Poovey, *Making a Social Body*, p. 35.

33 T. M. Devine, 'Urbanisation and the Civic Response: Glasgow 1800–1830', in A. J. G. Cummings and T. M. Devine (eds), *Industry, Business and Society in Scotland since 1700: Essays Presented to John Butt* (Edinburgh, 1994), p. 193.

34 Devine, 'Urbanisation', pp. 193–4.

35 D. Smith, 'Colonel A. B. McHardy: The Transformation of Penality in Scotland, 1885–1909', *Scottish Economic and Social History*, 9 (1989), 50, 47.

36 Foucault, *Discipline and Punish: The Birth of the Prison* (London, 1991), pp. 285–6.

37 Gatrell, 'Policeman-State', pp. 252–3.

38 J. B. Thompson, 'The Psychology of the Criminal', *Journal of Mental Science* (1870), quoted in M. J. Wiener, *Reconstructing the Criminal: Culture, Law and Policy in England, 1830–1914* (Cambridge, 1990), p. 233.

39 See H. Zehr, *Crime and the Development of Modern Society: Patterns of Criminality in Nineteenth-century Germany and France* (London, 1976), p. 9, for a discussion of Durkheim and crime.

40 C. Booth, *Life and Labour of the People of London, vol. 1* (London, 1892); B. S. Rowntree, *Poverty. A Study of Town Life* (London, 1901).

41 Hall *et al.*, *Policing*, p. 188.
42 Donnachie, 'Darker Side', p. 11.
43 Gatrell, 'Policeman-State', p. 278.
44 Quoted in A. L. Goldsmith, 'The Development of the City of Glasgow Police, *c.* 1800–1939', Unpublished Ph.D thesis, University of Strathclyde, 2002, p. 196.
45 Donnachie, 'Darker Side', p. 20.
46 Donnachie, 'Darker Side', p. 21.
47 Donnachie, 'Darker Side', p. 10.
48 C. Emsley, *Crime and Society in England, 1750–1900* (London, 1987), p. 27.
49 Farmer, *Criminal Law*, pp. 110–11; A. B. McHardy, 'The Economics of Crime', *Juridical Review*, XIV (1902), 48.
50 McHardy, 'Economics of Crime', p. 48.
51 W. H. Fraser and I. Mavor, 'The Social Problems of the City', in W. H. Fraser and I. Mavor (eds), *Glasgow, Vol. II: 1832–1912* (Manchester, 1996), p. 384.
52 Farmer, *Criminal Law*, pp. 113–14.
53 D. Jones, *Crime, Protest, Community and Police in Nineteenth-Century Britain* (London, 1982), p. 23.
54 Fraser and Mavor, 'Social Problems', pp. 383–4.
55 McHardy, 'Economics of Crime', p. 54.
56 C. N. Johnston, 'The Punishment of Crime', *Juridical Review*, XX (1908–9), 328.
57 Goldsmith, 'Glasgow Police', p. 355.
58 Goldsmith, 'Glasgow Police', p. 195.
59 *Reports from Commissioners and Inspectors: Reformatories and Industrial Schools*, BPP LII, 1881, p. 24; Johnston, 'Punishment', p. 328.
60 R. Swift, 'Heroes or Villains?: The Irish, Crime and Disorder in Victorian England', *Albion*, 29 (1997), 403.
61 Emsley, *Crime and Society*, pp. 49–50.
62 Fraser and Mavor, 'Social Problems', pp. 385–6.
63 Emsley, *Crime and Society*, p. 29.
64 J. Cameron, *Prisons and Punishment in Scotland: from the Middle Ages to the Present* (Edinburgh, 1983), p. 144.
65 S. Hall and P. Scraton, 'Law, Class and Control', in M. Fitzgerald, G. Mclennan and J. Pawson (eds), *Crime and Society: Readings in History and Theory* (London, 1994), pp. 483–4.
66 S. Gunn, 'The Spatial Turn: Changing Histories of Space and Time', in S. Gunn and R. J. Morris (eds), *Identities in Space: Contested Terrains in the Western City since 1850* (Aldershot, 2001), p. 9; P. Jess and D. Massey, 'The Contestation of Place', in P. Jess and D. Massey (eds), *A Place in the World? Places, Cultures and Globalisation* (Oxford, 1995), p. 134; J. Anderson and I. Shuttleworth, 'Spaces of Fear: Communal Violence and Spatial Behaviour', Paper presented to the Centre for Research in the Arts, Social Sciences and Humanities, Cambridge, January 2003.
67 E. McFarland, 'Marching from the Margins: Twelfth July Parades in Scotland,

1820–1914', in T. G. Fraser (eds), *The Irish Parading Tradition; Following the Drum* (Basingstoke, 2000), p. 62.

68 The National Archives [NA]: HO45/3472/E001.

69 NA: HO45/3472/E001.

70 Glasgow Magistrates Report on the Anti-Catholic Riots, 8 August 1851 (HO45/55).

71 N. Jarman, *Material Conflicts: Parades and Visual Displays in Northern Ireland* (Oxford, 1997), p. 56; McFarland, 'Marching', p. 61.

72 M. W. Dewar, *Orangeism: A New Historical Appreciation* (Belfast, 1973), p. 83, quoted in McFarland, 'Marching', p. 61.

73 NA: HO45/9/ 472/A19903.

74 NA: HO45/9/472/A19903.

75 *The Times*, 21 August 1883.

76 *The Times*, 10 February 1887.

77 Gunn, 'Spatial Turn', p. 5.

78 J. M. Bradley, 'Wearing the Green: A History of Nationalist Demonstrations among the Diaspora in Scotland', in Fraser (ed.), *The Irish Parading Tradition*, p. 114.

79 McFarland, 'Marching', p. 72.

80 E. Dye, *Tales of Old Dundee* (Dundee, 1947), p. 35.

81 N. L. Tranter, 'The Cappielow Riot and the Composition and Behaviour of Soccer Crowds in Late Victorian Scotland', *International Journal of the History of Sport*, 12 (1995), 127–8.

82 B. Murray, *The Old Firm: Sectarianism, Sport and Society in Scotland* (Edinburgh, 1984), p. 165.

83 C. Simon, 'Fever Pitch', *History Today* (May 1999).

84 D. Grant, *The Thin Blue Line: The Story of the City of Glasgow Police* (London, 1973), pp. 51–3.

85 M. Foucault, *Discipline*, pp. 285–6.

86 Hayes, *People and the Mob*, p. 119.

87 NA: HO45/6340.

88 Sir A. Alison, *My Life and Writings Vol. 2* (Edinburgh, 1883), p. 214.

89 A. B. Campbell, *The Scottish Miners 1874–1939, Vol. 1* (Aldershot, 2000), pp. 303–7.

90 Campbell, *Scottish Miners*, p. 276.

91 Fraser, 'Patterns of Protest', p. 271; Logue, *Popular Disturbances*, p. 199.

92 *Glasgow Herald*, 3 October 1907.

93 *Glasgow Herald*, 4 October 1907.

94 E. Gordon, *Women and the Labour Movement in Scotland, 1850–1914* (Oxford, 1991), pp. 177, 179, 192.

95 Gordon, *Women and Labour*, pp. 209–10.

96 S. Jex-Blake, *Medical Women: A Thesis and a History* (Edinburgh, 1886), p. 92.

97 E. King, *The Scottish Women's Suffrage Movement* (Glasgow, 1994), p. 24.

98 *The Times*, 16 January 1838.

99   Anon., *Report of the Trial of the Students on the Charge of Mobbing, Rioting and Assault at the College* (Edinburgh, 1838), pp. 70, 36.
100 Nenadic, 'Middle-Class Protest', p. 77.
101 McBain, *Arbroath*, pp. 103–4.
102 Alison, *My Life*, pp. 360–1.
103 Alison, *My Life*, pp. 370–1.
104 D. Barrie, '"Epoch Making" Beginnings to Lingering Death: The Struggle for Control of the Glasgow Police Commission', *Scottish Historical Review*, LXXXVI (2007), 261.
105 Fraser, 'Patterns of Protest', p. 279.
106 Fraser, 'Patterns of Protest', p. 279; K. Carson and H. Idzikowska, 'The Social Production of Scottish Policing, 1795–1900', in D. Hay and F. Snyder (eds), *Policing and Prosecution in Britain, 1750–1850* (Oxford, 1989), p. 273.
107 Devine, 'Urbanisation', p. 192.
108 Alison, *My Life*, p. 424.
109 Carson and Idzikowska, 'Social Production', p. 274.
110 C. J. Guthrie, 'Our Punishment of Crime – An Admitted Failure', *Juridical Review*, XIII (1901), 133–4.
111 Knox, *Industrial Nation*, pp. 94–103.
112 M. Billinge, 'A Time and Place for Everything: An Essay on Recreation, and Re-creation and the Victorians', *Journal of Historical Geography*, 22 (1996), 450.
113 Billinge, 'Time and Place', p. 450.
114 *Acts of Parliament Relating to the Glasgow Police* (Glasgow, 1913), p. 100.
115 *Acts of Parliament Relating to the Glasgow Police*, p. 342.
116 Wiener, *Reconstructing*, p. 215.
117 J. S. Davis, 'Prosecutions and their Context: The Use of the Criminal Law in later Nineteenth-century London', in Hay and Snyder (eds), *Policing and Prosecution in Britain* p. 426.
118 S. Reynolds, B. Woolley and T. Woolley, *Seems So* (1911), pp. 86–7, quoted in R. D. Storch, '"A Plague of Black Locusts": Police Reform and Popular Resistance in Northern England, 1840–1857', *International Review of Social History*, 20 (1975), 90.
119 L. Mahood, *Policing Gender, Class and Family: Britain 1850–1940* (Edmonton, 1995), p. 142.
120 S. H. Palmer, *Police and Protest in England and Ireland, 1780–1850* (Cambridge, 1988), pp. 449–50.
121 *Regulations for the Glasgow Muster of Police* (Glasgow, 1816), p. 14.
122 Gunn, 'Spatial Turn', p. 5.
123 *The Times*, 24 December 1908.
124 Storch, 'Plague of Black Locusts', pp. 61–90.
125 P. Gordon, *Policing Scotland* (Glasgow, 1980), p. 23.
126 City of Glasgow, *Regulations, Orders and Instructions* (Glasgow, 1857), pp. 21, 23.
127 Gordon, *Policing Scotland*, p. 19.
128 Palmer, *Police and Protest*, p. 453.

129 Grant, *Thin Blue Line*, p. 29.
130 Anon., *Report of the Trial*, p. 93.
131 A. Brown, writing as 'Shadow', *Midnight Scenes and Social Photographs, Being Sketches of the Life in the Streets, Wynds and Dens of the City* (Glasgow, 1858), p. 107.
132 Campbell, *Scottish Miners*, p. 277.
133 J. Bell and J. Paton, *Glasgow. Its Municipal Organisation and Administration* (Glasgow, 1909), pp. 111–12.
134 Jones, *Crime*, p. 22; Gatrell, 'Policeman-State', p. 283.
135 Gatrell, 'Policeman-State', p. 286.
136 Storch, 'Plague of Black Locusts', p. 71.
137 N. Elias, *State Formation and Civilization* (Oxford, 1982), p. 313.
138 L. Stephen, 'The Decay of Murder', *Cornhill Magazine*, 20 (1869), 722–33 quoted in Wiener, *Reconstructing*, p. 225.
139 Gatrell, 'Policeman-State', p. 289.

Chapter 8

New Spaces for Scotland, 1800 to 1900

R. J. Morris

IDENTITY AND ANTHROPOLOGICAL SPACE

John Mackay Wilson's *Tales of the Borders. Historical, Traditionary and Imaginative* were much read and reprinted in nineteenth-century Scotland and beyond. They are little to modern taste, but his 'Vacant Chair' first published in 1834 is worth re-reading for it encapsulates many of the insecurities of space, identity and social action faced by the Scots as the century opened. The tale centres on Peter Elliott, who was born at Marchlaw, 'a grey-looking farm-house' straddling the border between England and Scotland. It was Peter's misfortune to have been born in the room over the kitchen, through which ran 'the debateable line', thus he had no idea if he was Scottish or English, despite his desire to be Scottish and having three ancestors who were Scots. They had been born in the room over the parlour, which was in Scotland. The tale involved family, speech patterns, mistaken identity, parting and re-union, even food, for roast beef was served at the English end of the kitchen table and haggis at the Scottish end. The story served an idea of space in which culture and identity was secure and localised. Space was bounded and prescriptive. This was an anthropological space which both gave and took meanings. It was the place of birth which was decisive for Elliott. These were meanings with historical depth. Stories were told and re-told, demanding belonging.[1] The 'Vacant Chair' was published as Scotland itself was re-emerging in its own consciousness. The re-making of Scottish culture involved the border to a remarkable degree, notably in the attention Scott, Burns and others gave to Border ballads. Scott especially made the Borders and 'the licence of the marchmen' central to the history and making of Scotland. The border was central to his project of ensuring that a glorious and romantic past looked towards a modern future consecrated by the Union of 1707. He believed passionately in the importance of the preservation and publication of these ballads for the identity of his Scotland of the Union. He attributed their survival to the prescriptive identities of space, to the town pipers who survived until the late eighteenth century and to instances where 'the same families have occupied the same possession for centuries'.[2] The prescriptive border survived in many practical ways, somewhat playfully in the Gretna Green marriages, but more substantially in the separate existence

of Scottish law, especially Scottish property law which made at least some
contribution to the specific nature of the built environment.[3]

Many entities brought these qualities of anthropological space into the
nineteenth century. They projected a sense of a world which was bounded
and secure. The individual and the landscape were bound together in a way
which was moral, mystical and eternal. Rituals of place survived to teach
the Scots who they were and where they were. Those involved knew the
places their ancestors had built. The qualities of anthropological space,
based upon practice, memory, prescription, tradition and the division of
those who belonged and those who did not belong, were evident in many
entities in Scotland. By 1800, such a notion of space was already being challenged by a modern concept of space based upon law, the market, and the
utilities of production, consumption, order and improvement. This contest
was evident in the burghs of Scotland. Some sixty-six Royal Burghs had survived to the Union of 1707. The legitimacy and prestige of their authority
depended upon several centuries of practice and charters from the Crown.
In other burghs, those of regality and barony, the charters had been granted
to landowners to assist urban development and control. In most burghs,
the councils were self-selecting or nominated by the patron. They managed
a variety of properties and privileges, especially those relating to trade. In
many places they were assisted by a variety of guilds and trades.

The modest size and growth of Selkirk meant that many older practices
survived into the 1830s. The boundaries were 'extensive' and Corporation
property included five farms, two extensive common grazings, several mills
and a salmon fishing. The 'burgesses' had the privilege of 'pasturing each a
cow upon part of the south common without paying any rent'. They could
also take sand and stone from the river and quarry building stone on the
common. Access to the status of burgess was controlled by the five incorporations that also controlled the privilege of trade within the burgh. They
showed 'great jealousy of any invasion, and legal proceedings are taken
against those who infringe them . . . [and] . . . Strangers are not entitled
to be admitted to the freedom of the incorporations.' The legitimacy and
wisdom of these practices was already under challenge: 'It is the opinion of
the late chief magistrate that the exclusive privileges, by which tradesmen
are prevented from entering the town, are not beneficial to the community
at large . . . other gentlemen think they do good to no-one, and should be
abolished.' None the less, when the Corporation was challenged over the
cost of election dinners and other entertainments, a major contribution to a
substantial deficit, they replied 'it has always been the practice for the burgh
to pay the expenses of these entertainments'.[4] In many places the burgh's
sense of space and belonging was still encapsulated in the practice of 'riding
the marches'. The real purpose of this practice was to defend the citizens,
rights to common land owned by the burgh and available to citizens for
grazing, but it was also linked to assertions of collective identity.[5] A number

of instances survived to be recorded in the Old and New Statistical Accounts of Scotland. In the royal burgh of Brechin, the practice was very specifically to defend the privileges of the market:

> At the time of Trinity and Lammas fairs, the youngest Baillie of Brechin, with a select company, goes on horseback to the North Water Bridge, which is about five measured miles from the market, in order to prevent for-stalling; as no cattle, horses or sheep can be sold within that distance without being liable to the usual customs. At the same time the citizens proceed on foot with great pomp and solemnity, drums beating, pipes playing and colours flying, to the Law of Keithoc, alias Hare-Cairn, which is mid way between Brechin and North Water Bridge. In the days of club-law, the Baillie of Brechin, and his company, often met with resistance in the execution of their office. For this reason, the citizens proceeded the length of the Law of Keithoc, or Hare-Cairn, in order to assist them, if there should be occasion for it, in preserving and maintaining the immemorial rights and privileges of the market, and this they were there to do on the shortest notice. In these civilized times, no violence is offered; the old custom, however, is still kept up.[6]

The Statistical Accounts recorded instances of riding the marches in Inveresk, Lanark and Linlithgow as well as in Hawick and Selkirk, although most of these records noted that such practices were in decline.[7]

MODERN BOUNDARIES

The nature of this move to modern boundaries was evident in the terms of reference and the conclusions of the Commission which determined the boundaries of the burghs involved in the reforms of parliamentary representation in 1832.[8] Viscount Melbourne instructed the Commission to operate 'without being controlled by local divisions or jurisdictions [and] assign such Boundaries as the circumstances of each Burgh may seem to require', in other words to ignore the past. In his report, Sir J. H. Dalrymple of Oxenfoord Castle, noted that the boundaries of the 'ancient royalties of several Scotch Burghs' 'regulated solely by certain ancient Charters or usages' had little relationship to existing patterns of 'Population, Property or other local circumstances'. He looked at the population in the immediate neighbourhood of the built up area of the town: 'Most of the larger towns are surrounded by Villas, or detached Dwellings of that description, occupied by Persons who either carrying on business in the Town, or who are intimately connected with it in various ways, that they are, in habits and character, an urban rather than a rural population.' In Glasgow and Edinburgh space was left for the expansion of the town. In all cases he looked for boundaries that were independent of changing economic and social circumstances. At Haddington, they used the river but rejected the fences which enclosed the fields surrounding the town; 'they are [not] of such a nature as to be considered permanent'. On the other hand, at Lauder the aristocratic fence 'the Park Wall of Thirlestane' was accepted, 'being an ancient Baronial residence and an entailed estate, [it] is not likely to be changed'. In many cases they used the surveyors' rod and prominent landmarks to complement natural features. The coast and the Hopetoun monument were used at Dunbar, the canal and the River Kelvin for Glasgow, Musselburgh took the seashore and the Magdalene Burn as well as Inveresk Church spire, Portobello required Nelson's Monument and Arthur's Seat in Edinburgh and Inch Keith in the Forth. The Commissioners also sought to make an integrated, interacting economic and social unit. Thus, Falkirk included the villas of Grahamstown and straggling buildings around the canal, and Ayr took in villas south of the town 'chiefly inhabited by people engaged in business in it.' Aberdeen was a rare example of using an historical boundary, the 'march of the parish of Old Machar'. Space was defined by measurement and current economic and social relationships and not by memory and tradition.

Much of the burgh legislation of nineteenth-century Scotland was concerned with the definition and development of the modern boundary. The nature and logic of this process can be seen at its most complex in Glasgow in the 1880s as the Municipal Corporation laid claim to neighbouring territories.[9] Reforms begun in the 1830s had achieved new spaces in which authority and legitimacy depended upon representation, or to be precise, the vote of selected predominantly male property holders. The wishes of those who paid property taxes replaced the charters of long dead kings. The self-direction of often small groups of ratepayers was given free reign in Scotland as a result of the provisions of the General Police Acts of 1850 and 1862.[10] The Scots held such self-determination in high regard, but it did have its limits. In the west, the result was that Glasgow became surrounded by a ring of police burghs, most of which were specific social and economic constituencies of the larger urban unit. The Municipal Boundary Commission of 1835 had already tried to lay down the principles for creating modern urban space. It was 'the important interests which the inhabitants of a town have in common' which created the need for a unified government. This was not just a matter of maintaining public order and protecting public health and safety, but a basis for resolving disputes:

> Their [the inhabitants] constant dealings with each other, and the collision of rights and interests occasioned by the contiguity and intermixture of small properties, seem almost to render it desirable that there should be one judiciary to which all should be equally subject and may equally appeal.[11]

Expansion meant that the town population that had 'the same common interests' was divided into 'two distinct and separate classes; the one bearing burdens and enjoying privileges and immunities because accident has placed them on one side of an arbitrary line'. This was quite different from places like Selkirk in the early nineteenth century, where the whole point of the 'arbitrary' lines inherited from the past was to keep outsiders out and to assure citizens and burgesses of their privileges. By the 1880s, when a parliamentary commission was appointed to examine these issues for the specific case of Glasgow, the 'arbitrary' lines, whether sanctioned by history or the self-determination of ratepayers, were being overwhelmed by issues of scale, contiguity and justice, but above all by the development of an urban technology of pipes, and wires and rails. The Loch Katrine water supply had arrived by pipe and aqueduct in 1855 and was expanded in 1885. The municipality had taken over the gas supply in 1869 and various acts between 1870 and 1885 had sanctioned 31 miles of tramway at a cost of £345,000. In many cases the suburban police burghs simply bought into the Glasgow system, but fragmented governance produced several inefficiencies. Glasgow had tried to charge higher rates for gas to those outside the municipal boundary. The result was the establishment of the Partick, Hillhead and Maryhill Gas Company in 1871.[12] Govan took water and gas from Glasgow, but had its own tramway system. Passengers had to change trams as they crossed the line. There were issues of scale for the small police burghs. Maryhill had splendid municipal buildings, but only one manual fire engine. When asked if this was adequate Provost Craig replied 'Well, for a small fire, I daresay it would be, but for a great blaze we would require more assistance.'[13] Contiguity demanded more coherence and coordination in matters of both human and animal health, as well as some standardisation of building regulations. There were issues of justice: 'The public parks founded by Glasgow contribute largely to the health and enjoyment of the residents in many suburban districts, it is therefore proper that they should contribute to the cost of their maintenance.' The Commission felt it was quite wrong that many smaller burghs had lower rates than Glasgow itself, but 'those who reside in these smaller burghs [even to a greater extent than those who reside in Govan, Partick and Maryhill] are in every way dependent on the prosperity, sanitary government, and police arrangements of the City of Glasgow'.[14] The modern notion of space promoted by the Commission sought a sense of belonging and responsibility derived from close economic and social interaction and dependence:

> We consider that it will much conduce to the harmony and good feeling of the great urban population within and around Glasgow, if it is felt that none are free from a fair share of burdens, while all are admitted to partake in the government of the united municipality within whose boundaries they live and labour.[15]

In Glasgow, the modern sense of space was to dominate. It was functional and strictly related to the present through legal, scientific and market mechanisms. In other areas, the balance proved very different. The Highlands and Islands of Scotland had long been subjected to market forces and the property transactions recorded in Register House in Edinburgh but their inhabitants, especially those in Gaelic-speaking communities, retained a sense of a moral economy related to the practice and occupancy of a remembered past.[16] There was a long history of sporadic evictions and resistance. By the early 1880s, economic crisis, intensified poverty, political organisation and social disorder brought matters to a head. A Commission of Enquiry was led by Lord Napier, diplomat, former Governor of Madras and Border landlord of a radical turn of mind. The Commissioners recognised they were dealing with two accounts of space. Much evidence was 'delivered by illiterate persons speaking from early memory, or from hearsay, or from popular tradition, fleeting and fallacious sources . . .' This was compared with 'The depositions of the superior order of witnesses, embracing proprietors, factors, farmers, clergymen, and members of other learned professions.' Napier noted the opinion 'that the small tenantry of the Highlands have an inherited inalienable title to security of tenure in their possessions, while rent and service are duly rendered, is an impression indigenous to the country, though it has never been sanctioned by legal recognition . . .' This claim was at first dismissed as 'a custom unknown to the Statute Book', but Napier admitted that 'a MacDonald, a MacLeod, a MacKenzie, a Mackay, or a Cameron, who gave a son to his landlord eighty years ago to fill up the ranks of a Highland regiment, did morally acquire a tenure in his holding more sacred than the stipulations of a written covenant'.[17] The Highland township had no 'lawful status' but 'does nevertheless possess a distinct existence in the sentiments and traditions of its component members, and by the customs of estate management'. The tensions created by the changing nature of space in Scotland were at their most acute in Skye where the authority of law, landlords and the state had been re-asserted by armed force. Napier went there to hear evidence. Angus Stewart talked of the loss of the Hill of Benlee to the deer forest. He based his claims upon the fact that his grandfather had been born and buried there and that 'the hill was part of their holdings in time past'. Lord MacDonald's factor dismissed Stewart as only the son of a crofter, but Napier listened because he was the elected 'representative' of his township. Samuel Nicholson claimed 'I can point out to the present day the shielings which the women had in my grandfather's time on the hill, and we were looking upon it that we had full right of grazing on Benlee'. Much of the evidence was about practical matters. It was about the quality and quantity of land, about how and if a living could be made, about families from elsewhere being placed on the crofts. It was about lambs, stirks, salmon, bolls of meal, drainage and thatch material, as well as rents and factors and removals. Space was identified with what it would yield and the resources it would provide. Place was identified with communities, their rights and practices and so back to what had been done in the past. This did not exclude modern ideas of improvements. Stewart, Nicholson and the rest knew all about fences, notably as the basis for better farming and for keeping out deer. Nor was their view of space a narrow one. They knew all about work in 'the south', and about Australia and North America.[18] In the event the government adopted crofting legislation based upon Irish Land Reform models. This proved an imperfect attempt by the state to transform this sense of legitimate possession through history and productive usage into a legal form that could be construed by the courts in Edinburgh. None the less, it involved a very different balance between anthropological space and modern space when compared with the legislation applied to Glasgow and the other Scottish burghs.

Anthropological spaces became more visible in nineteenth-century Scotland for the simple reason that they were threatened. In 'The Vacant Chair', 'the boundaries of Peter's farm, indeed, were defined neither by fields, hedges, nor stone walls'. In fact, the countryside of the 1830s was already marked by dykes and hedges and strongly built farmhouses. Property boundaries were secure in the documents of the Register of Sasines and a well-organised labour and property market ensured continual movement, especially among wage labour. Change was marked by the double meaning of belonging. Will Fyfe and others might sing 'Glasgow belongs to me', but Glasgow actually belonged to those whose property deeds were in Register House in Edinburgh.

The nature of the threat to any sustained sense of anthropological space can be traced field by field and glen by glen, but the fundamental nature of change can be seen not by looking at the damaged spaces of the countryside but by examining the new spaces of urban industrial Scotland.

MODERN SPACE AND THE URBAN

If any individual had had the unlikely experience of being resurrected at hundred-year intervals from 1700 onwards and been able to travel across the landscape of Scotland, one of the most striking changes they might have observed would have been the existence, growth and changing nature of Scotland's urban places. This can be expressed most simply in terms of population figures. Between 1831 and 1891, the proportion of the Scottish population living in places of more than 5,000 people rose from 31 per cent to 54 per cent. By 1911, it was nearly 60 per cent, the second most urbanised country in Europe.[19] Before 1800 information is sparse, but there is enough to show that the proportion living in places over 10,000 in the 1690s was 9 per cent and by the Statistical Accounts of the 1790s was 20 per cent. There was an equally important change in the urban hierarchy driven not only by growth in trade and population, but also by the technologies, organisation and the products of industrial growth. By the 1790s, Paisley and Greenock had joined the top six Scottish towns and Falkirk the top twelve, while the likes of St Andrews and Haddington had long settled for a middle ranking.[20] By 1901, Govan, Coatbridge and Partick had joined the top group, while the populations of the big four exceeded 100,000, with Glasgow within expanded municipal boundaries counting 761,709. The scale exceeded anything experienced in earlier centuries.

Figure 8.1   *Alloa from William Roy's Military Survey of Scotland, 1747–55.* © *The British Library Board (Roy Map 16/1).*

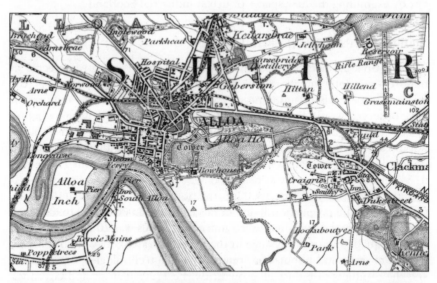

Figure 8.2   *Alloa, 1904 from* Third Edition Ordnance Survey of Scotland, 1903–1912, *Sheet 39. Scale: one inch to one mile. Reproduced by permission of the National Library of Scotland.*

An alternative look is provided by the increasing number of maps of Scottish towns and cities. The small burgh of Alloa on the north shore of the River Forth experienced none of the extremes of a Glasgow or a Motherwell, but the changes were profound. When General Roy's surveyors visited in the 1750s, they recorded a compact little burgh dominated by the parkland of its aristocratic patron, the Earl of Mar.[21]

By the time the Ordnance Survey had completed its revision of the 1859–63 survey in 1904, Alloa had acquired a port, an industrial area (including brewing, woollens, engineering, glass and an iron foundry), a respectable suburb to the north, several railways as well as a number of roads laid out by the surveyor's rod.

The object of study must be the urban industrial system. Crieff and St Andrews were as much part of the story as Motherwell and Kirkcaldy. In all these places lamp posts were lit, ceramic and iron pipes were laid and income streams brought building and investment. The products and services brought for sale were those of the industrial urban system. Observant visitors to the Hall of Heroes in the Wallace Monument near Stirling will see among the poets and ministers, the bust of Ayrshire-born, William Murdoch, engineer and inventor of gas lighting, presented by the North British Association of Gas Managers. This group had as profound an impact on the use of space as any in Scotland.

THE RE-MAKING OF THE STREET

The dynamics of the Scottish urban industrial system created a variety of new spaces which shared characteristics that were very different from the historical, traditional and imaginative spaces of the royal burgh or the highland clans. One of the most important outcomes of the urban industrial system was the re-invention of the street. This was a Scottish, a European and, indeed, a North American phenomenon, and it was very evident to those who used Argyle Street in Glasgow.

When Joseph Swan engraved his picture of the street in the 1820s, there was already a division between the paved walking area and the granite setts of the roadway for wheeled and horse-drawn vehicles, but the division was imperfect (Figure 8.3).[22] The roadway was still an area for street traders, pedestrians and conversation. By the time Valentines of Dundee published their photograph in the 1900s, the street was firmly divided between the crowded walking areas, the central roadway for the electric trams and the side of the road for the horse-drawn rulleys (Figure 8.4).[23] Spatial division was clear and disciplined. In part, this was the outcome of the organic processes of a greatly increased population. In part, it was the outcome of new technologies: Glasgow was now a place of pipes and wires. In part, it was the result of the regulation of the street. The central figure in the foreground is probably the policeman directing traffic.

VIEW OF TRONGATE & ARGYLE STREET,

from Foot of Nelson Street.

Figure 8.3 *View of Trongate and Argyle Street, Glasgow from John Leighton*, Select Views of Glasgow and its Environs engraved by Joseph Swan *(Glasgow, 1828)*.

Figure 8.4 *Argyle Street, Glasgow, from* Bonnie Scotland. Leng's Portfolio of the Scenic Beauties of Scotland *(Dundee, 1907). This photograph was taken c. 1898.*

Argyle Street was a much observed street. It was subjected to the multiple rhythms and regularities of urban industrial society as it responded to the pressures of growing size and density and the multiple purposes of those who used the street. The first 'look' comes from Alexander Brown, journalist and evangelical in 1858.[24] The word pictures were as important as the engravings and photographs:

> SUNDAY has passed away; the merchant has returned from the coast, and the industrious mechanic to his weekly toil. Despite the repose of the previous day, an apathy and a languor characterise the people.
>
> 'Saint': Monday! Groups of idle workmen hang about the corners of the streets. Nearly all have small black pipes in their mouths, and stand in a careless attitude, with their hands in their pockets, conversing with each other. A rollicking hard-fisted young fellow, apparently a son of St. Crispin, accosts a coterie of these idlers 'Well, how goes it to-day?' 'Mondayish,' is the cool reply of one of the number, as he salutes the pavement with a mouthful of filthy expectorations. 'Mondayish' is the word which drops from the lips of another youth, slightly inebriated, as he reluctantly withdraws his dirty fist from his pockets to meet the pressing exigencies of a certain member of 'the human face divine'. 'She has just missed it by a neck,' we say, as a lady unexpectedly sweeps on her way in glacé silk and finery, congratulating herself on a narrow escape from an accident, arising from the paucity of handkerchiefs amongst the lower orders of this manufacturing city of the west.
>
> As evening approaches, the difficulty in making a-head through the crowd, is greatly increased. In the confusion there is nothing but 'bobbing around' and personal collision on every hand, with the usual 'beg pardon' audibly muttered by respectably dressed people in too much haste to be punctiliously polite. 'Right hand to the wall' is not in my vocabulary of observances, says a philosophical-looking elderly gentleman, gazing up at the moon, with a huge umbrella under his arm, and a pair of galoshes over his shoes, prepared for any extent of deluge by sea or land, as he suddenly brings to the ground a stout middle-aged dame, fresh from the coast, covered head and shoulders by a bloomer of extraordinary dimensions. 'Right hand to the wall!' exclaims a Pickwickian English tourist, as he is crushed in a state of fearful nervous excitement, between a gigantic plated glass window and a brace of swells obscuring the path with clouds of smoke emitted from delicately scented cigars. 'Watchman, what is the meaning,' we inquire, 'of the streets being so unusually crowded to-night?' 'Big-pay week, sir, big-pay week,' is the ready reply.[25]

Like all purposeful journalists, Brown wanted to shock and grab attention with his accounts of noise, drunkenness, squalor, outdoor sleepers and half naked women in rags, but he also provided vignettes of ordinariness to highlight the gothic horror of poverty and moral ignorance. Places like Argyle Street provided a focus which intensified all the processes of the urban place. There was a constant bombardment of sight and sound, sometimes threatening, often defying understanding, which later urbanists saw as the basis of a blasé urban consciousness.[26] Observers like Brown did strive to identify patterns especially the rhythms of seasons, of days of the week and times of day:

> We have sometimes thought we could tell the day of the week from the appear-ance of the streets . . . Here is Tuesday, for instance, in this great mercantile city, in the first week of the month, and a 'cash-day,' with a sober earnestness about it, intent on business. The better class of merchants has only just come up from the coast, fresh and invigorated by nearly three days' rest . . . Towards evening as we take our accustomed stroll, the streets assume a gayer appearance. A number of working men with their wives, and lads, with their sweethearts, are seen, cleanly washed, and dressed in their Sunday's coat and hat, taking their evening walk. As they pass along the great thoroughfares of the city, the husband, should he have a literary turn, stops to look in at the bookseller's window, 'just for a minute!' to see *Punch*'s cartoon of 'Pam's Last Trick!' 'Well, really, there is no use coming out with you' impatiently vociferates his better half 'there is no getting past these horrid shops!' After sundry little pokings in the ribs with a small parasol, the husband makes a move. A few paces more, and the wife in turn is spell-bound before a huge plate-glass window. 'Stop, dear! did you ever see such a love of a bonnet! mine has got so shabby' – a speech in which she is interrupted by the unceremonious husband, 'Well, that is always the way with you; I daresay you would like all the shop if you could get it!' This 'game at cross purposes' over, a young olive branch, if such should form a portion of the group, is next impatient to be shown the great wax-work exhibition, as she thrusts her little finger into the eye of Daniel Dancer the miser, or some criminal celebrity, displayed at the bottom of a stair to tempt the passer-by.

The street was at once a place of entertainment, instruction, commercial enticement and the contests of gender.

Each part of the town created its own movement and meaning: Blythswood Square for calm; St Enoch Square with the attractions of the Corn Exchange and Stockwell was the rural come to town with 'shrewd, well-dressed, respectable-looking yeomen'.[27] The area around the Broomielaw had its own rhythm to add to the noise and bulk of the great ships:

> Retracing our way a little, and directing our course southwards, we are struck with the appropriate characteristics of the locality. Young men, in respectable attire, and of a business air, are wending their way, with impatient step, homeward. They are quitting the close confines of the city, where they have been breathing a dusty pestiferous atmosphere, in pent-up shops and warehouses, for ten or twelve hours together, to betake themselves to the purer air of this more healthy vicinage. What a blaze of light each side of the street presents, as we pass along the busy thoroughfare, amid a confusion and jostling enough to make the head dizzy! The rival establishments are evidently those of the publican and victual dealer. In

almost every shop-window of the later there is the long brass gas-pipe crossing the window, with as many as twenty-lights, shadowing forth to the passer-by a rich and attractive display of meat, boiled and unboiled, – hams of every description, – flour, meal, barley, eggs, &c., &c., all shown with an effect most tempting to a hungry stomach, and still more provoking if accompanied by an empty purse. Inside may be seen a few trim smart-looking housewives addressing the young shopman, whose blythe fresh countenance, and prepossessing appearance, a pretty young lass seems to say, as she enters, are in themselves no mean attraction to the establishment. A few paces more, and the eye is dazzled by another blaze of gas light – it is the shop of the publican. Outside are some miserable-looking crouching women, holding rather an angry altercation. Two or three children are hanging about, cold and ragged.[28]

Again the street was the place in which gas light and plate glass provided the stage props for movement and commercial enticement. By Saturday the Broomielaw had gained a different meaning:

A WEEK of toil has all but ended! 'Oh, what a blessing!' say a thousand happy faces that we meet. The merchant has deserted his counting-house, and the mechanic his workshop; the former to join his family in some marine retreat; the latter, with not less happiness, to enjoy a short sail on the Clyde, a trip on the railway, a game on the Green, or in such other way as fancy prompts. Railway station, coach office, and steam-boat wharf, alike are crowded with half-day excursionists. The Broomielaw, in particular, is besieged. Warm greetings are every where exchanged with friends arrived, and anxious looks are turned towards those expected . . . The boats, in rapid succession, arrive with their precious freight; and what with the smoke of funnels, the long rows of spectators looking down from Glasgow Bridge, and others lining the margin of the Wharf, the scene smacks a little of the picturesque. Again the roar of steam, the shouting of seamen, and the wide-spread but subdued hum of many voices emanating from the dense multitude, render it one of unusual animation. A few minutes more, and the thousands of excursionists are lost, as a drop in the ocean, in the busy throng of the streets.

What a life-book does the city unfold on this most notable night of the week, Saturday! Everybody seems to have turned out to look at everybody, and to do business with everybody. Even excursionists, loud in their praises of half holidays, have joined in the general persecution of young men still behind counters, at desks, or in warehouses. All are as busy as bees, as if they had not another minute to live – or as if, in this pious land, everyone grudged God and himself the blessed Sabbath that follows. What a 'dead set' is made at workmen's wives, and workers generally, as they lounge about the draper's door, or gaze up at his window, with manifest discomfort at having money in their pockets! Never did the fair sex appear more interesting, seems to say an oily-faced old bachelor, as he pushes his nose into the bonnets of pretty girls as they pass – telling them, with a confidential air, 'The only piece left ma'm!' – 'a sweet thing this ma'm!' 'first of the season ma'm!'

A poor woman is doling out, at a corner of the street, mugfuls of milk to the drouthy customers as they quit the public-house, or perhaps to drouthy ones of a different class, who are desirous of instituting a healthy opposition. Seeing everyone in a bit of excitement, 'Charley' sees no reason why he should not get excited too, and he forthwith breaks out upon the old woman and her customers, . . . she is moving off with her pitchers – 'Oh, its jist the nasty pollice, they winna let me sell my milk!' . . . The din of the streets has by this time reached its climax.[29]

The discipline of the streets was not simply a matter of pipes and rails. The policeman played an equal part in Brown's account to that of the gas light.

Glasgow in 1901 by James Hamilton Muir was written for visitors attracted to the Glasgow International Exhibition of that year. It was in fact the work of three journalists. The street was presented as a place of entertainment, culture and consumerism. Argyle Street was a place of 'waxworks and thieves'. All types of 'merchandise' from sugar to 'two-penny watches' was there as were the 'loafers' and the Saturday night 'stagger' from public houses. Entertainment was increasingly technologically driven with French, English and American films.

This account was more relaxed than that of Alexander Brown. It followed

Figure 8.5 *'Variety Theatre, Argyle Street, Glasgow', from James Hamilton Muir,* Glasgow in 1901, *reprinted by White Cockade Publishing (Oxford, 2001) with an introduction by Perilla Kinchin. © Estate of Sir Muirhead Bone. All Rights Reserved, DACS 2009.*

the subtle status gradations of Glasgow's major streets. Buchanan Street was where women from the suburbs of Kelvinside and the Great Western Road came to do their shopping:

> there is prepared for her the best shops and a broad pavement whereon groups may gather and show that it is possible to converse without shouting, for the cars do not clatter down it, and its surface is of tar macadam. It is the only street in Glasgow where you can hear your own voice. There was an arcade and tea rooms.
>
> The stucco goddesses that from their post at the Arcade front simper down upon the crowd could recall (if they had the mind) many a lovers' meeting held on the pavement at their feet. The stockbroker's clerk has long since commenced business for himself, and has married Miss So-and-So, of Hillhead, who used to meet him here at four o'clock of a fine afternoon. Now he has clerks of his own, is rather elderly, and she no longer slim, but they use the same trysting place when now they plan at Christmas to take the children to a matinee at the pantomime. The street is the chief haunt of the strangers and tourists who find their way to the city, and there is abundance of trinkets and souvenirs in it for their attention. Also it contains everything that the Glasgow man of means requires in the leisure he allows himself. Here is the maker of guns and fishing tackle, the theatrical booking-office, the confidential cigar divan, the jeweller's where he can buy things as dear as anywhere else, the bookseller who sells the kind of literature you may read on the 'Columba.'
>
> Glasgow has no leisure class, but it has its leisure hour . . . a little after noon. For an hour you may see the tea-shop doors ever on the swing . . . another hour and the street is half deserted again and the office doors are clanging again.[30]

These two looks were each mediated by a particular eye and purpose, but beneath both were general patterns. Spaces like the street were produced by structures, structures of class, of gender, of urbanism and governance. In turn, such spaces produced structures that gave regularity and made sense of the multiplicity of sight and sound and smell. They were spaces for walking, for looking and for knowing.

In part, the structuring of these spaces had a formality that was based upon law and regulation. The policeman, the curb edges and the naming of pavement and roadway appear almost without comment in both visual and written accounts. The nineteenth century saw a massive and continued increase in the formal regulation of the street, all designed to minimise potential conflict between those who used the spaces of the street and to maximise the success of their multiple purposes, shopping, entertainment, public health and public order, or just the simple tasks of movement. James Valentine was clerk of police for Aberdeen, and in 1871 he attempted to guide his fellow citizens through the growing complexity of regulation. His immediate inspiration was the Aberdeen Municipality Extension Act of 1871, which enlarged the boundaries of the burgh and enabled the municipal takeover of water works, gas and police. Authority was also drawn from the Aberdeen Police and Waterworks Act of 1862, the Aberdeen Roads Act of

1865, the General Police and Improvement Supplemental (Scotland) Act of 1866 and the Aberdeen Harbour Act of 1868. Valentine found 711 clauses still in operation covering everything from the width of streets, the laying of pipes and drains, the numbering of houses, the clearing of snow, the provision of public water closets, privies and urinals, the ownership of manure, the selling of milk and other commodities and the raising of taxes to pay for all this. The salaries and powers of those who were to ensure and enforce this order and regulation were themselves regulated. There were treasurers, collectors, clerks, inspectors, surveyors and engineers, armed with both legal authority and technical expertise who ensured the order of the street.[31] Some of this was specific to Aberdeen, but the Scottish burghs copied and adapted from each other as well as using general legislation like the 1866 Act. Valentine acknowledged the guidance of James D. Marwick, then Town Clerk of Edinburgh but soon to move to Glasgow.

Many Scottish burghs had begun the century with a division of authority between the Municipal Burgh, which embodied corporate interests, managed property and represented the economic and political interests of the burgh, and the Police Committee, which managed the general imposition of order on the burgh as well as the formal enforcement of law and order.[32] These two authorities had gradually merged over the century. In many places the maps and the census returns still showed municipal space and police space with their different and appropriate boundaries. One of the purposes of the 1871 Aberdeen Act was to bring these two forms of authority together, thus creating a municipal and police burgh.

Alexander Clark published his *Reminiscences of a Police Officer in the Granite City* in 1873. The book was full of anecdote and opinion and illustrated many ways in which the multiple purposes of the users of the street were reconciled and regulated. He disliked having to arrest lads and boys for making 'slides' along the public roads and pavements during times of snow and frost; 'Yet, what could we do? Douce, decent people would fall and get injured . . .' Clark believed 'our proper duty in regulating street traffic or usages was to endeavour, as far as possible, to prevent or suppress what was dangerous to the lieges'. Prominent was 'furious driving' and the practice 'in those days [c. 1840s] for dealers in horse flesh to turn these out when a buyer wished to see their paces, although this was clearly illegal and dangerous too, as there is no time a spirited animal is more likely to lash out than when he is held in leish and urged by his trainer running alongside . . . [this was] directly contravening a distinct clause in the Police Act'. Applying these regulations often ran counter to popular values. Arresting 'the loons' for making slides was greeted by crowds of women abusing and harassing the police as they attempted to take those arrested to the police station to be charged, just as the arrest of a horse dealer was opposed by fellow dealers.[33] The daily order and authority of the street could be very fragile at times.

The formality with which the spaces of the street were named, numbered and regulated to accommodate the multiple purposes of those who used it ran alongside other less formal but clearly understood patterns. The accounts of Argyle Street all recognised the time of day, the day of the week, the seasons of the year and specific events. Social groups identified and made allowances for each other. The experience of the street taught and guided behaviour in ways that were self-directed and group-directed quite independent of policemen and bylaws.

THE HISTORY OF WALKING

The history of the street as a space for walking, for looking, for knowing and for learning is not as easy to trace as the history of regulation and policing. Argyle Street and the braes between Union Street and the harbour in Aberdeen represented many of the processes and spaces of the street in an urbanising modernising Scotland, but such places show these processes at their most intense and developed. The dimensions of change across time can be explored by looking at smaller, less developed places and by exploiting a particular Scottish genre, the reminiscence and recollections. They provide a backward look and an account of walking and knowing that was significantly different from Glasgow and Aberdeen.

The changing nature of the street was reflected in the changing nature and meaning of 'walking'. In the Argyle Street of 1858, the walk was still an element of the regularities of leisure; 'towards evening we took our accustomed walk'. Working men and their wives took 'their evening walk'. Those on the street identified each other as groups, but there was little communication other than the mutually understood attempt to avoid collisions. Appearance, especially in matters of clothing and cleanliness, was the basis of judgement. The English tourist was labelled because he looked 'Pickwickian'. By 1900, there was less sense of the street as a regular walk. Meeting was identified with the special spaces of the 'tea shop'. Walking was very different in mid-century Inverness. Isobel Harriet Anderson in a memoir significantly titled *Inverness before the Railways* was able to observe the change. Before the Inverness and Nairn railway arrived in 1855:

> the usual hour for a 'constitutional' walk in Inverness was three o'clock, for of course, as almost all the townspeople lived above their offices and shops, and could not otherwise obtain fresh air, the daily walk was quite an institution. At three o'clock, or a little earlier, many gentlemen might be seen issuing from their doors, accompanied by their wives and daughters – Banker Wilson being one who seldom missed his daily promenade – and it was a source of pleasure to guess what friends one might meet, difficult for those to realise who now always meet the same faces on the same road as they go to or return from town.
>
> Sometimes, in summer, these walks were taken at a later hour, but not by the lawyers. Almost all of them took a rest at home between dinner and tea, and then

returned to their offices from tea time till supper time – a custom which is now impossible, owing to late dinners and villas out of town. The Millburn Road was always a favourite resort for the afternoon walk . . .[34]

The street in Inverness invited a walk among a known community of identifiable individuals. Although much of the rhythm of the street was managed by the elite and middle classes, it was not without its perils. There was the gentleman of 'high position' who became involved in a 'street row' and ended up in jail. Significant was the manner in which this became rapidly known and the man released. Walking demanded skills which had to be learnt. This was very evident to Jessie Saxby who grew up in the third quarter of the century. The street in Lerwick was still a place for learning and for seeing and being seen:

> In Unst I had never seen anything resembling a street . . . no policeman, no public house, no place of assemblage but the kirks and schoolrooms; no bakery.
>
> I learned my first lessons in the ways of the world that morning when we went out walking. 'Don't look behind you Jessica; it isn't proper – at least in town!' said Miss Ogilvy, as I wheeled about to study the garb of some French Officers who had just passed. '. . . don't dance along on your toes, everybody is looking at you' said my sister next.

Again it was not without its perils; we 'passed along The Street which looked as if it were closing on us . . . Two drunk men occupying the breadth of the street at one spot, and a country cart blocking the way at another . . .'.[35]

As the pressures of urbanism grew the walk changed from being an activity taken among a known community. New walking spaces emerged. The eighteenth and early nineteenth centuries had produced promenades like the 'ladies walk' between Ness Bank and Bellfield created by Provost Nicol in Inverness.[36] By mid-century, many urban places were creating 'parks', special spaces apart from the street.

By the 1890s, there was fundamental change. Those who announced they were 'going for a walk' now signalled that they were heading away from the urban towards open countryside and mountains. They sought individual fulfilment, escape and the companionship of selected friends. The *Scottish Mountaineering Club Journal* was first published in 1893. The President's account of a walk was very different from that of Isobel Harriet Anderson and Alexander Brown:

> Gentlemen, what is our great and glorious bond of union in this Club? It is the love of nature in every form, and especially of the hills; a sense that, after all sports and games have been tried and enjoyed, the most universal, most lasting, most healthful of all diversions, is that of walking in pure air and over beautiful country. Not being carted by train, or car, or tram, like so much merchandise; not confining ourselves to street, or road, or path; but to roam over the untrammelled

country, far from smoke and din, drinking in draughts of air as it rolls to us over a hundred hills; and, best of all, 'to put a stiff back up the stae brae' of stone or heather or snow, and on to that top which has so long eluded us, where we seem to breathe something else than air, and from which we look down on every side upon a scene untainted by work of man, just as it came fresh from the Creator's hand . . .

IMAGINE the darkness of night falling on a lonely Highland glen; the mountains – white with snow – towering overhead till lost in the rolling mist; the swollen river, sweeping along its wide stony channel. Not a house in sight, not a sound of man nor beast, not the twinkle of a star to illumine the dark breast of the night; everything solitary, cold, and cheerless; mist and drizzling rain distilling over all nature.[37]

The same issue had walks along Glen Sannox and Buchaille Etive. Paradoxically, as the President implied, such walks were a direct product of urban experience and culture.

THE FIRST NON-SPACE: THE RAILWAY STATION

The street as a space had been remade in response to the opportunities and pressures of urban industrial society, but the railway station was a space of a very new sort. Few places better marked the nature of urban industrial society. It was a place of order and discipline. It was a place where it was essential to read and write, a place of communication for parcels, letters and the telegraph as well as passengers and their luggage. It reflected the essence of industrial technologies. It was a definition of 'modern'. The early days of Scottish passenger railways reflected an uncertainty about what a railway station actually was. The engravings of the opening of the Garnkirk and Glasgow Railway show spaces that were a mixture of a stage-coach halt and a canal basin with warehouses, platforms and offices.[38] As the inter-city railway system reached Scotland around 1850, the railway station had adopted an assertive architecture of varied historical styles. The street face announced entrance to something important. This blended with very modern materials of glass, iron and steel in the distinctive new form of the train shed. The grand façade of the entrances were linked with spectacular station hotels, statements of luxury.[39] The railway companies were fierce exponents of brand recognition as architectural and heraldic details were built into the fabric. The railways and above all the railway station acquired huge amounts of urban space.[40] The station was not simply a remaking of space, but an intrusion of a new and disturbing kind into the urban landscape. This was evident from the uproar created by the proposals for Waverley Station in Edinburgh's Nor Loch.[41]

Again Glasgow showed the full development of this new industrial form. *The Railway Magazine* published an account of Central Station in 1907.[42]

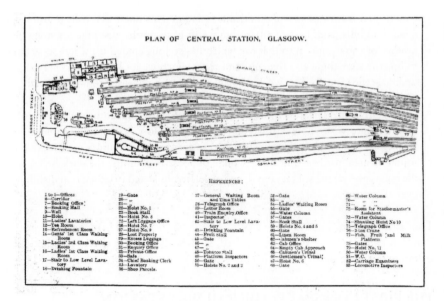

PLAN OF CENTRAL STATION, GLASGOW.

REFERENCES:

Figure 8.6 *Plan of Central Station, Glasgow, 1907, from* The Railway Magazine, *January 1907, pp. 1–8. Reproduced by permission of the National Library of Scotland (NLS: NH.308).*

This space was not only highly specialised, but divided by several major boundaries and barriers which could be crossed only on certain conditions. The most important barrier was between general public circulating space and the platforms which gave access to the trains. There were areas for railway employees. There were division of class and gender. There were many features which were linked only indirectly to travel, but rapidly became associated with the railway station: the urinal, the fruit, tobacco and book stalls and the refreshment room. Much thought was given to the smooth flow of people and goods. This was evident in the picture of the Caledonian Railway Goods Offices in Buchanan Street, organised for the orderly flow of horses and rulleys and goods.[43] At all points the written word assisted with instructions and the identity of this space with the Caledonian Railway. In both passenger and goods areas, text-based information gave form and purpose.

There was a wide range of evidence on the form and purpose of the railway station, but less evidence on what people actually did there. In the 1860s, Jules Verne, a technologically aware author if ever there was one, visited Scotland. He wrote a novel called *Backward to Britain*, which was not published in his lifetime. It was a trivial bit of writing, a half concealed account of Verne's own tour of Scotland, but the limited references to railway stations were instructive:

To reach the departure platform, they had to cross the station over a kind of covered bridge below which engines roared. Jonathan bought tickets for Glasgow,

EXTERIOR OF THE CALEDONIAN RAILWAY'S GOODS OFFICES AT BUCHANAN STREET.

Figure 8.7 *Caledonian Railway goods offices, Buchanan Street, from* The Railway Magazine, *September 1907, p. 223. Reproduced by permission of the National Library of Scotland (NLS: NH.308).*

which cost him three shillings and six pence for a second class fare. The railway attendants were so unpleasant and in such short supply he found it very difficult to decide which was the right train . . .

The moment they stepped out of the station [at Glasgow], the two travellers found themselves on an attractive square with a small enclosed garden where they could vaguely make out a few columns adorned with statues.

[at Balloch on Loch Lomond] They dashed out of the station and down onto the jetty, where they boarded a steamer, the *Prince Albert*; they bought two passages to Inversaid on the far side of the lake, paying two shillings and sixpence each.

[back in Edinburgh] An hour later they were back at the station . . . Passengers were besieging the ticket offices, and the employees could not handle the requests fast enough. A constant hum dominated occasionally by shouts and yells filled the station. With a struggle Jonathan thrust his way to the counter and asked for two seats to London. He never worked out how much he paid for them . . . in a dark corner they spotted their luggage vanishing into a bottomless pit. 'It seems we must register it', Jacques said, 'I suppose we just ask for a receipt.' But the attendants refused to consider such an indiscreet request . . . This Monstrous, riotous, endless train was, alas, an 'excursion' train taking back to London a crowd of English trippers.[44]

The experience of the station was dominated by the purchase and price of tickets, and rightly so as these were the means of passing access barriers to trains and travel. There was a hunger for information. It was a place of anxiety, but above all a place of transition. There were calmer views. Craigendoran Station on the north shore of the Clyde estuary was the place

CRAIGENDORAN STATION.

Figure 8.8 *Craigendoran Station, from* Mountain, Moor and Loch on the Route of the West Highland Railway *(London, 1895).*

where commuters from Glasgow might leave the train, or where the tourist would change from Clyde steamer to the West Highland Line. This station was a place of calm and order as befits a picture drawn from publicity for the North British Railway.[45] Porters and luggage were much in evidence as was the Refreshment Room. The platform was well lit with elegant iron Corinthian columns. Stations were places of waiting and transition and like a modern bookshop café seem to have been places where women felt comfortable. The Glasgow journalists of 1901 reported:

> Queen Street is not romantic simply, but also agricultural. Something in the dear old comfortable, unpretentious look of it tells you as much. It is more like a tavern – a battered caravanserai – than a station, its waiting-room quite like an inn parlour, with space for four tolerably stout farmers, and a dark polished, mahogany table. There is passage, too, for a porter should he wish to bring coals, but he never does, and so the illusion of the inn-parlour is maintained. Out on the platform there is a spring of water, at which Ne'er Day people will mix their drink. Also there are benches, and this, may be, is why city people like to come here hours before their time, out of the rain, and discuss where the holiday shall be spent. From the station, too, little parties of sightseers from the country set out, and hither they return long before their train will leave. Then 'wee Maggies' and tired 'Maws' – dazed wi' the lichts an' croods – may be settled on the benches with the 'trumphery,' and forgotten, what time the 'Paws' are growing unco fu' and happy at a neighbouring public-house. What with whisky and fruit and newspapers, it provides more than any other place in the city for tired holidaymakers from the country. On feein' days the smell in it is richly of the soil, and many little scenes of yokel fun are enacted there, like the more decent passages in Teniers' pictures. The officials, if they ever wish to enforce decorum, remember that theirs is the Waverley route, and stay their hand. On

market days the farmers may be traced from M'Coll's (where they have ended with apple dumpling) to the station by the hay-seed and corn samples fallen from their pockets.[46]

Stations were places of anxiety and waiting, but they were also places of departure and arrival with all the mixture of emotion and expectation that this entailed. There was no better place to gain insights into this process than in the correspondence columns of *The Scotsman*. There were complaints about pickpockets and complaints that the refreshment rooms were not open on Sunday morning at 6 am to greet the London trains. Soldiers and sailors passing through in 1914 were more fortunate as they were greeted at all hours of day and night by groups of women offering them food 'on special terms'. The whole was organised by the Navy League and the National Service League.[47] The most graphic account, because it was the most ordinary account, came from the Provost of Elgin:

> Railway stations at the best are cold and draughty, and it is rather hard, after walking through a long, cold, covered station, to find oneself on a wet, sloppy platform, exposed to a heavy shower of rain, or it may be a blinding storm of sleet or snow.[48]

He wanted more cover for the platform so passengers did not have to enter the trains wet. Modernity and the Scottish weather were evenly matched.

The railway station aroused that mixture of anxiety, excitement and dislocation because it was urban society's first non-place.[49] By this is meant that, unlike the street, the railway station had no history. It had no identity, unlike the burgh boundaries and highland grazings. It was a space with no social relationships. No one belonged there. Entry was by means of ticket and contract and status was defined by such documents. Continual guidance and discipline was required in the form of text and layout. The station was part of a system which subverted the sense of time and space, hence all the clocks, timetables and direction notices.

There were other spaces which shared some of these characteristics, notably the sports ground and the department store. These new places, always threatening to become non-places were places of uncertainty and anxiety. Individuals required continual guidance and direction. There were street names and house numbers, required by law. Each rail station required its name to be written and displayed. Maps and guides were not new but they multiplied with great rapidity. These were places for the individual as an individual to weave their way around. If anyone paused on the railway station, sports ground or in the department store, to ask 'Who am I?', the answers were simple: I am looking for the London train and I have paid for my ticket; I am an Hibernian football club supporter and I have bought my ticket; I have purchased the latest fashion made by a seamstress who has been to London and so on.

PLACES OF MEMORY

This growth of non-places was accompanied and related to a growth of places of memory.[50] It was a feature of the modernity of the urban industrial system, that constant demands were made for visible signs of what used to be, that the past was continually brought into the present. This was seen at its most dramatic and inventive in the architectural styles of the Scottish Baronial. The first statements of the baronial derived from a series of country houses in the 1840s, but the style spread in the 1860s to suburban villas, quality tenement buildings, urban improvement schemes, office developments and institutional buildings. Crow-stepped gables, bartizans, turrets, oriels, armorial panels often decorated with thistle and saltire appeared in many and varied locations, reminders that this was Scotland.[51] The anxiety of the anonymity and non-place of the modern was replaced by the confidence of imperial, commercial and industrial success. Such assertion had its artisan and municipal forms. Those who lacked a villa or country house could still live in a tenement where the armorial panels contained the name of the developer and the date.[52] Those who walked the paved and regulated streets were reminded of the world of pipes and drains beneath by access panels bearing the plumber's name. The battle to assert identity against the anonymity of modern space took many forms.

There was a spread of statues which made and remade history. Walter Scott made a spectacular appearance in Edinburgh as did William Wallace in Aberdeen.[53] More subtle messages came with the often ignored statue of the Duke of Buccleuch, which gazes down on the comings and goings of St Giles' Cathedral and the Law Courts in Edinburgh. The Duke is entitled to be there because of the family contribution to the creation of Edinburgh's coal port at Granton, and his ubiquity in the charities and institutions of the city, but the bronze story boards around the statue provide a reminder of the depth of family and Scottish history.[54] The Duke offered a prospect of endeavour and permanence.

The growing importance of spaces of memory for Scotland may be illustrated by two contrasting events in Edinburgh. Mid-century Edinburgh saw the publication of the now inspirational *A Letter to the Lord Provost of Edinburgh on the Best Ways of Spoiling the Beauty of Edinburgh* written by Lord Cockburn.[55] His protest was directed at the demolition of Trinity College Church to make way for the expansion of facilities around Waverley Station by the North British Railway. What is often forgotten is that Cockburn lost the argument. In an act of tokenism one of Scotland's finest medieval churches was demolished, the stones numbered and placed in a yard by Calton Hill, where they were pilfered before the rebuilding of a truncated and much reduced church began in 1872.[56] But 1872 was a different era. In 1849 the dominant 'modern' view was that of Revd James Begg, evangelical minister of the Free Church in suburban Newington:

Figure 8.9   *Edinburgh lamppost, Market Street. © R. J. Morris.*

Figure 8.10   *Crawford the Plumber, Fleshmarket Close, Edinburgh. © R. J. Morris.*

Many more will be very sceptical as to the wisdom of your pathetic lamentations over the fate of Old College Church . . . the church was latterly of little use – was half buried by railway operations at any rate – and £16,000 was rather a tempting price for a bankrupt city . . . what we want is a clearing out of the dens of filth and better houses for the poor . . . [not] the madness of spending the money in the erection of a church for which there is no congregation.[57]

The changes and the logic of the changes made to Edinburgh Castle were very different. The dominant visual impact of Edinburgh Castle in the early twenty-first century was created between 1850 and the 1930s. In 1850, the Great Hall was the barracks hospital, the Portcullis Tower was the armourer's shop and St Margaret's Chapel the powder store. By 1900, St Margaret's was again a twelfth-century chapel, the Great Hall a magnificent ceremonial space and the Portcullis Tower a grand entrance topped out with a third storey that had all the trimmings of the Scottish Baronial. This had been sanctioned by the War Office and largely financed by William Nelson, wealthy industrialist, printer, publisher and devout evangelical. He was especially keen to remake the spaces in which the 9th Earl of Argyll had spent his last night before execution in 1685. His adviser on all this was Daniel Wilson, one-time secretary of the Society of Antiquaries of Scotland and Professor then Principal of Toronto University.[58] In 1885, Wilson expressed the ambitions of the two men:

> here as elsewhere, all that is really old and genuine must be preserved; at the same time the prominent position of this gateway tower, in the general view of the Castle, suggests the desirability of treating it in such a way as may best accord with the picturesque outline of the fine old fortress, so long as this can be done without sacrificing any genuine ancient feature. It will of course be an indispensable condition in any restoration that the chamber in which Argyle passed his last hours be preserved intact. No new architectural feature, however admirable could compensate for the loss of a building enriched by such historical association.[59]

At the turn of the century, Gerald Baldwin Brown, Professor of Architecture and Fine Arts at Edinburgh University expanded on the logic of such inspirational 'restorations', adding a dimension of race and empire:

> The mother country must always remain the soil in which are rooted all the traditional memories of the race. Now these memories are of incalculable advantage in keeping alive throughout the Empire the sense of unity of the stock, and relics that evoke them may be envisaged as one of our imperial assets . . . the ancient assets that sheltered the forefathers of our common race . . . [these] structures . . . are living witness of the history through which the nation has grown strong enough to flourish itself and to send forth branches to cover the earth.[60]

Here indeed was a place of memory for a nation and an empire that was reimagining itself. It was an aspect of being a stateless nation that the Scots increasingly learnt their history from place. George Eyre Todd was a Glasgow-based journalist, an active member of the Scottish Patriotic Society and Glasgow St Andrew's Society. He advised the traveller with a good stick and a light knapsack to take their holiday in Scotland for 'hardly a step can be taken without treading on historic ground'. His readers were led around Scotland acquiring a distinctive and disjoined history.[61] Much of the agenda had been set by Walter Scott, 'the Wizard of Abbotsford'. Indeed, many of the postcards which the tourist of the 1900s might buy were based upon scenes engraved in the 1840s and inspired by the novels and poetry of Scott.[62] Several had been painted by Turner. Melrose Abbey, Fingal's Cave, Loch Coruisk and Loch Katrine were key points in the itinerary.[63] Few could visit without a copy of the *Lady of the Lake* and *Marmion*. Many would take *Scotland (part one) Edinburgh, Glasgow and the Highlands* from the 'Through Guide Series' by Mountford John Byndon Baddeley. At Callander, the sardonic old schoolmaster advised his readers on the best hotels and led them through the landscape of the great stag hunt across the bens and glens. He halted where Roderick Dhu had challenged Fitzjames, but warned they must substitute 'the great sluice of the Glasgow Waterworks' for 'Coilantogle Ford' – a somewhat brutal meeting of the romantic historical with the modern spaces of Scotland.[64] By 1900, the Scots had produced many places of memory, some like the Wallace Monument are still much loved, others like the Covenanter's Monument at Bothwell Bridge sit less easily in the Scottish identity of the early twenty-first century. It was all part of a process through which the Scots relearnt and continually revised their identity and history through the complex and fractured history of place.

The dimensions and direction of change in the spaces of everyday life in Scotland were clear. Movement and meaning were sanctioned in ways which moved from the self-evident stories, customs and moral assertion of the anthropological to the rational rule-based functionality of the modern, which in turn met the comforting amelioration of the 'spaces of memory'. These three dimensions of space emerged from a variety of sources. Each were created for specific, often extra-ordinary, purposes, the evangelicals desire to shock, the journalists need to entertain and gain attention, the municipal official wanting to inform local government decisions and the migrant craving for nostalgia. The extensive quotes enable the historian to extract the everyday from the extra-ordinary, the window shoppers in Argyle Street and the anxious railway traveller buying a ticket. The crofter before the Napier Commission was not just expressing anger in a political battle but looking over his cattle each day, looking up at the hill where shielings had once been and thinking how useful some fencing would be. Each specific account reflected the rhythms of the everyday, rhythms of the seasons, of the hour of the day and day of the week. The three dimensions of change outlined in this chapter present a neat account of change in which one destroys or conceals the other. In practice, although the modern and the places of memory came to dominate and compete with each other, there was rarely any neat replacement of one by the other. Indeed, new spaces might gather the moral certainty and sense of the eternal and permanent of the anthropological space. The gendered spaces of home and department store were especially powerful in this respect. Equally the quotes and memoirs showed multiple and competing meanings for each set of actors. The Argyle Street of the window shopper, the milk seller, the policeman, the tourist and the lads just having fun were very different. There was a railway station for the daily commuter, the tourist, the porter and the railway manager. Lastly, these changes were both Scottish and universal to industrial society. Places of memory and street regulation spread across Europe from Brussels to Budapest, but Wallace, thistles, saltires and the crofter's sense of the hill were very specific. Unpicking the sources showed clear general directions but the changing experiences, assumptions and compulsions of the everyday showed a variety of competing and overlapping spaces.

Notes

1 A. P. Cohen, *Whalsay. Symbol, Segment and Boundary in a Shetland Community* (Manchester, 1987).

2 W. Scott, *Minstrelsy of the Scottish Border consisting of Historical and Romantic Ballads* (London, 1869). The first edition was published in Kelso in 1802; see A. Lincoln, *Walter Scott and Modernity* (Edinburgh, 2007).

3 R. Rodger, *The Transformation of Edinburgh. Land, Property and Trust in the Nineteenth Century* (Cambridge, 2001), pp. 3–122.

4 *Royal Commission to Inquire into the State of Municipal Corporations in Scotland: Local Reports*, Parliamentary Papers (PP), 1836 XX, pp. 395–9; J. M. Gilbert (ed.), *Flower of the Forest. Selkirk: A New History* (Selkirk, 1985).

5 K. R. Bogle, *Scotland's Common Ridings* (Stroud, 2004); G. K. Neville, *The Mother Town. Civic Ritual, Symbol and Experience in the Borders of Scotland* (Oxford, 1994).

6 Old Statistical Account [OSA], vol. 5, p. 124.

7 OSA, pp. 15, 45 [Lanark]; New Statistical Account [NSA], 1834–5, vol. 2, p. 1778 [Linlithgow], p. 268 [Inveresk].

8 *Reports from Commissioners upon the Boundaries of the several Cities, Burghs and Towns in Scotland in Respect to the Election of Members to Serve in Parliament*, British Parliamentary Papers (PP), 1831–2 XLII.

9 *Glasgow Boundaries Commission, 1888: Report of the Glasgow Boundaries Commissioners, vol. 1 with Appendix*, PP, 1888; I. Maver, 'Glasgow's Civic Government', in W. H. Fraser and I. Maver (eds), *Glasgow. Vol. Two: 1830–1912* (Manchester, 1996), pp. 44–485.

10 *Glasgow Boundaries Commission*, vol. 1, p. xvi.

11 *Glasgow Boundaries Commission*, vol. 1, p. vii.

12 *Glasgow Boundaries Commission*, vol. 1, pp. xii–xiii.

13 *Glasgow Boundaries Commission*, vol. 1, p. xvii.

14 *Glasgow Boundaries Commission*, vol. 1, p. xxviii.

15 *Glasgow Boundaries Commission*, vol. 1, p. xxix.

16 E. Richards, *The Leviathan of Wealth. The Sutherland Fortune in the Industrial Revolution* (London, 1973), and *Patrick Sellar and the Highland Clearances*

(Edinburgh, 1999); J. Hunter, *The Making of the Crofting Community* (Edinburgh, 1976); W. Orr, *Deer Forests, Landlords and Crofters* (Edinburgh, 1982); E. A. Cameron, *Land for the People. The British Government and the Scottish Highlands, c.1880–1925* (East Linton, 1996).

17 *Royal Commission of Inquiry into the Condition of Crofters and Cottars in the Highlands and Islands of Scotland*, PP, 1884 XXXII, part 1, pp. 2–9.

18 *Royal Commission of Inquiry*, PP, 1884 XXXIII. From evidence taken at The Braes, Skye, 99, 1–547.

19 R. J. Morris, 'Urbanisation and Scotland', in W. H. Fraser and R. J. Morris (eds), *People and Society in Scotland, vol. II: 1830–1914* (Edinburgh, 1990), pp. 73–102.

20 I. D. Whyte, 'Scottish and Irish Urbanisation in the Seventeenth and Eighteenth Centuries: A Comparative Perspective', in S. J. Connolly, R. A. Houston and R. J. Morris (eds), *Conflict, Identity and Economic Development* (Preston, 1995), pp. 14–28.

21 T. C. Smout, 'The Erskins of Mar and the Development of Alloa, 1689–1825', *Scottish Studies*, 7 (1963), 57–74; W. Roy, *The Great Map. The Military Survey of Scotland, 1747–55* (Edinburgh, 2007) with introductory essays by Y. Hodson, C. Tabraham and C. Withers.

22 J. M. Leighton, *Selected Views of Glasgow and its Environs*, engraved by Joseph Swan (Glasgow, 1828), p. 1.

23 R. J. Morris, *Scotland 1907. The Many Scotlands of Valentine and Sons Photographers* (Edinburgh, 2007), p. 66.

24 A. Brown, writing as 'Shadow', *Midnight Scenes and Social Photographs, being Sketches of the Life in the Streets, Wynds and Dens of the City* (Glasgow, 1858).

25 Brown, *Social Photographs*, pp. 37–9.

26 D. Frisby and M. Featherstone (ed.), *Simmel on Culture* (London, 1997), pp. 137–69 ('The Sociology of Space') and pp. 174–86 ('The Metropolis and Mental Life').

27 Brown, *Social Photographs*, p. 59.

28 Brown, *Social Photographs*, p. 62.

29 Brown, *Social Photographs*, pp. 96–8.

30 James Hamilton Muir, *Glasgow in 1901* (Glasgow, 1901), reprint with introduction by P. Kinchin (Oxford, 2001), pp. 238–44.

31 J. Valentine, *Aberdeen as it Was & Is Being an Analysis of the Census for 1871, and a Retrospect*; with an appendix by J. Valentine and an illustrative map by A. Gibb (Aberdeen, 1871) and *A Classification and Arrangement of the Several Local Acts of Parliament Regulating the Police, Water, and Gas of the City of Aberdeen, with Index and Other References, and a Map*, prepared for the use of the Town Council by J. Valentine (Aberdeen, 1872); W. H. Fraser and C. H. Lee (ed.), *Aberdeen, 1800–2000. A New History* (East Linton, 2000).

32 G. Morton, *Unionist Nationalism. Governing Urban Scotland, 1830–1860* (East Linton, 1999), pp. 35–46.

33 A. Clark, *Reminiscences of a Police Officer in the Granite City* (Aberdeen, 1873), pp. 66, 86–7.

34 I. H. Anderson, *Inverness before the Railways* (Inverness, 1885), p. 29.
35 J. M. E. Saxby, *Auld Lerwick. A Personal Reminiscence*, printed for the Lerwick Church Improvement Scheme Bazaar, 8, 9, 10 November 1894.
36 Anderson, *Inverness*, p. 73; E. Cameron, 'The Construction of Union Street, Inverness, 1863–65', *Scottish Local History Journal*, 44 (Winter 1998), 13–18.
37 The President's address at the first annual dinner, *Scottish Mountaineering Club Journal*, 1:1 (12 December 1889), available at: www.gdl.cdlr.strath.ac.uk/smcj/smcj001.
38 D. O. Hill, *Views of the Garnkirk and Glasgow Railway* (Edinburgh, 1832).
39 J. Richards and J. M. MacKenzie, *The Railway Station. A Social History* (Oxford, 1986), pp. 19–36.
40 J. R. Kellett, *The Impact of Railways on Victorian Cities* (London, 1969), pp. 208–43.
41 D. Robertson, *The Princes Street Proprietors and other Chapters in the History of the Royal Burgh of Edinburgh* (Edinburgh, 1935), pp. 37–46.
42 J. T. Lawrence, 'Notable Railway Stations. No. 37 – Glasgow Central Station (Caledonian Railway)', *The Railway Magazine*, (January 1907), 1–8.
43 M. Waddell, 'The Caledonian Railways Diamond Jubilee. The Goods Department', *The Railway Magazine*, (September 1907), 223.
44 J. Verne, *Backwards to Britain* (Edinburgh, 1993), pp. 59, 79, 127, 137 and 157. My thanks to Sian Reynolds for this reference.
45 *Mountain, Moor and Loch on the Route of the West Highland Railway* (London, 1895), p. 31.
46 Muir, *Glasgow in 1901*, pp. 237–8.
47 *The Scotsman*, 2 November 1872, 13 August 1895 and 12 December 1914.
48 *The Scotsman*, 18 December 1872.
49 M. Augé, *Non-places: Introduction to an Anthropology of Supermodernity* (London, 1995).
50 This account follows the work of P. Nora, *Les Lieux de Mémoire* (Paris, 1994). The English translation is slightly different in content, A. Goldhammer, trans., *Realms of Memory* (New York, 1996), but both show the enormous variety of locations for this cultural process.
51 M. Glendinning, R. MacInnes and A. MacKechnie, *A History of Scottish Architecture from the Renaissance to the Present Day* (Edinburgh, 1996), pp. 274–85.
52 Rodger, *The Transformation of Edinburgh*, pp. 461–70.
53 G. Morton, *William Wallace. Man and Myth* (Stroud, 2001), p. 83.
54 *The Scotsman*, 7 February 1888.
55 H. T. Cockburn, *A Letter to the Lord Provost of Edinburgh on the Best ways of Spoiling the Beauty of Edinburgh* (1849), T. Levinthal and H. Suslak (eds) (Edinburgh, 1998).
56 J. Gifford, C. McWilliam and D. Walker, *The Buildings of Scotland. Edinburgh* (London, 1984), pp. 171–2.
57 J. Begg, DD, *How to Promote and Preserve the True Beauty of Edinburgh being a few hints to the Hon Lord Cockburn* (Edinburgh, 1849).

58 R. J. Morris, 'The Capitalist, the Professor and the Soldier: the re-making of Edinburgh Castle, 1850–1900', *Planning Perspectives*, 22 (January 2007), 55–78.

59 National Library Scotland Mss 1734, f 128, 12 December 1885.

60 G. B. Brown, 'Urban Legislation in the Interests of Amenity at Home and Abroad', *Journal of the Royal Institute of British Architects*, 12:2 (1904), 69–78.

61 G. Eyre-Todd, *Scotland Picturesque and Traditional. A Pilgrimage with Staff and Knapsack* (London, 1895), p. 19. It was the sort of book frequently given as a school prize.

62 Morris, *Scotland 1907*, pp. 13–26.

63 J. Reed, *Walter Scott: Landscape and Locality* (London, 1980); G. Finlay, *Landscapes of Memory. Turner as Illustrator of Scott* (London, 1980).

64 M. J. B. Baddeley, *Thorough Guide Series. Scotland (part one) Edinburgh, Glasgow and the Highlands* (London, 1908), pp. 51–7.

Chapter 9

Identity Out of Place

Graeme Morton

Nature was sparing in her gifts to Scotsmen. She gave to Scotland a poor, sterile soil as a rule, and compelled them by constant and painful toil to extract from her rugged bosom even a humble subsistence. Her children if they were to have comfort and independence in even a moderate measure, must of necessity be sturdy and frugal and hard-working. For centuries, Scotland was harassed with the inroads of Scandinavian hordes in the North and West, and with obstinate attacks of Saxons and English on the South and East. The industry, the energy, the shrewdness, the caution, the reliability, the noble daring and unbending sense of honour that Scotchmen have carried with them to the ends of the earth, are the direct result of this struggle for existence which the ruggedness of their native soil and the persistent attacks of the Northern and Southern foes imposed upon them [which they] could not avoid if they were to have social and political independence. Such is the priceless heritage, dearly bought with her best blood and brain, that Scotland has handed down to her sons of more modern times, and has equipped them with the energy and the ability with which they have displayed through the kindness of God in the service of their nation in various parts of the world.[1]

Scattered throughout the British Empire, Scottish migrants found regular opportunities to ponder the personal reverberations of departure from their native land. From his vantage point in Canada, for much of the nineteenth century the most popular of those destinations, Revd Neil Macnish reflected that 'character' had long empowered the Scottish people in overcoming an inhospitable land and politics to embrace the opportunities that emigration could offer. Writing from outside of Scotland, and therefore out of place, he wrapped the industrious Scot within the religion and religiosity that dominated in the land left behind. Others, unwilling to contemplate a life overseas, believed the industriousness that seemingly so defined the Scottish people could still be found and applied at home. In a letter to a cousin who had emigrated from Paisley during the downturn in cotton- and thread-making of the 1830s, John Brough encouraged his return: 'I think you had better come home to one [job] here & by your own labours you could support yourselves very well as work is now quite plenty here . . . '[2]

This debate could be found among many families of short- and long-distance migrants who proffered their labour, skills, training and knowledge into and out of a re-aligning economy. A dramatic drop of 40 per cent in agricultural jobs was accompanied by a growth in the industrial sectors, producing a net increase of around 760,000 jobs for men and 285,000 jobs for women in the years 1841 to 1911.[3] Widespread disturbance in working lives would be a consequence affecting those at home acting as an imperative to move. Unease and delight over the choice of emigration was expressed in letters that would then be passed around extended kin. There was encouragement for others to become pioneers: 'I never was happier', wrote James Good in 1841, 'and Magdalene [his sister] was never happier in all our lives, money is scarce but meat is plenty . . . A Canadian farmer is the happiest man in this world.' Looking back on that year, he had experienced his 'happiest summer ever' and 'Magdalene would not go to Paisley for the world – [she's] sorry she was not here 18 years ago'.[4] This was a man who was content with his lot. Others, of course, were not so easily pleased. John Robertson was disappointed with the land he was offered in the 1830s: 'Three plots, but out of the way of the market, with bad roads . . . too much water in spring, not enough in winter; even with wells, oxen wouldn't drink.' He gave up with Upper Canada and contemplated his next move to Ohio.[5] Between 1825 and 1914 it is estimated that 1.84 million people left Scotland for non-European destinations, with around 44 per cent heading for America, 28 per cent Canada and 25 per cent Australia and New Zealand.[6] Their life choices tell of a mobility now understood by historians as a known reality for many families in these decades, matched by frequent short and temporary movements within Scotland and with a history stretching back into earlier periods.[7] One consequence of the creation of new settlements overseas was the use of identity markers in the form of clubs and societies organised for purposes of philanthropic aid, merriment and pleasure, religious observance and cultural formation.[8] In St Andrew's societies, Caledonian clubs, Sons and Daughters of Scotland benevolent societies and in groups and dinners formed in honour of Walter Scott and Robert Burns there were regular opportunities to justify and lament the choice of emigration. From scattered beginnings, the flow of Scottish societies quickened during the 1830s in the Maritimes and Upper and Lower Canada, in the 1840s and 1860s in Australia, from the 1860s in New Zealand and during the 1870s in South Africa and western Canada.[9] Through this associational introspection were expressed feelings of loss and regret mingled with an optimism that grasped a sense of place left behind. Introducing his deliberations on the Scottish character in a sermon preached to a society of Scotsmen gathered to celebrate St Andrew's Day in Ontario, Macnish fell upon the well-known lines of the expatriate's Psalm (136, lines 5–6): 'If I forget thee O Jerusalem, let my right hand forget her cunning. If I do not remember thee, let my tongue cleave to the roof of my mouth: If I prefer not Jerusalem above my chief joy.'[10] Those same lines were also chosen when William McIntosh preached 'True Patriotism' before the St Andrew's Society of Ottawa two years later. Their sentiment led him to find parallels with the Jewish people, the greatest diaspora of all, where there are 'features of resemblance between the people who inhabit the heather hills of Scotland and the rocky fastness of Judea'. Both had a 'fondness for making and keeping money' and each had a 'love of their country that directed their actions at all times'. He identified the love of the Scottish people to Britain, and their respect for the English and the Irish, but importantly 'the patriotism of the Scot, like the Jew, was a religious one'. It was a love of landscape certainly, the 'land of brown heath and shaggy wood', but more so was it 'the religion of her firesides, the Gospel of her churches. Scotland is the land of the Sabbath, the land of the Bible and the Bible study'. His was a confident Presbyterianism, rooted in home and a sense of how that home had been transplanted in a community far away. And while some might mark the Scots as 'a race called cold, even solid' for their religious rootedness, to McIntosh their character was 'rather like the resistless onrush of sea waves, as has been shown in many a frightful contest, both by sea and land'.[11]

Blessed with little of God's natural bounty, these migrants thought of themselves as people of solid character, fundamentally religious, but also charitable, educated, industrious and free from the intellectual and emotional fancies that might detract from steadfastness. Even when the nearest Church of Scotland service in Upper Canada was three miles in one direction (in Preston) and four miles in another (in Galt), and not well attended, John Good could describe his contemporaries as 'every man for himself, but sober and industrious'.[12] Offering the clarity of distance, though not free from the romanticisation of a reality that was left behind, for the historian of the everyday his observations and others like them help to capture the contemporary expression of Scottish identity from afar. These boasts were not about exceptionalness. Contemporaries such as these were not attempting to capture the outlandish Scot. Their aim was to characterise the everyday facets of their humanity, the incessant basics of their life, their origins as 'Jock Tamson's bairns'.[13] Their use of associational culture to mobilise and encapsulate their identity was a reflection of their (predominant) Presbyterianism and their continued attachment to how life was lived at home. The theoretical and historical explanation for why and how Scotland maintained an identity within the British nation-state has been explained through the social structure of the nation, its civil society.[14] It has had little to say about 'blood and belonging', headlining instead an early form of national identity sustained by a broad range of institutions.[15] T. C. Smout's observation that it was a sense of place rather than a sense of tribe has neat summative power. Within the civic parameters something approaching 'tribe' could be used as a reaction to economic and social dislocation in the peripheral highlands and in the revival of a late-century pan-Celtic identity.[16] Ethnicity would also inform elements of associational culture in the diaspora, in Burns, Caledonian and St Andrew's societies when familial lineage, blood and kin, was prioritised. However, in none was it used with sufficient strength to undermine the associational rationale behind their formation.[17] These manifestations of identity that developed overseas – out of Scotland, out of place – remained inextricably sourced to home, to Scotland, to place.

The strength of this civil society was the banality which marked it out as everyday in thought and deed. This was not borne by ubiquity, although an important factor, but by the values and identities embodied and organised around the fundamentals of morality and religion, ideals that so permeated the lives of these people in its practice, observance and even in its rejection. Something very pervasive – religiosity – something fundamentally banal – civil society – mirrored and carried the dominant identities of the Scots abroad as at home. To focus on the banal is to attempt to look beyond a concept of identity applicable only to nation-states in periods of crisis such as war or points of commemoration such as royal coronation or the monarch's birthday. Instead, it offers a route to identity creation as it occurred on a daily basis, suggesting that the beliefs and ideologies that form any number of identities are sustained in mundane ways that are widespread and thus powerful. Nationalism, as the politicisation of one of those identities, is far from being an intermittent mood in established nations, but rather an endemic condition, always an influence, and daily the nation is indicated, or 'flagged' in the lives of the people.[18] Michael Billig develops the late-Victorian notion that 'forgetting' was just as essential to the formation of the nation as 'remembering' the past.[19] Importantly, this is not just a collective forgetting of the past, but also a collective forgetting of the present.[20] We look but we do not see the signs of the nation around us, so ordinary are they. Whereas national flags may at times be clear signifiers, such as when draped over a military coffin, or lowered to half-mast at times of death or national mourning, 'the majority of national flags likely to be seen by the modern citizen in the course of a lifetime will not be signalling a specific message'.[21] And if an identity that is state-captured can be understood through banal and mundane routines, one can hypothesise that an identity forged in civil society is no different and, indeed, that it can be a route to understanding better the 'Scottish character' of the nineteenth century.

To begin to explore the construction of identity in the everyday structures of Scotland's civil society, two themes will be followed in this chapter. The first has already been mentioned, the prevalence of religion and morality within Scotland's associational life in time of change. The second is the culture formed in and of attachment to place, to Scot-*land* within Scotland. Both were part of the people's construction of self, and both were reactions to the apparent loss of the everyday. Those that had left these shores bestowed direction upon us: the Scottish identity – whether at home or away – was formed out of place.

TIME

There was no shortage of contemporary comment upon the pace of change in the nineteenth-century world. As historians, we still debate how unprecedented this was and the extent to which the majority were or could be conscious of a 'Victorian Age', but to some well-placed contemporaries it seemed that movement was exhaustive. In mid-century, Charles Dickens satirised a life where *getting on* was an end in itself, where elbows were brandished in the search for something that was progress. Paradoxically, he chose from the feminised half of the 1707 Union, a Scot, to parody how modernity was epitomised by education based on facts 'and yet more Facts', tumultuously gathering their own momentum under the tutelage of the schoolmaster Mr McChoakumchild, 'If he had only learnt a little less, how infinitely better he might have taught much more'.[22] In contrast to what he had penned before, *Hard Times* presented the inhumanities of Victorian civilisation underpinned by an aggressive philosophy of unchecked progress and inhuman spirit.[23] To some writers at least, Great Britain was losing sight of what its people represented and the ordinariness of life was disappearing under exceptional changes. They were changes that would in turn become ordinary, but that awareness was yet to come. John Stuart Mill, the philosophical radical of Scottish parenthood, had difficulty reconciling the demands of being a gentleman with the concerns of material life in mid-Victorian society, failing to be 'charmed with the ideal of life held out by those who think that the normal state of human beings is that of struggling to get on'. He railed against those who believed 'the trampling, crushing, elbowing, and treading on each other's heels which form the existing type of social life, [was] the most desirable lot of human kind'; was it, he queried, 'anything but the disagreeable symptoms of one of the phases of industrial progress?'[24] In Robert Owen's *Report to the County of Lanark* in 1821, modernity and its inequalities of income were similarly faulted:

> Of all our splendid improvements in arts and science, the effect has hitherto been to demoralise society, through the misapplication of the new wealth created. The arrangements to which your Reporter now calls the attention of the Public, present the certain means of renovating the moral character, and of improving, to an unlimited extent, the general condition of the population, and while they lead to a more rapid multiplication of wealth than the present system permits to take place, they will effectively preclude all the evils with which wealth is now accompanied.[25]

The Scots knew first hand the problems of urban life. Their tendency to live in single- or two-room flats to a degree greater than was found elsewhere in Britain fostered high densities in Scottish towns and cities.[26] Glasgow, the urban city *par excellence*, continued to throw up tales that all too easily shook sensibilities despite their familiarity. Lamenting the height and scale of the tenements in Edinburgh which made cleaning so difficult, with 'common stairs, sometimes as filthy as the streets or wynds to which they open', it was Glasgow that most perturbed Edwin Chadwick in 1842, where in one part of the city next to Argyle Street 754 of the 5,000 cases of fever had been located the previous year.[27] His observations were part of any number of peering eyes that spied on the new and present threat, to health, morality and political stability that unregulated urbanisation was fostering. Some sought answers in science. John Kay, the educational reformer who was influenced by Thomas Chalmers, 'took the traditions of the statistical movement in Scotland to his enquiries in English towns', applying the moral and civil imperatives of a Scottish upbringing to the inspectorate of the civil service as it was formed in 1830.[28] The statistical department in the Board of Trade was launched in 1834 and the *Journal of the Statistical Society of London* published its first issue four years later, gaining a Royal moniker in 1887. Scotland's Poor Law was reformed on the recommendations of the evidential gatherings of a Royal Commission which reported in 1844. And, in an attempt to revise the statistics produced by the General Register Office in England, the Medico-Statistical Association produced its first report in 1852, using returns from a number of medical practitioners in Edinburgh and Leith.[29] Both were part of the impetus behind the legislation creating the Registrar General Office for Scotland in 1855, charging it with recording all of Scotland's births, deaths and marriages and bringing the collating of this information into line with English practice of the previous eighteen years. These were developments in rational bureaucracy summed up by *The Social Science Review* in 1862, marking its first issue by stating confidently that the 'advancement of social sciences in the last few years has been remarkable'.[30] The Scots though were apparently sceptical of some new ways of thinking about the world. The President of the Anthropological Society, Dr James Hunt, expressed his trepidation over travelling to Dundee from the south of England because of the many letters he had received from 'north of the Tweed telling me that the people of Scotland had made up their minds to declare war against [this] branch of science . . .'[31] Other scientific investigations attracted even more attention and George Combe the Edinburgh phrenologist, who led the movement in Britain, was prepared to offer some pseudo-scientific quantitative study, contrasting the industrious poor with those more feckless. Identifying differences as a flaw in personal morality, it was a thesis developed most notably in *The Constitution of Man* (1828) and highlighted throughout his work for the Phrenological Society from 1820 until his death in 1858.[32]

The development of the sciences, in all their forms, had particular impacts in Scotland. The university system found its emphasis on general studies undermined by the 'social expediency' of 'exact knowledge' in reforms debated in 1830, 1876 and more completely within the Universities Commission of 1889, resulting, G. E. Davie contends, in 'Scottish intellectualism [being] eclipsed'.[33] The most explicit connection between the physical and moral world in this period can be found in Patrick Geddes' studies of human evolution in the test case of Edinburgh. The link between urban and human preservation and renewal was developed in his conception of 'civics'. Much urban development in the late Victorian years focused on moral improvement through regularised street patterns, single-use precincts and class-demarcated order. As the chapter from R. J. Morris makes clear, new urban spaces, and use of those spaces, was an attempt to establish administrative governance over towns and cities that had grown up so quickly. It was an attempt to bring cultural influences to bear on the utilitarianism of rapid, and at times unfettered, urban growth. Geddes wrote of the modern life led by both the capitalist and the labourer being 'decidedly a poor affair . . . For both, life is equally bland at present; the capitalist in his big ugly house is no happier than the labourer in his little ugly one; if one has more fatigue, the other has more worry'.[34] The influence of the arts and crafts movement on Charles Rennie Mackintosh's early work is rooted in the sense of loss of an idealised past in these urban environments. His use of the baronial style as part of an eclectic Scottishness is important, just as gothic had taken over from classicism as a more organic basis for architectural expression. Macintosh's stencilled designs for the Cranston tearooms in Glasgow came in 1897,[35] and helped prioritise the social ritual of tea consumption in contrast to the dominance of the tavern and the ale house with the attendant detritus of people that surrounded them. The creation of the tearoom, and the social conventions that built up around it, was very much part of the Scottish urban experience, but so too has been the civic, national and artistic pride that has since followed Macintosh's creations.

These were chimes for the ordinariness of life in the face of exceptionalness; they are suggestive that small changes were charged with much hope. In his biography of the Scottish naturalist Thomas Edward, Samuel Smiles tells his readers that 'The History of the humblest human life is a tale of marvels.'[36] There is power in the meekest to face down modernity and Edward was the product of increasing interest in cataloguing a natural and societal life that was to be canonised before it was lost. Walter Scott offered his *Tales of a Grandfather* (1828) to instruct the young with historical yarns of how life was, and perhaps still should be, presented as memories of experience and of a previous age. His defence of the Scottish bank note was fuelled by a sense of national pride for something that was part of Scots' daily life as well as the practicalities of national commerce.[37] The hunting and gathering of manuscripts by the bibliographical clubs took inspiration from him and were replicated in many aspects of culture, such as the Iona Club's aim in 1834 to 'investigate and illustrate the History, Antiquities, and early Literature of the Highlands of Scotland'.[38] Many aspects of Scottish life were similarly logged: the antiquities gathered under the patronage of David Steuart Erskine (1742–1829), the ancient geology and Gaelic of Fingal in Mendelssohn's *The Hebrides* (1829), the product, wildlife, vegetation and spoils of Empire collected by the curators of the Royal Edinburgh Museum, its foundation stone laid in 1861, the flora and fauna of Angus hunted down by the Arbroath Horticultural and Natural History Society from 1884, the chapbooks brought to Lauriston Castle by William Robert Reid and John A. Fairley, and the systematic collection of the Scottish and English ballads in five volumes by F. J. Child (published 1882–98). Even the urban help directed to the poor of Highland and Borders Scotland, and the rural preservationists that were inspired by English concerns of industrial over-run in the unrelenting push to feed the cities, based on the communitarian ideas from a golden age, used the techniques of rational classification back upon itself. To these contemporaries at least, it appeared that the faster society was to change, and the more exceptional was that transformation, then the more the ordinariness of the day, and the stability of that day secured to times gone past, was called to the fore.

Almost pleading for the present to remain and not be propelled to times lost was a powerful counter current to the path of modernity. Many Scots of this period, it would seem, had a clear sense of themselves as unwavering and principled, and it was a belief that bathed their actions with a sense of purpose that comes only from routine familiarity. The combination of industry and ethos has remained one of the compelling analyses of Victorian Scotland. It is clear that the nation's impressive economic advance could not have been enacted without the opportunities of Empire and the availability of liquid money, entrepreneurship, accessible primary resources and cheap labour.[39] Yet the culture of industriousness was forged from an enveloping Calvinism manifest in thrift and self-help, especially from the second half of the century. It came to define a sense of self, a moral code that developed most strongly in response to the opportunities and disorder of economic transformation. Self-help was not found only in the writings of Smiles, uplifting as his biographies and morality tales were to contemporaries. The co-operative movement was one notable aspect of working-class life built around a strong sense of social responsibility.[40] The Savings Bank of Glasgow was another, with 117,000 depositors and £3,500,000 in its accounts at the end of 1881, making it the largest trustee savings bank in Britain.[41] Analysis of those predominantly skilled workers who opened new accounts in that year shows 56 per cent born in Ireland, and offers some challenge to contemporary rhetoric of the Irish labourer as drunk and improvident.[42] The latter remained a powerful narrative, part of Scotland's creation of 'other' against which to project itself, but this evidence indicates the cultural pervasiveness of the industrious ideal upon personal saving, family budgeting and the importance of regular paid employment.

As they were translated into associational activity, these ideals have been conceived as a programme of piety, with the Church of Scotland along with the other denominations engaging clerical and lay philanthropy in response to signs of secularisation.[43] This application of religious principles outside formal preaching was premised upon communal traditions, sustained most powerfully by the writing, oratory and direct action of Thomas Chalmers, notably his evocation of the 'Godly Commonwealth'.[44] Morality permeated much of labour action, both within the nascent trades unions and throughout the workplace. The link between religion and Chartism in the 1830s was strong and although the majority of the workforce did not attend church, the skilled worker would dominate congregations. As a result, Scottish worker radicalism, so William Knox tells us, developed an emphasis on social rights and brotherhood over class antagonism, and an emphasis on friendly societies rather than unionisation, with a strong pull of temperance within the Chartist leadership. Temperance began as a movement in Glasgow in the late 1820s and 1830s, promoted through the energy of John Dunlop, its impact developed by activating the local through the associational ideal.[45] Estimating that £2.5 million was spent upon spirits alone at mid-century, it was suggested by one campaigner that among the many productive alternatives that could be purchased for this sum were 1 million yards of linen at 1s. 3d. per yard, amounting to £62,000, or 4,800,000 loaves of bread at 5d. per loaf, amounting to £100,000.[46] Temperance was the sheen of moral respectability that cut across the classes, especially at times of social organisation and political debate.[47] In 1882, Major Henry Edwards searched out suitable accommodation to establish the Salvation Army in Parkhead, confirming his belief that it offered fertile ground for recruitment. Women would find the Band of Hope a more secular mix of temperance, respectable leisure and Sunday school. It lasted into the twentieth century and women especially enjoyed singing, the magic lantern and the cinema, giving them a 'good night out'.[48] Women were active proselytisers in both groups and there is evidence of 'three Salvation Army lassies' being 'keen propagandists' in Barr's soft drinks factory in 1896.[49]

From 1800, the associations of the Enlightenment had 'reached full maturity as a powerful and pervasive social institution' to the extent that 'they were already anticipating those self-consciously serious middle-class societies which shaped civic and class identities in Victorian Britain'.[50] Reflecting on its charitable work, it was suggested of the Broughton Place United Presbyterian Church in Edinburgh that 'the history of the congregation's benevolent institutions is, to a considerable extent, its own history'. It was activity determined by 'an indisputable maxim, that the amount of effort in the cause of Christ is the measure of love to Christ'.[51] At home, its Canongate Mission was characterised by 'firm confidence in the promises of God'. Their missionary in 1856 was James Peddie. He engaged the local population in prayer, in visiting their homes and in promoting the virtues of the lending library and the savings' bank. Such work was often bleak, but illustrations of God's work were forthcoming. In one tenement, heavily divided into apartments, another missionary, Mr Hancock, befriended a family from

Aberdeen whose child lay dying. Led by the churchman, the use of prayer greatly impressed the father, but the next day whisky was the choice of the mother once the infant had passed away. The visitor knew not whether to cry for the child, the drunken mother, or the brother who refused to let go of his deceased younger sister. The urban mission provided the coffin and the shroud for the child and it was deemed a humbling site of destitution caused by intemperance. A few days later, the family had moved on, leaving their neighbours in almost equal poverty.[52]

These societies tell us about the kinds of values created among those who established, ran and funded them: sympathy was offered, while temperance, cleanliness, discipline and the habit of regular work was coaxed. They also give insight into the lives of those who were to experience their benevolence. Most especially we learn how Godliness was sought for 'saved' lives, for then and for the future. Invariably the middle-class moralists had confidence in their interventions; that they were based on imperfect knowledge shaped by their own ideals appeared rarely to shake their convictions. Yet the working classes, Smout reminds us, were not 'tricked' into taking on these values because 'thrift sobriety and education . . . were functional in [their] lives'. Indeed, he argues, 'with this working-class ethic of respectability went an emphatic rejection of middle-class condescension'.[53] Corroboration can be found in the case of the 'ragged' education movement. The Aberdeen House of Industry and Refuge was one example, hailed a British success thanks to the work of Sheriff William Watson.[54] Governed by the municipal and civic leaders of the city, with the Provost as President and its vice presidents comprising Watson, advocate Thomas Burnett and local MP Alexander Bannerman, its aim was to inculcate clearly understood virtues:

> Perhaps no charity in Aberdeen commends itself more readily to the sympathy of the benevolent . . . *Eight hundred and seventy-eight* individuals, of both sexes, of all ages, and under every diversity of circumstance and condition, have, during the past year, enjoyed, more or less, the food and shelter and discipline of the House – the latter helpful to mind, as well as to body.[55]

Success was getting those in the House out to a productive life. Emigration remained an option, with six leaving for Australia in the previous year and a family of six having gone to America in 1841. Perhaps the most important mode of disposal was securing places of service in the town and country for the younger inmates. With the total cost for each inmate being £8 6s. 2½d. per year making up a total expenditure of £866 11s. 6½d., the public were canvassed to donate further to allow the House's aims to be met. We learn from the annual reports that inmate No. 818, an orphan girl aged thirteen, was brought in reluctantly after being charged with petty theft. The Society boasted she was taught to read and write, if only a little, and then sent into service 'where she has continued ten months, and gives satisfaction to her master'. Another, inmate No. 1098, was described as a female aged thirty, who was rescued from attempts at 'self-destruction' and 'extreme destitution'. She was admitted to the Society then placed into employment 'in which she has continued six months'. For many others, the Society simply helped to establish their claim upon the parish for relief, including removal and boarding. If a claim could not be established, and no one came to remove an inmate despite relatives being contacted, then it was not uncommon for them to stay in the House for five or more months, having their basic needs met and their spiritual well-being nourished by the occasional visit of a minister.

Support for some of the most basic requirements of Aberdeen's poorest residents could also forge a feeling of the collective. Civic pride was forthcoming from the city's associations with a movement in whose formative development it had played a major role. Indeed, it was noted 'That Aberdeen had become more celebrated for Industrial Schools than for anything else she possesses.'[56] First developed in Portsmouth by John Pounds, it was Thomas Guthrie who helped to promote ideas of free schooling for working-class children in Edinburgh with his *Plea for Ragged Schools* (1847) and the alliance of Free Churchmen, with a 'sprinkling' of Established Church and United Presbyterians brought together for its implementation.[57] Sheriff Watson had first tried to send the children to the burgh school, but the teachers were not welcoming. Having established Aberdeen's industrial school for boys in 1841, he helped to create a school for girls two years later and a mixed school a further two years after that. The Female Penitentiary was established in the

Figure 9.1 *A hive of activity greets the visitor to the Aberdeen School of Industry, Chronicle Lane, Aberdeen, c. 1850. © Aberdeen City Council, Arts & Recreation Department, Library & Information Services. Licensor www.scran.ac.uk.*

city to give 'outcast females' an 'opportunity of regaining a respectable place in society, and the means of turning from their sinful course to seek for salvation'.[58] Its Matron, Miss Donaldson was chosen for her intense 'religious principle and sincerity', although the job was of such magnitude that she shortly resigned and Miss Morton was put in her place.[59]

Before long, William Chambers took himself from his Edinburgh publishing house to enquire into the scheme, aware of the need for social intervention: 'I know of no town, at least in the northern part of the United Kingdom, in which the condition of the poor and their offspring has not, up till the present moment, been a scandal to a Christian community'.[60] As was the intention, philanthropy had stepped in where 'public duty has been remiss'. At the end of its first year, of the 280 child beggars (under fourteen years old) in Aberdeen, 77 of them, of whom only half could read, had been in prison in the last twelve months. Chambers describes their routine:

Meet at seven o'clock in the morning for religious instruction according to their capacities.
Then geography and natural history until 9 am.
On two mornings each week an hour is devoted to vocal instruction.
9–10 am breakfast, porridge and milk.
10 am return to school and employed in different kinds of work until 2 pm.
2–3 pm dine, usually on broth, beef and bread, occasionally on potatoes, soup, etc.
3–4 pm they either work in doors or out in the garden, partly for recreation, if the weather allows.
4–7 pm they are instructed in reading, writing and arithmetic.
At 7 pm they get supper, same as breakfast; and are dismissed to their homes for the night at 8 pm.

There was a half-day holiday on Saturday after lunch, while on Sunday morning 'the scholars assemble at half past eight o'clock, get breakfast at nine, attend public worship in the house of refuge during the forenoon, and after dinner return home, to enable them, if so disposed, to attend church with their relations'. At five o'clock they meet again in school, and 'are catechised; get supper at seven; and are dismissed as on other days'. With work, money could be made: net-making rewarded the boys at the rate of a penny an hour, with visitors impressed by how quiet the boys were as they acquired the habit of industry. At the girls' school, sewing, cooking and other household skills were taught in preparation for entering service. Observations of the female school of industry found 'the inmates treated to tea and some musical entertainments by the lady patronesses, as a reward for good conduct; and it was gladdening to see the pleasure which universally beamed in their rosy countenances'.[61] That many of the girls did not stay the night was regarded as a positive, enabling them to 'pass on good teachings' to their parents.[62] It was the quiet acceptance of the habits of industry, and outward signs of thankfulness for the patronage and interest shown by the middle classes, that so dominated the message of the society's management and also the report of Chambers.

In making these observations, the publisher was aware that no matter how successful this response to the problem of urban destitution was, and how bombastic the propaganda of this association and other middle-class reformers, there remained a huge challenge. Chambers reflected that 'If it be a duty of the state to pay for the *punishment* of crime, should it not with equal reason pay for its *prevention?*' The city's progress in this debate caused discussion in Bath where Sheriff Watson's brother (Dr Watson) was resident. At a public meeting there in 1849, Alex Thomson was called to 'tell of the success of ragged schools in Aberdeen'.[63] It was deemed instructive for a school which started out with £4 that in one year the working classes gave up to £250 compared with the wealthy giving less than £150. The scheme was judged to be not only morally uplifting, but also cost-effective, the £5 required to send a boy to school compared with the £25 it cost to send him to prison. The Revd W. C. Osborn, chaplain of Bath jail, had visited the schemes in Aberdeen and also those in Glasgow and Edinburgh. He thought that what he had seen was worthwhile, but 'the Scottish character was different to ours' and thus the failure of ragged industrial schools in England was because its children were 'more bold and enterprising, more addicted to vagrancy; thence they are more difficult to control and redeem to regular habits of industry'.[64] It was assumed that a moral life would develop from the regular and industrious habits that came from regular employment. Others concurred. In his submission to Chadwick's investigation into the labouring population, Mr Wood contrasted the clothing, diet and habits of working-class families in receipt of between 15s. and 22s. per week. He was quite convinced that 'above a certain amount, say 12s. or 14s. of weekly income, wages alone, without intelligence and good habits, contribute nothing towards the comfort, health and independence of the working population'. The solution was for them to be 'taught and trained to habits of industry, frugality, sobriety, cleanliness, etc'. If able to live within his means, a man 'deserves happiness at home, and he stands forth in his neighbourhood a noble example of honest independence'.[65]

These were discussions about Scottish society and the place of Christianity within it. Similar debates are found between those advocating an interventionist 'social gospel' and traditionalists, who argued that such an emphasis came 'at the expense of God, spiritual growth, and the afterlife' (see Chapter 4, above, p. 137). The cultural persistence of Presbyterianism was central to the daily activities of the children, as it was to their salvation and to the motives of so many of those who supported them. It was instituted for the children of the poor and funded – more than in other voluntary societies

– by donations from the industrious working classes. Watson's schools continued throughout his lifetime and he extended his philanthropy to involve
himself in a children's asylum committee that oversaw a marked reduction
in crime in 1875.[66] Women would be engaged in the Ladies' Committee of
similar societies and associations throughout Scotland, including superin-
tending the female department of Aberdeen's Refuge.[67] The moral effrontery
that the existence of such distress could engender was sufficiently common
to be regarded as the endemic condition.

It was not so much the existence of these social interventions or their
influence, for good or ill, as the application of an idealised Scottish character
formed in a thought-world imbued with the lingering Calvinism of a wider
culture of Christianity. Much, of course, depended on the willingness of
individuals to internalise these values into their everyday lives. The quick
change-about in matron for the Aberdeen Female Penitentiary brought the
realisation that 'not many of the wretched poor women will realise their sin-
fulness in sight of God', with the result that 'many have turned into a threat
to the other inmates'. In its first year of operation when thirty-two girls were
admitted, seven were dismissed from the Institution, four from their own
repeated desire, three because of rule infractions, and eight deserted for
periods that ranged from two weeks to eight months.[68] In the next year, of
the thirty-three admitted, nine absconded after staying for between two and
four months.[69] As Aberdeen's Mechanics' Institute reported in 1844, 'unless
pupils are prepared to apply themselves with energy, then progress cannot
be expected'.[70]

It is impossible to tell how many of those who came within the purview
of bourgeois associations took on the mores proffered to them. What is
well documented is that many among the labouring population were highly
instrumental in using philanthropic help for their own ends, playing off
one urban missionary against the next. In dispensary hospitals, as with
Sunday schools, there were those prepared to work through the proselytis-
ing to secure a meal, some clothing or warmth, any education that was on
offer, while perhaps shamelessly, perhaps not, smudging the fine doctrinal
divisions that to the rest of the world marked Protestantism in Scotland.[71]
Research by Linda Mahood on Magdalene societies has unearthed the
decision-making abilities of some of the most vulnerable girls in Victorian
towns and cities. The 'Glasgow System', which combined Magdalene institutes and Lock hospitals, was built on the Glasgow Police Act of 1862 and
was renowned for its effectiveness compared with the Contagious Diseases
Acts of 1866–9. Magdalene institutes had been in Scotland since the turn
of the century, in Edinburgh in 1797 and Glasgow in 1812.[72] Their respectability mid-century was sufficient for Victoria to be named Patroness of
the Edinburgh society formed to help the local Magdalene institution.[73] In
his 1842 enquiry into their effectiveness, Dr William Tate saw much in the
contrast between the hardened prostitute and she who was a 'victim' brought

down by circumstance.[74] While the Lock hospitals treated venereal disease, once free from infection those who were deemed worth saving, meaning an emphasis on women newly fallen into prostitution, or part-time prostitutes, rather than more experienced and older women, entered the moral and industrial instruction of the Magdalene institute. Between 1860 and 1890, evidence suggests that the Edinburgh and Glasgow institutions achieved 55 per cent and 40 per cent success rates, respectively, meaning respectable employment was obtained.[75] But it was saving only those who, it was felt, could be saved, a practicality recognised within the reformatory schools where 'children of bad character, or some other cause, remained unprovided for'.[76] The schemes themselves could be, and at times were, abused by those who ran them. Evidence finds younger women entering the system for little more than provocative or high-spirited behaviour, or for dressing in a way that might be deemed risqué, or for being out and about without suitable supervision. Sexual discipline had become a means for perpetuating patriarchy within the voluntary principle.[77] Nor was all charitable help equally attractive. As Houston points out, philanthropic support for lunacy in Scotland was hindered by moral objections of support for those who were physically active as well as by reluctance to offer support for those who may have transgressed other societal norms.[78]

Contemporaries were not unaware that the construction of 'self' reflected in these associations was narrowly conceived. It was bourgeois-led and while it has been argued that emulation can be found in acceptance of these values, living out an industrious, temperate and pious life was in practice inconsistent or even simply out of reach. There was understanding that those fixed to the wrong side of the divide would never cross into this particular social world. But rather than undermine the associational ideal, or readily confirm state centralisation as the alternative, it served to reinforce identities forged from 'others', giving credence to social intervention among those who 'could' be saved. The feared loss of morality, of social stability, and the inculcation of industrious and temperate habits mobilised and sustained the religiosity of the Scots, counteracting the anticipatory signs of secularisation. It was a response rooted in the identification of Scotland as a place where religious virtues prevailed among its people. The many dislocations of the times brought it sharply into focus. That the Scots also identified themselves with the locality of place, embedded in dense networks of bounded communities, is our next concern. Evidence comes from maps, festivals and a monarch's claim upon ordinariness.

PLACE

Just as identity values were forged upon the axis of us and them, so identities of place are best observed at their boundaries. Scotland shares only one land border with another nation and its political geography has remained remarkably static. The last major accession was Shetland in 1469 and while the border with England has experienced greatest uncertainty, most obviously Berwick's numerous sixteenth-century swings in ownership, it was without lands changing by more than a few miles. The Scotland found in maps was also little altered, but such depictions of the nation offer some compelling evidence of what the Scots knew, or imagined they knew, about their land and of the cognitive world in which they lived. Such coherence did not stop misunderstanding. There was some interesting eighteenth-century debate about what exactly North Britain looked like, with John Cowley, factor to the Duke of Argyll, commenting in 1734 that 'no less than five or six Geographers of good repute, disagree not only in the Form of the Coast, the Situation and Courses of Navigable Rivers or Lochs, Bays and Rivers: but also in degrees of latitude of the most noted Capes or Heads of Land . . .'[79] There was no quick fix to this uncertainty, despite the value of accurate maps being known to government as much as to landowners. The British Ordnance Survey was formed in the decade after Culloden to gather detail of Jacobite strongholds, but there was little further government mapping until it published a Trigonometrical Survey in 1805. The Scottish influence in this work came from Alexander Dalrymple, younger brother of Lord Hailes and first Hydrographer of the Navy, with the coastlines of Orkney and Shetland being the earliest to be done, most extensively from the 1820s and 1830s by George Thomas.[80] It was a move to gather more information for a state influenced by Sir John Sinclair's *Statistical Account of Scotland* (1791–9) and the inauguration of the decennial census in 1801.[81] Becoming a separate department in 1841, the Ordnance Survey (OS) moved beyond the measure of military ordnance to provide the kind of information needed for land transfers and civil engineering as Chapter 1 explains.[82] Yet there was no overnight trumping of local knowledge and custom. Prior to the boundary survey begun by the OS in 1841, 'chaotic administrative geography' prevailed, and it was not until 1881 that a standardised and reliable topographical map for Britain was available.[83]

Maps were for more than just practical military or legal purposes, they also had strong cultural power, notably for the creation of belonging. As Charles Withers charts their development out of Enlightenment thought, such maps where clearly part of the nation's historical identity, seen initially in David MacPherson's *Geographical Illustrations of Scottish History* from 1796 and its rationale that 'Geography is one of the eyes of history'.[84] Their interplay with culture was often more relevant than their hoped-for exactitude. The writings of Walter Scott were admired as much for the descriptions of the Trossachs as for the historical accuracy of his imagination; certainly it was that aspect that would spawn the nascent tourist industry of Thomas Cook. Victoria was likely not alone in having chosen *Bride of Lammermoor* (1819) as an early novel, and for her it helped to build the centrality of Scotland to her life, most conspicuously the lease in 1848 and then purchase four years later of the hunting lodge at Balmoral in Deeside. First visiting in 1842, she was to project her entanglement with this land and its people in text and watercolour. In 1865, she commissioned Kenneth MacLeay to paint portraits of her retainers, and then of the Highland chiefs, publishing the plates with a commentary by Amelia Murray MacGregor in 1870, then, two years later, as a single-volume edition illustrated with lower-cost sepia prints.[85] As much as that was impressionistic, she also offered snippets that rendered her life in unparalleled detail. *The Scotsman* had warned back in 1848 over the impending arrival of the Aberdeen-based *Balmoral Correspondent* and plans to supply the provincial newspapers with 'daily details of her Majesty's movements and the festivities of Balmoral', that royal gossip was 'an offence against public taste'.[86] Yet the greatest appeal of *Leaves from the Journal of Our Life in the Highlands* was to be its descriptions of everyday life around the lodge and its environs since the first acquisition of the royal retreat. Published in 1868, its success was immediate, with its peek into the 'domestic life of the Royal Family' described as being 'of great and peculiar interest' by the now less moralistic Edinburgh newspaper.[87] Its wide popularity spawned a Portuguese translation and encouraged a sequel in 1884.[88] In the preface to the first volume, Victoria offered up 'its simple records of the never-to-be-forgotten days spent with "him who made the writer's life bright and happy"' – telling how her heart had 'improved and cheered by the excursions and incidents it recounts, as well as by the simple mountaineers, from who she learnt many a lesson of resignation and faith in the pure air and quiet of the beautiful Highlands'.[89] It offered what was then a unique insight into the routines, protocol and the life behind the veil of a monarch who had withdrawn from public life following the death of Albert in 1861. According to one commentator, Victoria regarded her regular visits to Scotland as the more 'authentic' parts of her life, enabling her to be 'free to pursue a life of domestic bliss – of sketching, walking with her family and, most of all, spending time with her husband – Victoria feels more "at home" when she is "away" in the Highlands'.[90] It showed, her editor suggested, 'the enjoyment of a life removed for the moment from the pressures of public cares'.[91]

It was an everyday 'home' built on the romanticism of Ossian and the Jacobite creationism of Scott; it was a celebration of nature that 'captured the soul of continental Romanticism, a love of the distant past . . . and a promotion of a distinctive folk tradition, complete with national costume and music'.[92] This staging of the Highlands was also Victoria's antidote to the shards of radicalism that developed in part from her seclusion; she opened parliament only sporadically in these years, and built on the sympathy that followed the seven attempts on her life, the first of which was in 1840. Her 1842 visit, during the time of the Chartist uprisings, had drawn the comment from *The Times* that Scotland was a 'country of a brave, wise, thinking, happy and industrious people, uncorrupted by the tenets of Chartism, Liberalism and all those innovations of doctrine by which men's minds are corrupted and disturbed'.[93] The journal's success allowed her to mimic the associational ideal of the urban clan societies: publication earnings were used to donate £2,500 to create school and college bursaries 'for the benefit of well-deserving scholars in the district around Balmoral'.[94] The royal touch of the banal was also important. One 1,500-acre estate for sale on Deeside was 'desirable' because a visit there by the late Prince Consort was mentioned in Victoria's journal; while Lady Smith was presented with a signed copy by the monarch on her 100th birthday, intertwining lives long lived.[95] Her sentimental account fitted the authenticity of the 'exotic ordinariness' Scotland projected in post-Ossianic Highland musings. The royal author was not immune from localised romance, readily quoting James Hogg the Ettrick Shepherd and James Beattie's *Minstrel*, locating in both her claim to belong. The published journal is interesting for Victoria's observations upon both the Scottish landscape and the people found in the villages and towns she visited. Both private and public trips were recorded. In Dalkeith in 1872, she admired the beautiful trees, especially the sycamores, that 'were everywhere in the neighbourhood'. She recorded her previous visit there in 1859, where she found 'colliers and miners, [who] are very poor', but then, driving down *Queen's Drive*, 'we collected again a goodly and most good-humoured crowd, and saw the little boys and girls rolling down the steep hill, and people pouring in from the town to get a sight of us'.[96] This entry was followed by descriptions of a rather wet visit to Edinburgh, commenting on the newspapers being full of 'an absurd conversation of mine with them, but none took place', enjoying the architecture before travelling beyond the city to Trinity where 'some good houses' were found and to Newhaven 'where we saw many fishwives who were very enthusiastic, but not in their smartest dress'. She concludes this leg of her journey through Leith by commenting that 'everywhere the poor people came out – and were most loyal'.[97] What makes this more than the observations of the most privileged, which, of course, they were, is that they came from a monarch who at least on some level was bound up in the social mores, conventions and aspirations of her day. She and her family came to represent the ordinariness of the bourgeoisie. When first photographed, for example, it was the family pose that was chosen, always without a crown, and Albert in top hat.[98] She 'perfected an image of herself as middle class and regal, alone yet containing multitudes'.[99]

In a number of ways, Victoria was the everyday signifier, the banal semaphore, of the nation. It would be going too far, Clyde Binfield suggests, to see her as a basic nonconformist consciousness informing the values of the age; but without doubt her family life was of contemporary fascination.[100] Victoria was the image for Great Britain used by 'Aleph' (William Harvey) in his maps of geographical fun, published in London in 1869. The use of she who embodied the new class of influence coupled with her fascination as the highland Queen was the obvious choice.[101] Consisting of twelve maps of European countries, each with a unique national stereotype for the outline and shape of the country, its author wanted to advance knowledge through 'geographical puzzles [that] excite the mirth of children'. The bagpiper, inevitably perhaps, was chosen to *be* Scotland.

In the Celtic construction of Scotland, where the nation's peripheral culture serves the consumptive and political needs of an external core, the use of the highland imagery to represent the whole of Scotland remained fundamental. Identities and counter-identities are conceived in this dialectic and reference to the land is central, 'where nature, landscape and environment are semiotic signifiers, deeply embedded in the cultural make-up of Scotland'.[102] The pull of the land is a constant given, creating indelible attachments that are as strong when lived just as they are when challenged, reflecting Billig's suggestion that identity is the endemic condition. Powerfully as society came to urbanise, and to mechanise and commercialise once labour-intensive farming practices ended, the commodification of landscape by external elites impacted upon identity production. Ossianic mixtures of nature and Celticism inspired the music of Schubert, Beethoven and Schumann in the early part of the nineteenth century. Ossian was a Scottish equivalent to the epic folktales *Nibelungenlied* (Germany) and *Kalevala* (Finland), and was translated and popularised throughout Europe and North America.[103] Less literary texts also evoked the Scots' ordinary lives. The rustic poetry of Robert Nicholl and Janet Little was a genre not dissimilar to the parochialism of the later-century Kailyard novels.[104] Writing in 1840, James Paterson described the latter as a poet delighted to record any local or passing event.[105] And Celticism was to come back into vogue in the last decades of the century in attempts to give its study an institutional presence in the universities with J. S. Blackie's campaign for a Chair at Edinburgh University and in a Celtic movement and revival in folklore.[106] In part, it was the search for a cherished ideal, the golden age of the everyday that Raymond Williams has remarked is so important to understanding the cultural relationship between the country and the city and, David McCrone adds, 'Still we use simple binary opposites to understand ourselves: "us" and "them" defines identity in any age.'[107] The feminisation of the Celt by Blackie as much as by Victoria was an image of the exotic, something unknown. But this is not the same as saying it was conceived as unique or magical. It was an undeveloped culture that was looked to for being 'ordinary'. As an everyday culture to compare against a core society celebrated and condemned in equal measure for *its* progress, Highland Scotland was exotic in its ordinariness. The Celtic periphery was admired not for its fragility, its imminent passing, but for its strength of place and the apparent continuity of an idealised past and much sought after present.

The link between core and periphery was thus much more than jaunts north by Victoria and other readers of the Waverley novels, or the appropriation of tartan as more than just highland dress; it was the crossing of a cultural border. Borders are never neutral, but are zones in which 'meanings and values are (mis)read or signs are misappropriated'.[108] This uncertainty is found at national boundaries, but also at local, regional and even parish divisions. The rationale for focus on the local by geographer Susan Smith comes from scepticism of grand-scale theorising. Instead, the boundary offers insight into localised struggles, 'recognizing that identity is shaped through the specific practices of everyday life'.[109] The locality is a constraint on behaviour, filtering our responses through 'familiar cultural spaces against the encroaching strangeness'.[110] The Glasgow Fair, for example, has been described as the 'central event in the popular culture of the city' in the nineteenth century, temporarily marking it off from others.[111] It is in particularly local events that Anthony Cohen argues that the ritual crowd is essential to symbolic boundary making.[112] They are all points where public space was contested through issues of authority, class and gender, where the results shaped the identities of the people of these places.[113]

Sustaining local identity in Scotland can be seen most clearly in the culturally rich festivals of the regions. In common ridings, most especially, the lineage projected is one of struggle over the boundaries of place.[114] In the medieval past, such ridings were a burgess' duty to maintain the right to buy and sell land.[115] Once the town is delineated, events within it and between it and others are remembered and projected. They were, as is show in Chapter 8, about keeping people within the boundary and enabling them to benefit from the privileges therein, while keeping others out. Most obviously in the Scottish Borders the battling history with England is recalled, but so sometimes are disputes with neighbouring counties.[116] The four main common ridings in Scotland are at Selkirk (origins dating from *c.* 400), Hawick (1703), Langholm (1759) and Lauder (1910). They inculcate identity claims by the very anachronistic nature of their proceedings, often added to in this period, such as Langholm's use of horsemen to ride the boundaries in 1816 and the election of the first Cornet the following year.[117] The deferential and ritual-bound symbols used in Selkirk have even been likened to the rituals of Roman Catholicism, and are thus an oddity in a very Protestant town because of their intricacy and rootedness in place.[118] These formulaic actions are perhaps best understood as bounded in the rituals of obligation to the lived community. Place is defined and used as the conduit between past and present and from it identities are forged. As G. K. Neville points out, 'goods and services are redistributed; people are moved about on the landscape; the town's identity is affirmed; and social cohesion is established and maintained'.[119] Common ridings and local festivals had a mixed history in the nineteenth century, some appearing, others dying out. West Linton was home to the Whipman Play begun in 1803 as a benevolent society for the families of those working horses and the plough; it too chose its top laddie and lass.[120] The Jedburgh Border Games date from 1853 and were similar to the Highland Games which became a distinct fashion in the second half of the century.[121] In 1859, the Braemar Gathering – with roots to the eleventh century – was moved to Balmoral, to be hosted there again in 1887, 1890 and 1898, becoming the Braemar Royal Highland Society Gathering in 1889.[122] Historical pageants were certainly popular throughout Britain at the end of the period. They offered easily absorbed historical knowledge to those without a consciousness of the past, although none in either England or Scotland, Readman points out, dealt with British history.[123] While contributing to the national sense of self, such local festivals are primarily based on personal and geographic identities, where there is a clear difference between 'local selves and proximate others' and particular histories of place are the basis for how they are constructed.[124] Founded in 1827, the St Ronan's Border Club led to the organisation of the annual St Ronan's Border Games following impetus from Edinburgh's Six Feet Club then visiting the area.[125] Their scope widened over the years and in 1901 the Cleikum Ceremony was introduced to familiarise the youth of the town with the tradition of St Ronan. Social events throughout the week culminated with the main ceremonies on the Friday evening when the town's Standard Bearer was installed and the Burgh Flag raised. In the Cleikum Ceremony 'St Ronan' is represented by the boy dux of the school. Much of the local association is founded on folklore, the strength and malleability of the belief coming directly from the paucity of evidence. Walter Scott's *St Ronan's Well* (1824) was of influence in Innerleithan and it is legend that claims St Ronan partook of the mineral waters of the town. As the local patron saint, he tends then to be depicted with his crook attacking Satan, 'cleiking the Deil', bringing the people together to face down the greatest of adversaries.

These events were seasonal and linked to agricultural and civic routines. Six months after Hallowmas, the start of the summer was celebrated in many places by the festival of Beltane, a fire festival in homage to the sun.[126] The Peebles Beltane originally celebrated the advent of the Summer Solstice in May and in folklore was a Celtic festival devoted to Baal, the God of Fire. The stone circles of Stenness and Callanish have long been sites of fire festivals, but fires were also used more informally as points around which cattle would gather and as a means to ward off evil.[127] They were still observed by Thomas Pennant in his tour of Scotland in 1772, but were generally dying out in the early decades of the nineteenth century, with those in Arran and Helmsdale (1820), North Uist (1829) and Reay (1830) no longer being lit.[128] With its 'Ganging of the Marches' and May fair having roots back to the seventeenth century, the modern Beltane ceremony in Peebles was revived in 1897, added to by the riding of the boundaries in 1899 and then the coronation of the Beltane Queen.[129] Its week of festivities opened with a religious service in and around Old Cross Kirk, with the civic leaders of the town participating alongside key figures in the festival and representatives of the local organisations.[130] By 1920, voices would cry 'And sing the auld-warld round-e-lay of "Peblis to the Play"', and, remembering those overseas, 'The exile oft wi' pride recalls the dear auld Border hame'.[131] Connecting the town with itself, and with those overseas, it spatialised their social life as Peebles, Borders, Scotland, diaspora.[132]

Fire was more commonly used in winter festivals, burning the old year out either on New Year's Eve or the day itself.[133] The swinging of fireballs in Stonehaven and the Up-helly-aa festival in Lerwick were perhaps the most visible of such events.[134] Callum Brown shows how many of these fire festivals had their origins in the seventeenth century or earlier, but only began to be documented in the towns and villages of the nineteenth and twentieth centuries.[135] He also shows how the construction of the term Up-helly-aa was linked to a narrative of simplicity, of fairies or primitive folk given Norse names, a view popularised in the late nineteenth century.[136] Then, and in the decades that preceded it, the event was often a 'primitive and boisterous affair' its main feature being 'the dragging by clanking chains of sledges containing at least three tubs of blazing tar and wood shavings, the youths who performed the ceremony cheering themselves on with frequent blasts of the horn'.[137] There were many claims upon the significance of the ceremony and it was even used for moral instruction with its 1870 incarnation sponsored by the Total Abstinence Society in a bid to deflect from the revelry of Hogmanay. This control would develop in 1874 when tar-barrelling was banned and in 1884 a torch-light parade instigated. Brown reminds us, importantly, that there was no simple (re-)creation of the event in the nineteenth century and that much of its activity was spontaneous from within the community.[138] Throughout this period, New Year's Day was a magnet for bonfires and beacons, with instances recorded in Inverness and Auchterarder, Wick and Biggar somehow marrying the druidic and Christian, Celtic and occasionally some Norse identities of the Scots.[139] As Hugh Miller had earlier remarked, 'It is a curious fact, that we meet among the Protestants of Scotland with more marked traces of the Paganism of their earlier, than of the Popery of their later ancestors.'[140]

Like fire festivals, sporting occasions have been strong identifiers of place. Shinty, or a form of it, was played throughout Scotland up until the seventeenth century, but was the preserve of Highland society and its culture when the Camanachd Association was formed in 1893.[141] The popularity of football from the 1870s and 1880s, with the first international between Scotland and England coming out as a scoreless draw in 1872 and the Scottish Football Association formed the next year, was tied closely to the fostering of local civic and religious rivalries between towns and cities and also within the bigger settlements of Glasgow, Edinburgh and Dundee. Prior to the formalisation of associational football, for which a professional league was set up in 1890, ball or ba' games of all forms were popular in localities such as Hawick, Jedburgh, Orkney and Wigtown. There could be special one-off matches: in 1815, a contest between Galashiels and Selkirk was staged to honour the victory at Waterloo, and in 1835 a match was staged between estate workers from Blairdrummond and Deanston Cotton mills.[142]

The Jedburgh Ball Game, known locally as the 'Jethart Hand Ba', was one of those all-town games with older roots and supposedly once played with the heads of English soldiers. Like its Orcadian counterpart, the game was split between the upper and lower parts of the town, the 'Uppies' and the 'Doonies'. In Jedburgh, the residential qualification was delimited by those living above and below the Mercat Cross at Candlemass and Shrove Tuesday; in Kirkwall, the 'Doonies' had to get the ba' into Kirkwall harbour, while the 'Uppies' had to get to the junction of Main Street with New Scapa Road: the boys' game would be in the morning, the men's in the afternoon.[143] The Orkney version dates from the mid-seventeenth century, although its origins are unknown. In 1800, it moved to the centre of the town, while by 1850 the ba' was picked up, no longer kicked, and in 1880 a Christmas Day game was added to the New Year's Day event; in 1892 the Youths Ba' was instigated for 'halflins' or 'those who are not quite yet men'.[144] Women-only ba' games have been held in the twentieth century, but there is note of individual

Figure 9.2 *This early photograph of the Orkney Ba' Game in Kirkwall, dating from around 1898, shows the all-encompassing community involvement not segmented or rule-based in the way that associational football had become.* © *National Museums Scotland. Licensor www.scran.ac.uk.*

women being influential in earlier engagements, as on Christmas Day 1886 when 'an Amazon who ought to have been at home with her mamma caught it and threw it down'.[145] The game spread from Kirkwall to Stromness in 1884 and built upon an attachment to place forged when away, as seen also with a group of Orcadians who gathered on New Year's Day in 1866 to play a match on Glasgow Green.[146]

While far from being unregulated, and certainly so in custom, the game lacked the intricate rule-based structure of associational football that would come to dominate, and its propensity to lead to injury and damage to property would gave reason for attempts in Jedburgh in 1849 to ban it. But this indicates how attachment to locality was developed and managed. Along with the local festivals these are outcomes of identities that were personal, forged in the relations of family and community. It reminds us that we cannot examine the everyday without placing into view its symbiotic contribution to calendric culture. What we need to understand, Bauman explains, is 'the deeply reflexive nature of such cultural performances . . . in which the *cultural meanings and values of a group* are embodied, acted out, and laid open to examination and interpretation in symbolic form'.[147] It is a way of understanding personal nationalism, the means by which people 'might think themselves into difference'.[148] It is a form of identity, Cohen argues, formed from 'my reading of history, my perceptions of the landscape, and my reading of Scotland's literature and music, so that when I "see" the nation, I am looking at myself'.[149] The regions offer the strongest evidence of personal identity formed in the peculiarities of locality. Importantly also, the Borders region offers points that signify all that is Scotland and not England while remaining peripheral to Scotland-the-nation, on the edge of the core central belt and excluded from Scotland's own national periphery, the Highland region.[150] The *natio*, we must not forget, is forged in and from a placeable community.[151] We grow up and develop personal and familial relationships that are formed in and of place, and we appear to need this fixed belonging.[152]

This was no politics of identity-making, national or otherwise, and this is appropriate for a nation that has lacked singularity in its national culture of independence in this century. It is appropriate also that the associational responses inspired by religious commitment to address the poverty and distress caused by insatiable change should focus on the ordinary folk. The common ridings, the fire and community festivals were also about the people. Choosing the best boy or girl in the village or town was most probably class or denominationally delimited, but it was at least nominally inclusive and was active before and after the festival days were played out. Analytically, the folk, the plebeians, the people and the working class are important components of the all-encompassing construction of the nation.[153] All such cultural formations reinforced existing class hierarchies and inequalities, gender especially, and they also strengthened attachment to place. Identity claims are both impossibly aspirational and dependent on seemingly inviolate inequalities; they are episodic and endemic. Much more has been written on the former, especially on national identity, searching for greater frequency of action or for more impressive numbers at gatherings commemorating Burns, the Jacobites, Bruce or Wallace. The character of the Scot has also been linked to those episodes, often with little evidence being unearthed. Yet as William McIntosh reminded us, the Scot is like the 'resistless onrush of sea waves, steady and relentless'. It suggests that there is much to be found in Scottish identity in its endemic form. Here we explored the narratives of character, of Calvinism, of temperance, of moral rectitude and philanthropic intervention. It was no matter that the reality could never match the idealised values and that many would reject them utterly. As an identity claim, this was how the Scots would situate and project who they thought they were. It was complemented by attachment to locality. Affirming the boundaries of place, delineating it in maps, constructing reminiscences of its history, replaying its culture in sports and festivals, there was a constant making of self. From sustaining the deep roots of Christianity in time, and in a commitment to place, identity was embedded in the everyday.

Notes

1 N. Macnish, *A Sermon preached at St John's Church, Cornwall, on the 26th November 1893, before the Sons of Scotland* (Cornwall, ON, 1894).

2 'Letter from John Brough, Nenthorn, 24 May 1841 to Cousin James Brough', *Brough Family Fonds* (University of Guelph), cited in A. Pipe, 'Voices from the Past: A Reconstruction of the Scottish Emigrant Experience (1830–1856)', *International Review of Scottish Studies*, 29 (2004), 80–1.

3 C. Lee, *Scotland and the United Kingdom: The Economy and the Union in the Twentieth Century* (Manchester, 1995), p. 25.

4 'Letter from J. and M. Good, Newhope 23 September 1841'; and '11 January 1842', University of Guelph Archives [UGA], *Good Family Correspondence*. See also: Pipe, 'Voices from the Past', p. 79.

5 UGA: 'Letter by John Robertson to his father, Gosford, Scotland, 21 April 1834, Niagara Township'.

6 M. Harper, *Adventurers and Exiles: The Great Scottish Exodus* (London, 2004), pp. 2–4.

7 E. J. Ravenstein, 'The Laws of Migration', *Journal of the Statistical Society of London*, 48:2 (June 1885), 181–3; T. C. Smout, N. C. Landsman and T. M. Devine, 'Scottish Emigration in the Seventeenth and Eighteenth Centuries', in N. P. Canny (ed.), *Europeans on the Move: Studies on European Migration, 1500–1800* (Oxford, 1994), pp. 76–90, 111–12.

8 P. E. Rider and H. McNabb (eds), *A Kingdom of the Mind: How the Scots Helped Make Canada* (Montreal and Kingston, 2006), pp. xvii and *passim*.

9   T. Bueltmann, A. Hinson and G. Morton (eds), *Ties of Bluid, Kin and Countrie: Scottish Associational Culture in the Diaspora* (Guelph, 2009).

10 Psalm 136 under the Septuagint system, while under the Masoretic system used in most modern Bible translations it is Psalm 137.

11 W. McIntosh, *True Patriotism: A Sermon Preached before St Andrew's Society, Ottawa, Ont. on December 2nd 1895* (n.p., n.d.).

12 'J. and M. Good to Dear Brother and Sister', 17 July 1842, UGA, *Good Family Correspondence*.

13 D. McCrone, *Understanding Scotland: The Sociology of a Stateless Nation* (London, 1992), pp. 90–1.

14 T. Nairn, *The Break-up of Britain* (London, 1977); McCrone, *Understanding Scotland*; L. Paterson, *The Autonomy of Modern Scotland* (Edinburgh, 1994); G. Morton, *Unionist Nationalism* (East Linton, 1999).

15 G. Morton, 'Scotland is Britain: the Union and Unionist-Nationalism, 1807–1907', *Journal of Irish and Scottish Studies*, 1:2 (2008), 130–1.

16 T. C. Smout, 'Perspectives on the Scottish Identity', *Scottish Affairs*, 6 (1994), 107.

17 G. Morton, 'Ethnic Identity in the Civic World of Scottish Associational Culture', in Bueltmann, Hinson and Morton (eds), *Ties of Bluid, Kin and Countrie*, pp. 33–45.

18 M. Billig, *Banal Nationalism* (London, 1995), pp. 5–6.

19 E. Renan, *Qu'est ce qu'une nation?*, trans. I. M. Snyder (Paris, 1882), pp. 26–9.

20 Billig, *Banal Nationalism*, pp. 37–8.

21 Billig, *Banal Nationalism*, p. 39.

22 C. Dickens, *Hard Times for these Times* (Warmsworth, 1854), p. 6.

23 F. R. Leavis, *The Great Tradition* (1948), cited in J. F. Links, 'The Close Reading of "Hard Times"', *The English Journal*, (1969), 212.

24 Quoted in M. J. Wiener, *English Culture and the Decline of the Industrial Spirit, 1850–1980* (Cambridge, 1982), pp. 32–3.

25 R. Owen, *Report to the County of Lanark, of a Plan for Relieving Public Distress, and Removing Discontent, by Giving Permanent, Productive Employment, to the Poor and Working Classes* (Glasgow, 1821), p. 16.

26 R. J. Morris, 'Urbanisation and Scotland', in W. H. Fraser and R. J. Morris (eds), *People and Society in Scotland, vol. II: 1830–1914* (Edinburgh, 1990), pp. 83–5.

27 M. W. Flinn (ed.), *Report On the Sanitary Condition of the Labouring Population of Gt. Britain, by Edwin Chadwick, 1842* (Edinburgh, 1965), pp. 97–8.

28 R. J. Morris, 'Victorian Values in Scotland and England', in T. C. Smout (ed.), *Victorian Values* (Oxford, 1992), pp. 33–4.

29 W. T. Gairdner, MD and W. J. Begbie, MD, *First Report of the Medico-Statistical Association* (Edinburgh, 1852), pp. 4–5.

30 *The Social Science Review*, 1:1 (14 June 1862).

31 'The Dundee Anthropological Conference', *Anthropological Review*, 6:20 (January 1868), 72.

32 See *Transactions of the Phrenological Society* (Edinburgh, 1824), p. 334;

'Acceptance and Display of Skulls', *Phrenological Society: Agreement between the Phrenological Society and Wm. Henderson's Trustees* (1856), p. 2.

33 G. E. Davie, *The Democratic Intellect: Scotland and her universities in the Nineteenth Century* (Edinburgh, 1964: 1999 edn), pp. 89, 105; C. Beveridge and R. Turnbull, *The Eclipse of Scottish Culture* (Edinburgh, 1989), pp. 81–2.

34 *On the Conditions of Progress of the Capitalist and of the Labourer* (1886), cited in H. Meller, 'Geddes, Sir Patrick (1854–1932)', *Oxford Dictionary of National Biography* (Oxford, 2004) available at: http://www.oxforfdnb.com/view/article/33361, accessed 13 February 2009.

35 A. Crawford, 'Mackintosh, Charles Rennie (1868–1928)', *Oxford Dictionary of National Biography* (Oxford, 2004), available at: http://www.oxforddnb.com/view/article/34764, accessed 18 July 2008.

36 S. Smiles, *Life of a Scottish Naturalist: Thomas Edward, Associate of the Linnean Society* (London, 1876), p. v.

37 *Thoughts on the Proposed Change of Currency, and Other Late Alterations, as they Affect, or Are Intended to Affect, the Kingdom of Scotland* (Edinburgh, 1826). See also his second and third letters (again 1826).

38 *Transactions of the Iona Club, Vol. 1, Part. 1* (Edinburgh, 1834), p. 3.

39 S. and O. Checkland, *Industry and Ethos: Scotland 1832–1914* (Edinburgh, 1984): The roots of the Calvinist influence on the Scottish economy is debated in T. M. Devine, 'Industrialisation', in T. M. Devine, C. H. Lee and G. C. Peden (eds), *The Transformation of Scotland: The Economy since 1700* (Edinburgh, 2005), pp. 54–6.

40 E. J. Yeo, 'Early British Labour Movements in Relation to Family Needs', in J. Kok (ed.), *Rebellious Families: Household Strategies and Collective Action in the Nineteenth and Twentieth Centuries* (Oxford, 2002), p. 36.

41 G. D. Pollock, 'Aspects of Thrift in East End Glasgow: New Accounts at the Bridgeton Cross Branch of the Savings Bank of Glasgow, 1881', *International Review of Scottish Studies*, 32 (2007), 117.

42 Pollock, 'Aspects of Thrift', p. 121.

43 O. Checkland, *Philanthropy in Victorian Scotland: Social Welfare and the Voluntary Principle* (Edinburgh, 1980), p. 30.

44 S. J. Brown, 'Thomas Chalmers and the Communal Ideal', in Smout (ed.), *Victorian Values*, p. 63.

45 I. Maver, 'The Temperance Movement and the Urban Associational Ideal: Scotland, 1820s–1840s', in G. Morton, B. de Vries and R. J. Morris (eds), *Civil Society, Associations, and Urban Places: Class, Nation, and Culture in Nineteenth-century Europe* (Aldershot, 2006), pp. 163–6.

46 *Sabbath [scored out 'for the Political Economy of the] Traffic in Intoxicating Liquors* (n.d.), Aberdeen University Archives: Thomson 327/69.

47 W. Knox, 'The Political and Workplace Culture of the Scottish Working Class, 1832–1914', in Fraser and Morris (eds), *People and Society in Scotland* pp. 152–5.

48 C. G. Brown, *Religion and Society in Scotland*, 2nd edn (Edinburgh, 1997), pp. 117, 127, 149.

49 G. D. Pollock, 'Saints and Sinners: Church Members in Glasgow's East End 1873–1885', *International Review of Scottish Studies*, 31 (2006), 6, 37.

50 P. Clark, *British Clubs and Societies, 1500–1800* (Oxford, 2000), p. 140.

51 *History of Broughton Place United Presbyterian Church, with Sketches of its Missionary Operations* (Edinburgh, 1872), p. 161.

52 *Broughton Place United Presbyterian Church*, p. 305.

53 T. C. Smout, *A Century of the Scottish People, 1830–1950* (London, 1986), pp. 248–9.

54 *Fifth Report by the Committee of Directors of the Aberdeen House of Industry and Refuge, 1840–1841. Instituted in 1836* (Aberdeen, 1841). See *Sheriff Watson of Aberdeen: the story of his life and his work for the Young* (1913) by his granddaughter Marion Emily Angus (1865–1946).

55 *Fifth Report, Aberdeen House of Industry and Refuge, 1840–1841*, p. 5 (original emphasis).

56 *Birmingham Conference on Juvenile Delinquency. Public Meeting at Aberdeen* (24 December 1851).

57 *Public Education: The Original Ragged Schools and the United Industrial School of Edinburgh: Being a Comparative View of their Recorded Results* (Edinburgh, 1855), p. 5.

58 *First Report by the Directors of the Aberdeen Female Penitentiary from 10th March 1842 to 1st January 1843. Presented to a Meeting of the Subscribers, held 16th January 1843.*

59 *First Report by the Directors of the Aberdeen Female Penitentiary*, pp. 7–8.

60 'Visit to the Aberdeen School of Industry' (From *Chambers's Edinburgh Journal*, 15 November 1845) Signed with initials W. C. and sent with the handwritten compliments of W. and R. Chambers.

61 'Visit to the Aberdeen School of Industry', p. 3.

62 *First Report of the Aberdeen Female School of Industry for the Year 1844. Meeting held 3 December 1844. Lord Provost in the Chair* (n.p., 1844).

63 'Ragged and Industrial Schools', From the *Bath and Cheltenham Gazette*, 14 March 1849.

64 'Ragged and Industrial Schools'.

65 *Sanitary Condition of the Labouring Population of Gt. Britain*, p. 209.

66 S. Wood, 'Education', in W. H. Fraser and C. H. Lee (eds), *Aberdeen, 1800–2000. A New History* (East Linton, 2000), p. 330.

67 *Notes on the Refuge, Aberdeen, and the Reformatory and Industrial Schools Connected Therewith* (1896).

68 *Aberdeen Female Penitentiary* (1843), pp. 8–9, 11.

69 *Second Report of the Aberdeen Female Penitentiary 1843. Presented to a Meeting of the Subscribers, held 30 January 1844* (Aberdeen, 1844), p. 6.

70 *The Nineteenth Report of the Committee of the Mechanics' Institution, Aberdeen* (1844), p. 7.

71 Morton, *Unionist Nationalism*, p. 85.

72 J. Stark, *Picture of Edinburgh, Containing a Description of the City and its Environs*, 4th edn (Edinburgh, 1825), p. 252; originally called the Edinburgh Philanthropic

Society, it was renamed the Society for the Support of the Magdalene Asylum in 1800.

73 *Report of the Society for the Support of the Magdalene Society for 1858* (Edinburgh, 1859), p. 3.

74 W. Tait, *Magdalenism: An Inquiry into the Extent, Causes and Consequences of Prostitution in Edinburgh* (Edinburgh, 1842), p. 323.

75 M. H. Ditmore, *Encyclopaedia of Prostitution and Sex Work* (Westport, 2006), p. 271.

76 'Visit to the Aberdeen School of Industry'.

77 L. Mahood and B. Littlewood, 'Prostitutes, Magdalenes and Wayward Girls: Dangerous Sexualities of Working class Girls in Victorian Scotland', *Gender and History*, 3:2 (1991), 165–6.

78 R. A. Houston, 'Poor Relief and the Dangerous and Criminal Insane in Scotland, 1740–1840', *Journal of Social History*, 40:2 (Winter 2006), 466.

79 Cited in C. W. J. Withers, 'The Social Nature of Map Making in the Scottish Enlightenment, *c.* 1682–*c.* 1832', *Imago Mundi*, 54 (2002), 50.

80 http://www.nls.uk/maps/early/info/admiraltycharts.html.

81 S. Daniels, 'Mapping National Identities: The Culture of Cartography, with Particular Reference to the Ordnance Survey', in G. Cubitt (ed.), *Imagining Nations* (Manchester, 1998), pp. 118–20.

82 The National Archives, *Ordnance Survey Records: Domestic Record Information*, 70 (2003).

83 D. Fletcher, 'The Ordnance Survey's Nineteenth-Century Boundary Survey: Context, Characteristics and Impact', *Imago Mundi*, 51 (1999), 132, 140–1.

84 Withers, 'The Social Nature of Map Making', p. 52.

85 *The Highlanders of Scotland: the Complete Watercolours Commissioned by Queen Victoria from Kenneth MacLeay of her Scottish Retainers and Clansmen* (London, 1986), pp. 12, 14.

86 *The Scotsman*, 6 September 1848, p. 3, and 27 September 1848, p. 3. My thanks to Erica German for this reference.

87 *The Scotsman*, 10 January 1868, p. 3.

88 *The Scotsman*, 19 June 1869, p. 7; A. Helps (ed.), *More Leaves from the Journal of a Life in the Highlands, from 1862 to 1882* (London, 1884).

89 A. Helps (ed.), *Leaves from the Journal of Our Life in the Highlands from 1848 to 1861* (London, 1868); Victoria was writing in the preface of the second volume, 22 December 1883, pp. v–vi.

90 K. McNeil, *Scotland, Britain, Empire: Writing the Highlands, 1760–1860* (Columbus, 2007), pp. 146–7.

91 Arthur Helps writing in its preface and quoted in *The Scotsman*, 10 January 1868, p. 3.

92 W. A. Everett, 'National Themes in Scottish Art Music, ca. 1880–1990', *International Review of the Aesthetics and Sociology of Music*, 30:2 (December 1999), 157.

93 Cited in M. M. Martin, *The Mighty Scot: Nation, Gender, and the Nineteenth-century Mystique of Scottish Masculinity* (Albany, 2009), p. 65.

94 *The Scotsman*, 18 May 1869, p. 2.
95 *The Scotsman*, 2 September 1870, p. 1; *The Scotsman*, 21 June 1873, p. 4.
96 *More Leaves from the Journal of a Life in the Highlands*, p. 119.
97 *More Leaves from the Journal of a Life in the Highlands*, p. 120.
98 M. Homans, *Royal Representations: Queen Victoria and British Culture, 1837–1876* (Chicago, 1998), p. 44.
99 A. Booth, 'Illustrious Company: Victoria Among other Women in Anglo-American Role Model Anthologies', in M. Homans and A. Munich (eds), *Remaking Queen Victoria* (Cambridge, 1997), pp. 76–7.
100 C. Binfield, 'Nonconformity's True Conformity', in Smout (ed.), *Victorian Values*, p. 82.
101 *Geographical Fun: Being Humorous Outlines of Various Countries, with an Introduction and Descriptive Lines*, by Aleph (London, 1869).
102 D. McCrone, 'Land, Democracy and Culture in Scotland', the 1997 McEwen Lecture on Land Tenure in Scotland (Perth, 1997), pp. 3–5.
103 Everett, 'National Themes in Scottish Art Music', p. 157.
104 P. Perkins, 'Little, Janet (1759–1813)', *Oxford Dictionary of National Biography* (Oxford, 2004), available at: http://www.oxforddnb.com/view/article/40635, accessed 1 February 2008.
105 J. Paterson, *The Contemporaries of Burns, and the More Recent Poets of Ayrshire, with Selections from their Writings* (Edinburgh, 1840), p. 88.
106 S. Wallace, *John Stuart Blackie: Scottish Scholar and Patriot* (Edinburgh, 2006), p. 272.
107 R. Williams, *The Country and the City* (New York, 1973); D. McCrone, *The Sociology of Nationalism: Tomorrow's Ancestors* (London, 1998), p. 58.
108 H. K. Bhabha, *The Location of Culture* (London, 1994), p. 34.
109 S. Smith, 'Bordering on Identity', *Scotlands*, 3:1 (1996), 20.
110 Michael Herzfeld, quoted by J. N. Gray, *At Home in the Hills: Sense of Place in the Scottish Borders* (Oxford, 2000), p. 14.
111 J. Burnett, 'Small Showmen and Large Firms: The Development of Glasgow Fair in the Nineteenth century', *Review of Scottish Culture*, 17 (2004–5), 72.
112 A. P. Cohen, 'Of Symbols and Boundaries, or does Ertie's Greatcoat hold the Key?', in A. P. Cohen (ed.), *Symbolising Boundaries: Identity and Diversity in British Cultures* (Manchester, 1986), pp. 4, 9; S. Smith, 'Where to Draw the Line', in A. Rogers and S. Vertovec (eds), *The Urban Context: Ethnicity, Social Networks and Situational Analysis* (Oxford, 1995), p. 149.
113 S. Gunn, 'The Spatial Turn: Changing Histories of Space and Time', in S. Gunn and R. J. Morris (eds), *Identities in Space: Contested Terrains in the Western City since 1850*, (Aldershot, 2001), pp. 9–11.
114 G. K. Neville, *The Mother Town: Civic Ritual, Symbol, and Experience in the Borders of Scotland* (Oxford, 1994), pp. 4–6.
115 Neville, *The Mother Town*, p. 45.
116 Gray, *At Home in the Hills*, p. 4.
117 F. M. McNeill, *The Silver Bough, Vol. iv: The Local Festivals of Scotland* (Glasgow, 1968), p. 136.

118 Neville, *The Mother Town*, p. 8.

119 Neville, *The Mother Town*, p. 4.

120 McNeill, *The Silver Bough, Vol. iv*, pp. 194–5.

121 G. Jarvie, *Highland Games: The Making of the Myth* (Edinburgh, 1991), pp. 3, 6.

122 G. Jarvie and I. A. Reid, 'Sport, Nationalism and Culture in Scotland', *The Sports Historian*, 19:1 (May 1999), 110.

123 P. Readman, 'The Place of the Past in English Culture, *c.* 1890–1914', *Past and Present*, 186 (February 2005), 170, 179.

124 Smith, 'Where to Draw the Line', pp. 151–3.

125 McNeill, *The Silver Bough, Vol. iv*, p. 108. Members of the sporting club stood at or above the requisite height.

126 F. M. McNeill, *The Silver Bough, Vol. ii: A Calendar of Scottish National Festivals, Candlemas to Harvest Home* (Glasgow, 1959), p. 55.

127 McNeill, *The Silver Bough, Vol. ii*, p. 73.

128 R. Hutton, *The Stations of the Sun: A History of the Ritual Year in Britain* (Oxford, 2001), p. 222; McNeill, *The Silver Bough, Vol. ii*, p. 58.

129 S. J. Smith, 'Bounding the Borders: Claiming Space and Making Place in Rural Scotland', *Transactions of the Institute of British Geographers*, New Ser., 18:3 (1993), 293.

130 McNeill, *The Silver Bough, Vol. iv*, pp. 170–1.

131 http://www.peeblesbeltanefestival.co.uk/html/the_beltane_song.html.

132 The term comes from R. Shields, cited in Smith 'Bounding the Borders', p. 293.

133 McNeill, *The Silver Bough, Vol. iv*, pp. 208–16.

134 C. G. Brown, *Up-helly-aa. Custom, Culture and Community in Shetland* (Manchester, 1998), p. 14; Hutton, *Stations of the Sun*, p. 43.

135 Brown, *Up-helly-aa*, p. 41.

136 Brown, *Up-helly-aa*, pp. 34–6.

137 McNeill, *The Silver Bough, Vol. iv*, p. 218.

138 Brown, *Up-helly-aa*, pp. 45, 126–51.

139 Hutton, *Stations of the Sun*, pp. 43–5.

140 Hugh Miller, *Scenes and Legends of the North East of Scotland; or, the Constitutional History of Cromarty* [1835], 16th edn (Edinburgh, 1881), p. 55.

141 I. A Reid, 'Shinty, Nationalism and Celtic Politics, 1870–1922', *The Sports Historian*, 18:2 (November 1998), 122.

142 T. Collins, J. Martin and W. Vamplew, *Encyclopaedia of Traditional Rural British Sports* (London, 2005), pp. 119–20.

143 McNeill, *The Silver Bough, Vol. iv*, pp. 217.

144 Collins, Martin and Vamplew, *Encyclopaedia*, p. 176; J. Robertson, *Uppies and Doonies: The Story of the Kirkwall Ba' Game* (Aberdeen, 1967), pp. 11, 39.

145 Robertson, *Uppies and Doonies*, p. 41

146 Robertson, *Uppies and Doonies*, p. 45; Collins, Martin and Vamplew, *Encyclopaedia*, p. 119.

147 Quoted in Neville, *The Mother Town*, p. 107. Emphasis added.

148 A. P. Cohen, *Self-Consciousness: An Alternative Anthropology of Identity* (London, 1994), pp. 156–8; A. P. Cohen, 'Personal Nationalism: A Scottish View of some Rites, Rights, and Wrongs', *American Ethnologist*, 23:4 (1996), 803.

149 Cohen, 'Personal Nationalism', p. 805.

150 Smith, 'Where to Draw the Line', p. 149.

151 H. K. Bhabha, *Nation and Narration* (London, 1990), p. 45.

152 R. Williams, *The Year 2000* (New York, 1983), p. 5.

153 B. King, *The New English Literatures: Cultural Nationalism in a Changing World* (London, 1980), p. 42.

Annotated Bibliography

INTRODUCTION: STRUCTURES OF EVERYDAY LIFE IN SCOTLAND, 1800 TO 1900

Among recent overviews of nineteenth-century Scotland, the following are especially useful: T. C. Smout, *A Century of the Scottish People, 1830–1950* (London and New Haven, 1986); S. G. and O. Checkland, *Industry and Ethos: Scotland, 1832–1914* (London, 1984); W. H. Fraser and R. J. Morris (eds), *People and Society in Scotland. Vol. II: 1830–1914* (Edinburgh, 1990); T. M. Devine, *The Scottish Nation, 1700–2000* (London, 1999); G. Morton and R. J. Morris, 'Civil Society, Governance and Nation, 1832–1914', in R. A. Houston and W. W. J. Knox (eds), *The New Penguin History of Scotland. From the Earliest Times to the Present Day* (London, 2001); and T. M. Devine, C. H. Lee and G. C. Peden (eds), *The Transformation of Scotland: The Economy since 1700* (Edinburgh, 2005).

To introduce the themes of this volume we first focused on economic changes, and here the analysis we made most use of comes from: E. P. Thompson, 'Time, Work-Discipline and Industrial Capitalism', *Past and Present* (December 1967); M. A. Bienefeld, *Working Hours in British Industry: An Economic History* (London, 1972); and G. R. Boyer, 'Living Standards, 1860–1914', in R. Floud and P Johnson (eds), *The Cambridge Economic History of Modern Britain. Volume II: Economic Maturity, 1860–1939* (Cambridge, 2004). Surveys of the period which place emphasis on the economic changes that were impacting on Scotland's culture include: W. H. Fraser, 'The Victorian Achievement', in G. Menzies (ed.), *In Search of Scotland* (Edinburgh, 2001), and I. G. C. Hutchison, 'Workshop of Empire: the Nineteenth Century', in J. Wormald (ed.), *Scotland: A History* (Oxford, 2005).

Urban growth is a major characteristic of the nineteenth century, with Scotland following not far behind European leader, England, as a highly urbanised place. To study these changes we recommend: R. J. Morris, 'Urbanisation and Scotland', in Fraser and Morris (eds), *People and Society in Scotland*; T. Hart, 'Urban Growth and Municipal Government: Glasgow in a Comparative Context, 1846–1914', in A. Slaven and D. H. Aldcroft (eds), *Business, Banking and Urban History* (Edinburgh, 1982); *Glasgow, Vol. II: 1830–1912* (Manchester, 1996), W. H. Fraser and I. Maver (eds); *Aberdeen, 1800–2000* (East Linton, 2000), W. H. Fraser and C. H. Lee (eds); R. Rodger, *The Transformation of Edinburgh. Land, Property and Trust in the Nineteenth Century* (Cambridge, 2001).

Religion, religiosity and morality are particular themes throughout a number of chapters. The best introduction to this literature comes from C. G. Brown, *Religion and Society in Scotland since 1707* (Edinburgh, 1997); C. G Brown, 'Religion, Class and Church Growth', in Fraser and Morris (eds), *People and Society in Scotland*; C. G. Brown, *The Death of Christian Britain* (London, 2001). For an outstanding introduction to the leading churchman of the age, see S. J. Brown, *Thomas Chalmers and the Godly Commonwealth* (Oxford, 1982).

An important part of Scotland's everyday life is found by analysis of speech and written language. On these developments there is particular value to be found from a number of essays collected in the *Edinburgh History of Scottish Literature, Vol. II* (Edinburgh, 2006), I. Brown, S. Manning, M. Pittock and T. Clancy (eds). William Donaldson has produced a number of influential works on the use of Scots in print, including *The Language of the People: Scots Prose from the Victorian Revival* (Aberdeen, 1989). The different use of language in popular and elite publications can be followed up in the work of E. J. Cowan and M. Paterson, *Folk in Print: Scotland's Chapbook Heritage 1750–1850* (Edinburgh, 2007) and E. Letley, *From Galt to Douglas Brown: Nineteenth-century Fiction and Scots Language* (Edinburgh, 1988); a superb survey of Scottish literature of this period, and others, is found in R. Crawford, *Scotland's Books: The Penguin History of Scottish Literature* (London, 2007).

The Scots in photography, still and moving, have benefited from some excellent recent publications, notably: V. Toulmin, *Electric Edwardians: The Story of the Mitchell and Kenyon Collection* (London, 2007); R. J. Morris, *Scotland 1907: The Many Scotlands of Valentine and Sons, Photographers* (Edinburgh, 2007); T. Normand, *Scottish Photography: A History* (Edinburgh, 2007); the popularity of the postcard along with the development of tourism in Scotland is analysed in A. J. Durie, *George Washington Wilson in St Andrews and Fife* (Aberdeen, 1994) and A. J. Durie, *Scotland for the Holidays: Tourism in Scotland, c.1780–1939* (East Linton, 2003).

The significance of a diary for recounting the events of the day is shown in *Journal of My Life and Everyday Doings, 1879–81, 1885–92, James Wilson, farmer in Banffshire*, P. Hillis (ed.) (Edinburgh, 2008) and C. A. Whatley (ed.), *The Diary of John Sturrock, Millwright, Dundee 1864–65* (East Linton, 1996). Both are important for offering insight into the daily lives of those who were otherwise silent. The remaining topics in this introduction are of course best followed by reading the chapters, and accompanying bibliographic essays, from the authors themselves.

CHAPTER 1: LAND, THE LANDSCAPE AND PEOPLE IN THE NINETEENTH CENTURY

This chapter considers some key changes in land use and the landscape of the nineteenth century and how these impacted on the people who still depended on the land. In doing so, it has drawn on a range of source material, both primary and secondary. For a scholarly and highly readable account of the themes of, and influences upon, everyday life for nineteenth-century Scots, T. C. Smout, *A Century of the Scottish People, 1830–1950* (London, 1986) is still indispensable. T. M. Devine, C. H. Lee and G. C. Peden (eds), *The Transformation of Scotland: The Economy since 1700* (Edinburgh, 2005) provides a useful synthesis of more recent material, including the chapter by Devine, 'The Transformation of Agriculture: Cultivation and Clearance'. The latter has produced many authoritative texts covering the social and economic transformation of Scotland. Most relevant to the themes addressed in this chapter are T. M. Devine, *The Transformation of Rural Scotland: Social Change and the Agrarian Economy, 1660–1815* (Edinburgh, 1994), particularly in covering the antecedents of the Improvement era and in following the process of change and how it affected the nature of the rural community into the nineteenth century. Most recently Professor Devine's collections of essays, *Clearance and Improvement: Land, Power and People in Scotland, 1700– 1900* (Edinburgh, 2006) examines the responses to change in both Lowland and Highland society.

The Highlands have attracted a wealth of excellent writing, most notably E. Richards, *A History of the Highland Clearances*, 2 vols (London, 1982), which concentrates overwhelmingly on the impact and process of rural change on the Highlands, and the nature of the Clearances. Then there is the highly readable, J. Hunter, *The Making of the Crofting Community* (Edinburgh, 1968). Alongside this is the in-depth account of the potato famine by T. M. Devine and W. Orr, *The Great Highland Famine: Hunger, Emigration and the Scottish Highlands in the Nineteenth Century* (Edinburgh, 1988). The development of the sheep industry and its relationship to deer forest development is ably covered by W. Orr, *Deer Forests, Landlords and Crofters: The Western Highlands in Victorian and Edwardian Times* (Edinburgh, 1982). Also of note in this respect is J. Hunter, 'Sheep and Deer: Highland Sheep Farming, 1850–1900', *Northern Scotland*, 1 (1973). A detailed account of shieling life in the central Highlands and its demise in the early nineteenth century is provided by A. Bil, *The Shieling, 1600–1840: The Case of the Central Scottish Highlands* (Edinburgh, 1990). Other worthwhile local Highland histories accounts include, P. Gaskell, *Morvern Transformed: A Highland Parish in the 19th Century* (Cambridge, 1996).

A very readable account of the life of the ferm-touns of the north-east of Scotland is provided by D. K. Cameron, *Ballad and the Plough* (Edinburgh, 1978). Also focusing on the north east is I. Carter, *Farmlife in Northeast Scotland 1840–1914* (Edinburgh, 1979). From an ethnological perspective, there is much to be gleaned about 'traditional' ways of rural life, from A. Fenton, *Scottish Country Life* (Edinburgh, 1976) and for the Highlands, from I. F. Grant, *Highland Folk Ways* (Edinburgh, 1965; reprinted 1995).

Less has been written on the physical alteration of the Scottish landscape and ecology during the nineteenth century. The more traditional historical geography approach has been provided by M. L. Parry and T. R. Slater (eds), *The Making of the Scottish Countryside* (London, 1980) and D. Turnock, *The Making of the Scottish Rural Landscape* (Aldershot, 1995). Of more relevance are the environmental histories that have emerged more recently, particularly from T. C. Smout. Although not specific to the nineteenth century, T. C. Smout, *Nature Contested: Environmental history in Scotland and Northern England since 1600* (Edinburgh, 2000) is a concise but comprehensive book, based on a series of lectures about how we have treated nature and is particularly relevant to the nineteenth century. For woodlands, there is now a wealth of authorative accounts of their history. For native woodlands, there is the seminal, T. C. Smout, A. R. Macdonald and F. Watson, *A History of the Native Woodlands of Scotland, 1500–1920* (Edinburgh, 2005). And for all woods, T. C. Smout (ed.), *People and Woods in Scotland. A History* (Edinburgh, 2003). An idiosyncratic but well-written account of forests through the ages is provided by J. Fowler, *Landscapes and Lives: The Scottish Forest Through the Ages* (Edinburgh, 2002). It provides a good account of the development of plantation forestry in the late nineteenth century.

Contemporary accounts and literature is supplied by Lord H. Cockburn, *Circuit Journeys* (Edinburgh, 1975 edn); J. Mitchell, *Reminiscences of My Life in the Highlands* (Newton Abbot, 1971); W. Alexander, *Johnny Gibb of Gushetneuk in the Parish of Pyketillim* (East Linton, 1995). Also, the delightful E. Grant, *Memoirs of a Highland Lady*, Vol. 1, A. Tod (ed.) (Edinburgh, 1988).

By the nineteenth century, the sources – particularly archival material – which can be drawn on to construct a picture of the landscape, country life and land management become richer, more detailed and more widespread. The more accessible sources include the Statistical Accounts of Scotland, available at: http://edina.ac.uk/stat-acc-scot. These offer the basis for some comparison between parish life in the late eighteenth and mid-nineteenth centuries. Though the accounts have been heavily criticised for deliberate bias, they none the less provide a good deal of information about the changing face of Scottish society. As a result, it is possible to chart the progress of improvement in agriculture and the impact this had on the parish and its population. Alongside these is the first edition of the Ordnance Survey, which provides perhaps the most accurate and detailed portrayal of the Scottish landscape before the twentieth century. These are available at: http://www.nls.uk/maps/os/6inch.

The county *General Surveys of Agriculture*, anxious to highlight both what was being done and what needed to be done, catalogue the state of agriculture at the beginning of the century. The influential contemporary *Transactions of the Highland and Agricultural Society of Scotland* is a voluminous source of material on agricultural experimentation and innovation. To hear the voice of the people, there are a plethora of government reports and parliamentary commissions set up to look into every aspect of Scottish life. I. Levitt and T. C. Smout, *The State of the Scottish Working Class in 1843* (Edinburgh, 1979), for example, utilised the report of the Poor Law Commission of 1844 to offer a picture of the state of the poor in mid-century. Also relevant for the Highlands is the *Report of the Royal Commission on the Highlands and Islands of Scotland*, 1884 (the Napier Commission).

CHAPTER 2: NECESSITIES IN THE NINETEENTH CENTURY

Routes in to the everyday life of consumption can be found in C. Palmer, 'From Theory to Practice. Experiencing the Nation in Everyday Life', *Journal of Material Culture*, 3:2 (July 1998) and H. Mackay (ed.), *Consumption and Everyday Life* (Milton Keynes, 1997). The changing impact on diet within the working-class economy can be seen in I. Levitt and T. C. Smout, *The State of the Scottish Working Class in 1843* (Edinburgh, 1979) and P. Johnson, *Saving and Spending. The Working-Class Economy in Britain 1870–1939* (Oxford, 1985).

Focus on diet, as well as the preparation of food, is discussed in A. Fenton, 'Hearth and Kitchen: the Scottish Example', in M. R. Schärer and A. Fenton (eds), *Food and Material Culture. Proceedings of the Fourth Symposium of the International Commission for Research into European Food History* (East Linton, 1998); H. Cheape, 'Pottery and Food Preparation, Storage and Transport in the Scottish Hebrides', in A. Fenton and E. Kisbain (eds), *Food in Change. Eating Habits from the Middle Ages to the present* (Edinburgh, 1986); R. H. Campbell, 'Diet in Scotland; An Example of Regional Variation', in T. C. Barker, J. C. McKenzie and J. Yudkin (eds), *Our Changing Fare. Two Hundred Years of British Food Habits* (London, 1966); A. Gibson and T. C. Smout, 'From Meat to Meal. Changes in Diet in Scotland', in C. Geissler and D. J. Oddy (eds), *Food, Diet and Economic Change Past and Present* (Leicester, 1993); D. N. Paton, J. C. Dunlop and E. M. Inglis, *A Study of the Diet of the Labouring Classes in Edinburgh Carried out Under the Auspices of the Town Council of the City of Edinburgh* (Edinburgh, 1902); A. Fenton, 'Place of Oatmeal in the Diet of Scottish Farm Servants in the Eighteenth and Nineteenth Centuries', in J. Szabadfalvi and Z. Ujváry (eds), *Studia Ethnographia et Folkloristica in Honorem Béla Gunda* (Debrecen, 1971); F. Dye, *The Cooking Range: Its Failings and Remedies* (London, 1888); and S. W. Mintz, 'The Changing Role of Food in the Study of Consumption', in J. Brewer and R. Porter (eds), *Consumption and the World of Goods* (London, 1993).

The culture of cooking within the home was part of wider changes in the function of rooms and in developments in popular understandings of privacy and separate spheres: G. Vigarello, *Concepts of Cleanliness. Changing Attitudes in France since the Middle Ages* (Cambridge, 1988); F. Dye, *The Cooking Range: Its Failings and Remedies* (London, 1888); E. Gordon and G. Nair, *Public Lives. Women, Family and Society in Victorian Britain* (New Haven, 2003); M. M. Brewster, *Household Economy. A Manual intended for Female*

Training Colleges and the Senior Classes in Girls' Schools (Edinburgh, 1858); J. Begg, *Happy Homes for Working Men, and How to Get Them* (Edinburgh, 1866); J. W. Laurie, *Home and its Duties; A Practical Manual of Domestic Economy for Schools and Families* (Edinburgh, 1870); E. Rice, *Domestic Economy* (London, 1879); F. Young, 'RLS's Bathroom', in S. Mackay (ed.), *Scottish Victorian Interiors* (Edinburgh, 1986). On housing more generally, see T. Chapman and J. Hockey, *Ideal Homes? Social Change and Domestic Life* (London and New York, 1999) and V. D. Dickerson, *Keeping the Victorian House. A Collection of Essays* (New York and London, 1995).

Clothing as necessity, and as it was changed by fashion, are discussed in C. Walkley and V. Foster, *Crinolines and Crimping Irons. Victorian Clothes: How they were Cleaned and Cared For* (London, 1978); L. Johnston et al., *Nineteenth Century Fashion in Detail* (London, 2005); P. Bourdieu, *Distinction: A Social Critique of the Judgement of Taste* (London, 1984); M. Carter, *Fashion Classics from Carlyle to Barthes* (Oxford, 2003); A. Godley, 'Homeworking and the Sewing Machine in the British Clothing Industry 1850–1905', in B. Burman (ed.), *The Culture of Sewing: Gender, Consumption and Home Dressmaking* (Oxford, 1999); and P. Bryde, *The Male Image. Men's Fashions in Britain 1300–1970* (London, 1979). For the earlier period, see: B. Lemire, 'Consumerism in Pre-industrial and Early Industrial England: The Trade in Second-hand Clothes', *Journal of British Studies*, 27:1 (January 1988).

Important analyses on shifts in societal attitudes are tracked in J. A. and O. Banks, *Feminism and Family Planning in Victorian England* (Liverpool, 1964); R. Q. Gray, *The Labour Aristocracy in Victorian Edinburgh* (Oxford, 1976); J. Fields, 'Erotic Modesty: (Ad)dressing Female Sexuality in Open and Closed Drawers, USA, 1800–1930', in B. Burman and C. Turbin (eds), *Material Strategies. Dress and Gender in Historical Perspective* (Oxford, 2003); K. C. Grier, 'The Decline of the Memory Palace: the Parlour after 1890', in J. H. Foy and T. J. Schlereth (eds), *American Home Life 1880–1930. A Social History of Spaces and Services* (Knoxville, 1992).

The development of retailing remains an important part of building up demand for consumption. For the themes examined in this chapter see: P. Mathias, *Retailing Revolution* (London, 1967); M. Moss and A. Turton, *A Legend of Retailing. House of Fraser* (London, 1989); C. Breward, *The Hidden Consumer: Masculinities, Fashion and City Life* (Manchester, 1999); K. Hudson, *Food, Clothes and Shelter. Twentieth-Century Industrial Archaeology* (London, 1978). Consumption as part of wider industrial changes can be found in G. P. Bevan (ed.), *British Manufacturing Industries* (London, 1876); R. L. Cohen, *A History of Milk Prices* (1936); S. W. Mintz, *Sweetness and Power. The Place of Sugar in Modern History* (New York, 1985); and J. Kinloch and J. Butt, *History of the Scottish Co-operative Wholesale Society* (Glasgow, 1981).

Some of the most informative detail on necessities of life in this period can be found within the returns of the New Statistical Account of Scotland. Local newspapers also provide growing coverage, while specific reference

294 Annotated Bibliography

to house and home can be gleaned from the *Report of the Select Committee on Public Houses in Scotland*, PP, 1846 XV and the Dundee Social Union's *Report on Housing and Industrial Conditions and Medical Inspection of School Children* (Dundee, 1905). Biography and autobiography, including working-class diaries, while rare, can be full of detail: A. Somerville, *The Autobiography of a Working Man* (London, 1855); D. Stevenson (ed.), *The Diary of A Canny Man 1818–1828. Adam Mackie Farmer, Merchant and Innkeeper in Fyvie compiled by William Mackie* (Aberdeen, 1991); J. Mackenzie, *Pigeon Holes of Memory. The Life and Times of Dr John Mackenzie (1803–1886)*, C. B. Shaw (ed) (London, 1988); C. A. Whatley (ed.), *The Diary of John Sturrock, Millwright, Dundee 1864–65* (East Linton, 1996); L. B. Walford, *Recollections of a Scottish Novelist* (Waddesdon, 1984); H. Cockburn, *Memorials of His Time* (Edinburgh, 1856); J. L. Story, *Early Reminiscences* (Glasgow, 1911). See also a number of essays within *The Scottish Home*, A. Carruthers (ed.) (Edinburgh, 1996). Useful detail can also be found in local histories: H. W. Drysdale, *Alva in the Time of Our Grandfathers* (Alloa, 1886); J. Strathesk, *More Bits from Blinkbonny. A Tale of Scottish Village Life between 1831 and 1841* (Edinburgh, 1885).

There were any number of instruction manuals offering advice, including: *The Cook and Housewife's Manual; Containing the Most Approved Modern Receipts for Making Soups, Gravies, Sauces, Ragouts, and Made Dishes; and for Pies, Puddings, Pastries, Pickles and Preserves, Also for Baking, Brewing, Making Home-made Wines and Cordials etc.* by Mrs Margaret Dods of the Cleikum Inn, St Ronan's (Edinburgh, 1826); *Cook and Housewife's Manual* (1829 edn), *The Home Book of Household Economy: or Hints to Persons of Moderate Income* (London, 1854); *Miss in the Kitchen or A Week's Misadventures in House Keeping* (Edinburgh, 1877); *Cassell's Household Guide: being a Complete Encyclopaedia of Domestic and Social Economy, and Forming A Guide to Every Department of Practical Life, Vol. 2* (London, 1873); *Girl's Own Paper* (1880); [Helen Greig Souter], *Aunt Kate's Book of Personal and Household Information* (London, 1895)

CHAPTER 3: RITUALS, TRANSITIONS AND LIFE COURSES IN AN ERA OF SOCIAL TRANSFORMATION

This chapter considers the changing character and patterning of life-course passages, an exercise that requires understanding both of the immediate circumstances surrounding baptisms, courtship, weddings and funerals and the broader historical and geographical context over which custom and practice varied.

The literature concerning rituals and the life course in nineteenth-century history is extremely diverse, the most useful material being either ethnological or demographic. Among the former, M. Bennett, *Scottish Customs: from the Cradle to the Grave* (Edinburgh, 1992) provides a wide-ranging collection of information about traditions pertaining to rites of passage, including a good deal of oral testimony. J. Beech, O. Hand, M. Mulhern and J. Weston (eds), *Scottish Life and Society, Vol. 9: The Individual and Community Life* (Edinburgh, 2005) contains a section on the life cycle, including contributions about 'Courtship, Marriage and Related Folklore' (F. MacDonald), 'Divorce in Scotland' (F. Wasoff) and 'Death and Associated Customs' (A. Gordon). See also G. J. West, 'Custom', in S. Storrier (ed.), *Scottish Life and Society, Vol. 6: Scotland's Domestic Life* (Edinburgh, 2006), pp. 562–80. Contemporary observers lend further detail – see particularly Revd W. Gregor, *Notes on the Folk-lore of the North-East of Scotland* (London, 1881) and Revd J. Napier, *Folk Lore: or, Superstitious Beliefs in the West of Scotland Within this Century* (Paisley, 1879) – while some ethnological evidence is available in the Scottish Life Archive of the National Museums of Scotland, which contains sources such as diaries and photographs, samples of which are accessible through www.scran.ac.uk.

Primary population data are abundant, but while statutory registers of births, marriages and deaths after 1855, and Old Parish Registers prior to this date, are accessible via www.scotlandspeople.gov.uk, the information from these cannot be understood without clear comprehension of the national and regional demographic context. M. W. Flinn (ed.), *Scottish Population History* (Cambridge, 1977) provides the starting point for this, with more refined demographic analysis provided by M. Anderson and D. Morse, 'The People', in W. H. Fraser and R. J. Morris (eds), *People and Society in Scotland, Vol. 2* (Edinburgh, 1990), pp. 4–45, and M. Anderson and D. Morse, 'High Fertility, High Emigration, Low Nuptiality: Adjustment Processes in Scotland's Demographic Experience, 1861–1914', *Population Studies*, 47 (1993), 5–25 and 319–43. Pertinent to both ethnological and demographic interests, the 'Old' Statistical Account (1791–9), and the New Statistical Account (1834–45) provide a comprehensive resource of comparable social evidence for every Scottish parish, including interesting snapshots of local social customs, 'character of the people' and the ecclesiastical state of each written by incumbent parish ministers. They may be accessed at http://edina. ac.uk/stat-acc-scot. Meanwhile, T. C. Smout's overview, 'Aspects of Sexual Behaviour in Nineteenth-century Scotland', in A. A. MacLaren (ed.), *Social Class in Scotland: Past and Present* (Edinburgh, 1976), pp. 55–85 brings alive the cultural implications of variations in courtship and marriage according to class, region, religion and ethnicity. His article 'Scottish Marriage, Regular and Irregular, 1500–1940', in R. B. Outhwaite (ed.), *Marriage and Society: Studies in the Social History of Marriage* (London, 1981), pp. 204–36 further points to the connection between customs and the law.

The parochial framework by which individual life events were formally processed reflects the dominant role of the kirk in such affairs. For a detailed overview of the relationships between religious perception and policy regarding such matters as courtship, illegitimacy, divorce and remarriage, see K. M. Boyd, *Scottish Church Attitudes to Sex, Marriage and the*

Family, 1850–1914 (Edinburgh, 1980) and A. Blaikie, *Illegitimacy, Sex and Society: Northeast Scotland, 1750–1900* (Oxford, 1993), which also considers the regional impact. On the role of the local kirk, and more particularly the changing nature of discipline regarding courtship, G. D. Henderson, *The Scottish Ruling Elder* (London, 1935) and I. M. Clark, *A History of Church Discipline in Scotland* (Aberdeen, 1929) supply useful orientation, with examples drawn from a range of parishes. Case studies of the eldership in action – both in the north-east, and covering urban and rural setting, respectively – are A. A. MacLaren, *Religion and Social Class: The Disruption Years in Aberdeen* (London, 1974) and A. Blaikie and P. Gray, 'Archives of Abuse and Discontent? Presbyterianism and Sexual Behaviour during the Eighteenth and Nineteenth Centuries', in L. Kennedy and R. J. Morris (eds), *Order and Disorder: Scotland and Ireland, 1600–2001* (Edinburgh, 2005), pp. 61–84. Although outside the period covered, R. Mitchison and L. Leneman, *Sexuality and Social Control: Scotland, 1660–1780* (Oxford, 1989), is a valuable study, allowing for close comparative analysis, and indicating the degree and nature of change in the treatment of courtship between early-modern and nineteenth-century Scotland. Kirk session minutes for Church of Scotland, Free Church and other denominations are housed in the National Archives of Scotland (available at: www.nas.gov.uk) and are currently (March 2009) being digitised (see http://www.scottishdocuments.com).

CHAPTER 4: BELIEFS AND RELIGIONS

While there is a rich literature on ecclesiastical politics, church–state relations and theological debates in nineteenth-century Scotland, much less has been written on everyday religious practices and popular beliefs. Several essays in C. MacLean and K. Veitch (eds), *Scottish Life and Society: a Compendium of Scottish Ethnology, Vol. 12: Religion* (Edinburgh, 2006) discuss religious beliefs and practices in the different Scottish denominations. There is also a rewarding chapter on 'Churchgoing' in T. C. Smout, *A Century of the Scottish People 1830–1950* (London, 1986), which takes a broad view of popular beliefs and practices. The changing social composition of the Scottish denominations, the extent of popular church adherence and the timing of secularisation receive expert treatment in C. G. Brown, *Religion and Society in Scotland since 1707* (Edinburgh, 1997).

For an engaging, though somewhat idiosyncratic survey of Scottish Christianity during this period, see A. L. Drummond and J. Bulloch, *The Scottish Church, 1688–1843: The Age of the Moderates* (Edinburgh, 1973), *The Church in Victorian Scotland, 1843–1874* (Edinburgh, 1975) and *The Church in late Victorian Scotland, 1874–1900* (Edinburgh, 1978).

The changing beliefs and worship in the Presbyterian denominations are eloquently described in A. C. Cheyne, *The Transforming of the Kirk: Victorian Scotland's Religious Revolution* (Edinburgh, 1983). For broader developments in nineteenth-century worship, see also D. Forrester and D. Murray, *Studies in the History of Worship in Scotland*, 2nd edn (Edinburgh, 1996). The distinctive Scottish Presbyterian tradition of the communion season is superbly interpreted in L. E. Schmidt, *Holy Fairs: Scottish Communions and American Revivals in the Early Modern Period* (Princeton, 1989). For the no less distinctive Presbyterian system of corporate discipline, see I. M. Clark, *A History of Church Discipline in Scotland* (Aberdeen, 1929).

While more work is needed on the role of women in Scottish religion, a good beginning has been made with L. A. Orr MacDonald, *A Unique and Glorious Mission: Women and Presbyterianism in Scotland, 1830–1930* (Edinburgh, 2000). C. G. Brown and J. D. Stephenson, '"Sprouting Wings?" Women and Religion in Scotland, c. 1890–1950', in E. Breitenbach and E. Gordon (eds), *Out of Bounds: Women in Scotland in the Nineteenth and Twentieth Centuries* (Edinburgh, 1992) provides a fresh understanding of the central place of religion in many women's lives at the close of the nineteenth century.

For popular Christianity in the Gaelic-speaking Highlands and Islands, the seminal works of Donald Meek are indispensable. See especially D. E. Meek, *The Scottish Highlands, the Churches and Gaelic Culture* (Geneva, 1996) and D. E. Meek, 'The Bible and Social Change in the Nineteenth-Century Highlands', in D. F. Wright (ed.), *The Bible in Scottish Life and Literature* (Edinburgh, 1988), pp. 179–91. The Highland Presbyterian tradition finds a sympathetic portrayal in D. Ansdell, *The People of the Great Faith: the Highland Church 1690–1900* (Stornoway, 1998), while for the tradition of 'the Men' in popular Highland Presbyterianism, see D. M. M. Paton, 'The Myth and Reality of the "Men": Leadership and Spirituality in the Northern Highlands, 1800–1850', *Records of the Scottish Church History Society*, 31 (2001), 97–144.

Non-Christian folk beliefs, including second sight, earth spirits and the evil eye, receive classic treatment in J. G. Campbell, *The Gaelic Otherworld: John Gregorson Campbell's Superstitions of the Highlands and Islands of Scotland (1900) and Witchcraft and Second Sight in the Highlands and Islands (1902)*, R. Black (ed.) (Edinburgh, 2005). For a rewarding study of these phenomena, see A. Ross, *The Folklore of the Scottish Highlands* (London, 1976).

CHAPTER 5: MOVEMENT, TRANSPORT AND TOURISM

Given the importance of movement to work, leisure and pleasure, it is not surprising that there is an immense and growing literature on nineteenth-century transport. Although transport history is nowadays relatively neglected in academic circles, the vacuum has more than been filled by the writing of enthusiasts, some very knowledgeable indeed, and from whom a great deal can be drawn and learnt. Scarcely an issue of the journal, *Scottish Local History*, appears without a contribution in this field, as for example in issue 70 (summer 2007), when J. Mitchell examined royal travel on the railways of Strathendrick. Due soon is Vol. 8 (*Transport and Communications*) in the fourteen-volume project of the European Ethnological Research Centre under the series title *Scottish Life and Society. A Compendium of Scottish Ethnology*; this promises to be an invaluable and weighty synthesis of recent writing on all aspects of transport and movement.

Of the making of books on railways in particular there is no end. The Oakwood Press is in the process of publishing a trilogy on the lines of East Fife, the first of which on the *St Andrews Railway* by A. M. Hajducki, M. Jodeluk and A. Simpson, has just appeared (Usk, 2008). Studies of this kind tend to be especially strong on how and where lines were built and what traffic, passenger or freight that they carried, regular services and excursions. The world of promotion, of the complexity of scheme and counter scheme, is analysed to an exceptional depth in J. McGregor's *The West Highland Railway. Plans Politics and People* (Edinburgh, 2005). A recent addition to the literature is P. J. G. Ranson's *Iron Road. The Railway in Scotland* (Edinburgh, 2007). Water transport, inland or coastal, has not lacked attention, with the construction and use of canals comprehensively reviewed by L. Paterson in his *From Sea to Sea, A History of the Scottish Lowland and Highland Canals* (Glasgow, 2006). For the Clyde steamers, A. Paterson's work is still of great value, and A. Brodie has performed a similar service for the east coast in his *Steamers of the Forth* (Newton Abbot, 1976). N. Robins and D. Meek's *The Kingdom of MacBrayne* (Edinburgh, 2006) is very important. It shows not just what the steamers of this company meant for business travellers, migrant workers and tourists, but also throws light on what the arrival of tourists meant for the receiving communities in the Highlands and Islands. The development of cycling and motoring in Scotland have yet to be fully examined, although there is a wealth of information in R. Grieves' commentary to his collection of postcards and photographs in *Scotland's Motoring Century* (Paisley, 1990). W. Plowden's *The Motor Car and Politics 1896–1970* (London, 1971) is still essential reading on such topics as to how to fund the roads system or regulate motorists so that they were less of a danger to themselves and the public. There is still no better treatment of what was happening in the larger cities whose streets were increasingly congested as horse-carriages, carts and trams competed for room, than that of J. R. Hume. His study, of 'Transport and Towns in Victorian Scotland' in *Scottish Urban History* (Aberdeen, 1983), ed. G. Gordon and B. Dicks (eds), remains authoritative.

What changing transport meant for tourism, whether that of Scots day-trippers or English holidaymakers, is covered in E. Simpson, *Going on Holiday* (Edinburgh, 1997) and in A. J. Durie, *Scotland for the Holidays: A History of Tourism in Scotland, 1780–1939* (East Linton, 2003). Travellers' accounts are a rich seam of information as to the experience of travel, but should not always, even those of Dorothy Wordsworth, be taken entirely at face value. More and more tourist journals, whether of English or American or Continental visitors, are being rescued from obscurity. It would be helpful indeed were a database to be compiled – and regularly updated – of these, as to which are held where, and if published. For the effect on sport, and the ways in which transport contributed to the emergence of modern commercial sport, it will pay to look at N. Tranter's pamphlet *Sport, Economy and Society in Britain* (Cambridge, 1998). This gives a magisterial overview of the relationship at national level, but draws heavily on evidence from sport in central Scotland. For examples of how better travel benefited particular sports, see D. Hamilton's *Golf; Scotland's Game* (Kilmacolm, 1998) and R. Eden's *Going to the Moors* (London, 1979). J. Burnett's publications, of which *Riot Revelry and Sport in Lowland Scotland* (East Linton, 2000) is but one, cover the whole spectrum of popular recreations.

CHAPTER 6: WORK, LEISURE AND TIME IN THE NINETEENTH CENTURY

Although historians acknowledge the strong associations between the experiences of work and leisure, these activities have tended to generate discrete literatures. That on work has a longer pedigree and has developed in line with changing perceptions of the nature and impact of industrialisation. The study of leisure, for long confined to the antiquarian or the folklorist, acquired academic respectability from the 1970s, as explanations for social change turned to examine wider cultural, rather than narrowly materialistic influences. The literature that resulted, concerned as it has been with the practices and values that help to shape social relations, shares many of the preoccupations of the everyday. In Scotland, it has generated a diverse, if patchy, body of work that, by enabling us to recognise areas of continuity and change within the everyday experience, provides the basis for the preliminary generalisations offered here.

Work

The impact of the Industrial Revolution continues to provoke debate. The general argument over whether innovation was confined to a few, 'modern' sectors of the economy or was more broadly based is set out in P. Temin, 'Two Views of the British Industrial Revolution', *Journal of Economic History*, 57 (1997); N. Crafts and C. Harley, 'Output Growth and the British Industrial Revolution: A Restatement of the Crafts–Harley view', *Economic History Review*, 2nd ser., XLV (1992); and M. Berg and P. Hudson, 'Rehabilitating the Industrial Revolution', *Economic History Review*, 2nd ser., XLV (1992). For a recent examination of the Scottish experience, see T. M. Devine, C. H. Lee and G. C. Peden (eds), *The Transformation of Scotland: The Economy since 1700* (Edinburgh, 2005), and the essays by Devine and Lee in the first two volumes of R. Floud and P. Johnson (eds), *The Cambridge Economic History of Modern Britain* (Cambridge, 2004). The implications of rapid urbanisation are explored in R. J. Morris, 'Urbanisation and Scotland', in W. H. Fraser and R. J. Morris (eds), *People and Society in Scotland, Vol. II: 1830–1914* (Edinburgh, 1990).

The impact of industrialisation on work and, by extension, class formation has generated an equally vigorous historiography. The 'traditional' view, that technological and organisational change transformed the work experience was forcefully restated for the classic phase of the Industrial Revolution by E. P. Thompson, 'Time, Work-Discipline and Industrial Capitalism', *Past and Present*, 38 (December 1967), and taken on into the later, more broadly-based sequence of change in E. J. Hobsbawm (ed.), 'The Formation of British Working-Class Culture,' and 'The Making of the Working Class, 1870–1914', in *Worlds of Labour* (London, 1984). From the 1970s, as part of a literature concerned with long-term economic decline, the limitations of change and the survival of traditional attitudes and practices came to be emphasised, a view summarised in W. Lazonick, 'Employment Relations in Manufacturing and International Competition', in R. Floud and D. N. McCloskey (eds), *The Economic History of Britain since 1700. Vol. 2*, 2nd edn (Cambridge, 1994). A more recent re-evaluation of the link between work and class identity is attempted in M. Savage and A. Miles, *The Remaking of the British Working Class, 1840–1940* (London, 1994). Work on Scotland has rarely engaged directly with this debate, but useful synoptic overviews which enable points of comparison to be developed are available in W. W. J. Knox, *Industrial Nation: Work, Culture and Society in Scotland, 1800–Present* (Edinburgh, 1999), and J. H. Treble, 'The Occupied Male Labour Force', in Fraser and Morris (eds), *People and Society, Vol. II*. Eleanor Gordon's essay on 'Women's Spheres', in the same volume as Treble, usefully opens up the female experience of work in this period.

An examination of the changing nature of work is more often pursued at the level of the individual sector. The nature of the rural labour market is neatly encapsulated in R. Anthony, *Herds and Hinds: Farm Labour in Lowland Scotland, 1900–1939* (East Linton, 1997). Alan Campbell's work on the coal miners pays due attention to the wider social context within which work was carried on: *The Lanarkshire Miners: A Social History of their Trade Unions, 1775–1874* (Edinburgh, 1974), and *The Scottish Miners, 1874–1939: Vol. One: Industry, Work and Community* (Aldershot and Burlington, 2000). This can usefully be supplemented by Angela John's work on the numerically marginal, but socially significant female pit workers, *By the Sweat of their Brow: Women Workers in Victorian Coal Mines* (London, 1980). Other studies of single industries with material of value include W. W. J. Knox, *Hanging by a Thread: the Scottish Cotton Industry, c. 1850–1914* (Preston, 1995) and W. M. Walker, *Juteopolis: Dundee and its Textile Workers, 1885–1923* (Edinburgh, 1979). The dynamics of the everyday within the workplace are perhaps most vividly captured through the parliamentary investigations of the time, in particular the 1833 Factory Commission (PP, 1833 XX), the reports of the Assistant Commissioners into the State of the Handloom Weavers in 1839 (PP, 1839 XLII), the Royal Commission on Children's Employment (Mines) (PP, 1842 XVI), the Royal Commission on Labour in the 1890s (PP, 1892 XXXIV–XXXVI), and the Departmental Committee into the Miners' Eight-Hour Day (PP, 1907 XV).

Leisure

Useful introductions to the historical analysis and conceptualisation of leisure are P. Borsay, *A History of Leisure: The British Experience since 1500* (Basingstoke, 2006), in which the chronological breadth encourages us to reconsider the ways in which the use of free time was understood, and, covering a narrower period, H. Cunningham, 'Leisure and Culture', in F. M. L. Thompson (ed.), *The Cambridge Social History of Britain, 1750–1950, Vol. 2: People and their Environment* (Cambridge, 1990). For Scotland, Hamish Fraser's, 'Developments in Leisure', in Fraser and Morris (eds), *People and Society in Scotland, Vol. II*, continues to provide a valuable overview. The interpretive framework within which the development of leisure in the nineteenth century has been understood is also set out in R. W. Malcolmson, *Popular Recreations in English Society, 1700–1850* (Cambridge, 1973), and P. Bailey, '"A Mingled Mass of Perfectly Legitimate Pleasures": the Victorian Middle Class and the Problem of Leisure', *Victorian Studies*, 21 (1977–8). Urban histories which have effectively located leisure within its immediate social context include R. J. Morris, 'Clubs, Societies and Associations', in F. M. L. Thompson (ed.), *The Cambridge Social History of Britain, 1750–1950, Vol. 3: Social Agencies and Institutions* (Cambridge, 1990), E. King, 'Popular Culture in Glasgow', in R. A. Cage (ed.), *The Working Class in Glasgow, 1750–1914* (Beckenham, 1987), and I. Maver, 'Leisure and Culture: The Nineteenth Century', in W. H. Fraser and C. H. Lee (eds), *Aberdeen, 1800–2000: A New History* (East Linton, 2000). R. Q. Gray, *The Labour Aristocracy in Victorian Edinburgh* (Oxford, 1976) is more broadly conceived, but has much to offer on the leisure culture of the respectable working class. These can be read alongside key contemporary texts, such as *Glasgow, 1858: Shadow's Midnight Scenes and Social Photographs* (Glasgow, 1976 reprint) and the ubiquitous C. A. Whatley (ed.), *The Diary of John Sturrock, Millwright, Dundee, 1864–65* (East Linton, 1998).

In tracing the development of particular leisure forms, a longer-term perspective is sometimes rewarding. Useful texts include R. Hutton, *The Stations of the Sun: A History of the Ritual Year in Britain* (Oxford, 1996), and N. Elias and E. Dunning, *Quest for Excitement: Sport and Leisure in the Civilizing Process* (Oxford, 1993). The development of modern sport is succinctly outlined in N. Tranter, *Sport, Economy and Society in Britain, 1750–1914* (Cambridge,

1998) and R. Holt, *Sport and the British. A Modern History* (Oxford, 1989). For Scotland, as yet, no text spans the nineteenth century. The early part of the period is chronicled in the works of John Burnett, including *Sporting Scotland* (Edinburgh, 1995) and *Riot, Revelry and Rout: Sport in Lowland Scotland before 1860* (East Linton, 2000). A useful examination of a durable, yet evolving activity, is J. Robertson, *Uppies and Doonies: The Story of the Kirkwall Ba' Game* (Aberdeen, 1967), while Neil Tranter's studies of Stirling offer insights into the impact of industrialisation on popular sporting practices, the most pertinent being 'Popular Sports and the Industrial Revolution in Scotland: The Evidence of the Statistical Accounts', *International Journal of the History of Sport*, 4 (1987). G. Jarvie, *Highland Games: The Making of the Myth* (Edinburgh, 1991), traces the development of Highland sporting culture across the later decades of the century. By contrast, studies of Scotland's most popular sport of the period remain, with few exceptions, the work of enthusiasts rather than academics. Honourable exceptions include J. Hutchinson, *The Football Industry: The Early Years of the Professional Game* (Glasgow, 1982) and N. L. Tranter, 'The Cappielow Riot and the Composition and Behaviour of Soccer Crowds in Late Victorian Scotland', *International Journal of the History of Sport*, 12 (1995). Nevertheless, club histories, for all their preoccupation with the recondite, can be made to yield points of value. The development of sport within Edinburgh is clarified somewhat by the histories of its two leading football clubs: A. Lugton, *The Making of Hibernian* (Edinburgh, 1999); A. Mackie, *The Hearts: The Story of the Heart of Midlothian F.C.* (London, 1959); D. Speed, B. Smith and G. Blackwood, (eds), *The Heart of Midlothian Football Club: A Pictorial History, 1874–1984* (Heart of Midlothian F.C. plc, 1984). Much work remains to be done in the newspapers of the period before the full story of Scotland's sporting development can be reconstructed.

The picture is equally variable when considering the popular entertainments of the time. Useful local studies include I. McGraw, *The Fairs of Dundee*, Abertay Historical Society No. 34 (Dundee, 1994), and the works of King and Maver above. As yet, the development of Scotland's popular visual culture, from the fairground shows to the early cinemas, has been only imperfectly sketched, although P. Maloney, *Scotland and the Music Hall, 1850–1914* (Manchester, 2003) offers an effective overview of the development of one key entertainment medium. The most complete survey of early Scottish film shows remains 'Fifty Years of Scottish Cinema, 1896–1946', *Educational Film Bulletin*, 33 (September 1946), although this has been supplemented of late by Janet McBain's work on the Green family of Glasgow, in particular, 'Green's of Glasgow: "We Want 'U' In"', *Film Studies*, 10 (Spring 2007) and Michael Thomson's survey of cinema exhibition in Aberdeen, *Silver Screen in the Silver City: A History of Cinemas in Aberdeen, 1896–1987* (Aberdeen, 1988).

The use of time to examine the relationship between work and leisure is exemplified by D. A. Reid, 'The Decline of Saint Monday, 1768–1876', *Past and Present*, 71 (May 1976) and H. J. Voth, *Time and Work in England, 1750–1830* (Oxford, 2000). Changes in working hours are set out in M. A. Bienefeld, *Working Hours in British Industry: An Economic History* (London, 1972), while the campaign for the nine-hour day can be traced through I. MacDougall (ed.), *The Minutes of Edinburgh Trades Council, 1859–1873* (Edinburgh, 1968). Time also casts important light on the experiences of women, a theme which oral histories of a more recent period have explored to some effect. Here, see particularly C. Langhamer, *Women's Leisure in England, 1920–60* (Manchester, 2000) and, for Scotland, J. Faley, *Up Oor Close: Memories of Domestic Life in Glasgow Tenements, 1910–1945* (Wendlebury, 1990) and H. Clark and E. Carnegie, *She Was Aye Workin': Memories of Tenement Women in Edinburgh and Glasgow* (Oxford, 2003).

CHAPTER 7: CRIME, PROTEST AND POLICING IN NINETEENTH-CENTURY SCOTLAND

Compared with the extensive research carried out in England and other European countries, as well as the United States the study of crime, protest and policing in Scotland is still in its infancy. Moreover, although scant, the published material has focused more on protest to the neglect of crime and policing, and more on the eighteenth century than the nineteenth. Thus, although an annotated bibliography such as this would in normal circumstances highlight the more important secondary sources, in many respects these are the only sources for Scotland. Place of publication is London unless otherwise stated.

Protest

An excellent starting point in thinking about crowd behaviour and popular protest is Gustav Le Bon, *The Crowd: A Study of the Popular Mind* (New York, 2002 edn) which sees this kind of action as irrational and violent. Correctives to Le Bon's irrationalism thesis can be found in E. Canetti, *Crowds and Power* (1973); J. Bohstedt, *Riots and Community Politics in England and Wales 1790–1810* (Cambridge, MA, 1983); M. Harrison, *Crowds and History: Mass Phenomena in English Towns, 1790–1835* (Cambridge, 1988); C. Melucci, *Nomads of the Present: Social Movements and Individual Needs in Contemporary Society* (1989); G. Rude, *The Crowd in History: A Study of Popular Disturbances in England and France 1730–1848* (New York, 1964); E. P. Thompson, *The Making of the English Working Class* (1963). The latter two write from a Marxist perspective and if one desires a different, more conservative approach then J. Stevenson, *Popular Disturbances in England 1700–1870* (1979) and R. Quinault and J. Stevenson, *Popular Protest and Public Order* (New York, 1975) are good examples of this. In terms of Scotland the best introduction to the question of crowds and riots can be found in K. Logue's unsurpassed, *Popular Disturbances in Scotland, 1780–1815* (Edinburgh, 1979); W. H. Fraser, 'Patterns of Protest', in T. M. Devine and R. Mitchison (eds), *People and Society in Scotland, Vol. 1: 1760–1830* (Edinburgh, 1988) and C. A. Whatley, *Scottish Society, 1707–1830: beyond Jacobitism towards Industrialisation* (Manchester, 2000). All these works adopt a highly empirical approach to the question and should be read in conjunction with some of the more theoretical works mentioned above.

Food riots were the most common source of public disorder between 1780 and 1840, and they are detailed in the previously mentioned work by K. Logue, but also see E. Richards, 'The Last Scottish Food Riots', *Past and Present*, Supplement 6 (1982) for its last fling. Strikes by industrial workers were also a common source of disturbance throughout the nineteenth century, but increasingly as the trades union movement became more respectable the focus was more on unorganised women and colliers. W. H. Fraser, 'The Glasgow Cotton Spinners 1837', in J. Butt and J. T. Ward (eds), *Scottish Themes* (Edinburgh, 1976) is perhaps the best example of this kind of social history for the first half of the nineteenth century. Riotous activity among the industrial proletariat is barely addressed by Scottish historians, but examples can be found in A. B. Campbell, *The Scottish Miners 1874–1939, Vol. 1* (Aldershot, 2000); W. W. Knox, *Hanging by a Thread: The Scottish Cotton Industry c. 1850–1914* (Preston, 1995) and E. Gordon, *Women and the Labour Movement in Scotland 1815–1914* (Oxford, 1991). For a general background to sectarian conflict in Scotland in the nineteenth century see W. Gallagher, *Glasgow: The Uneasy Peace* (Manchester, 1987). Sources of the conflict between Catholics and Protestants can be found in E. McFarland, 'Marching from the Margins: Twelfth July Parades in Scotland, 1820–1914', in T. G. Fraser (ed.), *The Irish Parading Tradition; Following the Drum* (Basingstoke, 2000) and N. Jarman, *Material Conflicts: Parades and Visual Displays in Northern Ireland* (Oxford, 1997). As middle-class protest was constitutional, it was only those members who were peripheralised such as women that engaged in public disturbances. See E. King, *The Scottish Women's Suffrage Movement* (Glasgow, 1994).

Crime

Professor Anne Crowther once remarked that Scotland was a country without a criminal past, and given the paucity of published material on the subject that holds true even for today. The only published data set covering the first half of the nineteenth century is I. Donnachie, 'The Dark Side: A Speculative Survey of Scottish Crime During the First Half of the Nineteenth Century', *Scottish Economic and Social History*, 15 (1995). England has fared better and there are a number of important studies which can be used to frame comparative questions of Scottish data. These include V. A. C. Gatrell, 'The Decline of Theft and Violence in Edwardian England', in V.

A. C. Gatrell, B. Lenman and G. Parker (eds), *Crime and the Law: The Social History of Crime in Western Europe since 1500* (1980); V. A. C. Gatrell, 'Crime, Authority and the Policeman-State', in F. M. L. Thompson (ed.), *Cambridge Social History of Britain, 1750–1950, Vol. 3: Social Agencies and Institutions* (Cambridge, 1990); C. Emsley, *Crime and Society in England, 1750–1900* (1987). Theoretical insights can be gained through a critical reading of M. Foucault, *Discipline and Punishment* (1991 edn) and *Society must be Defended: Lectures at the College de France, 1975–76* (New York, 2003).

Policing

The issue of policing and pacifying urban and rural Scotland has been given little attention by historians with few published sources. Most of what exists consists of institutional celebratory histories such as D. Grant, *The Thin Blue Line: The Story of the City of Glasgow Police* (1973). However, there are a number of histories that examine the struggles mainly in Glasgow for control of the police commission. See D. Barrie, '"Epoch Making" Beginnings to Lingering Death: the struggle for control of the Glasgow Police Commission', *Scottish Historical Review*, LXXXVI (2007), and his latest book (sadly too late to be used in this chapter) *Police in the Age of Improvement: Police Development and the Civic Tradition in Scotland, 1775–1865* (Devon, 2008). Unpublished material in the form of theses and dissertations can be used to broaden the picture. See, for example, A. I. Goldsmith, 'The Development of the City of Glasgow Police, c. 1800–1939', unpublished Ph.D. thesis, University of Strathclyde, 2002. For developments in rural Scotland there is K. Carson and H. Idzikowska, 'The Social Production of Scottish policing, 1795–1900', in D. Hay and F. Snyder (ed.), *Policing and Prosecution in Britain, 1750–1850* (Oxford, 1989). None of these texts deal with the important issue of legitimacy or how the police were used to regulate everyday life in the cities and countryside. England is much better served in this respect see, for instance, R. D. Storch, '"A Plague of Black Locusts": police reform and popular resistance in Northern England, 1840–1857', *International Review of Social History*, 20 (1975). S. Gunn, 'The Spatial Turn: Changing Histories of Space and Time', in S. Gunn and R. J. Morris (eds), *Identities in Space: Contested Terrains in the Western City since 1850*, (Aldershot, 2001) and P. Jess and D. Massey, 'The Contestation of Place', in P. Jess and D. Massey (eds), *A Place in the World? Places, Cultures and Globalization* (Oxford, 1995), show how the regulation of everyday life was to a large extent dependent on the reorganisation of space by the police.

CHAPTER 8: NEW SPACES FOR SCOTLAND, 1800 TO 1900

There is no established literature around this topic which combines a number of theoretical and historical approaches and requires the continued interrogation of historical sources (many of which are available in reprint and on web sites) and historical landscapes (many of which survive).

A. P. Cohen, *Whalsay: Symbol, Segment and Boundary in a Shetland Island Community* (Manchester, 1987), presents a sense of place, place and boundaries or insiders and outsiders created by stories, language and actions. Its methodology can be fruitfully applied to many historical sources.

M. Augé, *Non-places: Introduction to an Anthropology of Supermodernity* (London, 1995), provides a concise and rather stark way into the modern spaces. The literature of modern spaces derived from the geographical tradition is massive but for a thoughtful, well-documented case study see R. Dennis, *Cities in Modernity: Representations and Productions of Metropolitan Space, 1840–1930* (Cambridge, 2008).

P. Nora's work has shown the variety of spaces and places in which memory, belonging and history are produced and located. See P. Nora, *Les Lieux de Mémoire* (Paris, 1994). The English translation is slightly different in content, A. Goldhammer, trans., *Realms of Memory* (New York, 1996).

The urban history of nineteenth-century Scotland has not been drawn together in a single publication, but see R. J. Morris, 'Urbanisation and Scotland', in W. H. Fraser and R. J. Morris (eds), *People and Society in Scotland, Vol. II: 1830–1914* (Edinburgh, 1990), pp. 73–102 and I. D. Whyte, 'Scottish and Irish Urbanisation in the Seventeenth and Eighteenth Centuries: A Comparative Perspective', in S. J. Connolly, R. A. Houston and R. J. Morris (eds), *Conflict, Identity and Economic Development* (Preston, 1995), pp. 14–28 for brief outlines and an introduction to an older literature. Recent years have produced a number of case studies of the big four, notably R. Rodger, *The Transformation of Edinburgh: Land, Property and Trust in the Nineteenth Century* (Cambridge, 2001); G. Morton, *Unionist Nationalism: Governing Urban Scotland, 1830–1860* (East Linton, 1999); W. H. Fraser and I. Maver (eds), *Glasgow, Vol. Two: 1830–1912* (Manchester, 1996); W. H. Fraser and C. H. Lee (eds), *Aberdeen, 1800–2000: A New History* (East Linton, 2000); L. Miskell, C. A. Whatley and B. Harris (eds), *Victorian Dundee: Image and Realities* (East Linton, 2000).

The literature on rural change in nineteenth-century Scotland is even greater than for urbanisation, although historians tend to concentrate on economic and social relationships rather than the spatial. Here is a selection: J. Hunter, *The Making of the Crofting Community* (Edinburgh, 1976); E. Richards, *Patrick Sellar and the Highland Clearances: Homicide, Eviction and the Price of Progress* (Edinburgh, 1999); E. A. Cameron, *Land for the People?: The British Government and the Scottish Highlands, c. 1880–1925* (East Linton, 1996); R. Anthony, *Herds and Hinds: Farm Labour in Lowland Scotland, 1900–1939* (East Linton, 1997); T. M. Devine, *Farm Servants and Labour in Lowland Scotland, 1770–1914* (Edinburgh, 1984).

In the very near future a chapter on 'space' in Scotland will have to include a section on the interaction of the social, economic and environmental. For two 'swallows' in this anticipated summer see T. C. Smout, A. R. MacDonald and F. Watson (eds), *A History of the Native Woodlands of Scotland, 1500–1920* (Edinburgh, 2005) and J. H. Dickson *et al.*, *The Changing Flora of Glasgow: Urban and Rural Plants Through the Centuries* (Edinburgh, 2000).

There is no substitute for walking the streets and fields of Scotland, nor for looking at the documentation of Scottish space.

CHAPTER 9: IDENTITY OUT OF PLACE

On aspects of Scottish identity the best starting point is the work of David McCrone, most notably his *Understanding Scotland: The Sociology of a Stateless Nation* (London, 1992) and the historical essay which begins the second edition published in 2001. Much of the debate originates from concepts best defined in T. Nairn, *The Break-up of Britain* (London, 1977). Explorations of the interplay between history and theory in Scotland's dual and multiple identities is well served in a short but important contribution by T. C. Smout, entitled 'Perspectives on the Scottish Identity', *Scottish Affairs*, 6 (1994); work by the present author on national identity and nationalism in this period can be found in *Unionist Nationalism: Governing Urban Scotland 1830–1860* (East Linton, 1999), 'What If? The Significance of Scotland's Missing Nationalism in the Nineteenth Century', in D. Broun, R. Finlay and M. Lynch (eds), *Image and Identity: the Making and Re-making of Scotland Through the Ages* (Edinburgh, 1998); and 'Scotland is Britain: the Union and Unionist-Nationalism, 1807–1907', *Journal of Irish and Scottish Studies*, 1:2 (2008).

The way that identity is related to everyday experiences of personal life is hypothesised in a number of influential works by Anthony P. Cohen, most notably *Self Consciousness: An Alternative Anthropology of Identity* (London, 1994), and 'Personal Nationalism: A Scottish View of Some Rites, Rights, and Wrongs', *American Ethnologist*, 23:4 (1996). The concept of the banal and how identity can be understood as endemic in the everyday is found in Michael Billig's much cited *Banal Nationalism* (London, 1995).

For the examination of industriousness and morality in this period, use as been made of a number of essays in T. C. Smout's *Victorian Values* (Oxford, 1992), notably R. J. Morris, 'Victorian Values in Scotland and England', Ann Digby, 'Victorian Values and Women', Stewart J. Brown, 'Thomas Chalmers and the Communal Ideal' and C. Binfield, 'Nonconformity's True Conformity'. On the concept of 'self-help', there are plenty of examples to choose from the writings of Samuel Smiles who popularised the concept, notably *Self Help* (London, 1859), *Thrift* (London, 1875) and *Character* (London, 1880). The role of Calvinism within notions of industriousness is prioritised in the analysis of S. and O. Checkland, *Industry and Ethos: Scotland 1832–1914* (Edinburgh, 1984); the ubiquity of thrift among the respectable working class is examined in one case study in G. D. Pollock, 'Aspects of

Thrift in East End Glasgow: New Accounts at the Bridgeton Cross Branch of the Savings Bank of Glasgow, 1881', *International Review of Scottish Studies*, 32 (2007); the changes in the Scottish economy within which these beliefs interacted is best examined through the contributors to *The Transformation of Scotland: The Economy since 1700*, T. M. Devine, C. H. Lee and G. C. Peden (eds) (Edinburgh, 2005). Changes in the world of work are explored in W. W. J Knox, 'The Political and Workplace Culture of the Scottish Working Class, 1832–1914', in W. H. Fraser and R. J. Morris (eds), *People and Society in Scotland, vol. II: 1830–1914*, and W. W. J. Knox *Hanging by a Thread: the Scottish Cotton Industry c. 1850–1914* (Preston, 1995).

On aspects of emigration, the most extensive contemporary analysis comes from E. J. Ravenstein, 'The Laws of Migration', *Journal of the Statistical Society of London*, 48:2 (June 1885). For the important history of emigration before the growth in movements to North America, see: T. C. Smout, N. C. Landsman and T. M. Devine, 'Scottish Emigration in the Seventeenth and Eighteenth Centuries', in N. P. Canny (ed.), *Europeans on the Move: Studies on European Migration, 1500–1800* (Oxford, 1994); for Scottish migration in the nineteenth century, see T. M. Devine (ed.), *Scottish Emigration and Scottish Society* (Edinburgh, 1992) and Marjory Harper, *Adventurers and Exiles: The Great Scottish Exodus* (London, 2003). The role of identity in the philanthropic and associational groups formed by Scots in the diaspora is explored in the range of examples found in *A Kingdom of the Mind: How the Scots Helped make Canada*, E. Rider and H. McNabb (eds) (Montreal and Kingston, 2006); and *Ties of Bluid, Kin and Countrie: Scottish Associational Culture in the Diaspora*, T. Bueltmann, A. Hinson and G. Morton (eds) (Guelph, 2009).

On association culture in Victorian society, see the work of R. J. Morris. Most notably his 'Clubs, Societies and Associations', in F. M. L. Thompson (ed.) *The Cambridge Social History of Britain, 1750–1950: Social Agencies and Institutions* (Cambridge, 1993), and his contributions to *Society, Associations, and Urban Places: Class, Nation, and Culture in Nineteenth-century Europe*, G. Morton, B. de Vries and R. J. Morris (eds) (Aldershot, 2006). The subject of temperance and association culture is analysed in Irene Maver's essay in this collection entitled 'The Temperance Movement and the Urban Associational Ideal: Scotland, 1820s–1840s'. The range of associational activities in this and earlier periods is found in P. Clark, *British Clubs and Societies, 1500–1800* (Oxford, 2000) and O. Checkland, *Philanthropy in Victorian Scotland: Social Welfare and the Voluntary Principle* (Edinburgh, 1980).

The fundamental issues driving the cultural importance of broad values of industriousness, thrift and self-help were the effects of rapid urbanisation and overcrowding on issues of health, the spread of disease and the threat of crime. The best introduction to Scottish urban history in this period is R. J. Morris, 'Urbanisation and Scotland', in Fraser and Morris (eds), *People and Society in Scotland*. The key contemporary analysis of the problem was the *Report On the Sanitary Condition of the Labouring Population of Gt. Britain, by Edwin Chadwick, 1842*, ed. M. W. Flinn (eds), (Edinburgh, 1965). In Scotland, the contrasting advantages of self-help, philanthropy and state intervention are explored in the debates between W. P. Alison, Professor of Medicine at Edinburgh University and Thomas Chalmers, Scotland's most influential churchman. See, in the first instance, W. P. Alison, *Observations on the Management of the Poor in Scotland and its Effects on the Health of the Great Towns* (Edinburgh, 1840).

For the best overviews of religion, see: C. G. Brown, *Religion and Society in Scotland*, 2nd edn (Edinburgh, 1997), S. J. Brown, *Thomas Chalmers and the Godly Commonwealth in Scotland* (Oxford, 1982) and his contribution to this volume. An insightful contemporary review of prostitution in Scotland comes from William Tait and his *Magdalenism: An Inquiry into the Extent, Causes and Consequences of Prostitution in Edinburgh* (Edinburgh, 1842). Dissecting Magdalene institutions within constructions of Victorian sexuality and social control is offered by Linda Mahood, *The Magdalenes: Prostitution in the Nineteenth Century* (London, 1990) and L. Mahood and B. Littlewood, 'Prostitutes, Magdalenes and Wayward Girls: Dangerous Sexualities of Working-class Girls in Victorian Scotland', *Gender and History*, 3:2 (1991). As these ideological constructions of relief were applied to the insane, see R. A. Houston, 'Poor Relief and the Dangerous and Criminal Insane in Scotland, 1740–1840', *Journal of Social History*, 40:2 (Winter 2006).

On the development of mapping in Scotland, see: C. W. J. Withers, 'The Social Nature of Map Making in the Scottish Enlightenment, c. 1682–c. 1832', *Imago Mundi*, 54 (2002); for the development of the Ordnance Survey, this chapter is indebted to S. Daniels, 'Mapping National Identities: The Culture of Cartography, With Particular Reference to the Ordnance Survey', in *Imagining Nations* (Manchester, 1998), G. Cubitt (ed.) and D. Fletcher, 'The Ordnance Survey's Nineteenth-Century Boundary Survey: Context, Characteristics and Impact', *Imago Mundi*, 51 (1999). The example used in this chapter is *Geographical Fun: Being Humorous Outlines of Various Countries, With an Introduction and Descriptive Lines*, by Aleph (London, 1869).

Commentary of Queen Victoria's projections of her Highland self can be found in a number of places, but the literature consulted here includes K. McNeil, *Scotland, Britain, Empire: Writing the Highlands, 1760–1860* (Columbus, 2007); W. A. Everett, 'National Themes in Scottish Art Music, ca. 1880–1990', *International Review of the Aesthetics and Sociology of Music*, 30:2 (December 1999); M. Homans, *Royal Representations: Queen Victoria and British Culture, 1837–1876* (Chicago, 1998); and references within M. M. Martin, *The Mighty Scot: Nation, Gender, and the Nineteenth-century Mystique of Scottish Masculinity* (Albany, 2009).

Victoria's own publications were: *The Highlanders of Scotland: The*

Complete Watercolours Commissioned by Queen Victoria from Kenneth MacLeay of her Scottish Retainers and Clansmen (London, 1986); *Leaves from the Journal of Our Life in the Highlands from 1848 to 1861* (London, 1868), A. Helps (ed.) and *More Leaves from the Journal of a Life in the Highlands, from 1862 to 1882* (London, 1884), A. Helps (ed.).

Conceptual explanations of the pull of the land in Scottish national identity are best started from D. McCrone, 'Land, Democracy and Culture in Scotland', the 1997 McEwen Lecture on Land Tenure in Scotland, Perth, 1997 and R. Williams, *The Country and the City* (New York, 1973). While analysis of late-century celticism comes from S. Wallace, *John Stuart Blackie: Scottish Scholar and Patriot* (Edinburgh, 2006); and H. K. Bhabha, *The Location of Culture* (London, 1994)

The strongest theoretical conclusions from analysis of the local Borders festivals have developed in the work of the geographer, Susan Smith, notably her 'Bounding the Borders: Claiming Space and Making Place in Rural Scotland', *Transactions of the Institute of British Geographers*, New Ser., 18:3 (1993); S. Smith, 'Where to Draw the Line', in A. Rogers and S. Vertovec (eds), *The Urban Context: Ethnicity, Social Networks and Situational Analysis* (Oxford, 1995); S. Smith, 'Bordering on Identity', *Scotlands*, 3:1 (1996). These should be read in conjunction with A. P. Cohen, 'Of Symbols and Boundaries, or does Ertie's Greatcoat Hold the Key?', in A. P. Cohen (ed.), *Symbolising Boundaries: Identity and Diversity in British Cultures* (Manchester, 1986). Still the best guide to local and national festivals is found in the work of Florence Marian McNeill, with two of her four volumes being used here: *The Silver Bough, Vol. ii: A Calendar of Scottish National Festivals, Candlemas to Harvest Home* (Glasgow, 1959); *The Silver Bough, Vol. iv: The Local Festivals of Scotland* (Glasgow, 1968). Further analysis of the Border festivals is found in G. K. Neville, *The Mother Town: Civic Ritual, Symbol, and Experience in the Borders of Scotland* (Oxford, 1994) and J. N. Gray, *At Home in the Hills: Sense of Place in the Scottish Borders* (Oxford and New York, 2000). The Scottish fire festivals are placed with their British context in R. Hutton, *The Stations of the Sun: A history of the Ritual Year in Britain* (Oxford, 2001) and a fascinating examination of the Shetland fire festival comes from Callum G. Brown in *Up-helly-aa. Custom, Culture and Community in Shetland* (Manchester, 1998).

A sociological interpretation of Highland Games is seen in G. Jarvie, *Highland Games: The Making of the Myth* (Edinburgh, 1991) and, for its place among other sports, see: G. Jarvie and I. A. Reid, 'Sport, Nationalism and Culture in Scotland', *The Sports Historian*, 19:1 (May 1999). The local attachment of ba' games is contextualised in T. Collins, J. Martin and W. Vamplew, *Encyclopaedia of Traditional Rural British Sports* (London, 2005) and the standard account of Orkney remains John Robertson, *Uppies and Doonies: The Story of the Kirkwall Ba' Game* (Aberdeen, 1967).

Notes on the Contributors

Andrew Blaikie is Professor of Historical Sociology at the University of Aberdeen. Informed by both sociological and historical perspectives, his research has ranged from demographic micro-linkage to the changing imagery of the life course. He has recently completed *The Scots Imagination in Modern Memory* (Edinburgh, 2010), an exploration of the relationships between perceptions of place, belonging and identity. Major publications include *Illegitimacy, Sex and Society: Northeast Scotland, 1750–1900* (Oxford, 1994) and *Ageing and Popular Culture* (Cambridge, 1999). He is co-editor of the journal *Cultural Sociology*.

Stewart J. Brown is Professor of Ecclesiastical History at the University of Edinburgh. His work over the years has explored the religious culture of Britain and Ireland since 1690, with a particular emphasis on Scotland. His books include *Thomas Chalmers and the Godly Commonwealth in Scotland* (Oxford, 1982), *The National Churches of England, Ireland and Scotland, 1801–1846* (Oxford, 2001) and *Providence and Empire: Religion, Politics and Society in the United Kingdom, 1815–1914* (London, 2008). He is currently working on the established Churches and Church–State relations in Britain and Ireland from 1846 to 1922.

Alastair Durie, formerly of Glasgow University, is now a part-time teaching fellow at the University of Stirling, with continuing research and publication activity in the fields of tourism, medical and sports history, dealing with such topics as the spas and the seaside, golf and grouse. Among his publications is *Scotland for the Holidays. Tourism in Scotland 1780–1939* (East Linton, 2003), to which he is currently writing a sequel on tourism from 1939 to 2000.

W. Hamish Fraser is an emeritus professor at the University of Strathclyde. Among his publications are *The Coming of the Mass Market* (Basingstoke, 1981), *Conflict and Class: Scottish Workers 1700–1838* (Edinburgh, 1988), *A History of British Trade Unionism 1700–1998* (Basingstoke, 1999) and *Scottish Popular Politics* (Edinburgh, 2000). He has also co-edited books on both the history of Glasgow and the history of Aberdeen. His forthcoming publications include *Britain since 1707* (with Callum Brown) and *Chartism in Scotland*.

Trevor Griffiths is Senior Lecturer in Economic and Social History at the University of Edinburgh. He has worked on aspects of working-class culture and society in Britain in the late nineteenth and early twentieth centuries, and developments in textile technology in Britain prior to and during the Industrial Revolution. His published works include *The Lancashire Working Classes, c. 1880–1930* (Oxford, 2001) and several articles in the *Economic History Review* and the *Journal of Economic History*. He is currently working on a study of cinema and cinema-going in Scotland in the first half of the twentieth century.

W. W. J. Knox is a Senior Lecturer in the Institute of Scottish Historical Research, University of St Andrews. His main publications include *Industrial Nation: Work, Culture and Society in Scotland, 1800–Present* (Edinburgh, 1999); edited, with R. A. Houston, *The New Penguin History of Scotland* (London, 2001), and is the author of *Lives of Scottish Women: Women and Scottish Society, 1800–1980* (Edinburgh, 2006). He is currently working on a social history of homicide in Scotland from 1700 to 1850.

Alan McKinlay is a Professor of Management at St Andrews University. He has written on historical and contemporary issues in management, collective bargaining and work organisation, particularly in Scottish heavy industry and American multinationals. He has a long-standing interest in developing and applying the philosophy of Michel Foucault.

R. J. Morris is Professor of Economic and Social History at Edinburgh University where he has taught for over forty years. His research interests include class formation and urbanisation. He edited *People and Society in Scotland, Vol. II* (Edinburgh 1990) with W. Hamish Fraser, and his publications include *Class, Sect and Party. The Making of the British Middle Class: Leeds, 1820–50* (Manchester 1990), *Men, Women and Property in England, 1780–1870* (Cambridge, 2005) and *Scotland 1907. The Many Scotlands of Valentine and Sons, Photographers* (Edinburgh 2007). Coming 'retirement' will be devoted to writing about the landscape and history of Scottish and Irish towns and growing historic varieties of apples in Berwickshire.

Graeme Morton is the Scottish Studies Foundation Chair and Director of the Centre for Scottish Studies at the University of Guelph. His research interests cover all aspects of Scottish national identity and nationalism, with a current focus on late Victorian migrations and diasporic associational culture. He is completing *Ourselves and Others: Scotland, 1832–1914* for Edinburgh University Press and his publications include *William Wallace: Man and Myth* (Stroud, 2004), *Unionist Nationalism* (East Linton, 1999) and *Locality, Community and Nation* (London, 1998). His editorial work includes *Ties of Bluid, Kin and Countrie* (Guelph, 2009), *Civil Society, Associations and*

Urban Places (Aldershot, 2006) and, since 2004, *The International Review of Scottish Studies*.

Mairi Stewart is a Research Fellow at the UHI Centre for History where she is currently working on a three-year research project entitled, 'The Social History of Forestry in 20th-Century Scotland'. She also works freelance on Scottish environmental history research, particularly woodland history. Among her publications are two chapters in *People and Woods in Scotland: A History*, T. C. Smout (ed.) (Edinburgh, 2003). With Fiona Watson she has also published *Mar Lodge Estate: Its Woods and People* (Edinburgh, 2004). Most recently, she contributed a chapter to *Greening History: The Presence of the Past in Environmental Restoration*, M. Hall (ed.) (London, 2009). She is joint organiser of the Scottish Woodland History Discussion Group.

Fiona Watson is a writer and historian. Brought up in Dunfermline, she studied Medieval History at the University of St Andrews and gained a Ph.D. in Scottish History at the University of Glasgow. She went on to become a Senior Lecturer in History and Director of the Centre for Environmental History at the University of Stirling before leaving to pursue a writing career in 2006. She is the author of *Under the Hammer: Edward I and Scotland, 1296–1305* (East Linton, 1997), *Scotland, A History* (Stroud, 2000), and is about to publish a book on the real Macbeth. She also fronted *In Search of Scotland*, a ten-part TV series in 2001, and has presented numerous radio programmes, including *Enlightenment* and *History File*.

Index

Edinburgh Castle, 250
Edinburgh Irish Mission and Protestant
    Institute, 13
Edinburgh Phrenological Society, 192n,
    261; *see also* phrenology
Edinburgh Protestant Publication Society,
    13
Edinburgh Review, 6
Edinburgh Six Feet Club, 276
Edinburgh Sunday Society, 187
education, 7, 12, 83, 117–18, 131, 133,
    137, 153–5, 205, 211, 215, 242, 251,
    260, 264–8, 273
eggs, 63, 76, 80–1, 237, 155, 237
Eglinton, 13th Earl, 183
Eglinton Tournament (1839), 183
Eighteenth Brumaire of Louis Bonaparte,
    198
elders (church), 90, 97, 103–8, 115n,
    123–4, 127–9
Elgin, 23, 36, 70, 77, 147, 157, 247
Elias, Norbert, 218
emigrant letters, 257
emigration, 8, 28, 34, 37–8, 40–2, 54, 91,
    99, 102, 108, 110, 110, 256–7, 265; *see
    also* migration
Empire (British), 30, 43, 50, 78, 250, 256,
    263–4
Empire (Russian), 134
employment, 3, 9, 14–15, 29, 36, 51–3, 83,
    94–5, 101, 133, 153, 170, 173, 178–9,
    186, 188, 257, 263, 266–70
Emsley, Clive, 203, 206
enclosure, xi, 32
engineering, 28, 174
England, 2, 48, 61, 77–8, 91, 111n, 121,
    134, 149, 165, 182, 197, 199, 203–5,
    206, 216, 261, 271, 275, 276–7
English, 5–7, 14, 39, 42, 47–8, 62, 65, 98,
    112n, 122, 134, 150, 155, 161–4, 176,
    197, 201, 203–5, 225, 235, 238, 241,
    245, 256, 258, 261, 263, 278
English Mechanic, 195n
English Prison Commission, 201–2
Erskine, Thomas, 118
Established Church (or Kirk), 12, 90–1,
    105–6, 111n, 116–17, 120, 129, 132,
    266; *see also* Church of Scotland
estate records, 25–6
ethnicity, 7, 17–18, 133, 205, 208–9, 258
Euchologion, or Book of Prayers, 121, 127
evangelicalism, 118, 138, 171, 183

everyday life, 19, 48, 89, 90, 103, 117, 142,
    150, 165, 170, 178, 189, 198, 199, 206,
    215, 251, 272, 275, 289, 292, 305
and change, xi, 55
and 'great events', xiii
and men, xii
problems of historical evidence, xii
study of history, x–xi
and women, xi–xii
excursions, 149–51, 157–8, 165, 181, 237,
    245, 272, 298
Exhibition (Aberdeen, 1840), 18
Exhibition (Glasgow, 1901), 238
Exhibition (London, 1851), 73, 77, 165
Exhibition (Paris, 1858), 73
exotic, 51, 68, 176–7, 192n
exotic ordinariness, 273–4; *see also*
    ordinariness
extended kin, 102, 257

FA Cup, 164
Fabian Society, 136
fairs (and markets), 70, 125, 175, 180–2,
    185, 227
Falkirk, 16, 70, 149, 228, 231
Falkirk Herald, 81
famine, 30, 37, 38–9, 53, 54, 62, 77, 95, 99,
    102, 132, 134
'Farewell to the Bens', 27
farm, 19, 24–5, 30–42, 45, 46, 48, 50, 52,
    62, 70, 94, 99, 106, 107–8, 125, 153,
    181, 225–6, 231
Farquharson, John, 32–3
fashion, 10, 61, 67, 247, 275
fears, xi
Fenton, Alexander, xi
fertility, 2, 3, 91, 95–6, 99, 107
festivals, 15, 18–19, 270, 275–9, 280
Fife, 24, 45, 48, 55n, 62, 157, 162, 172,
    178, 188, 298
Fife, 4th Earl, 45
Findhorn (river), 30, 41–2
Finney, Charles Grandison, 135
fire engines, 229
fire festivals, 15, 276, 277
fire grates, 10, 66, 67
fireplaces, 75
First World War, 60, 165–6
fish, 10, 63, 73, 140, 151, 153–4
fishermen, 101
fishing, 14, 38, 46, 63, 73, 99, 123, 140,
    147, 154–6, 182, 226, 239

Index

Wester Ross, 37
Westminster Confession of Faith, 11–12, 117–20, 131
Westminster Directory, 120, 126
wet nurses, 33
Whatley, Christopher, 196, 197, 198
Whipman Play
whisky, 45, 49, 65, 68, 75, 211, 246, 265
Wierling, Dorothee, xiii
Wight, Andrew, 31
Wigtown, 277
Wild Sports and Natural History of the Highlands, 42
Williams, Raymond, 274
Wilson, Charles James, 179
Wilson, Daniel, 250
Wilson, James, 13–14
Wilson, Washington, 8
wines and spirits, 68, 81, 84, 124, 264
women
  births, 96–7, 99, 104–6, 128
  children, 29, 41, 99, 128, 157, 165, 188
  consumption, 64–5, 68
  crime, 200, 203
  disorder, 16, 205, 208, 210, 211–12, 215–18, 235, 237, 240, 269
  drink, 64, 200
  gang members, 209
  home, 4, 67, 83–4, 165, 178, 188–9
  leisure, 15–17, 68, 137, 151, 157, 165, 183, 189, 264, 269, 278–9
  marriage, 93

  morality, 128–9, 149, 200, 237, 269–70
  religion and beliefs, 135, 137, 141, 178, 297
  shopping, 16–17, 68, 239, 246
  sport, 41
  time, 178
  work, 15, 19, 29, 30, 41, 154, 170, 181, 188–9, 210–11, 230
Women's Social and Political Union, 211
woodland, 48–51
Wordsworth, Dorothy, 149, 155, 298
work, 3, 14–15, 28, 34–5, 39, 42–6, 53, 62–3, 67, 79, 97–101, 125, 132–7, 153–5, 170–4, 178–82, 185, 188–90, 197, 200–7, 231, 256–7, 262–4, 268–9, 274
  agricultural, 39–40, 44, 178, 180–1
  disciplines, 173, 185–8
  industrial unrest, 209–10
  seasonal, 36, 52, 179
working class, 1, 6, 60–1, 63, 67, 71, 74, 75, 78–84, 99, 110, 117, 121–3, 133, 153, 157–8, 162, 165, 172, 176, 189–90, 198, 200–1, 206, 214, 215–18, 265–8, 279; *see also* class (social)
wringers, 76
Wyllie, James, 37

Yeats, W. B., 141
Yeo, Stephen, 136
Yester (Haddingtonshire), 180–1
York, 203